F

Caribbean Hideaways!

"It's a pleasure to read your descriptions—especially since you are a discriminating reviewer, unlike many others who simply praise every place they include in their books." (L. Long, New York City)

"*Caribbean Hideaways* has been my travel bible for years..."
(L. Silverstein, Marina del Rey, California)

"It's a pleasure in this day to find an honest appraisal of a commercial subject." (H. Cole, Los Angeles, California)

"Your books are my vacation bibles..."
(Mrs. J. Epstein, Narberth, Pennsylvania)

"...you take the time to describe the little details about each inn—such as how a room is decorated, or what the surroundings are like. This helps in knowing a place sounds 'right' for us." (M. Roeske, Des Moines, Iowa)

"I have read many other guides to inns and hotels... but none of the others is comparable to yours in humor and insight."
(L. Fanning, Fort Worth, Texas)

"...your recommendations made our trips super."
(T. Ollendorff, San Francisco, California)

Other books by Ian Keown

Ian Keown's European Hideaways

Very Special Places: A Lover's Guide to America

Ian Keown's
Caribbean Hideaways
1988-1989 Edition

Featuring the 98 most romantic inns, hotels and resorts from Anguilla to Tobago

With additional material by Eleanor Berman, Sharon Flescher, Elizabeth Murfee and Cynthia Proulx

Illustrated by Claude Martinot

Harmony Books/New York

Published by Harmony Books, a division of Crown Publishers, Inc., 225 Park Avenue South, New York, New York 10003 and represented in Canada by the Canadian MANDA Group

HARMONY and colophon are trademarks of Crown Publishers, Inc.

Manufactured in the United States of America

Design by Ron McCutchan

Library of Congress Cataloging-in-Publication Data

Keown, Ian.

Ian Keown's Caribbean hideaways.

1. West Indies—Description and travel—1981-   — Guide-books.

I. Berman, Eleanor, 1934–

II. Title. III. Title: Caribbean hideaways.

F1609.K46   1988   917.29′0452   87-14926

ISBN 0-517-56764-4

10 9 8 7 6 5 4 3 2

Second Revised Edition

Contents

Acknowledgments/xv

Introduction/1

Belize/23

The Belizean *(Ambergris Caye)*/25

Cayman Islands/29

Hyatt Regency Grand Cayman *(Grand Cayman)*/32
Tortuga Club *(Grand Cayman)*/34
Added Attractions/36

Jamaica/37

Sundowner *(Negril)*/40
Tryall Golf and Beach Club *(near Montego Bay)*/41
Round Hill *(near Montego Bay)*/43
Half Moon Club *(near Montego Bay)*/46
Plantation Inn *(Ocho Rios)*/48
Jamaica Inn *(Ocho Rios)*/50
Sans Souci Hotel Club and Spa *(Ocho Rios)*/52
The Admiralty Club *(Port Antonio)*/55
Trident Villas and Hotel *(Port Antonio)*/57

Haiti/61

Added Attractions/63

The Dominican Republic/71

Casa de Campo *(La Romana)*/73
La Posada *(Altos de Chavon)*/76
Added Attraction/78

The U.S. Islands/79

Hyatt Dorado Beach *(Dorado, Puerto Rico)*/82
Palmas del Mar *(Humacao, Puerto Rico)*/86
Gran Hotel el Convento *(Old San Juan, Puerto Rico)*/88
Caneel Bay *(St. John)*/90
Point Pleasant *(St. Thomas)*/93
Pavilions & Pools Hotel *(St. Thomas)*/95
Harbor View *(St. Thomas)*/96
Carambola Beach Resort and Golf Club *(St. Croix)*/99
Cormorant Beach Club *(St. Croix)*/102
The Buccaneer Hotel *(St. Croix)*/105
Added Attractions/107

The British Virgins/109

Long Bay Hotel *(Tortola)*/112
Peter Island *(Tortola)*/114
Guana Island Club *(Guana Island)*/118
Little Dix Bay *(Virgin Gorda)*/121
Biras Creek *(Virgin Gorda)*/124
The Tradewinds *(Virgin Gorda)*/126
Bitter End Yacht Club *(Virgin Gorda)*/129
Drake's Anchorage *(Virgin Gorda Sound)*/131
Added Attractions/133

The Dutch Windwards/135

Oyster Pond Yacht Club and Hotel *(St. Maarten)*/138
Pasanggrahan Royal Guesthouse Hotel *(St. Maarten)*/141
Mary's Boon *(St. Maarten)*/143
The Caravanserai *(St. Maarten)*/144
La Samanna *(St. Martin)*/147
Captain's Quarters *(Saba)*/149
The Old Gin House *(St. Eustatius)*/151
Added Attractions/153

The Queen's Leewards/155

Malliouhana *(Anguilla)*/159
Cinnamon Reef Beach Club *(Anguilla)*/162
The Mariners *(Anguilla)*/164
The Golden Lemon *(St. Kitts)*/166

Rawlins Plantation *(St. Kitts)*/169
Nisbet Plantation Inn *(Nevis)*/171
Hotel Montpelier *(Nevis)*/173
Golden Rock *(Nevis)*/175
Jumby Bay Resort *(Antigua)*/177
Blue Waters Beach Hotel *(Antigua)*/179
Curtain Bluff *(Antigua)*/181
Copper & Lumber Store *(Antigua)*/184
The Admiral's Inn *(Antigua)*/188
The Inn at English Harbour *(Antigua)*/190
Half Moon Bay Hotel *(Antigua)*/192
St. James's Club *(Antigua)*/194
Added Attractions/197

The French West Indies/203

Castelets *(St. Barthélemy)*/206
Hotel Manapany *(St. Barthélemy)*/209
Filao Beach Hotel *(St. Barthélemy)*/211
Hotel Guanahani *(St. Barthélemy)*/213
El Sereno Beach Hotel *(St. Barthélemy)*/215
Hamak *(Guadeloupe)*/218
Auberge de la Vieille Tour *(Guadeloupe)*/220
Auberge des Anacardiers *(Terre-de-Haut, Guadeloupe)*/222
PLM Azur Los Santos *(Terre-de-Haut, Guadeloupe)*/223
Hotel Plantation de Leyritz *(Martinique)*/225
Hotel Bakoua Beach *(Martinique)*/228
St. Aubin Hotel *(Martinique)*/230
Manoir de Beauregard *(Martinique)*/231
Added Attractions/232

The Queen's Windwards/235

Steigenberger Cariblue Hotel *(St. Lucia)*/239
Cunard La Toc Hotel and La Toc Suites *(St. Lucia)*/240
Anse Chastanet Beach Hotel *(St. Lucia)*/243
Dasheene *(St. Lucia)*/246
Ginger Bay Beach Club *(Barbados)*/248
Crane Beach Hotel *(Barbados)*/250
Sandy Lane Hotel *(Barbados)*/252
Coral Reef Club *(Barbados)*/254
Glitter Bay *(Barbados)*/257
Cobblers Cove Hotel *(Barbados)*/260

Arnos Vale Hotel *(Tobago)*/262
Mount Irvine Bay Hotel *(Tobago)*/264
Added Attractions/267

St. Vincent-Grenadines and Grenada/269

Young Island *(St. Vincent)*/273
Grand View Beach Hotel *(St. Vincent)*/276
Spring on Bequia *(Bequia)*/277
Friendship Bay Hotel *(Bequia)*/279
Frangipani Hotel *(Bequia)*/281
The Cotton House *(Mustique)*/282
Palm Island Beach Club *(Palm Island)*/286
Saltwhistle Bay Club *(Mayreau)*/288
Petit St. Vincent Resort *(Petit St. Vincent)*/291
The Calabash *(Grenada)*/294
Secret Harbour *(Grenada)*/296
Horse Shoe Bay Hotel *(Grenada)*/298
Spice Island Inn *(Grenada)*/299
Added Attractions/300

The Dutch Leewards/303

Divi Divi Beach Hotel *(Aruba)*/306
Tamarijn Beach Hotel *(Aruba)*/308
Hotel Bonaire *(Bonaire)*/310
Flamingo Beach Hotel and Casino *(Bonaire)*/312
Avila Beach Hotel *(Curaçao)*/315

The Rates—and how to figure them out/317

Reservations and Tourist Information/331

Update/335

Contents

Listed Alphabetically by Island

Anguilla

Malliouhana/159
Cinnamon Reef Beach Club/162
The Mariners/164
Added Attractions/200

Antigua

Jumby Bay Resort/177
Blue Waters Beach Hotel/179
Curtain Bluff/181
Copper & Lumber Store/184
The Admiral's Inn/188
The Inn at English Harbour/190
Half Moon Bay Hotel/192
St. James's Club/194
Added Attractions/202

Aruba

Divi Divi Beach Hotel/306
Tamarijn Beach Hotel/308

Barbados

Ginger Bay Beach Club/248
Crane Beach Hotel/250
Sandy Lane Hotel/252
Coral Reef Club/254
Glitter Bay/257
Cobblers Cove Hotel/260
Added Attractions/267

Belize

The Belizean/25

Bequia

Spring on Bequia/277
Friendship Bay Hotel/279
Frangipani Hotel/281

Bonaire

Hotel Bonaire/310
Flamingo Beach Hotel and Casino/312

Cayman Islands

Hyatt Regency Grand Cayman/32
Tortuga Club/34
Added Attractions/36

Curaçao

Avila Beach Hotel/315

The Dominican Republic

Casa de Campo/73
La Posada/76
Added Attraction/78

Grenada

The Calabash/294
Secret Harbour/296
Horse Shoe Bay Hotel/298
Spice Island Inn/299
Added Attractions/300

Guadeloupe

Hamak/218
Auberge de la Vieille Tour/220
Auberge des Anacardiers/222
PLM Azur Los Santos/223

Guana Island

Guana Island Club/118

Haiti

Added Attractions/63

Jamaica

Sundowner/40
Tryall Golf and Beach Club/41
Round Hill/43
Half Moon Club/46
Plantation Inn/48
Jamaica Inn/50
Sans Souci Hotel Club and Spa/52
The Admiralty Club/55
Trident Villas and Hotel/57

Martinique

Hotel Plantation de Leyritz/225
Hotel Bakoua Beach/228
St. Aubin Hotel/230
Manoir de Beauregard/231
Added Attractions/232

Mayreau

Saltwhistle Bay Club/288

Mustique

The Cotton House/282

Nevis

Nisbet Plantation Inn/171
Hotel Montpelier/173
Golden Rock/175
Added Attractions/197

Palm Island

Palm Island Beach Club/286

Petit St. Vincent

Petit St. Vincent Resort/291

Puerto Rico

Hyatt Dorado Beach/82
Palmas del Mar/86
Gran Hotel el Convento/88

Saba

Captain's Quarters/149

St. Barthélemy

Castelets/206
Hotel Manapany/209
Filao Beach Hotel/211
Hotel Guanahani/213
El Sereno Beach Hotel/215
Added Attractions/232

St. Croix

Carambola Beach Resort and Golf Club/99
Cormorant Beach Club/102
The Buccaneer Hotel/105
Added Attractions/107

St. Eustatius

The Old Gin House/151

St. John

Caneel Bay/90

St. Kitts

The Golden Lemon/166
Rawlins Plantation/169
Added Attractions/199

St. Lucia

Steigenberger Cariblue Hotel/239
Cunard La Toc Hotel and La Toc Suites/240
Anse Chastanet Beach Hotel/243
Dasheene/246

St. Maarten/St. Martin

Oyster Pond Yacht Club and Hotel/138
Pasanggrahan Royal Guesthouse Hotel/141
Mary's Boon/143
The Caravanserai/144
La Samanna/147
Added Attractions/153

St. Thomas

Point Pleasant/93
Pavilions & Pools Hotel/95
Harbor View/96
Added Attractions/107

St. Vincent

Young Island/273
Grand View Beach Hotel/276

Tobago

Arnos Vale Hotel/262
Mount Irvine Bay Hotel/264

Tortola

Long Bay Hotel/112
Peter Island/114
Added Attractions/133

Virgin Gorda

Little Dix Bay/121
Biras Creek/124
The Tradewinds/126
Bitter End Yacht Club/129
Drake's Anchorage/131

Acknowledgments

As they say in Bonaire, *masha danki* (thank you) to scores of friends and colleagues for tips and suggestions; to readers who took the trouble to send me comments and critiques; to island hoppers in airports and bars who shared their experiences; to innkeepers who took time, reconfirmed flights and helped me get to the airport on time.

There are too many people to name individually, but for special efforts I'd like to offer a special thank-you to the following (in, of course, alphabetical order): Bruce Baxter, Scott Calder, Watti Chai, Leslie Cohen, Lisa Cutick, Elyse Elkin, Susan Esposito, Dave Fernandez, Dunster Fontainelle, Jacqueline Goldson, Arlene Gross, Marianna Hoppin, Richard Huff, Gayle Knopfer, Sue McManus, Jane MacNeil, Yvonne Maginley, Marilyn Marx, Phil Miles, David Mitchell, Madge Morris, Alan O'Neal, Nina Onishi, Joe Petrocik, Merle Richman, Joe Scott, Virginia Sheridan, Gillian Thompson, Nikki Tromp, Robb Volgers, Neal de Weaver, Hilary Wattley, Paul Zar. Likewise, I herewith acknowledge the professionalism and what-would-I-do-without-her dependability of Sheila Keenan, who did most of the dirty work—editing, proofreading, keeping track of bits of paper and brochures, deciphering my scribbles, and even the tedious chore of checking out some hotels.

Finally, to colleagues and contributors who braved the midday sun to visit yet one more hotel and flush one more toilet: Eleanor Berman (*E.B.*) is the author of several books, including the *Away for the Weekend*™ series of guides, also published by Crown; her byline also appears frequently in leading magazines and newspapers throughout the United States. Sharon Flescher (*S.F.*) has a Ph.D. in art history from Columbia University, writes scholarly articles on the French Impressionists and works for a philanthropic/arts foundation. Elizabeth Murfee (*E.M.*) has her own public relations company and is closely involved with the arts in New York. Cynthia Proulx (*C.P.*) was my coauthor on *Guide to France for Loving Couples* and has contributed her peppy prose to several of my other guidebooks.

Introduction

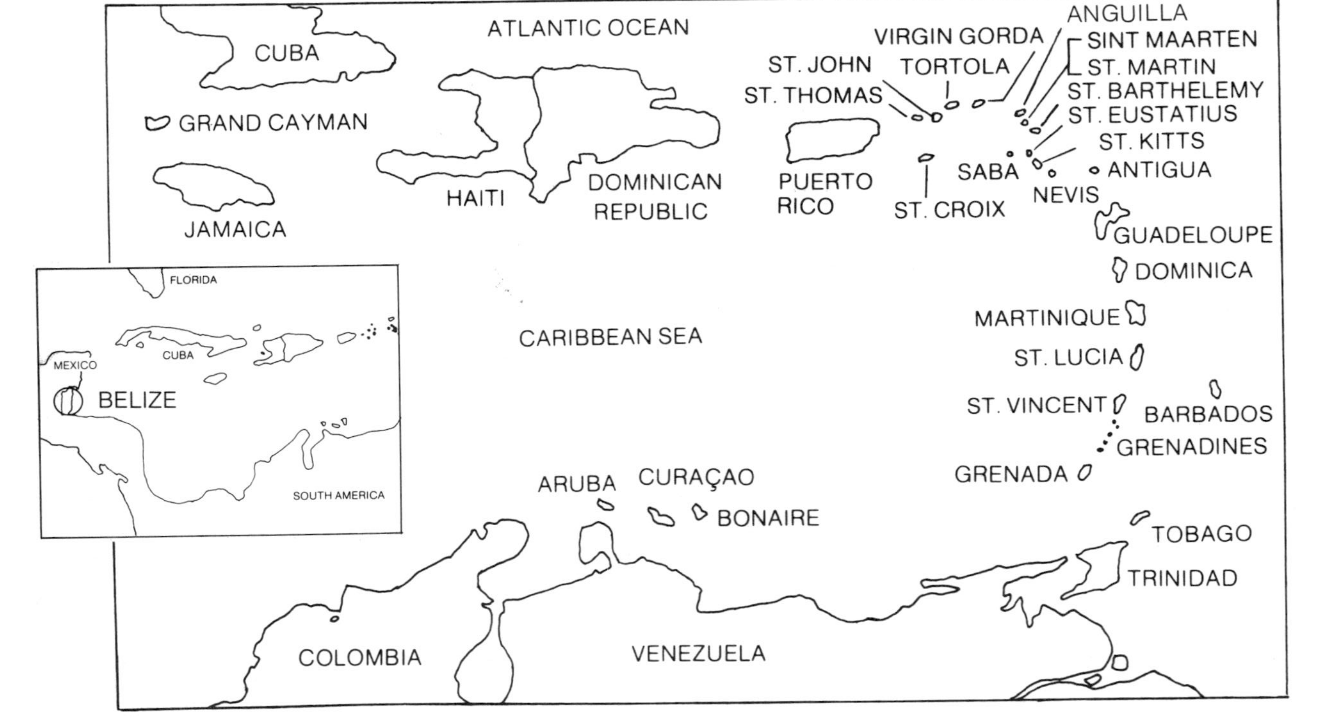
ATLANTIC OCEAN
CUBA
GRAND CAYMAN
JAMAICA
HAITI
DOMINICAN REPUBLIC
PUERTO RICO
ST. JOHN
ST. THOMAS
VIRGIN GORDA
TORTOLA
ST. CROIX
ANGUILLA
SINT MAARTEN
ST. MARTIN
ST. BARTHELEMY
ST. EUSTATIUS
ST. KITTS
SABA
NEVIS
ANTIGUA
GUADELOUPE
DOMINICA
MARTINIQUE
ST. LUCIA
ST. VINCENT
BARBADOS
GRENADINES
GRENADA
CARIBBEAN SEA
ARUBA
CURAÇAO
BONAIRE
TOBAGO
TRINIDAD
COLOMBIA
VENEZUELA
FLORIDA
MEXICO
CUBA
BELIZE
SOUTH AMERICA

Introduction

You've dreamed the dream a hundred times: you, someone you love, a quiet beach, a row of palms; warm sand beneath your tummy, sand in your toes, sand in your ear; that delectable sensation of hot sun and cool breezes playing hide-and-seek on your back, the first chilly glop of suntan lotion, playful fingers spreading the glop around and around; the murmur of surf, sunflares in your eyes when you roll over, the heat in your cheeks long after you've moved into the shade; siestas, love in the afternoon, the quiet whirring of a four-bladed fan; rum punches at sundown, a table for two beneath the palms, candles flickering in the trade winds, tree frogs courting. After dinner, a walk on the beach, barefoot through the surf, the moon shimmering on the sea. Early to bed, early to love.

For all you dreamers and lovers, here is another book of nice places, a guide for lovers of all kinds and inclinations—Romeo and Juliet, Romeo and Romeo, Juliet and Juliet, rich lovers, poor lovers, newlyweds and newly unweds, bosses and secretaries, actresses and bodyguards, mums and dads who would still be lovers if only they could get the kids out of their hair for a few days. In other words, it's for anyone who has a yen to slip off for a few days and be alone in the sun with someone he/she fancies, likes, loves, has the hots for, or simply wants to do something nice for.

Whatever your tastes or inclinations, you'll probably find something that appeals to you in these pages. This is a fairly eclectic selection. Some of the resorts are on the beach, others in the mountains; some are on big islands, some on islands so small you won't find them on a map; some large resorts are included because there are lovers who prefer the anonymity a large resort affords (but none of them so vast as to be tourist processing factories); some have nightlife of sorts, most of them don't even have a tape recorder; some are for lovers who want to dress up in the evening, others are for lovers with cutoff Levi's and beat-up sandals. But these hotels and resorts all have something special going for them. It may be seclusion (Palm Island Beach Club or Petit St. Vincent Resort, both in the Grenadines), it may be spaciousness (Caneel Bay on St. John, Casa de Campo in the Dominican Republic) or nostalgia (Avila Beach on Curaçao, Pasanggrahan on St. Maarten), charm (Nisbet Plantation Inn on Nevis, The Golden Lemon on St. Kitts), a sense of the past (Plantation de Leyritz on Martinique) or luxury (Malliouhana on Anguilla or Jumby Bay on Antigua).

They may be here because they have some of these qualities and are, in the bargain, inexpensive (Frangipani on Bequia, Sundowner in Negril).

In most cases, they're a combination of one or more of these characteristics, and in almost every case they're places where you can avoid neon, plastic, piped music, air-conditioning, casinos, conventions, children and that peculiar blight of the Caribbean—massed cruise ship passengers.

Above all, none of these hotels try to disguise the fact that they're in the Caribbean; none of them try, the minute you arrive in the Caribbean, to transport you instantly to back-street Hong Kong or ye olde pubbe in Ye Olde Englande (well, one or two of them maybe, but you'll read about their follies in these pages so that you won't be startled when you get there). They are hotels that don't make you line up for breakfast in an air-conditioned dining room and then line up immediately afterward to make a reservation for the first or second seating at dinner. They're not the sort of hotels that entice you with promises of soft air and trade winds, and then seal you into a box where you're not allowed to leave the balcony door open to let in the promised soft air and the trade winds.

Pet Peeves

Curmudgeons of the world unite! There are innkeepers who believe in some of the standards you try to uphold. I quote: "Please do not let your wife wear those ghastly hair curlers out of your room"; or " . . . May we ask you please to assist us in maintaining our standards by not wearing hair curlers in the public areas?"; or "Transistor radios can be very disturbing to other people. Guests are requested not to play them in public areas"; or "No jeans and tank tops in the dining room."

AIR-CONDITIONING For me, and I'm sure for a lot of you, louvers and ceiling fans are more romantic than whirring, dripping, throbbing, rusting, shuddering, grinding air-conditioning units, so most of the hotels in this guide either do not have air-conditioning or use it only as a backup system. There is, of course, another side to the air-conditioning debate: in some hotels, the gadget is necessary to block out extraneous noises such as stray dogs, roosters and roisterers, and on occasion you may welcome the background hum to keep your own noises *in;* moreover, one of my colleagues, who shall remain nameless, claims air-conditioning is a necessity for after-lunch lovemaking in the tropics. Therefore, when a hotel has air-conditioning as a backup system the fact is noted in the listings—*but please don't take this as being a commendation at the expense of hotels without air-conditioning.*

 CRUISE SHIP PASSENGERS Presumably you're going to the

Caribbean to find a quiet, secluded beach that won't remind you of Coney Island on the Fourth of July, but you can forget that idea if a few hundred old salts arrive in ankle socks and T-shirts. Some hotels encourage these visits because they represent instant profit; others ban them unequivocally, and still others are beginning to learn that after they've cleared up the litter and tallied up the missing souvenirs, cruise ship passengers aren't worth the trouble. ("They buy one Coke, then use the toilet, and the profit on the Coke is less than what I pay for the water.") Most of the hotels in this guide ban cruise ship passengers—or at least limit the numbers.

PIPED MUSIC If you take the trouble to search out a hideaway, as opposed to a big swinging resort, you probably don't want your peace and quiet to be disturbed by piped noise, especially when it's music that has no connection, harmonic or otherwise, with the setting—such as dining by candlelight on the veranda of a centuries-old inn and having to listen to a record of a chanteuse singing, "It's so-o goo-oo-ood."

OTHER MUSIC Piped noise is not the same thing as discreet background music that's carefully selected by the management to match the mood of the guests or the setting; but any kind of music, taped or live, combo or steel band, should be avoidable (that is, if you don't want to listen, you should be able to go to another lounge or patio where you can't hear it), and it should never keep guests from their sleep. Also, any hotel that plays "Island in the Sun" more than six times in one evening should lose its license. Another ubiquitous blight these days is Bartender's Radio. He's bored, standing around all day serving drinks to a bunch of frolicking foreigners, and he wants his music—usually noisy with an insensate beat. It's a pain for owners, too: "I can see the bartender scurrying to turn down the radio every time he sees me approaching; I agree with you, guests shouldn't have to listen to the bartender's music." The "all" in getting away from it all includes other peoples' radios. That wish should be respected. Worst offense of all, of course, is amplified music—singer, combo, native band or, horror of horrors, *steel* band. Quite apart from the fact that the music is often so loud you can't hear yourselves whisper sweet nothings, the sound systems usually distort the music itself—too much *kaBOOM-kaBOOM,* not enough *trala-trala.* Too often, I suspect, loud music is managerial camouflage to distract guests' attention from the wishy-washy food.

In this guidebook, loud music is tolerated (but with the greatest reluctance) only *if* the hotel offers alternative facilities for imbibing and dining away from the noise; but if the kabooming follows guests all the way to their beds or balconies, or lasts beyond, say, 11:00 P.M., that place loses points. Hotel people often boast about the days when their guests were entertained to impromptu performances by a Noël Coward or a Cole Porter: but Coward and Porter never went *kaBOOM-kaBOOM.* Yet presumably people still managed to enjoy their vacations back in the days before combos carted their own power stations around.

Please, please: when you resent the music or the volume of the music, take the manager aside and explain that you paid all that money and took that long journey to get some peace and *quiet.* Remind him or her, gently, that it's considered bad manners to talk so loudly that people at the next table can't enjoy their own conversation. Ditto a band that plays too loudly.

PAGING SYSTEMS Even worse than intrusive music is the paging system around the swimming pool and bar; if you're trying to escape telephones and reminders of the office, it doesn't do much for your spirits to know that the people around you are wanted on the phone. Any man or woman who tips a telephone operator to be paged at the pool should be sealed in a phone booth! I can think of only one hotel in this guide with a paging system, and even then it's used sparingly.

CHILDREN Some hotels ban them altogether, like cruise ship passengers; others shunt them off to a far corner of the property and feed them separately. It's not really the children who are the problem. It may be the parents, who are trying to have a vacation themselves and have allowed family discipline to break down until it reaches the point where it can be restored only by a public shouting match—usually on the beach or around the pool. As one innkeeper puts it, "Kids around pools mean *noise*—so we don't allow them at the pool." In any case, many couples in hideaways are parents trying to get away from their own families for a day or two, so they're hardly enchanted to be surrounded by other people's squawking youngsters. Rowdy families are less of a bother in the Caribbean than they are back home because parents can't just pile everyone into a car and drive off to the islands. Sometimes there's a lot to be said for stiff air fares.

CONVENTIONS The object of a convention or sales conference is to whip people into a frenzy of enthusiasm; but frenzied enthusiasm is something you don't need when you're trying to escape the business or urban world. Very few of the hotels in this guide accept conventions; if they do, the groups are either small enough to be absorbed without trace, or so large they have to rent the entire hotel. However, most of the hotels in this guide will accept small, seminar-type groups in the off-season, and in many cases they have to do so to stay in business; but that kind of group shouldn't interfere with your privacy and pleasure. In some cases, it's an advantage: while the group is cooped up studying or discussing its specialty, you have the beach, windsurfers and tennis courts all to yourselves.

Signing In

"If we worried about whether or not our guests were married, we would lose maybe one-third of our clientele," seems to be a fairly general attitude among innkeepers in the Caribbean. Even in some of the most famous resorts, it's not unknown for the management to smuggle "Mrs. John Smith" down a ladder from the balcony when the real Mrs. John Smith arrives unexpectedly at the front door.

So, these hotels are hideaways where you won't be embarrassed if you forget to sign in as Mr. and Mrs., or even if you simply sign in with your own names; where bellhops won't snicker if the initials on your luggage don't match (a safe bet in the Caribbean where you'll be lucky if you find bellboys in the first place, and if you do, they'll probably be too drowsy to notice things such as initials); where the front-desk clerk won't look askance if you ask him/her to reconfirm your airline tickets and it turns out they have different names on them. Some hotels don't even bother to have you sign a register; few of them, if any, will ask to see passports or other identification.

Some managers prefer that you sign in with your real names, even if they don't match; others prefer you to sign as a couple because it's simpler for the staff. Unless you have strong views one liberated way or another, the simplest procedure is to write the noncommittal M/M—that is, M/M John Smith, M/M Ian Keown, and so on.

However, at least one of you should use your real name. If it's absolutely imperative that you both travel incognito, then at some point you'd better take the manager aside and explain that "Mr. John Smith" will be paying his bill with checks or credit cards in the name of whatever your name is.

If you're on an illicit adventure and don't want anyone to find out about it six months later, before you leave the hotel *ask the manager to make sure your name does not appear on any mailing lists for Christmas cards, newsletters and such.*

The Rates

This is the most hazardous chore in putting together a reliable guidebook. Most of the hotels in this guide were visited during the fall and winter of 1986–1987, when many managers or owners had not yet established their rates for winter 1987–1988. Unlike some guidebook writers, however, I feel that rates are indispensable in such a publication; therefore, to simplify the production of the guidebook and ensure that you get the most up-to-date figures possible I've listed all the latest rates in a special chapter at the end of the guide. This way you can scan the list more easily and compare resort A with resort B. Moreover, to give you some indication of what sort of place you're reading about, I've also included, with the description of each hotel, a symbol ($) for *approximate* costs. (See chart page 14.) The symbols (please note this carefully) are based on *high season MAP rates for two people, with breakfast and dinner*—that is, the cost of room plus breakfast and dinner. They are high season rather than summer rates because they happened to be the most reliable figures available when the guidebook was compiled; please remember, the dollar symbols would look much less ominous if they represented summer figures, and if you are considering a summer trip, I suggest that as a rule-of-thumb you chop off one $, except in the case of the lowest category.

Reservations

It's nice to pack a bag and just go on the spur of the moment, and if the moment happens to spur in the off-season, you may be able to drop in on some of these hotels and get the best room without a reservation.

But is it worth the risk? Think of it: you fly down there, take a long, costly taxi ride to the other side of the island, only to discover that by some fluke this happens to be the weekend when a bunch of people have come over from an adjoining island and have filled every room, or that the owners decided to close down for the weekend because they had no reservations. For the impetuous, I've listed telephone numbers, most of them direct-dial (first three digits are area codes for the island). Call ahead at least. In any case, at peak seasons it's imperative that you also reserve your *flight* weeks in advance.

For lovers who think ahead, there are several alternatives:

1. TRAVEL AGENT The agent who books your flight can also arrange your hotel reservation, probably at no extra charge; he/she will also attend to the business of deposits and confirmations. However, travel agents often have their own favorite islands and resorts, sometimes places involving no complications in terms of flights or reservations; if your agent tries to sell you a bigger island or resort, by all means consider it, but if you feel strongly about your own choice, dig in your heels.

2. HOTEL REPRESENTATIVE You pick up the telephone, call someone such as David B. Mitchell & Company or Scott Calder International, tell them where you want to stay and they can let you know (often right there and then) if your hotel is full or otherwise; they'll make your reservation, and, if there's time, send you confirmation—at no extra charge, unless they have to telex or telephone. You'll find a list of the leading hotel reps (who generally handle two or more hotels in this guide) at the end of this guide; individual hotel representatives and phone numbers are listed under the hotel itself.

3. TELEX You can contact the hotel directly, using a telex address, which is listed under each hotel. Telex is fast and simple because the message goes directly to the reservations office of the hotel and you can get a reply within minutes. It's also cheaper than telephoning. Moreover, a telex is more reliable than the telephone because both parties have the reservation and confirmation *in writing*. (You can send telexes via Western Union, ITT, or RCA offices.)

4. LETTER The least efficient. You could be senile by the time you get a reply.

Whatever method you choose, you must be specific; know the number of people in your party, date of arrival, time of arrival and flight number if possible; number of nights you plan to stay, date of departure; whether you want a double bed or twin beds, bathtub or shower; least expensive or most expensive room or suite, sea view or garden view or whatever; whether you want an EP, MAP or FAP rate (these terms are explained at the end of this guide). Finally, don't forget your return address or telephone number.

Deposits

Once you get a reply to your request for a reservation, assuming there's time, you'll be expected to make a deposit (usually one, two or three days, depending on the length of your stay). Of course it's a nuisance—what if you want to change your mind? That's just the point. The smaller hotels can't afford to have reservations for a full house, turn down other reservations in the meantime, only to have half of their expected clientele chicken out at the last minute.

From your point of view, the deposit guarantees your reservation. People sometimes goof down in the Caribbean, especially with reservations, but if you have a written confirmed reservation in your hand *with proof of a deposit* you're not going to be turned away from your hotel.

If you're going down there in the peak season, you should always allow yourself time to send a deposit and get a *written* confirmed reservation. Again, you're better off using a telex, which gives you and the hotel a reservation/confirmation record.

How to Lick High Costs

So long as people insist on scuttling south to the sun at the first hint of frost or snow, hotel rates will remain astronomical in the Caribbean during the winter months. The December-through-Easter period is the island inns' chance to make a profit and they grab the chance with a vengeance (remember, the owners have to pay wages and overhead in spring, summer and fall, too—even if *you're* in Maine or Europe).

Here are a few suggestions for keeping your budget within bounds:

1. AVOID THE PEAK SEASON Obviously, it's great to get some Caribbean sun when the frost is nipping up north, but March and April are not so hot in northern climes either, and it's often very pleasant to escape to the islands in October, November and early December; some people head south in May and June to get an early start on a suntan; even during summer, the Caribbean has its attractions, and more and more people are discovering them. Oddly enough, summer in the Caribbean islands can be *cooler* than in stifling northern cities; while northern beaches and facilities are overcrowded in summer, the beaches in the Caribbean are half empty; and while the northern resorts are charging peak-season rates, the Caribbean is available at bargain rates. So remember that the peak season lasts only four months (usually December 15 through Easter), *and for eight months of the year rates are one-quarter to one-half less.*

2. CHOOSE YOUR RESORT CAREFULLY Some resorts throw in everything with the rate—sailing, waterskiing, tennis, snorkeling gear and so on; others charge extra for almost everything. Compare, for example, Curtain Bluff and St. James's Club on Antigua—free scuba and waterskiing at the former, you pay for them at the latter. Obviously, if you *don't* want to scuba dive or water-ski, you may be better off at St. James's Club, in this case. But this sort of situation also occurs with tennis, windsurfing—even snorkeling gear.

3. DODGE TAXES Some islands have no tax on tourists, others are as high as 8 percent; not much as a percentage, true, but on a two-week vacation it can add up to a few hundred dollars. Taxes are listed in the section on rates at the end of this guide. So are service charges: read these details carefully for they can save you a small bundle. Not simply because some service charges are 10 percent, others 15 percent, but because in many cases the service charge relieves you of the need to tip. For example, this reminder from Antigua's Curtain Bluff: "A 10 percent service charge is added to all accounts. Therefore, TIPPING IS NOT ALLOWED." Their capitals. (This does not mean that guests cannot express their appreciation: "Curtain Bluff has a fund for the community of Old Road. If you want to donate funds, please see a member of the management.")

4. DRINK RUM On rum-producing islands, rum is less expensive than Scotch or bourbon, and in a thirst-building climate this can make a noticeable difference when the tab is tallied up at the end of your stay. However, some island governments clamp such enormous duties on soda or tonic that your rum may cost less than its mixer. In that case, drink the local beer.

The best way around big bar tabs is to buy a tax-free bottle of your favorite liquor at the airport before you leave. This may be frowned upon in smaller hotels, but in any case you should *never* drink from your bottle in public rooms. Several of the hideaways in this guide have a bottle of rum and mixers waiting for you in your room—on the house.

5. KITCHENS No one wants to go off on vacation and spend the time cooking, but a small kitchen is useful for preparing between-meal snacks, lunches and drinks, without running up room service charges. Several of the hotels listed in this guide have refrigerators and/or kitchenettes and/or fully equipped kitchens, and a few of them also have minimarkets on the premises. They can save you a lot of dollars without a lot of extra effort.

6. DOUBLE UP Consider the possibility of trotting off to the islands with your favorite couple and sharing a suite or bungalow/cottage/villa. If you do this in a place such as, say, Tryall in Montego Bay, you can enjoy a villa with kitchen, sitting room and two bedrooms with two complete bathrooms. You'll find many examples of such cost-cutting options in this guide.

7. PACKAGES These are special rates built around the themes of honeymoons, water sports, tennis, golf. "We have people coming back every year for five or six years on the honeymoon package," sighs one hotelkeeper. In fact, some couples have arrived on a honeymoon package with all their children in tow, looking for reduced rates for them, too. Honeymoon packages usually include frills such as a bottle of champagne, flowers for the lady, or a half-day sail up the coast. Check them carefully—you may be better off with a regular rate. Sports packages usually *are* a good deal. They will probably include free court time (carefully specified) for tennis players, or X number of free rounds for golfers. If you're a sports enthusiast, check with the hotel rep or your travel agent for the nitty-gritty details.

8. TOUR PACKAGES Dirty words to some people but they needn't be. A tour package is not the same thing as an escorted tour: it can mean simply that 10 or 20 people will be booked on the same flight to take advantage of a special fare; they may be given their choice of two or three hotels on the island, so you may never see them again until you get to the airport for your return flight. Local sightseeing is sometimes included, sometimes it's an option; some packages include boat trips and barbecues. If you don't feel like taking part in these activities, you may still be ahead of the game because the special rates you will be paying for hotels and flights may be such good deals. The advantages of package tours are that you may qualify for lower air fares (always with conditions, but you can probably live with them), and the tour operator may have negotiated lower hotel rates; in winter, tour operators may have "blocked off" a group of hotel rooms and seats on jets, and package tours may be your only hope of finding reservations.

Few of the hotels in this guide are likely to be overrun with package tours, but some of them do in fact accept small tour groups, a fact that is noted under the P.S. at the end of each hotel listing. Look into the tour brochures of some of the airlines—say, American, BWIA, Eastern or Pan Am—and you may find special packages built around some of these hotels—the Caravanserai and Grand Case Beach Club of St. Maarten/St. Martin, the Half Moon Club in Jamaica, Cobblers Cove in Barbados and Casa de Campo in the Dominican Republic.

The Ratings

All the hotels and resorts in this guide are above average in one way or another, but some obviously are more special than others. To make choosing simpler, I've rated the hotels (using symbols) for romantic atmosphere (palm trees), food and service (knives and forks), sports facilities (tennis balls) and cost (dollar signs). The ratings are highly personal and subjective—the fun part of compiling the guide, my reward to myself for scurrying around from island to island and hotel to hotel when I could just as easily have been lying on the beach.

PALM TREES represent the *romantic* atmosphere of a hotel or resort more than the quality or luxury or facilities. Of course, the two go together, and here we're talking also about setting, decor, size, efficiency, location, personality, welcome—the intangibles.

KNIVES AND FORKS evaluate not just the quality of the food, but the overall emphasis and attitude toward dining, the competence of the waiters, the way the food is placed before you. *This is a specifically Caribbean evaluation*—it takes into consideration the special circumstances in the islands. In other words, any hotel that promises "the finest in gourmet dining" or "the ultimate in continental cuisine" almost certainly gets a low score because this is a vain promise: "the finest continental cuisine" is something you find at a three-star restaurant in France. Caribbean islands just don't have access to the market gardens and meat markets to match those standards. There are times, in fact, when you get the impression that all the meals in the Caribbean are coming from some giant commissary in Miami (even fish); so hotels that list local dishes, such as conch pie, *keshi yena* or *colombo de poulet riz* on their menus, even if only occasionally, stand a better chance of getting a higher rating than most hotels trying to emulate continental cuisine (unless they do it really well).

Any hotel that forces you to dine indoors in an air-conditioned restaurant ranks badly (there are only two or three of them in this guide, and although one of them is Dorado Beach, which gets a four-knives and forks rating, at least it gives you the option of dining alfresco in a second restaurant, or on your room balcony). It seems to me that one of the great pleasures of dining in the Caribbean is to be in the open air, surrounded by the sounds of the tropical night or the sea, in an atmosphere of palms and stars—not in some third-rate interior designer's concept of an English pub or Manhattan nightspot. Wine does not enter into consideration in this guide. The conditions, usually, are all wrong for storing wine and caring for wine, and by the time it has been trans-shipped three times, it's overpriced. Most of the hotels that rate highly for food have passable to good wine lists; otherwise it's a hit-and-miss affair (except, perhaps, on the French islands, or in special cases such as Curtain Bluff hotel in Antigua, Malliouhana on Anguilla and Biras Creek on Virgin Gorda, all run by oenophiles).

In the listings following each hotel, you'll occasionally find the term *family style.* This doesn't mean that you all sit down with the kiddies; it means, rather, that you don't get a menu, you take what's offered, and usually all the guests sit down to dine at the same time, perhaps at communal tables. Sometimes you will be offered a choice of dishes, sometimes not; if you have problems with your diet, check with the manager each morning, and if he's planning something you don't fancy, he'll probably prepare a steak or some other simple alternative. If you're fussy about food, skip places serving family-style meals. Moreover, you may not want to dine with strangers each evening.

While on the subject of dining: please note that under each hotel listing I spell out the evening dress code. I've seen too many hapless vacationers either laden with wardrobes they have no opportunity to show off or, conversely, the male has to borrow tie or jacket to get into the dining room. Although most of these hideaways set their code as casual or informal this does not mean sloppy—and for most places that means no shorts, no tank tops or T-shirts in the evening, cover-ups and no wet swimsuits at lunchtime. My personal preference is to have the option of dressing or not, depending on my mood; I have obviously included some places that expect guests to dress up every evening, but they either have alternative dining areas or can arrange for you to have dinner on your private patio or balcony.

TENNIS BALLS offer you a quick idea of the availability of sporting facilities, but you'll also find the actual facilities spelled out at the end of each hotel. I tried originally to include prices for each activity, but this became too cumbersome; however, you will learn from the listings whether a particular sport is free or whether you have to pay an additional fee.

Remember, no matter how well-endowed the hotel, sports facilities are *less crowded in the nonwinter months.*

DOLLAR SIGNS Use these as a rough guide only, primarily for comparing one resort with another. For detailed rates, turn to the special chapter at the end of the guide. The $ symbols are based on *winter rates for two people;* since the most accessible rate for comparison between hotels is the *MAP rate,* this is the one that is used (that is, for room, breakfast and dinner). Each $ represents roughly $50; where a hotel overflows into more than one category, I've used the lower category, assuming that this represents a reasonable proportion of the available rooms. For a quick guide to *summer* rates, you will not be far off the mark if you reduce the higher ratings by one $.

Here are the ratings:

	A port of call
	A long weekend
	Time for a suntan
	A place to linger
	Happily ever after
	Sustenance
	Good food
	Something to look forward to
	As close to haute cuisine *as you can get in the Caribbean*
	Some diversions
	Lots of things to keep your mind off sex
	More diversions than you'll have stamina for
	All that and horseback riding, too
$	*$150 or under, MAP for two*
$$	*$150 to $250 MAP for two*
$$$	*$250 to $350 MAP for two*
$$$$	*$350 to $450 MAP for two*
$$$$$	*$450 and over, MAP for two*

Added Attractions

A special feature in this guide is *Added Attractions* at the end of some islands. These are, for the most part, hotels, inns and resorts that we visited as possibilities but which didn't quite measure up; in some cases they are hotels that were rated in earlier editions of the guide but have since lost some of their appeal or changed management. But they may help fill a few gaps for you, especially since several of them are relatively inexpensive. If you visit any of them and think they deserve to be featured and rated, please let me know.

Double Beds

Some Caribbean hoteliers seem to have installed twin beds in most of their rooms. However, most hotels of any size have some rooms with double, queen- or king-size beds, and all but the tiniest hideaways can arrange to push two twins together to make a double—*if you give them advance notice.* If this is the case, however, check before indulging in any trampolining, because if the beds are pushed together and sheeted lengthwise rather than crosswise they may part like the Red Sea and you may end up in a voluptuous heap on the floor.

Creepy-Crawlies and Other Hazards

Snakes, spiders, tarantulas are no problem. Mosquitoes, no-see-ums and sand flies have been sprayed almost to oblivion on most islands; however, they do sometimes appear in certain types of weather, so if you have the sort of skin that can rouse a dying mosquito to deeds of heroism, take along a repellent.

Sea urchins are a hazard on some islands, depending on tides or seasons or something I don't understand. Every hotel seems to have its solution, but, for what it's worth, here is the traditional remedy of the island of Saba: "Count the number of spines sticking in you, then swallow one mouthful of sea water for each spine." Since sea urchin stings are painful, check with the hotel staff before venturing into the sea.

Drinking water is *not* a problem on most islands, but it *is* chemically different from what you're accustomed to, and if your system is touchy about such things, ask for bottled water.

Sun is something else altogether. Naturally, you want to get a quick tan, and of course you love lying on the beach—but remember, your reason for slipping off together is love, and love can be a painful affair if you both look like lobsters and feel like barbecues.

Remember, too, the Caribbean sun is particularly intense; one hour a day is enough, unless you already have a hint of tan. Some enthusiasts forget they can get a sunburn while *in* the water; if you plan to do a lot of snorkeling, wear a T-shirt. If you do get a burn, stand in a lukewarm shower. Some people recommend compresses of really strong tea; one of the beach boys on Aruba has quite a sideline going rubbing on the leaf of the aloe plant; the Greeks recommend rubbing on yogurt. For heat prostration, Sabans again seem to have the endearing answer: "Rub the body with rum, particularly around the stomach."

Muggings and Other Vexations

Each time I set out to research this guide, friends keep cautioning me about the horrible things that might happen to me in the Caribbean—robbery, mugging, assault, battery, anti-Americanism, fascism, racism and other everyday hassles.

Nothing has happened so far. There are probably plenty of statistics around to prove that things *can* be unpleasant in the Caribbean, but it has never been immediately obvious to me.

Piracy on the High Roads

Caribbean taxi drivers. Now there's a motley, shameless, scurrilous bunch of brigands! They begin hectoring you the second you leave the plane, follow you, if they can, through customs and immigration, and before they take time to welcome you to their lovely island in the sun they're already trying to make you "reserve" them for sightseeing tours and the trip back to the airport. (There are, of course, exceptions, and I hereby apologize to the one taxi driver in a hundred who is pleasant, courteous, punctual, honest.)

Their gross behavior can get your amorous tryst off to an unpleasant start, and the way around this is to ask your hotel to assign one of its pool of "approved" drivers to meet you at the airport; the hotel will send you his name when confirming your reservation, in which case, you simply ask for Sebastian or whatever his name is when you get there. If there's no time to send his name before you arrive, the hotel may post a message for you on the airport notice board, telling you to ask for Sebastian. (This procedure is not the same thing as sending over a hotel limousine; you may still have to pay the regular taxi fare, but at least it will be the official rate and not whatever the driver thinks he can get away with.)

Taxis can cost you an arm and a leg in the Caribbean, and the driver may go for the shoulder and thigh too. That's why I've included the cost of the taxi ride from the airport in the list of nitty-gritty following each hotel.

The drivers' point of view is that their costs are unusually high—imported cars, imported gas, imported parts, highways that knock the hell out of the cars, stiff insurance rates, and so on. Fine. What's not so understandable is why island governments kowtow to the drivers, who won't allow anyone else to operate a bus or limousine service; the result is that you, the visitors, have to pay perhaps $10 to $12 for a taxi ride, when you could be paying only $2 to $3 for a minibus or limousine. On some islands authorities quite blatantly post lower rates for residents. In some cases, taxis operate on a "seat available" basis—that is, you pay a share of the cost with other people going in the same direction; but if only six people get off an interisland flight they may not be going in your direction, and in any case by the time the immigration officer has finished scratching his head and stamping your passport, all the "seat available" taxis may have mysteriously left. Your best bet, if you have a long taxi ride, is to ask your hotel to have a taxi and driver waiting for you at the airport.

Some Caribbean Comments

WATER You'll be constantly reminded of the old Caribbean adage—"Water is the gold of the Caribbean," or as it's less eloquently phrased on some signs, "On our island in the sun we don't flush for number one." In deluxe resorts with their own catchments and reverse osmosis plants, the cost to the hotel for one shower may be $3.50—your two showers each per day account for $15 of your rate; hotels that have to import water will have a still higher bill. Be sparing. Shower together.

HOT WATER Most of the hotels in this guide supply hot water, but a few don't (noted in the listings for that hotel). Don't let that turn you off; the water pipes are just below the surface and the midday sun warms the water before it reaches the tap. In the early morning, just cling to each other.

CARIBBEAN SERVICE Don't expect the staff to rush around. It's all right for you—you're there for only a few days, but the people who live there don't find the glaring sun so appealing day after day. They'll operate at normal Caribbean pace no matter how much you tip, and at *less* than normal pace if you shout and snap your fingers and stamp your feet. You just have to learn a few tricks. For example, always *anticipate* your thirst: order your drinks about 10 minutes before you'll be gasping for them. Also, place your order in simple English; the islanders don't want to figure out what you're trying to say—it's too hot to bother.

Escape Routes to the Caribbean

There are several hundred flights a week from the North American mainland to the Caribbean islands, and it's about time you were on one of them. But which one? What with deregulation and mergers, it's a hassle trying to keep up with airlines these days. You'll find a quick summary of the major services to the various islands, or groups of islands, at the beginning of each chapter in this guide; please note that this information is based on *winter schedules,* and lists only nonstop or direct (that is, with no change of aircraft) flights from major North American departure points.

The major multidestination carriers to the islands are still *American, Eastern, Pan Am, Air Canada* and *British West Indies Airways (BWIA),* but they have been joined by others such as *Delta* and *TWA.* If you live in or transit via the northeast, American and Pan Am are the carriers with most flights to the islands, and they should be your first choice; most Caribbean flights from Miami are flown by Eastern. Both Eastern and American have expanded their Caribbean services by introducing new regional divisions—*Eastern Metro* and *American Eagle* respectively, both based in San Juan and fanning out from there to other islands. These new services are among the best things that have happened to the Caribbean in recent years. Both airlines are plugged into the parents' computers, so reservations are much easier than with most Caribbean-based airlines; both airlines have above-average concern for considerations other Caribbean carriers seem to find a nuisance—such as on-time takeoffs and honoring reservations; both airlines are flying modern fleets of twin-engined prop or turboprop planes. Remember (and I've said this elsewhere because it's important) when using these regional services that the smaller aircraft do not have capacious overhead bins or racks for garment bags, so luggage that would normally be considered carry-on will have to be checked. That probably means a little more care in packing.

Of the Caribbean-based carriers, BWIA (known affectionately or patronizingly, as the case may be, as BeeWee) is a sort of national carrier; it probably has to serve too many islands (and, therefore, too many governments) for its own good—Antigua, St. Lucia, Barbados, Trinidad and Tobago (and, off and on, St. Kitts/Nevis). *Air Jamaica* flies all up and down the eastern states and provinces and sometimes the west coast, garnering passengers for Montego Bay and Kingston. It scored a lot of points with upscale vacationers last winter by chartering a British Airways Concorde every Saturday and sweeping vacationers off to Montego Bay in more style than they're accustomed to on Caribbean runs. Let's hope it does it *every* winter. Let's hope other airlines follow suit.

ALM (Antilleanse Luchtvaart Maatschappij) is the flag carrier of the Netherlands Antilles, linking Miami and New York with Aruba, Bonaire and Curaçao (with occasional service to Haiti), with interisland services to St. Maarten, San Juan and Trinidad.

Airlines Within the Caribbean

Apart from Eastern Metro and American Eagle, mentioned above, it may be necessary to finish your trip to your chosen hideaway on a local island-hopper. Here's where the fun begins—*if* you have a bottomless sense of humor. I recently planned to fly on a new carrier called *Air Puerto Rico.* When I got to the check-in counter, the flight had been canceled. Why? Because they were changing insurance companies. I'm still waiting for my refund—three months later. If they ever straighten out their insurance, they may be operating between Miami, San Juan, Mayaguez, plus Casa de Campo in the Dominican Republic. But don't break your neck getting to the check-in counter.

Windward Island Airways is my favorite interisland carrier. St. Maarten-based, it shuttles between Juliana Airport and Saba, St. Eustatius, St. Kitts, St. Barthélemy and Anguilla. This very efficient little outfit, run by a Dutchman, operates a complex "bus service" (more than a thousand flights a year to Saba alone) with a few DeHavilland Twin Otters, that short takeoff and landing (STOL) workhorse, the engines of which are washed every morning—*inside* and out. There are only six pilots in the entire world licensed to land on Saba, and they all fly with Windward.

Air Guadeloupe, Air Martinique and *Air Barthélemy* are handy, fairly dependable commuter lines linking the French islands with each other and with outsiders such as Barbados, Antigua, St. Thomas, San Juan, St. Vincent and the Grenadines.

The biggest operation in the Caribbean is *LIAT,* Leeward Islands Air Transport. In terms of departures/arrivals per day it's actually one of the largest airlines *in the world.* It's always been a sort of laughingstock, and in the last edition of this guide I quoted some of the scathing comments associated with its acronym—Leave Island Any Time, etc. Truth is, LIAT is a much-improved airline. Serving so many independent islands with the kind of frequency (45,000 takeoffs and landings a year) LIAT has to maintain is a momentous task. Recently, the management called in specialists from *Aer Lingus* to study the airline's operations and make recommendations. The result is that LIAT now has a first-rate on-time record (officially, although it's hard to believe when you're on a flight, as I was earlier this year, leaving one hour early and heading north instead of south). Moreover, the line has recently introduced new aircraft—updated versions of its warhorse Hawker-Siddeley Avro 7s (you no longer feel like you're about to sink through the worn cushions to the floor) and the nifty DeHavilland Dash propjets. They may Leave Island Any Time but once in the air you're in good hands.

For short flights to the smaller islands, it may be smart to charter a small plane. The local hotels will make the arrangements for you, teaming you with other couples to cut costs. These shared charters are common practice in St. Kitts/Nevis and the Grenadines. For St. Kitts/Nevis or other islands around St. Maarten or Antigua, you can arrange to have a Beechcraft or Partenavia of *Carib Aviation* waiting for your jet. From Antigua to Nevis is a quick flight (10 minutes or so), costs only a few dollars more when shared and can save hours waiting for a scheduled LIAT flight. In St. Vincent and the Grenadines, most hotels will arrange to have you met at Barbados by a representative of *Air Mustique* or *Tropicair,* who will escort you to your small plane and make sure your luggage is aboard. The alternative is probably a connecting flight via St. Vincent or Grenada, which could take forever.

Most Caribbean airlines do not have the sophisticated electronic reservations systems, or even the alert staffs of U.S. airlines, so always double-check tickets—date, flight number, check-in times, and so forth. In the case of LIAT—double-double-check.

Even if you're taking a 10-minute flight with only half a dozen passengers to be boarded you'll be expected to check in *an hour and a half* before departure. I questioned this with one airline executive, and his disarming reply was: "Because the flight may leave early." He wasn't kidding, either. Moreover, to be sure of your seat, get to the check-in desk as early as possible, even if your ticket is reconfirmed—and make sure the check-in attendant sees it. Don't assume that being *in line* on time is enough to guarantee your seat.

Always reconfirm your flight 48 hours before departure. This is very important, because some of the lines have a tendency to overbook, and some passengers have a tendency not to turn up; so the airline may simply decide that if you don't reconfirm you're not going to turn up and they'll give your seat to someone else. In the case of LIAT, double-reconfirm. Many hotels will handle your reconfirmations, but there's nothing they can do if you wait until it's too late.

Also, a reconfirmed ticket doesn't mean a thing until it's in the hands of the ticket agent. You can be standing politely in line, ticket in hand, and still lose your seat. The people huddled around the check-in counter may not have tickets—they may be waiting for someone not to show up. You, for example. Push your way to the front.

If you're taking along carry-on luggage, remember that what may qualify as carry-on size on a 747 may have to be checked on smaller island-hopping aircraft, so make sure it is locked and labeled. Also, luggage allowances on U.S. carriers may not be acceptable to local carriers, and you may find yourself paying excess baggage charges on some stretches. If you anticipate problems, see your travel agent before you leave.

Island-Hopping Stopovers

This is really something you have to take up with your travel agent, but I mention it here to remind you of some of the possibilities you may be overlooking for visiting several islands for the price of one. A full-revenue ticket from New York to, say, Barbados may entitle you to stop off for a few days in Antigua on the way down, in Martinique or Guadeloupe on the way back. Likewise, with a full-revenue round-trip ticket from New York to Haiti in your pocket you may be able to visit Santo Domingo and/or Puerto Rico, at no extra fare; a round-trip ticket Miami–Tobago may also take you to St. Lucia and Trinidad. The actual stops will depend on the type of fare, day of week, season, and so on—but the prospect of seeing twice as much Caribbean for the same price is certainly worth the time it will take you to ask about island stopovers.

Boat Travel

Several of the islands or groups of islands are linked by seagoing ferries.

In the Virgin Islands, the M/V *Bomba Charger,* M/V *Native Son* and M/V *Speedy's Fantasy* operate 90-passenger, air-conditioned multihulls between Charlotte Amalie in St. Thomas and West End, Road Town and Virgin Gorda in the British Virgins. Fares: $13 per person each way.

Another twin-hull ferryboat, M/V *Alisur Amarillo,* sails between St. Maarten's Philipsburg and St. Barthélemy, leaving 9:30 A.M. and returning at 4:00 P.M., 30 minutes and $20 each way. The same vessel also operates picnic/tour excursions to Saba and Anguilla, for $65 and $50, respectively.

Belize

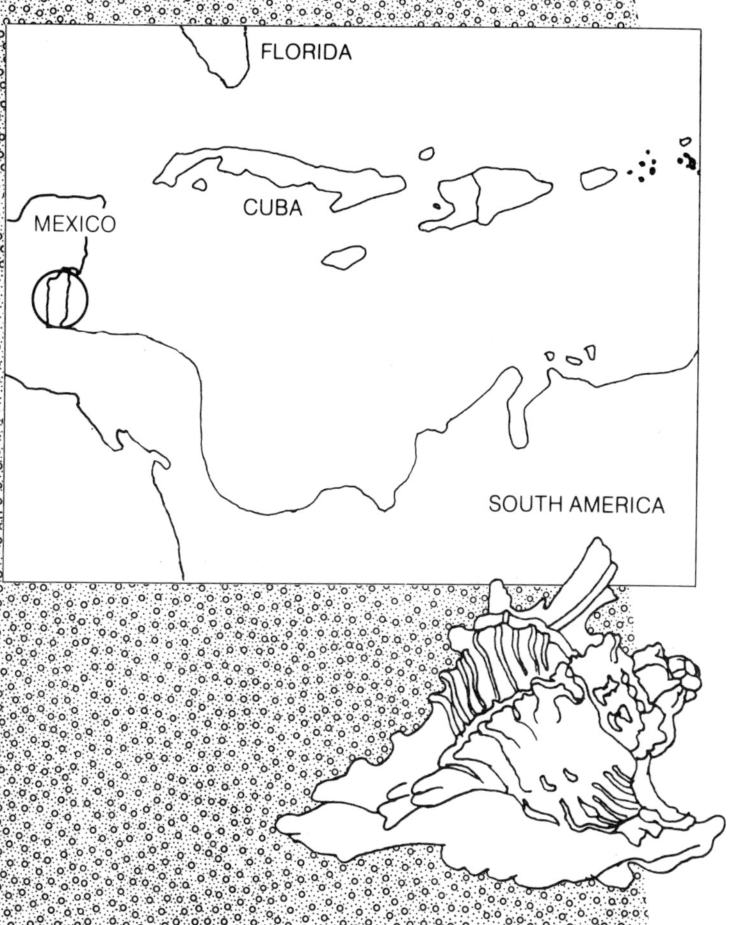

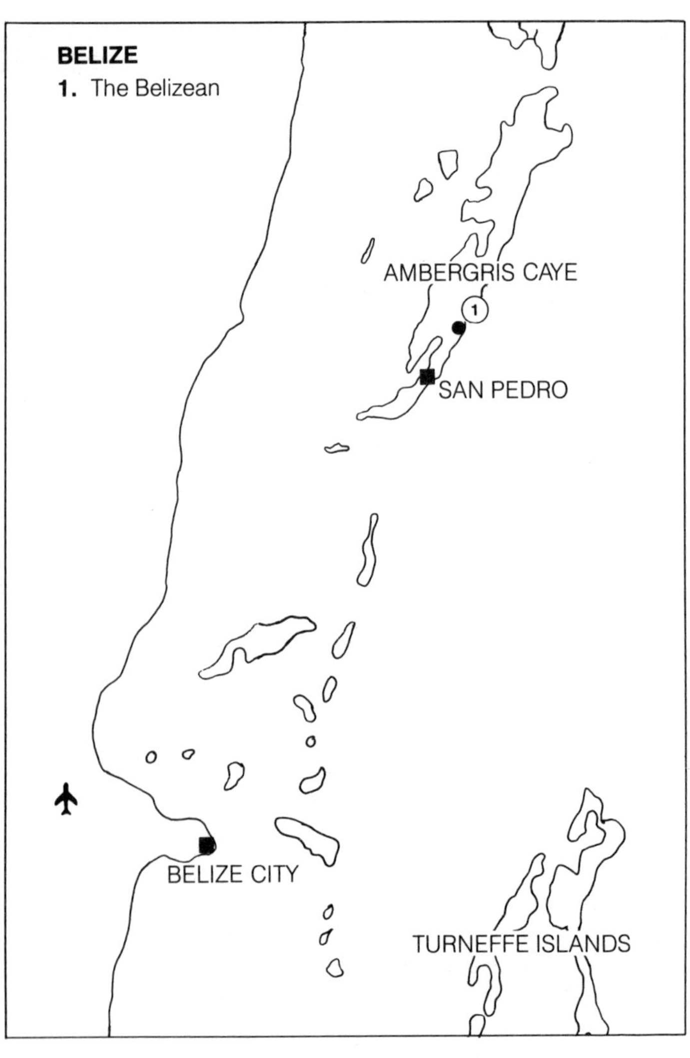
BELIZE
1. The Belizean
AMBERGRIS CAYE
1
SAN PEDRO
BELIZE CITY
TURNEFFE ISLANDS

Belize

It's the country just to the south of Mexico on the Caribbean coast—and nowhere near all the goings-on down that way. In fact, Ambergris Caye, which you'll be reading about below, is so close to the Yucatán you could almost walk from one to the other. Belize is a most unusual country—part Mayan, part Spanish, part Creole, part British (a member of the Commonwealth, English is the official language and the bobbies don't carry guns).

It's population could fit easily into one big apartment complex in Manhattan, sharing a land twice the size of Massachusetts. Its hilly jungle-clad hinterland is noted for ruined Mayan temples and towns, but its main tourist attraction has always been its 150-mile barrier reef, second in size only to Australia's Great Barrier Reef. Of the reef's 175 islets, or cays, Ambergris is the best-known and most developed for visitors—mostly people interested in scuba diving and sport fishing.

HOW TO GET THERE Easy. Miami is less than 2 hours away, with flights to Belize City three times a day on three airlines—TACA, TAN and Challenger. There are also scheduled flights from New Orleans, Houston and Los Angeles, all jets.

If you're bound for Ambergris Caye, your hotel can arrange to have Tropic Air meet you with a twin- or single-engine plane for the 15-minute flight to San Pedro ($45 round trip).

The Belizean

Ambergris Caye

$$$

Until late 1986, when The Belizean hosted its first guests, visiting Ambergris Caye meant settling for spartan to modest accommodations geared for fishing and diving devotees. Now Ambergris Caye has a small deluxe resort that puts this backwater islet on a par with most of its fellow islands to the east.

It's the dream come true of a multilingual, cosmopolitan Belgian named Paul den Haenen, who acquired Poland Springs mineral water in Maine, boosted sales and revenues, then sold the company to Perrier (a family he's related to). Five years ago, he fell in love with Ambergris Caye, bought 18 acres just beyond the fishing village of San Pedro and set about building his own private getaway. It wasn't long until he elaborated his plans to incorporate a small top-flight inn that reflects his own elegant, international style and his passion for detail.

Three years and $4.5 million later, The Belizean opened its handsome mahogany and beveled-glass doors. Quietly, without fanfare. A wise move, as you'll see. But word is leaking out anyway about this great little place down near Mexico somewhere, and it didn't hurt that Harrison Ford stayed here while filming *Mosquito Coast.*

What Ford found here was anything but primitive. Three white stucco buildings with contemporary lines, topped with roofs of azure Mexican tiles and split-level ceilings with fanlights. Wall-to-wall mahogany-framed windows with French doors open onto broad, expansive decks where guests lounge or dine beneath sun umbrellas. In front of the main lodge stands a small, rather formal fountain in Spanish colonial style; and out on the lawn, near the beach, Mayanlike steps lead to a platform 20 ft. high and supporting not a somber temple, but a swimming pool decorated with plant-filled terra-cotta urns and mahogany deck chairs swathed in thick blue-and-white cushions.

As you enter your high-ceilinged room through gleaming mahogany doors, your eyes feast on gleaming mahogany everywhere—a two-poster or four-poster bed and a massive chest that opens to reveal an old-time secretary with nooks and drawers and a silver-and-crystal inkstand. The chest's upper doors conceal a 19-in. TV with remote control and stereo speakers, while the lower doors open to a VCR unit. The small hallway leading to the sumptuous tile bath is dominated by an oversize armoire with a six-drawer chest inside. The bathroom, equally oversize and equally impressive, sports Kohler double vanities, a 6-ft. reclining tub, a glass-enclosed shower and a bidet. The thick peach towels are hand-monogrammed, the soap is hand-milled, the passion fruit *bain moussaint* is from Aix-en-Provence. As we said, Ambergris Caye has never known anything like this.

All the rooms are more or less the same, except for the beds: book numbers 2 or 5 if you want a king-size bed, numbers 3 or 4 if you don't want a connecting door (not 100 percent soundproof) between you and the couple next door. On the other hand, numbers 5 and 6, farthest from the pool, are the most private.

The main lodge is an even grander version of your guest room, with plump white pillows on plump white sofas in the living room, onyx chess set and backgammon boards set up invitingly in the games room. The centerpiece of the dining room is a formal table for eight, complete with three-taper silver candelabra and Lierre Lauvage china. If you prefer whispery privacy, ask for one of the smaller tables nestled in alcoves. Either way, you'll find it hard to believe that this seaside oasis is carved from a coconut plantation, or that ocelots still prowl the remaining jungle behind the inn. Not that the food is so outstanding. Your meals may range from delectable lobster salad for lunch and mouth-watering shrimp for dinner to dry and disappointing lobster tails and vegetables. You can't expect the Grand Véfour here. The kitchen is the bailiwick of the den Haenen family cook from Brazil, Anne Marie, who cooks by instinct with a soupçon of acquired traditional French. The hotel has its own vegetable garden, the juices are freshly squeezed, the fish as fresh as fish can be.

All is not yet perfect, as you can tell, in this implausible would-be paradise. Even partner/manager Ingeborg Sorensen will concede that point (she is also the ex-wife but still best friend of den Haenen). The service, though warm and friendly (Belizeans seem to truly enjoy having visitors in their midst), is not yet up to top-resort standards—or even up to the elegant surroundings. The landscaping, too, in an early experimental stage, needs more hibiscus and bougainvillea, especially to entwine and camouflage the out-of-place rough-hewn railings around the decks. But all these things will come. "Everything will be in order in time for the upcoming season," says Ms. Sorensen. And having sampled the best the world has to offer, she has a clear-headed vision of what's needed.

In the meantime, your attention is diverted from such start-up shortcomings by the inimitable Ingeborg, by the luxury of the rooms, by the sheer incongruity of the place. It's this incongruity that sets The Belizean apart. Each day you wake in the lap of luxury, each night you tumble into bed in the lap of luxury. Between, you can stroll a primitive shoreline (some sand, some reef, some mangrove) or explore a wondrous reef (most islands would give their all for just one mile of it). You can putter around the unpaved, wood-framed fishing village of San Pedro.

Best of all, you can ask the manager to set up an excursion to the mainland to explore jungle rivers and Mayan ruins. At Altun Ha or Xunantunich, Chaa Creek or Chetumal. Most guests go by plane. Be adventurous; take a boat to Altun Ha or Chetumal. This is, after all, seafaring country. And you can still get there and back to your tub-for-two before dinner. *(E.M.)*

NAME: The Belizean

OWNERS/MANAGERS: Paul den Haenen, Ingeborg Sorensen

ADDRESS: San Pedro, Ambergris Caye, Belize

LOCATION: Just over 3 miles north of San Pedro and a 5-minute launch ride from the San Pedro airstrip (the hotel will meet your plane)

TELEPHONE: 501-026-2128

TELEX: 494107

RESERVATIONS: First Resorts Management, New York

CREDIT CARDS: American Express, MasterCard, Visa

ROOMS: 6, in 2 bungalows, all facing the beach, all with large decks, air-conditioning and ceiling fans, refrigerators, satellite TV/VCR, clock radios, cassette players, telephones, bathrooms with large tubs, separate showers, bidets, hair dryers

MEALS: Basically whenever guests feel like eating, but officially breakfast 7:30–9:30, lunch noon–2:00, dinner from 7:30 (in the main lodge or on the veranda, approx. $40 for 2); informal but stylish dress; room service to 9:00 P.M. (charcoal grills are also available for guests' use)

ENTERTAINMENT: Piano player Saturday evening (maybe other evenings too), occasional folk dance groups (Garifuna, Warribaggabagga), taped music (classical, jazz, Brazilian, French), nighttime launch service to San Pedro for reggae or disco—and, of course, your choice of movies from the resort's $30,000 film library

SPORTS: Beach (largely manmade, not so good for swimming except near the reef), swimming pool, snorkeling, windsurfing, Sunfish sailing, aqua scooters, jet skiing, dune buggies—all free; scuba diving, fishing, waterskiing, sailing trips on native fishing boats called scamps—at extra charge

Cayman Islands

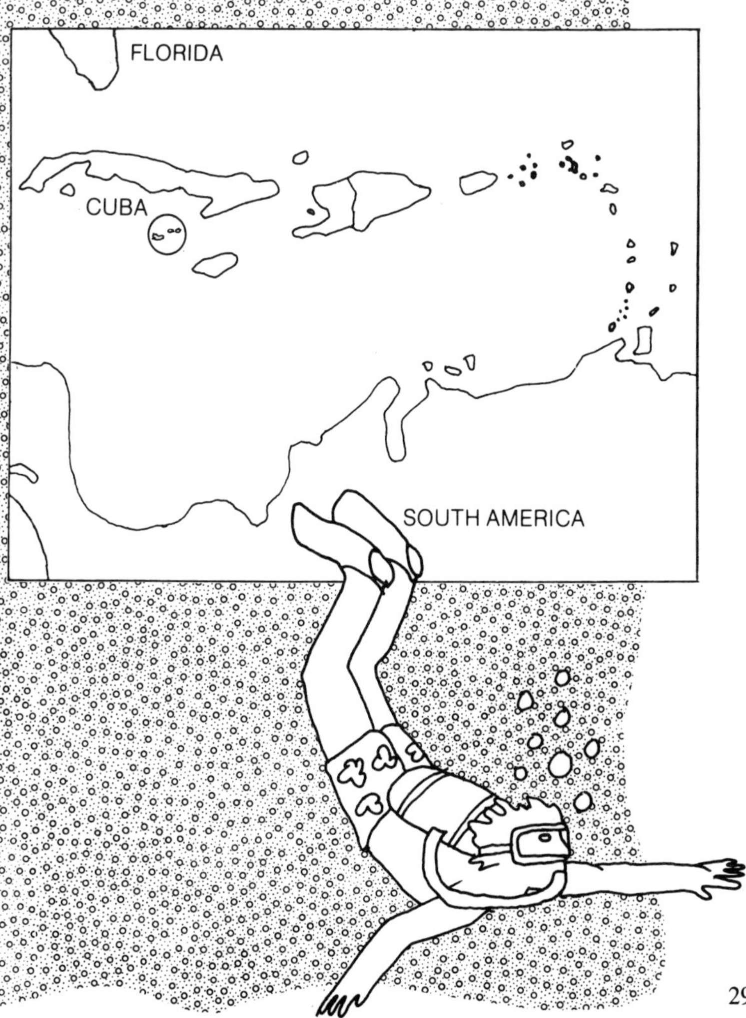

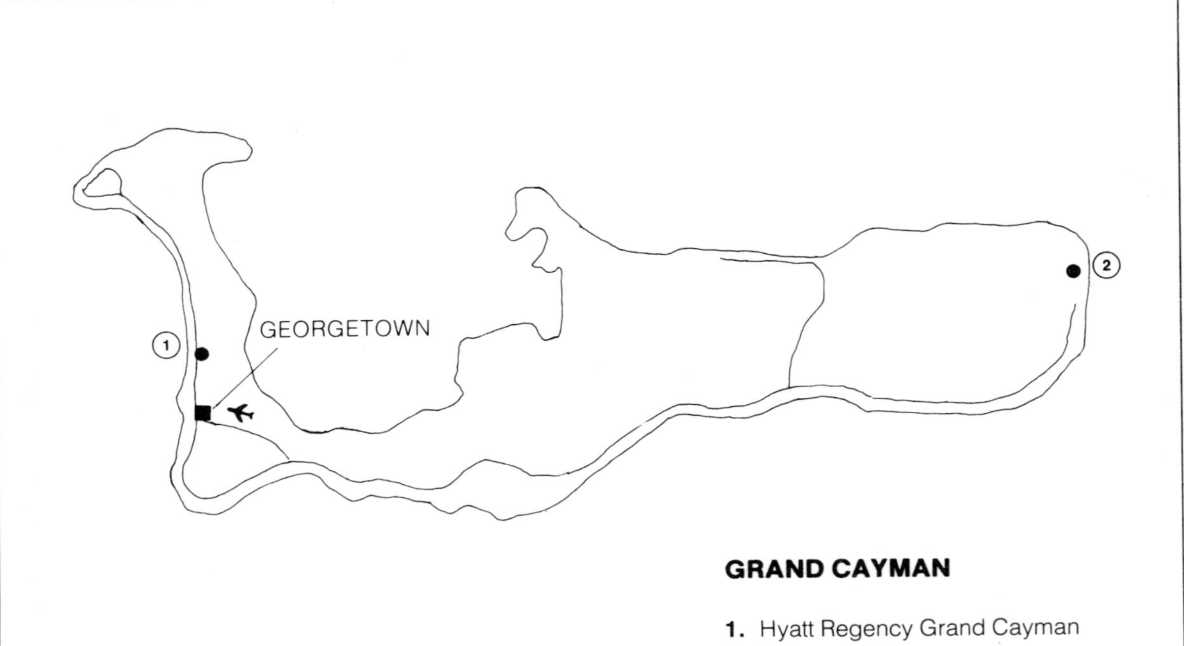
GEORGETOWN
1
2
GRAND CAYMAN
1. Hyatt Regency Grand Cayman
2. Tortuga Club

Cayman Islands

There are three of them—Grand Cayman, Little Cayman, Cayman Brac—together they're a British Crown Colony that will probably remain that way for some time because, as one local taxi driver put it, "If we got independence we'd only end up with a lot of politicians."

Otherwise, the Caymans can't seem to make up their mind what they want to be. On the one hand, the colony claims to be, as the brochures put it, "as unspoiled as it was the day Columbus sailed by"; on the other hand, a banking boom has "transformed George Town from a sleepy village into a dynamic financial capital." At last count there were about 400 banks for a population of less than 20,000 plus who knows how many megabucks wheeler-dealers skulking among the sea-grape trees searching for the perfect offshore banking. The islands are touted as a tax haven, but everyone seems to forget to mention that it's taxless only for people who live there or buy condominiums there; the poor visitors get zapped with a 6 percent tax on rooms, a $5 departure tax (but they *have* fixed up the airport nicely), another fee for a local driver's license, and the aftereffects of an import duty that has sent prices soaring alarmingly ($1.50 for a ginger ale, for example).

All of this would be easier to take if Grand Cayman, the largest of the trio, were something special. But this is no lofty, luxuriant Jamaica or St. Lucia. It's flat, swampy and characterless (well, what else can you call a place whose prime tourist attraction is a turtle farm?). True, there are lots of beaches, most notably Seven Mile Beach running north from George Town, but they're lined with an uninspired collection of hotels and condominiums (none of them, it should be noted, higher than the palm trees, so no one can accuse the authorities of ruining the place).

What the Caymans do have—in abundance—are miles, fathoms, leagues of coral reefs, with water so clear you can spot an angel fish 200 ft. away. I have it on the unimpeachable authority of world-class diver Helga Gimbel that diving in the Caymans is "AAA + . . . absolutely spectacular."

HOW TO GET THERE Daily nonstop from Miami on Cayman Airways, Eastern and Northwest, from Houston on Cayman Airways; in winter, charter flights once or twice a week from New York, Chicago, Detroit, Atlanta, Boston, Philadelphia, Tampa, St. Louis and Minneapolis (and possibly others); flights once or twice daily from Grand Cayman to Cayman Brac.

Hyatt Regency Grand Cayman

Grand Cayman

$$$

You won't find many chain hotels represented in these pages, but, like its sister resort at Dorado Beach in Puerto Rico, this $54-million newcomer eschews the Hyatt formula.

The architecture, described as British colonial, is really more Birthday Cake colonial, with white iron verandas and decorative trim "icing," a pastel-blue facade accented by flower boxes and decorative fanlights. After dark, the *mise-en-scène* becomes positively magical, what with a zillion lights gleaming through French windows, bathing the reflecting pools and fountains, spotlighting the fountains and festooning the ficus trees.

The Hyatt is just one corner of an 88-acre resort development known as Britannia, which will, when completed a few years down the line, have scores of condos, its own beach club and marina, as well as the current hotel and one-of-a-kind golf course. The hotel itself is comprised of a courtyard of lawns, pools and fountains surrounded by the seven wings of the hotel, the tallest of which is five stories high. At 235 rooms, it is, for my money, a hundred rooms too big, but it brings to the Caymans a touch of luxury hitherto found only in a few of the island's condominiums. The guest rooms are tastefully designed, as you'd expect from Hyatt, and equipped with all the trimmings, such as minibars and bathrobes. Color schemes reflect the aquas and corals of sea and sand, with flashes of lilac and pink tossed in; travertine marble layers the foyers, bathrooms and oval bathtubs, the custom-designed furniture features mostly upholstered rattan and wicker (the only complaint here is that in the standard rooms a two-seat couch crowds the room without adding much in comfort or convenience, unless you plan to watch hours of television). For a view of the sea (about 300 yards away) you'll have to check into the top 2 floors; if you want private sunning space, ask for 1 of the 12 Terrace Rooms. The most attractive accommodations are probably the Studio Suites (with sleeping galleries, brass beds, wet bar and 3 telephone extensions); but for as much seclusion and privacy as you can muster in a hotel this size, check into the 2 wings housing the premium Regency Club and ask for a room overlooking the golf course.

Generous in all things, the Hyatt people give you a choice of dining spots—the veranda of the golf course clubhouse, the soon-to-open beach club and the Garden Loggia Café (the main dining room, stylishly decorated in bleached ash paneling with latticed ceilings, French windows opening to the alfresco garden extension). Menus are hardly predictable Hyatt fare, the German chef producing a masterly combination of continental, American and Caribbean dishes—tenderloin of veal with braised bok choy and grilled swordfish with passion fruit butter. (Remember to make reservations for dinner: the Hyatt is now the most stylish dining spot along Seven Mile Beach and popular with nonresident diners.)

Even Hyatt's water-sports facilities are a notch beyond the usual with a flagship 65-ft. catamaran designed specifically for cruising around the Caymans and equipped with spacious decks, comfortable seating, stereo, bar, two restrooms and underwater glass panels for fish watching.

But what heaps most attention on Britannia is its golf course. Jack Nicklaus not only designed the 9-hole links-style course, he also designed the special Cayman Ball, a sphere that claims to do something my own tee shots have been doing for years—going half as far as they should. The advantage of the Cayman Ball in a resort like this is that players can get in 18 holes in half the time, on a course that requires space for 9 rather than 18 holes. Figure that out. The links (as beautiful as anything Nicklaus has designed) also function as an 18-hole executive course weekday afternoons, as a 9-hole regulation course on weekends. It may not be St. Andrews but at least it's another reason besides scuba diving for going to the Caymans.

NAME: Hyatt Regency Grand Cayman

MANAGER: Denis O'Flannery

ADDRESS: P.O. Box 1698, Grand Cayman, B.W.I

LOCATION: On the Britannia resort development, across the main road from Seven Mile Beach, 2 miles outside of George Town, 12 minutes and $10 from the airport

TELEPHONE: 809-949-1234

TELEX: 4334 Hyatt CI

RESERVATIONS: Hyatt Worldwide, 800-228-9000

CREDIT CARDS: All major cards

ROOMS: 235, including 43 Regency Club rooms, 9 studio suites, 2 deluxe suites, some with terraces or patios, some with small verandas, all with ceiling fans and air-conditioning, fully stocked minibar (wet bars in suites), satellite TV, alarm/radio, direct-dial telephone, bathrobes, amenities baskets; suites are duplexes with sleeping lofts and canopy beds

MEALS: Breakfast 7:00–10:00, lunch 11:30–2:30 (everything from sandwiches to complete meals, at any of 3 indoor/outdoor locations), afternoon tea 4:00–5:00, dinner (7:00–10:00, in the fan-cooled indoor/outdoor Garden Loggia Café, $50–70 for 2); light snacks until midnight, Sunday champagne brunch buffet 11:30–2:30; jackets appropriate in the Garden Loggia Café, otherwise informal; piano player with breakfast and dinner; no-smoking area in dining room; room service 7:00 A.M.–10:00 P.M., no extra charge

ENTERTAINMENT: 6 bars and lounges, live music 2 or 3 evenings a week

SPORTS: Beach (i.e., a section of the popular Seven Mile Beach across the road), beach club, freshwater swimming pool (with swim-up bar), Jacuzzi, tennis (2 Plexipave courts, with lights)—all free; snorkeling gear, catamaran and Sunfish sailing, windsurfing, paddleboats, scuba and day-sails on the resort's private 65-ft. catamaran for a fee; private 9-hole golf course that can be played three ways, including 18 holes with the Cayman Ball (pro shop, green fees $35 for 18 holes)

P.S.: At any season (at least for the first few years) you may encounter some groups that come perilously close to behaving like conventions

Tortuga Club

Grand Cayman

$

Kick off your shoes the minute you arrive—the only thing you wear on your feet here is flippers. Walk four steps across your patio and you're on the sand; a few steps more and you're in a huge lagoon formed by a reef that runs as far as the eye can see. And just about all that the sun-parched eye can see is reef, lagoon, beach, palms and blue sky. You don't notice terra firma again until you walk out the main door on your way home.

It's built in simple island style—a string of low one-story cabanas; an open lobby and bar lead to a drinking deck, a breezy dining room, the Hammock House, a thatched *bohio* on the beach hung with three or four hammocks. And that's it. Just 14 rooms and all that sand and sea and sky.

Simple decor, too—khuskhus rugs woven by blind people in Tobago, tables made from local mahogany; the dining room of beamed ceilings on columns of shells and coral rock.

There's nothing, glorious nothing, to do between meals except slip back to your cabana for a siesta, lounge in the Hammock House, sail a Sunfish across the lagoon, play tennis, go snorkeling or scuba diving. The Tortuga Club is a place for lovers who are content to stroll along the empty beaches, gathering shells and sea anemones, while the ocean tosses a white spray beyond the lapping fringe of the lagoon. But be prepared for relaxed management, which may present frustrations lovers don't need, such as lethargic plumbing, hot water that isn't. Neither the aborted condos next door nor the vintage towel-draped telly in the lobby do much to enhance the welcome, but if you take along a desert-island frame of mind you'll probably love the seclusion and camaraderie.

NAME: Tortuga Club

MANAGER: Frank Connolly

ADDRESS: P.O. Box 496, Grand Cayman, B.W.I.

LOCATION: On the cool windward coast, 1 hour from the airport, about $35 by taxi

TELEPHONE: 809-947-7551

TELEX: None

RESERVATIONS: Cayman Islands Reservation Service

CREDIT CARDS: American Express, Visa, MasterCard

ROOMS: 14, all with patios facing the beach, air-conditioning

MEALS: Breakfast 8:00–10:00, lunch noon–2:00, snacks 2:00–5:00 (served in a breeze-through beachside pavilion); casual dress at all times (jacket and tie definitely *not* required)

ENTERTAINMENT: Nothing scheduled (unless there's a group in the house), but there's endless conviviality

SPORTS: Lagoon beach, table tennis, pool table, tennis (1 court, no lights)—all free; snorkeling gear and scuba extra

Added Attractions

Cayman Kai
Grand Cayman

Cayman Kai's 26 rooms are known as Sea Lodges because of their unusual design—triangular screened patios and white tentlike roofs that make them seem like something out of a concrete Arabian Nights. But their tiled floors, ceiling fans, louvers, hammocks, loungers and island decor are a perfect backdrop for Caribbean nights. You can spend most of your time in your tent, since they all have kitchens (deliveries daily from the resort's private commissary) and venture into the sunlight only for water sports and strolls along Cayman Kai's 1½-mile beach (wild, undeveloped coral strand). If you feel in the mood for dining out, you don't have to walk more than a few paces to the resort's handsome bar/lounge and so-so restaurant, and you don't have to dress up to go there, either. (You could go farther afield for dinner, of course, since you have the freedom of a room-only rate—but you would spend about $40 in taxi fares getting to and from the nearest dependable restaurant.) 26 rooms. Avoid numbers 1–10 as they are too close to the public areas, ask for numbers 11, 17, 18 or 24. *Cayman Kai, P.O. Box 1112, Grand Cayman, B.W.I. Telephone: 809-947-9556.*

Tiara Beach Hotel
Cayman Brac

The brac is the rugged bluff that distinguishes this particular Cayman, the Tiara is just the sort of hotel to help you enjoy the quiet and solitude of this unspoiled island. Since the main attraction of this small, two-story hotel is the Peter Hughes Dive Center, most of the guests are underwater nuts, and the colorful room decor seems to be trying to outdazzle the reefs. Besides scuba, there are windsurfers, paddleboats, a tennis court, beachside pool and bicycles. Cuisine is undistinguished, but even the divers surface for the Sunday buffet brunch, with every dish cooked *alfresco* beside the pool. 40 air-conditioned, balconied rooms and luxury apartments. *Tiara Beach Hotel, Cayman Islands, B.W.I., reservations via Divi Hotels in Ithaca. Telephone: 607-277-3484.*

Jamaica

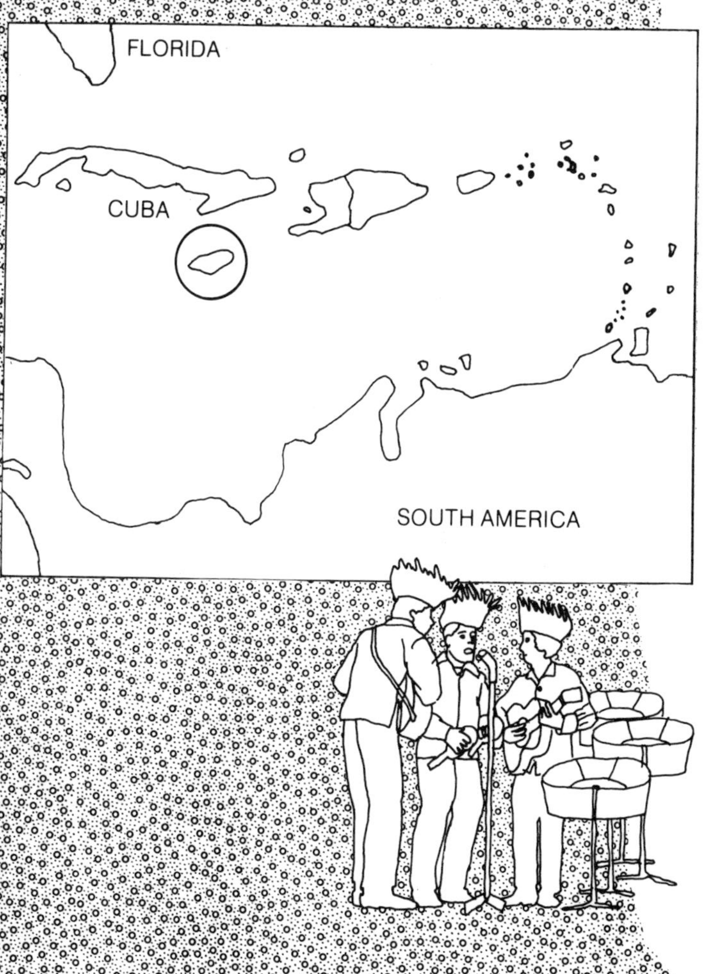

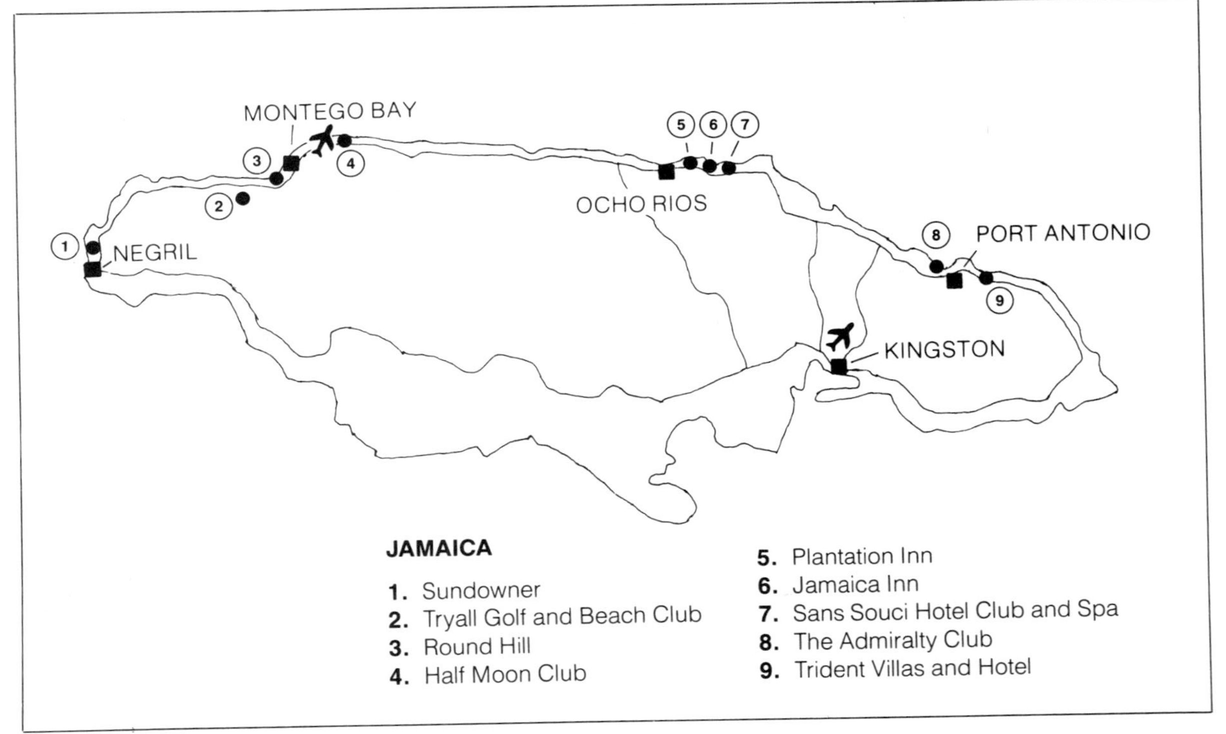
MONTEGO BAY
OCHO RIOS
PORT ANTONIO
NEGRIL
KINGSTON
1
2
3
4
5
6
7
8
9
JAMAICA
1. Sundowner
2. Tryall Golf and Beach Club
3. Round Hill
4. Half Moon Club
5. Plantation Inn
6. Jamaica Inn
7. Sans Souci Hotel Club and Spa
8. The Admiralty Club
9. Trident Villas and Hotel

Jamaica

It's the stuff travel posters are made of—rafting down the Rio Grande, frolicking in waterfalls, limbo dancing and reggae, aristocratic plantations and elegant villas. That sort of thing. No wonder Jamaica used to be the one island everyone went to sooner or later. A few years ago, things turned sour and surly, however. Tourists stayed away. Hotels closed. Now, happy to say, my recent visits convince me that the Jamaicans are offering a genuinely friendly welcome. For one thing, the government has been dunning into them that the island needs tourism and the sure way to attract tourists is to ensure they're treated well. Sure there are irritations (even the government has been goaded to do something about overzealous street vendors), but hardly threatening situations. Even Kingston, the teeming Antillean capital, has pulled its socks up, cleaned its streets, spruced up its hotels and built new shopping centers and an impressive national gallery.

Where to go? Most flights from North America touch down in Montego Bay before continuing to Kingston, so MoBay's the place to begin. Once a quiet honeymooners' haven, it's now crowded with tour groups, cruise ship passengers and honky-tonk. But there's still much to enjoy—in town and in the surroundings—so begin with a few days at one of the three classy resorts just outside town. Two hours east along the north shore, Ocho Rios is a scaled-down version of MoBay, with three more of the island's top resorts and oodles of activities, from scrambling up Dunn's River Falls to touring Prospect Plantation to polo—spectating or playing—at not one but two locations. Port Antonio is the least developed of the three resorts, although visitors drive from all over the island to go rafting down the Rio Grande. You can also go horseback riding on the estate of Patrice Wymore Flynn, the widow of movie star Errol Flynn. At the opposite end of the island, the once sleepy village of Negril is now a sprightly resort, especially popular with the young, the laid back and the swingers; its Seven Mile Beach is the finest stretch of sand on the island.

A tip on planning: If you find choosing where to stay as difficult as I do, begin with a few days at one of MoBay's top resorts, with a day trip to Negril. Then, since your plane is probably going to stop at Kingston anyway (where you'll probably have to disembark while the aircraft is serviced), I suggest you sightsee your way to the airport—driving along the north shore, spending a night or two in Ocho Rios and/or Port Antonio on your way to the airport in Kingston. If you stop over in the capital itself, be sure to visit the new national gallery and the crafts boutiques, café and restaurant at Devon House.

The selection in these pages begins in the west, in Negril, and moves east toward Port Antonio.

HOW TO GET THERE Jamaica is now one of the easiest islands to get to from North America. Air Jamaica has nonstop or direct flights from Atlanta, Baltimore, Miami, New York, Philadelphia, Washington and Toronto (not all daily but at least frequently); American has daily nonstop flights from New York, Eastern has several flights a day from Atlanta and Miami, and there's additional service from Toronto on Air Canada.

Best of all, during the peak winter months Air Jamaica will repeat its innovative *Concorde* service to Montego Bay from New York. The service operates only on Saturdays, cuts flying time in half (maybe more, if Castro allows the plane to overfly Cuba at supersonic speed), but even without the faster time the Concorde service is a treat. Special Concorde lounge at JFK; special baggage handling at MoBay (although you may still be caught in a line for immigration if your arrival coincides with a slowpoke 747); special in-town terminal for return flights. It's expensive, of course, but you might as well begin your vacation before you leave the ground.

Sundowner

Negril

$$

The sea is calm as a paddling pond, the beach is narrow and white and runs for 6 or 7 miles without a break, the Sundowner borders the beach in a sun-dappled garden, with dining terraces beneath palm trees. For such an enviable setting it's not the most imaginative hotel (two-story motellike structure, balconies facing the sea, tanks of freshwater tropical fish, bar tables put together from barrels and filled with seashells). The guest rooms are functional: asphalt tile floors, functional furniture, tiled bathrooms with tub and shower, jalousied windows and doors, air-conditioning if you want it. The 10 superior rooms upstairs have higher ceilings, king-size beds and midget-size refrigerators. Rumor has it that the owner plans to upgrade the guest rooms, but you're not coming to the Sundowner for something special in the way of love nests. Rather you're coming because it's there—on a great beach, in a lazy-making setting, far from the hassles of the city.

NAME: Sundowner

OWNER/MANAGER: Rita Hojan

ADDRESS: P.O. Box 5, Negril, Jamaica, W.I.

LOCATION: On the west coast, 1½ hours by car from Montego Bay, $50 by taxi with minimum of 5 people

TELEPHONE: 809-957-4225

CABLES: Sundown Jamaica

RESERVATIONS: American International and Jamaica Reservation Services in United States; Wolfe International in Canada

CREDIT CARDS: MasterCard, Visa, American Express

ROOMS: 26, facing the beach, with air-conditioning, ceiling fans, balcony or veranda

MEALS: Breakfast 8:00–10:00, lunch 12:30–2:30, dinner 7:45–9:30 (approx. $36 for 2); informal dress

ENTERTAINMENT: Calypso band; weekly barbecue

SPORTS: Beach; snorkeling, scuba, tennis, horseback riding available nearby, all extra

P.S. Regret! Children under the age of eight not accepted

Tryall Golf and Beach Club

Near Montego Bay

$$$

Tryall is 2,000 acres of lush Jamaican plantation that long ago switched from sugar to the sweet life. The 200-year-old Great House is a stylish 44-room inn, perched on a low hill a few hundred yards inland from the beach and surrounded by sumptuous villas and championship fairways.

Golfers know Tryall well—they see it every December in live telecasts of the Mazda Seniors Tournament. It's an appealing layout. Waterholes lined with coconut palms. A sixth fairway that skirts a centuries-old, still-turning waterwheel. And there are so many fruit trees lining the course—star apple, orange, breadfruit, mango—the caddies are not only expert in which clubs to play, but also in having perfect timing when it comes to knowing which fruits are ripest.

Other guests never leave their knolltop for days on end. Why should they? A few paces from their Great House they have well-tended tennis courts. A few steps in the opposite direction, they can plunge into one of the Caribbean's most spectacular swimming pools, complete with waterfall and swim-up bar.

Tryall's guest rooms flank the driveway leading to the Great House, linked by wooden arcades draped with morning glories. The so-called Garden Terrace rooms look out on lawns and fairways, the pricier Deluxe quarters frame views of seashore, fairways and the coast all the way to distant Montego Bay—distant enough to preserve Tryall's seclusion, accessible enough for occasional junkets into town to shop, dine or hit the reggae clubs (why not?—Prince Andrew went discoing in MoBay without bodyguards). Upper level deluxe rooms have private balconies, while the lower level rooms compensate for lack of thorough ventilation (and growling air-conditioning units) with both shaded lanais and lawn patios.

All 44 guest rooms are different but spacious, comfortable, practical, in two basic color schemes—sea blue and canary yellow—with sitting areas, antiques and four-posters carved from Jamaican hardwoods. The real star up here, though, is the single-roofed, native-stone Great House itself, its parquet floors polished to within an inch of their lives. Chandeliers and antiques fill the sitting room, the upholstered wicker armchairs fill up around 4:00 when guests gather for afternoon tea (tea bags, tsk, tsk) and finger sandwiches. The recently extended alfresco terrace is almost as popular for its views as the cuisine of Swiss chef, Thomas Pfister—inventive even at breakfast time. How about coconut pancakes topped with Jamaican rum syrup? Or Eggs Caribe—like Benedict but with local lobster instead of the ham?

Guests are so pampered here they don't even have to make a reservation for dinner (villa guests and outsiders most certainly do). Early-bird sunrise watchers find coffee waiting for them on the veranda at 6:30 A.M. And even that lovely championship golf course is now reserved for villa owners and Tryall guests exclusively.

NAME: Tryall Golf and Beach Club

MANAGER: Josef Berger

ADDRESS: Sandy Bay Post Office, Hanover Parish, Jamaica, W.I.

LOCATION: On the North Shore, 12 miles west of Montego Bay, 35 minutes and $30 by taxi from the airport

TELEPHONE: 809-952-5110/1

TELEX: 5346 Cocores JA

RESERVATIONS: Scott Calder International, New York

CREDIT CARDS: All major cards

ROOMS: 44 Great House rooms, all with balconies or patios, air-conditioning *and* ceiling fans, direct-dial telephones, amenities baskets; most of the 57 villas, beside the beach or in the hills, are available for rent as complete units, a few with 2 bedrooms, most with 3 or 4 bedrooms

MEALS: Breakfast 7:00–9:30 (continental 9:30–10:30), lunch noon–3:00 (in beachside pavilion, salads and sandwiches at Ninth Hole Bar, pool or golf clubhouse), afternoon tea, 4:00–5:30, dinner 7:00–9:30 (in the open dining terrace, approx. $70 for 2); Friday evening barbecue on the beach, Monday seafood buffet; jackets in the evening in winter; room service during kitchen hours, no extra charge (Great House only); small combo or folksinger (amplified) most evenings

ENTERTAINMENT: Lounge/bar, manager's cocktail party on Monday (guests and homeowners), music for dancing every evening, VCR in meeting room, parlor games

SPORTS: Freshwater pool at Great House, 51 villa pools, beach, snorkeling, Sunfish sailing, windsurfing, paddleboats, glass-bottom boats, tennis (6 Laykold courts, 2 with lights, pro shop), golf (18 championship holes, full pro facilities)—all free; scuba, sport fishing, horseback riding, day cruises to Negril can be arranged

Round Hill

Near Montego Bay

$$$$

The sweeping, casuarina-lined driveway says "class." And when you get to the crest of the hill and take in the gardens and the view of coves and mountains, it's easy to understand why this elegant resort has been hosting the rich and famous for 30 winters.

Of all the resorts along Jamaica's fabled north shore this is probably the one that still comes closest to the glory years of everyone's memories. Its villas and servants have beckoned the likes of the Oscar Hammersteins, the Moss Harts and, in Villa 25, Adele Astaire. As if that weren't cast enough for one resort, Cole Porter and Noël Coward (Villa 3) used to entertain the entertainers. Ever since, the upper crust of show business, high society, big business and the aristocracy has been chauffeured up that driveway in loyal streams, among them Kennedys (Jackie's favorite, Villa 10) and Bernsteins. Last winter, the Aga Khan and his family settled in for a lengthy stay, but the place was so full Paul McCartney, among others, had to be turned away.

Many visitors to Round Hill have to bed down in three two-story wings alongside the beach, hitherto known as The Barracks but now rechristened Pineapple House after what passes in these conservative parts as a major renovation (new pencil-post beds handcrafted from local mahogany, new clay tile floors, better views, more space by incorporating the balconies into the rooms). In other resorts, they'd probably be the most desirable rooms because of their beachfront location; but the true Round Hill is to be found on the bosky bowl rising from the beach, what seems to be 23 acres of tropical garden planted with villas rather than the other way around. Each whitewashed, shingle-roofed villa is privately owned, but each is designed in such a way that it can be rented as an individual suite, each with a bedroom with louvered shutters opening to a covered outdoor patio framed by bougainvillea and croton and mahogany trees. Since they're privately owned, each one is different. Unless you book now for winters two or three years down the line, you will almost certainly have to settle for whatever is available, but if I were specifying lodgings these are some of the villas I'd bid for: Number 8 (new owners have spent a bundle installing marble floors, silk rugs, walls hand-stenciled by a specially imported Japanese craftsman, a canopy bed with pink chintz); number 13 (also new owners, who have installed a large deck, pool and the resort's only Jacuzzi); number 6 (frilly boudoir with chinoiserie living room); number 18 (a particularly attractive high-ceilinged, arched living room, with fabrics to match the anthurium and elephant ear in the garden).

But what sets Round Hill apart is probably the service. Life here may be the closest you can come in this hemisphere to experiencing the pampering of the British Raj in India. When you rouse yourselves in the morning, your maid sets the terrace table and prepares breakfast. Your gardener (there are 40 of them!) has already cleaned the pool and positioned your loungers to catch the morning sun. If you opt for the cove, each time you paddle into the sea you'll find a beach boy has edged your chaise around to face the sun. At the lunchtime buffet, an army of waiters totes your laden plates to your table, whisks away the empties when you're ready for refills, recharges your water glasses, holds chairs for the ladies. Laundry? Just drop it in the basket and the maid will take care of it (no charge, other than tip). Room service? If you can't be bothered trotting down the hill, the dining room will send your dinner up. There are drivers to get you to and from your rooms when you don't feel like walking, ball boys to retrieve stray serves on the tennis courts.

Many people have misconceptions about Round Hill, so let me correct three myths: it's *not* formal, it's *not* stuffy, it's *not* prohibitively expensive. Black tie is requested for Saturday's gala evenings, but only a handful of men actually dress up; other evenings, dress is informal (but stylishly so, of course). Everyone who wants to mingle, mingles—marquises and marchionesses included. During the peak season, manager Michael Kemp makes a point of inviting hotel guests to the frequent cocktail parties put on by villa owners. And with the Jamaican dollar slightly groggy as of this writing, Round Hill's rates are almost a bargain. Compare rates here (and elsewhere in Jamaica, for that matter) with some other islands; for what some down-island resorts charge for room only, Round Hill throws in a suite, personal maid and all meals.

There are only two drawbacks to all this. All those upper-crust guests lose interest in the Caribbean come Easter, so Round Hill goes full tilt for a limited season. However, spring, summer and fall the villas are still available for solitude seekers, complete with maids who'll prepare meals, beach boys who'll mix your piña coladas—and you might have the tennis courts all to yourself.

The other minor drawback: on weekends in winter, regular jet services are augmented by charter flights that occasionally shatter your sense of seclusion (they're not supposed to fly over the resorts and the owners are trying to do something about it).

But that's no reason to forego the lap of luxury, because *once* in a lifetime at least everyone should sample a week in, say, Lady Rothermere's hillside villa, with its plush outdoor living room, a pool shared only with one other couple, an enormous deck shaded by an even more enormous cotton tree, a gardener to move your lounger around with the sun, a personal maid to bring you afternoon tea.

NAME: Round Hill

MANAGER: Michael J. Kemp

ADDRESS: P.O. Box 64, Montego Bay, Jamaica, W.I.

LOCATION: On a promontory west of Montego Bay, about 10 miles, 25 minutes and $25 by taxi from the airport

TELEPHONE: 809-952-5150/5

TELEX: 5418

RESERVATIONS: Distinguished Hotels and Elegant Resorts of Jamaica

CREDIT CARDS: All major cards

ROOMS: 101, including 36 rooms in Pineapple House plus 65 suites in 27 villas; rooms in Pineapple House have walls of shutters facing the bay, standing fans or ceiling fans, telephones; villas have maids and gardeners, ceiling fans (air-conditioning in some suites), balconies or patios, gardens or lawns, indoor/outdoor living rooms, telephones, kitchens (for maids' use), private or shared pools

MEALS: Breakfast 8:00–10:00, lunch (buffet or à la carte) 1:00–2:30, snacks 11:00–7:00, dinner 7:30–9:30 (on the beachside patio beneath the almond trees, $70 for 2); picnic on the beach Monday evenings, barbecue Wednesdays; dress informal, except jacket and tie on Saturday (black tie is "requested"); room service, no extra charge; music (amplified until 11:00) for dancing most evenings

ENTERTAINMENT: Local band for beach picnic and barbecue; library, parlor games, VCR

SPORTS: Private beach (60 or 90 yards depending on the tides, but hardly spectacular), 16 pools, snorkeling, floats, tennis (4 courts, lights, pro)—all free; waterskiing, windsurfing, Sunfish sailing, paddleboats from the beach; golf and horseback riding 40 minutes away

P.S.: Open in summer; new beachside pool, added in winter 1987–1988.

Half Moon Club

Near Montego Bay

$$$$

The beach is indeed an almost perfect half moon, shaded by sea grape onshore, sheltered by a reef offshore, and marred only by a glimpse of the upper floors of a gauche Holiday Inn on the next cove. The first upper-crust vacationers settled around their half moon in the fifties in a cluster of private cottages, each different from its neighbor. Later expansions included undistinguished two-story wings of beachside rooms and suites and, in the past year, the tastefully renovated studios and apartments that were once the neighboring Colony Club Hotel. The total tally, almost 200 rooms, is spread out along 1½ miles of beach, which in turn is a mere corner of a 400-

acre estate that includes a working ranch and a Robert Trent Jones golf course.

Which of these varied accommodations you stay in may depend on what you want to do with your days as much as with price. If you like to step directly from your cottage into the sea, check into one of the original cottages around the beach (some of which also have semiprivate patio pools); the two-story wings of rooms and suites are closest to the tennis courts; if you want seclusion, opt for the beachside cottages opposite the tennis courts (again, with semiprivate pools, but the lagoon here is not much good for hearty swimming) or the new suites in the neo-Georgian villas of the former Colony (each of which has a private maid and a kitchen, which can be stocked from the commissary across the driveway).

Despite the rambling nature of the place, the Half Moon staff still manages to offer service in the old Jamaican tradition, and chances are maître d's and waiters will have your name down pat on your second visit to their breeze-cooled beachside domain, even if it's not Bush or Bronfman—to name just a couple of recent guests.

That lovely half moon beach may have been what first lured people to this spot, but the resort's sports facilities have to be a major attraction today. Where else do you get to play a Robert Trent Jones at no extra charge (and without having to rent golf carts)? And how many resorts that promise free tennis actually give you a chance to get in a game by providing not 1 or 2 but *13* courts? Free, with lights, too.

The Club has just emerged from a $2-million rehabilitation sprouting new jumbo gateposts, a new Nautilus gym and new stables. Kingston architect/decorator Earl Levy (owner of the Trident in Port Antonio) has totally transformed the public areas with striking success, adding cupolas and courtyards and bold tropical colors. The guest rooms, more of a touch-up job, are less than breathtaking. Frankly, most of the villas are boring and outlandishly overpriced, even if they *are* next to the best beach (some are actually squashed between the beachside villas and the road), even if they *do* have kitchens and pools. For what you pay for a villa suite here, you can have a villa *and* meals at Round Hill.

But, if you plan to play lots of golf or tennis (no extra charge for either), Half Moon's room-only rates in winter may be a godsend—especially if you stay in one of the suites with kitchens and have your maid prepare breakfast and a light lunch.

NAME: Half Moon Club

MANAGER: Heinz Simonitsch (part-owner/managing director)

ADDRESS: P.O. Box 80, Montego Bay, Jamaica, W.I.

LOCATION: 9 miles from town; 7 miles from the airport, 10 minutes and $12 by taxi

TELEPHONE: 809-953-2211

TELEX: 5326

RESERVATIONS: Robert Reid Assoc., Elegant Resorts of Jamaica in the United States

CREDIT CARDS: All major cards

ROOMS: 197, including 99 studios and superior rooms, 60 suites and 35 villas, all with air-conditioning, some with air-conditioning *and* ceiling fans, balconies or patios, refrigerators, direct-dial telephones, some with kitchens, some with private or semiprivate pools

MEALS: Breakfast 8:00–9:30, lunch noon–6:00, dinner 7:30–9:30 (on the open beachside patio, new covered dining room or the Clubhouse Grill at the golf course, $40–60 for 2); long-sleeved shirts after 6:00 in winter, jacket and tie requested on Saturdays, otherwise informal (but "shorts, T-shirts and jeans are not allowed"); room service in some rooms only, small extra charge; live music for dancing most evenings

ENTERTAINMENT: Bar/lounge/terrace, live music most evenings (combo, calypso, steel band), floorshows, crab races ("with pari-mutuel betting")

SPORTS: Beach, 19 freshwater pools (17 private or semiprivate), tennis (13 courts, 4 with lights, pro shop), golf (18 holes, pro shop), sauna, Nautilus gym, squash (4 courts)—all free; water sports on the beach (windsurfing, new Mistral windsurfing school, Sunfish sailing, scuba, snorkeling), horseback riding (with guide), massage—at extra charge

P.S.: Some children, some seminar groups, up to 120

Plantation Inn

Ocho Rios

$$$

For 25 of the last 30 years, Plantation Inn was one of the grand names in Jamaican resorts. Up there on a par with Round Hill and Jamaica Inn. Then it slumped in the early eighties. But now it's bouncing back with new owners and a new manager heading up a seasoned team that includes many long-serving waiters and chambermaids.

The most recent addition to the inn is a four-story wing of rooms and suites right on the edge of the beach. It doesn't do much for the setting when seen from the beach, but from the rooms the views are impressive—across the bay to Jamaica Inn and east along the coast. The suites here are impressive, two of them with Jacuzzis in the bathtub, some with wet bars, one with a four-poster bed. The regular rooms are pretty but undistinguished. Rooms in the original wings are more tropical, with lots of hardwoods and louvers (they're also less expensive, which is a bonus).

The white-columned porte cochere, on the other hand, may strike you as more Carolinian than Caribbean, the tiny dark-hued lounge just off reception is more Mayfair than Antillean, but once you step beyond the lobby to the terrace the setting is pure Jamaica. Masses of hibiscus and bougainvillea drape walls and railings, vines twine around 100-year-old silk cotton trees. Flights of steps lead down to a small swimming pool, then continue down to an expanse of soft, white sand. Problem is, because of the bluff, the sun's rays get snared in the branches of the towering trees and you have to spend the afternoon dodging shadows. But you can't say it isn't peaceful and private down there. And you don't even have to come up for lunch and piña coladas.

The brochures note that Plantation Inn has been named "one of the 300 best hotels in the world." Hardly. It still needs some fine tuning to bring it back to par with Jamaica Inn. And you'd think that owners who impose such a fussy dress code in their dining room could at least present guests with something better than dog-eared menu cards.

NAME: Plantation Inn

MANAGER: Paul L. Koster

ADDRESS: P.O. Box 2, Ocho Rios, Jamaica, W.I.

LOCATION: Just east of town, 1½ hours and $75 by taxi from Montego Bay airport, or $22 per person round-trip by air-conditioned minibus, making stops along the way

TELEPHONE: 809-974-2501

TELEX: 7452 PlanInn JA

RESERVATIONS: Elegant Resorts of Jamaica

CREDIT CARDS: American Express, Visa, MasterCard, Diners Club

ROOMS: 77, including rooms, junior suites and deluxe suites, all with air-conditioning *and* ceiling fans, balconies overlooking the sea, telephones, some with wet bars and refrigerators, 2 with Jacuzzis

MEALS: Breakfast 7:30–9:30, consommé on the beach 11:00, lunch 1:00–3:00, afternoon tea 4:00–5:00, dinner 8:00–9:30 (on the terrace or in the covered dining pavilion, $60 for 2); jackets required Monday through Thursday, jacket and tie Friday and Saturday in winter, jackets only on weekends in summer; room service at no extra cost

ENTERTAINMENT: Bar/terrace, calypso music, folklore show Thursday, VCR in main lounge, card room with parlor games; live and amplified music for dancing 6 nights a week

SPORTS: Beach (reef-protected for good swimming and snorkeling), freshwater pool, Sunfish sailing, windsurfing, tennis (2 courts, 1 lighted)—all free; golf, scuba, horseback riding and polo nearby

P.S.: No children under 12 nine months of the year, no children under 7 in summer; some groups and seminars year round

Jamaica Inn

Ocho Rios

🌴🌴🌴🌴🍴🍴🍴😊😊$$$

The loggias alone are larger than rooms in most hotels. Better furnished, too, with padded armchairs, ottomans and overstuffed sofas, breakfast tables, desks, desk lamps, fresh flowers and drying racks for soggy swimsuits and beach towels. Have a swim before lunch and you'll find a fresh supply of big, bulky beach towels waiting for you in your rooms; have a nap or something after lunch, then a dip and, sure enough, the maid has straightened out your mussed-up bed by the time you get back. Your nap or whatever may take place in a romantic little pencil-post bed, in a tropical boudoir of cool pastel blues and greens and yellows, the sunlight filtered by green and white drapes, the breezes filtered by louvered windows and doors, the terrazzo floors softened by white rugs.

The West Wing is best—with your loggia right on the edge of the water, your front door facing the beach and garden. If you want to be right on the beach, choose the Beach Wing and you can step from your patio over a shin-high balustrade right onto the sand. If you can afford the best, ask for the Blue Suite, a self-contained cottage right on the beach; if the *very* best (and you remember to book, say, a couple of years in advance), then ask for the White Suite, where Winston Churchill stayed in the fifties—it has its own small pool with a circular ramp, and a path over a private promontory to a very private sun terrace right above the sea.

The inn, once the private hideaway of a Texas millionaire, has two one-story and two two-story wings, all a pretty pastel blue, strung out along a private 700-ft. beach, in 6 acres of lawns, wild banana, sea grape, hibiscus and bougainvillea, and very tall coconut palms. The covelike beach (one of the most beautiful on the island), the clear water (as cool and inviting as the bedrooms), the placid tempo and elegance of the place have been attracting devoted fans for a quarter of a century. Service is exemplary, mainly because one of the Morrow family is sitting right there in the "Morrow Seat" on the terrace, with an uninterrupted view of reception, lounge, bar, dining terrace and beach.

But ask the fans what they like most about Jamaica Inn and they'll probably tell you the food. For 20 winters, Chef Battista Greco has crossed over from Europe to supervise the kitchen here, turning out meals with a cosmopolitan choice of cuisines—American, Italian, French, Jamaican (his lunchtime buffets are bountiful and beautiful). He leaves again in the spring, but his spirit and recipes stay behind to satisfy less affluent off-season palates. It's not just the food, though, that makes dining at Jamaica Inn so pleasurable; dinners are served on a broad lamplit terrace with an ornamental balustrade, by the edge of the sea, beneath the stars. It's the classic Caribbean setting—and you're expected to dress accordingly. With the crêpes suzette or zabaglione, there's dancing under the stars on that balustraded terrace. Nondancers often retire to the croquet lawn for a moonlit duel. But there's always that big tempting loggia with the big, comfy sofa, sheltered by wild banana and serenaded by the surf.

NAME: Jamaica Inn

OWNERS: The Morrow Family

ADDRESS: P.O. Box 1, Ocho Rios, Jamaica, W.I.

LOCATION: On the eastern edge of town, $75 by taxi from Montego Bay (alert the hotel and they'll have a "reliable driver" there to meet you)

TELEPHONE: 809-974-2514

TELEX: None (962400 in United States)

RESERVATIONS: Ray Morrow Associates

CREDIT CARDS: American Express

ROOMS: 45, all with air-conditioning plus fans plus breezes, large loggias, telephones

MEALS: Breakfast 8:00–10:00, lunch 1:00–2:30, dinner 8:00–9:30 (beneath the stars, approx. $60 for 2); jacket and tie (and often, by preference of the guests, black tie) in winter, jackets only in summer, $3 charge for room service (off-season) 8:00 A.M.–10:00 P.M.

ENTERTAINMENT: Dancing to a moderately amplified four-piece combo every evening, library/lounge with masses of jigsaw puzzles

SPORTS: Beach (good swimming and snorkeling), freshwater pool, Sunfish sailing, croquet—all free; 1 tennis court (no charge) at adjoining hotel; scuba, boat trips, golf, horseback riding, polo (for players, learners—and sometimes the managers cart all the guests off to a match for a jolly afternoon of spectating) nearby

P.S.: No groups, no conventions ever, no children under 14

Sans Souci Hotel Club and Spa

Ocho Rios

$$$

From the driveway it looks like a very pink, very private hideaway on the Italian Riviera; from the sea it's a great, multitiered palazzo—splashes of pink stucco in 35 cliffside and beachside acres of tropical greenery, gazebos and traceried terraces. Steps guide you gently past fountains and lawns, mineral pool and freshwater pool to the waterside play area with its giant chess set.

This is the newest part of Sans Souci. New owners, Jamaicans Maurice and Valerie Facey, have turned one gazebo into a canvas-shrouded massage room, a second suite of cabanas into Charley's Spa. A brand-new sea-level pavilion functions as a duplex, open-to-the-breezes exercise room with Nautilus equipment looking so formidable it contradicts the name of the hotel—"Carefree."

The mineral pool, the core of the spa, is fed by a secret stream that emerges from a grotto with a big and venerable green turtle called Charley.

There's another pet in the lobby, a raucous Brazilian macaw with, apparently, a tin ear: when flautist James Galway stayed here he serenaded the feathered fool with one of his golden flutes but Sir Walter Raleigh merely squawked louder than ever.

Raleigh's domain is your first glimpse of the $4-million restyling of Sans Souci—an inviting, curving salon with French doors opening to the patio,

and a raftered ceiling hung with oversized white baskets, all 16 of them trailing greenery that's replenished once a month. Beyond, a pair of arches lead to the Balloon Bar and dining room, but the most popular spot for sampling the kitchen's homemade pasta is the big cliff-top terrace, level with the tops of lofty flame trees, the tables shaded by umbrellas of coral-pink-and-white stripes.

This is real snuggly-poo territory, and the owners keep nudging your thoughts in the right direction: the restaurant, for no apparent reason, is called the Casanova, there's the mineral pool and spa for toning up your muscles—and big bouncy beds for showing them off in. Plumply upholstered guest rooms come in one of two color schemes—bananaquit yellow or the ubiquitous Sans Souci coral pink. Valerie Facey, a decorator by profession, had the fabrics custom designed and printed right here on the island and redesigned the bathrooms with marble (and the quietest flushers you've ever heard). A one-bedroom suite, D20, is one of the hotel's most desirable aeries, sort of a penthouse with 30 ft. of red-tiled terrace, loungers at one end, dining table for six beneath a wooden pergola and views past the palms to the sea *and* westward to the mountains and sunsets. Since Sans Souci's guest rooms are spread out along paths and stairways, it might be smart to ask for lodgings, depending on your tastes, closer to the beach and tennis courts or closer to the pools and spa. On the other hand, location hardly matters if, like Capt. Mark Phillips, Princess Anne's husband, you'll be spending most of your time on the polo fields at nearby Chukka Cove.

NAME: Sans Souci Hotel Club and Spa

MANAGER: Kenneth S. Kennedy

ADDRESS: P.O. Box 103, Ocho Rios, Jamaica, W.I.

LOCATION: 2 miles east of town, 60 miles from Montego Bay airport ($75 by taxi direct, or $22 round-trip per person in an air-conditioned minibus that may make several stops along the way)

TELEPHONE: 809-974-2353

TELEX: 7496

RESERVATIONS: Elegant Resorts of Jamaica

CREDIT CARDS: American Express, Visa, MasterCard

ROOMS: 72 rooms and suites in 5 two-story and three-story wings, all but 1 with balcony, ceiling fan *and* air-conditioning, telephone, tea/coffee makers

MEALS: Breakfast 7:30–10:00 (continental 10:00–11:30), lunch noon–3:00, afternoon tea 4:00–5:00, dinner 7:00–9:00 (approx. $50–60, on the terrace beneath the stars or in the fan-cooled Casanova Restaurant); jackets in winter ("no shorts or jeans"); room service 7:00 A.M.–9:00 P.M., no extra charge; music (amplified) from the next terrace down

ENTERTAINMENT: Piano player in Balloon Bar, live music in band shell, folklore shows, backgammon, chess, Scrabble, satellite TV in separate lounge

SPORTS: So-so beach, 2 pools (1 mineral spring), tennis (4 courts, 2 with lights, pro shop)—all free; water sports concession on beach (waterskiing, sailboats, windsurfing, scuba, snorkeling trips, paddleboats, picnic cruises), spa (operated by Chris Silkwood—sauna, weights, whirlpool, massage, facials, exercise programs), extra charge; golf (18 holes), horseback riding and polo (clinics, instruction, rentals) nearby

P.S.: Some children during holidays, a few seminars, special pro-am tennis week in mid-January

The Admiralty Club

Port Antonio

🌴 🍴 🎾 $

Trembly Knee Cove is, according to the welcome brochure, a "clothes optional beach."

Crusoe's Beach, the alternative, is a stretch of windswept, reef-rimmed sand with a palm-thatched bar, a wooden jetty with a sundeck at the tip and steps into a sandy-bottomed swimming hole.

To get to either beach you have to walk—4 or 5 minutes maximum—because the only vehicle on this islet is a beat-up blue Jeep used for hauling luggage and furniture.

In other words, you're not basking in the lap of luxury here, except for those ineffable luxuries of seclusion: a private cay, secret pathways through your own mini-rain forest, coral outlooks you share with only 30 or so fellow escapists.

Half of those guests check into seven beachside studios—individual wood-framed bungalows with two walls of louvered shutters that fold right back to join the veranda as one large living space. The sturdy wooden furniture is handmade, right there in the workshop beneath the clubhouse; the beds are topped by canopies of mosquito netting (more romantic than functional). Remaining accommodations are in wood-and-louver cottages with two or three bedrooms, except for "Firefly," a one-bedroom charmer opening directly onto the sea and just three or four steps from a bikini-size patch of sand. From your "Firefly" deck you can practically touch the banana boats edging through the deepwater channel into Port Antonio. On the far side of the channel sits the former Titchfield Hotel, an aging structure that was once the home of movie bad boy Errol Flynn, who discovered the beauty of Port Antonio after riding out a hurricane in his yawl, *Zaca.* He made Titchfield his home for many years and played on your private cay, Navy Island.

Now Flynn's hideaway playground is the fiefdom of a Hollywood publisher and his wife, who have owned a vacation cottage here for many years. They've added a pleasant new dining room and yacht-clubby bar/lounge that rises on stilts above the water's edge, with just the right amount of fancying up for a castaway's cay.

The lounge, like the cottages, faces *north*—not out to sea but back toward the mountains, the town and the harbor. Water taxis (free to guests) shuttle you back and forth around the clock for shopping, dining or an evening of reggae in a local bar. Rafting on the Rio Grande is one of the most popular attractions in these parts—especially appropriate in this case since it was Flynn himself who first adapted the rafts that hauled the bananas down the river for the delight of his Navy Island guests.

If all that sounds too worldly, you can always stroll through your private jungle to Trembly Knees Cove, where there's nothing between you and the sand and nothing but ocean between you and forever after.

NAME: The Admiralty Club

MANAGER: Burkhard Klein

ADDRESS: P.O. Box 188, Port Antonio, Jamaica, W.I.

LOCATION: On Navy Island, 5 minutes across the harbor by water taxi; 2 hours and $80 by taxi from Kingston, or 20 minutes by air ($100 per plane)

TELEPHONE: 809-993-2667

TELEX: None

RESERVATIONS: Own office in North Hollywood, 800-225-3614; in California, 818-766-4343

CREDIT CARDS: MasterCard, Visa

ROOMS: 10 rooms, including 7 studio bungalows and 5 bungalow suites (1 of them with 1 bedroom), all with ceiling fans, louvered walls and doors, mosquito nets, balconies or verandas, small refrigerators and hot plates in studios, some suites with kitchenettes

MEALS: Buffet breakfast 8:00–10:30, lunch 10:30–5:00, dinner 7:00–9:00 (in the breeze-cooled dining pavilion, $35 for 2); informal dress, "but not scruffy"; room service for breakfast only in studios only (10 percent extra); suites have their own maids to prepare breakfast; taped background music (classical)

ENTERTAINMENT: Bar (with radio), folksinger, beach party Wednesday evening, VCR, Errol Flynn movie nights, backgammon, checkers, library

SPORTS: 3 beaches (1 for water sports only), tennis court—all free; waterskiing, knee boarding, windsurfing, snorkeling gear, small sailboats for rent

Trident Villas and Hotel

Port Antonio

White breakers come plunging through, under and over the craggy coral. A winding pathway leads to a gazebo for two that seems to float in the middle of the sea spray. Farther along the coast, scores of waves spume and fume, the Blue Mountains crowd the shore, the narrow road winds among villaed coves and lush green headlands. This is one of the more dramatic corners of Jamaica and Trident makes the most of its setting. Of all the small luxury hideaways along Jamaica's north shore, here is the one that most magically puts you into another world. Screened from the roadway by garden walls, it's a whitewashed, shingle-roofed enclave of gardens and courtyards, with most of its villas strung out along the edge of the shore, cuddled in bougainvillea and allamanda. Australian pine trees have been coaxed and

cajoled into an exuberance of topiary, with silver butterwood to add a touch of color. At one end of the garden, a big circular swimming pool sits atop the coral, at the other, a columned doorway leads to a secluded cove with private beach and lagoon.

The main lodge has something of the look of one of those whitewashed, black-trimmed staging-post inns in England's Lake District. Even the interiors are more English country house than Antillean resort, the drawing room decked with striped fabrics and wingback armchairs, the dining room with Oriental rugs and Baccarat flambeaux. The villas and rooms display many of the grace notes associated with its owner, Jamaican architect Earl Levy—peaked shingle roofs, roughcast stucco, lattice window grills and ornamentation, gazebos and clay tile patios.

Villa 1 is still my favorite nest here, 20 paces from the lodge, screened from its neighbors by hedgerows and shrubbery. The French doors of the living room open to a patio for wave watching, a dainty gazebo (lovely spot for breakfasts for two), a patch of lawn separated by a low wall from the coral. In the bedroom, a bay window forms a sunny reading nook with an armchair, foot stool and reading lamp. The living room sports color-coordinated wicker chairs and sofas (custom-made on the Patrice Wymore Flynn estate), tile floors, louvered windows and an antique desk and end tables, every flat surface a potential setting for vases of fresh tropical flora, plucked that morning by the maids. Colors and furnishings vary from suite to suite, but each is a minor masterpiece, no concessions to untropical carpeting or air-conditioning. The most impressive accommodations are the Presidential and Imperial Suites, the latter a duplex in the Tower Wing—dining room and living room downstairs, a twisting white stairway swirling up to a capacious bedroom where three more mahogany steps put you onto the mammoth four-poster bed.

In previous editions of this guide I questioned whether vacationers would want to dress up every evening, dine indoors in an air-conditioned, chandeliered salon, consuming seven-course, fixed-menu dinners served by white-gloved waiters. Well, apparently they do. Even Monty Python's John Cleese and actor Kevin Kline, Broadway stars Betty Buckley and Tommy Tune, fashion stars Klein and Blass, princes, princesses and duchesses. They even seem to welcome the Tia Maria that comes with the coffee after each dinner. (The meals are nicely paced, with small portions, classic cuisine accented with local variations such as ackee pâté and red snapper patties; the menu is posted each morning in the lobby, if you're on a diet you can order substitutes.)

Perhaps Trident's distinguished guests enjoy their dinner hours because here's a resort that doesn't feel obliged to regale you with amplified music. A pianist plays in the drawing room, a local trio known as the Jolly Boys—

guitar, rumba box and banjo—plays on the terrace. (They have an amazing repertoire, including their own compositions, such as the impish "Philip, Dear," about an intruder in the Queen's bedroom.)

And that's about it as far as nightlife is concerned, unless you trot into town for a night of reggae at the Roof Club, or guests like Betty Buckley and Tommy Tune entertain you after dinner in the drawing room.

Not least of Trident's attractions for many repeat guests is manager Josef Forstmayr, an aristocratic young Austrian who is not only a polished innkeeper but a natural host. He guards your privacy, if that's what you want (and it seems to be what most of the guests want), but it's not unknown for Forstmayr to round up a party of guests and take them rafting on the Rio Grande, riding on the Flynn ranch or hiking to a secret waterfall for a picnic and swim. But wherever you disappear to by day, be back on the terrace by 4:30, when Mrs. McHardy, a gracious Queen Mum of a lady, oversees afternoon tea. Silver pots. Wedgwood china. Finger sandwiches and home-baked cake. Peacocks and peahens preen expectantly—Oscar, Otto, Ophelia, Ozzie and the newcomer, the dazzlingly white Lancelot. It's all very civilized, very garden partyish. Even the breakers calm down.

NAME: Trident Villas and Hotel

MANAGER: Josef Forstmayr

ADDRESS: P.O. Box 119, Port Antonio, Jamaica, W.I.

LOCATION: A few miles east of Port Antonio, 2 hours and $80 by taxi from Kingston, 20 minutes by air ($100 per plane, included in the hotel rate if you stay 7 nights or more); the Port Antonio airstrip is about 15 minutes from the hotel

TELEPHONE: 809-993-2602 or 2705

TELEX: None

RESERVATIONS: First Resorts Management

CREDIT CARDS: American Express

ROOMS: 30 rooms, including 15 villas, 13 junior suites and 2 deluxe suites, all with ceiling fans and louvers, balconies or patios, telephones; all villas have refrigerators and wet bars, some have kitchenettes

MEALS: Breakfast "from 7:30 on," lunch "whenever," afternoon tea 4:30–5:30 (all served on the awning-covered terrace), dinner 8:00–10:00 ($80 for 2, in the main dining room, cooled by fans or air-conditioning); Jamaican buffet Thursdays; jackets required, jacket and tie preferred; room service for breakfast and lunch only, no extra charge

ENTERTAINMENT: Bar/lounge, piano player, calypso trio every evening ("no amplification ever"), occasional folklore shows, parlor games in drawing room

SPORTS: Beach, freshwater pool, snorkeling, Sunfish sailing, tennis (2 courts, no lights)—all free; massage, windsurfing, scuba can be arranged, horseback riding (with guides) on the Patrice Wymore Flynn Ranch

P.S.: "Children any age, any time," but it's not really suitable for young children; no groups ever

P.P.S.: The owner is currently completing another 8 junior suites in the hotel plus 3 suites and 4 tower rooms in a contemporary "castle" a few coves along the coast—when completed (probably by the time you read this guide) they will be among the most striking rooms in Jamaica

Jamaica P.S.

In the iffy world of Caribbean resorts, few resorts have been as iffy as the Port Antonio white elephant once known as Dragon Bay, most recently as the Marbella Club. The original 95-room resort has a beautiful location, around a scenic cove with a sheltered beach; it was initially designed as a series of private villas, with living room and master bedroom upstairs, guest rooms (cramped and stuffy) downstairs—a layout that doesn't work well as a hotel. A few years back, Prince Alfonso von Hohenlohe, of the original highly touted Marbella Club in Spain, came along and took the place over, planning to turn the dragon into a unicorn. He didn't. Currently (spring 1987), the resort is closed, with everyone suing everyone. I mention this only in case some astute reader says "But what about that swank place opened by that Spanish prince?" If you want to keep posted on what's happening there, you can call the resort's NewYork reps, Leading Hotels of the World, at 212-838-3110 or 800-223-6800.

Haiti

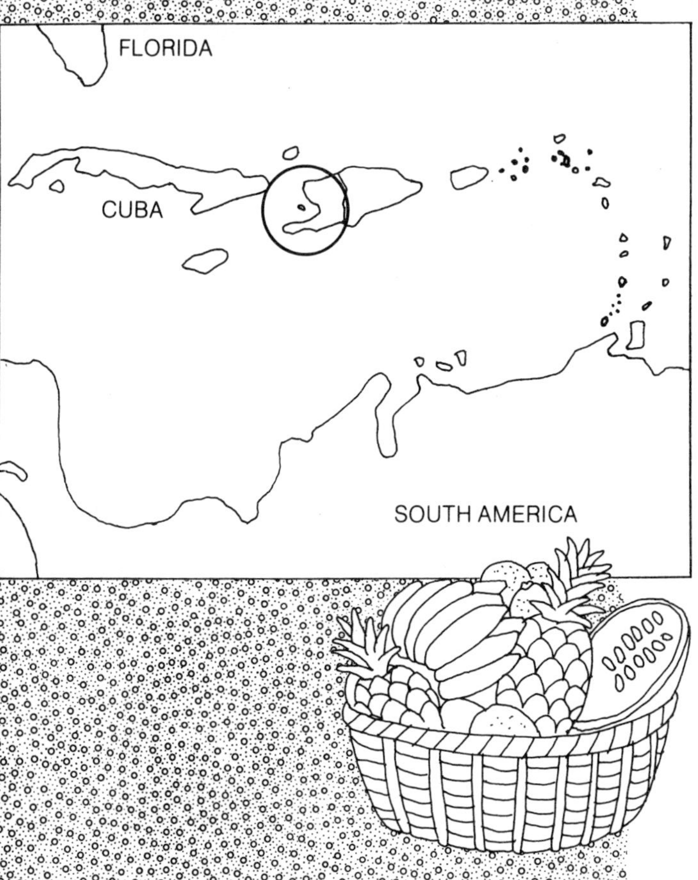

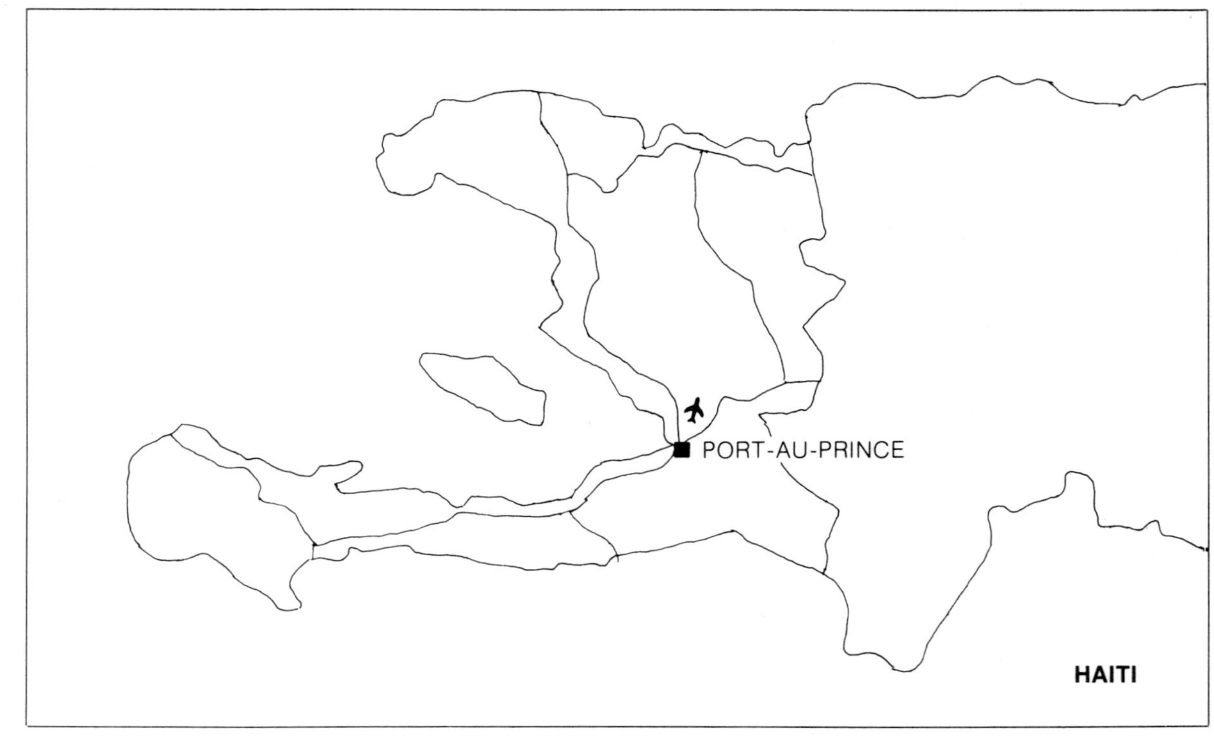
PORT-AU-PRINCE
HAITI

Haiti

As readers of previous editions of this guidebook well know: I'm a big fan of Haiti. It's everything people say it is. Mysterious. Vibrant. Hot. Spooky. Damp. Poor. Fun-loving. Sensual. Edgy.

Haiti, more than any other Caribbean island, is an *experience*. Darkest Africa just a few hundred miles to the south. I wish I could exhort you to go there, but I hesitate to rate most hideaways in Haiti, especially with the demise of the beloved Oloffson. Because of the unsettled state of the nation since the departure of former President—and now Exile-for-Life—Baby Doc Duvalier, there seems to be little enthusiasm on the part of tourists to go there. (American tourists, that is. Haiti still has a loyal following among Europeans.) Consequently, most (but not all) hotels have been holding back on renovations and refurbishing. Since conditions there can change at any time, for better or worse, I skipped a research trip to Haiti this time round. What you have in the following pages, therefore, are reminders rather than recommendations, based on previous visits to the island. Updated information on Haiti will appear at appropriate times in my newsletter, *Very Special Places* (see page 336).

HOW TO GET THERE From New York, daily nonstop flights on American, one-stop flights on Pan Am; from Miami, nonstop on Pan Am, Eastern and Air France; from Montreal, once-a-week nonstops on Air Canada.

Added Attractions

Le Relais de L'Empereur

Petit-Goâve

At first glance, it doesn't look like a hotel. Its imposing three-story colonial facade and the flag unfurled above the entrance seem to herald a town hall. But don't drive past; it is the ensign of the Relais de l'Empereur, the latest creation of Parisian Oliver Coquelin, the inspired founder of the legendary but now defunct Habitation Leclerc. Once again, Coquelin's vision and taste have produced a jewel, a precious if slightly impractical gem fit for an emperor (in this case, Haitian emperor Faustin I, who lived in this very building between 1849 and 1856).

Inside, it may remind you more of a French country inn than a tropical resort. Everything is solid and cozy, with only the terraces open to the breezes. There are just 10 guest rooms, each exquisitely furnished with antiques, their beige walls accented by ceiling beams and heavy, dark wooden terrace doors. Each room has a terrace facing either the mountains or the village square with the blue bay beyond. Ceiling fans spin softly in the rooms (there's no air-conditioning, nor is it needed most of the time). There are no windows, only the louvered terrace doors, and when they are closed some people might find the effect a mite somber, even claustrophobic.

But no one will fault the marvelous king-size four-posters that dominate the rooms—some brass, others mahogany, all with plenty of room for maneuvering. As if that's not enough, the spotlight is shared by huge porcelain bathtubs ornamented with gold-plated fixtures. Real sybarites' dreams, these. In most rooms the tubs (and washbasins, also with gold-plated fixtures) are accorded a place of honor on a platform within the bedroom itself; but for those guests who want more privacy when bathing and mystery when dressing, or just don't like tubs anyway, there are two guest rooms with enclosed shower stalls.

The atmosphere is peaceful and serene, except, that is, when punctured by street noises. This is, after all, a *relais* in the heart of a typically Haitian town, charming, unspoiled, but tropical and exuberant.

There's not much to do in Petit-Goâve, which you can explore in half an hour. It's certainly no place for anyone who demands activity or lively nightlife. There's no swimming pool on the premises, only a lovely, leafy courtyard with caged birds and tables shaded by *ombrelles*. So, what do you do?

Coquelin has thought of that too: he loads his guests into a powerboat for a half-hour trip to Cocoyer Beach, a long sliver of white sand with clear blue water framed by coco palms (or *cocoyers*). The only way to get to this Eden is by boat, and although a few day-trippers from hotels in Port-au-Prince usually go along, too, you can enjoy delicious privacy once you're there. The beach barbecue (free to hotel guests) is complemented with punch and fresh coconuts.

Back at the Relais, glowing from hours in the sun (and, perhaps, the bathtub), guests gather for apéritifs and dinner, elegantly served, and quite outstanding—real Haitian cuisine prepared by a local chef, François. You dine family-style at 8:30, seated with other guests, unless you request a table for yourselves. Since the Coquelin coterie usually attracts a variety of

interesting, urbane travelers, most guests share tables, and you may find yourselves dining with European journalists, movie directors, people who are something in finance, or, perhaps, a sprinkling of royalty.

The Relais, like Petit-Goâve itself, is not for everyone, but it most certainly is an experience for the special few who appreciate hideaways off the beaten track, who prefer the charm, say, of a mews house to the open space of a penthouse, who appreciate elegant appointments and the special mystique of Haiti. *(S.F.)* 10 rooms. *Le Relais de l'Empereur, P.O. Box 11399, Carrefour, Haiti, W.I. Telephone: 509-350-810. No credit cards.*

Hotel Ibo Lélé

Pétionville

Entering the 70-room Ibo Lélé is like stepping into a Haitian painting: the salmon pink walls almost throb with brightly colored murals by local artists Antonio Joseph and Tamara Baussan, wife of the architect-owner. For some people, the atmosphere of Ibo Lélé may be almost as exuberant as the decor, but the guest rooms themselves are more secluded, staggered across the terraced hillside. Some of the most attractive (and least expensive) rooms are the "standard" accommodations in the entrance patio; some of them have striking doors and headboards hand-carved from local hardwoods, and small balconies overlooking the garden. There's not much to do up here except relax in the springlike temperatures or make forays into Port-au-Prince; if you want to enjoy a more sporty life you can exchange a few nights here for a few nights at the Baussans' Ibo Beach resort on Cacique Island, where you'll find three lighted tennis courts, three pools, windsurfers, pedal boats, and just about every water sport you could ask for, including scuba diving. Accommodations are in small, basic but attractive "chalets" (each with private bath and terrace); but Ibo Beach is also a popular spot for day-trippers and on a busy day it is as peaceful as St. Tropez in August. Still, two days by the beach in Cacique and two in the hills of Pétionville make an interesting mix. 70 rooms. *Hotel Ibo Lélé, P.O. Box 1237, Port-au-Prince, Haiti, W.I. Telephone: 509-370-845.*

Hotel Mont Joli

Cap-Haitien

At its best, the hotel lives up to its name, a pretty mountain setting of gardens and vine-covered terraces overlooking the bay, the town and the great gleaming dome of the cathedral. The dome was constructed by the father of the Mont Joli's present owner, and Mont Joli was the family home until it became a hotel in 1956. The oldest (and prettiest) of the 30 rooms are furnished with 100-year-old French colonial beds, wardrobes and chairs, mostly in sturdy mahogany; the remaining 6 rooms are in two-story wings, and a dozen new minisuites in the terraced garden at the rear. Room 1, in the old wing, is particularly attractive, separated from the others by a porch, with a small terrace overlooking the sea; Room 2 sports a canopied bed. All rooms have air-conditioning (rarely necessary at this elevation—200 to 300 ft. above the sea—for cooling but helpful for shutting out the sounds of crowing cocks and barking dogs). 30 rooms. *Hotel Mont Joli, P.O. Box 12, Cap-Haitien, Haiti, W.I. Telephone: 509-320-300.*

Hotel Beck

Cap-Haitien

You've heard of hotels with their own nurseries, others that make their own furniture, but here's a remarkable little inn with its own nursery, workshop *and* its own lime kiln. The rooms are constructed from stones dug up and fashioned by hand right here on the plantation, the furniture is handcrafted in the inn's workshop from mahogany trees grown on the estate. Even the drinks are cooled by "spring-fed" ice cubes, and the same spring supplies the water for the big swimming pool.

This self-sufficient hotel, like its near neighbor, the Mont Joli, started out as a private home for the family that has been running the plantation for four generations. The family chef has been here more than 20 years, and since the Becks were originally German, the menus are likely to feature *sauerbraten* and *marmorkuchen* alongside chicken Haiti-style.

The guest rooms are solidly comfortable, furnished throughout with estate-grown mahogany, the best of the batch being the half dozen new rooms above the pool area. All the rooms have air-conditioning, although most of the time you won't need it. "This is the coolest spot in town," claims Kurt Beck, but even without the mellowing effect of the mountains, trees and deep verandas, this is a refreshing garden to return to after an expedition up the Citadelle. 16 rooms. *Hotel Beck, P.O. Box 48, Cap-Haitien, Haiti, W.I. Telephone: 509-320-001.*

Hotel Cormier Plage

Cap-Haitien

Your first impression says no-frills beachcombers' resort, and your second impression confirms it. The surprises come later. The parking lot seems to merge with the beach; the front office is a small *bohio* with screen walls; the

gentleman with Jacotte the parrot perched on his big toe is Jean-Claude the co-owner. Ahead of you, a massive almond tree shades a score of wooden loungers; a few hammocks are strung up between the palms and sea grapes; and beyond them half a mile of sand and reef, with a few native fishing boats hauled up on the beach. The 30 guest rooms (or most of them) are scattered among the garden's 26 varieties of hibiscus; 10 small thatch-and-wattle cottages modeled on the native huts you passed on the way from town, plus 20 rooms in two new wings, each with terrace. They're furnished with French colonial antiques, and have straw-matted doors; bedspreads and lamps are covered with voodoo motifs; each room is equipped with louvers and table fan.

While you're having dinner, a quartet of the fishermen you saw on the beach earlier in the day (and who probably caught the snapper or lobster you had for dinner) settle down outside the lounge to play haunting Haitian songs. (Ask them to play "Ibo Lélé" and you'll see what I mean.) To top it all off, when you return to your cottage, you find that your chambermaid has turned down the bed, replenished your ice bucket and put a match to the bug-repelling candle. Your first impression was right: Cormier Plage is a beachcombers' resort—but with many extra attentive little touches. 30 units. *Hotel Cormier Plage, P.O. Box 70, Cap-Haitien, Haiti, W.I. Telephone: 509-320-300.*

Hotel Roi Christophe

Cap-Haitien

In a historic byway such as Cap-Haitien you may want to forego an inn by the beach or a room with a view of sea or mountains and check into a hotel that captures something of the character of this offbeat town. The Hotel Roi Christophe more than fits the bill: Built in 1724, once the home of the French governor, M. de Chatenoy, its sturdy stucco walls rise two stories from lush tropical gardens. Modern facilities, air-conditioning and private bathrooms complement old-world features such as ceilings and arcaded halls, wooden beams and elaborate chandeliers. But it's the cloisterlike gardens that will surely capture your heart. Strolling in them or sunning yourselves beside the Olympic-size pool, it will hardly seem possible that this 18-room inn is right in the center of town. Although the inn is full of character and charm, not all of the rooms are what you would hope for: the "standard" rooms tend to be small and somber, more suitable for the governor's underlings than for his excellency in person. The 6 superior rooms, on the other hand, are outstanding—yet still reasonably priced.

Many visitors consider the beamed dining room of the Roi Christophe to be the best in Cap-Haitien—its ambitious cuisine, a combination of Creole and French, beautifully prepared and presented. As a Frenchman, old Governor Chatenoy might well be proud of what's become of his home. *(S.F.)* 18 rooms. *Hotel Roi Christophe, P.O. Box 34, Cap-Haitien, Haiti, W.I. Telephone: 509-320-414.*

Hotel La Jacmélienne

Jacmel

You reach Jacmel from Port-au-Prince by driving south past some of the greenest, lushest scenery in all of Haiti. First, the sugar plantations, then the mountains, with their dizzying, winding roads, clear air, and views that seem to go on forever. Not too long ago the trip took all day, but a new superhighway gets you there in about 2 hours. It's a demanding drive nonetheless, and once in Jacmel, you will probably want to stay awhile. The perfect place: La Jacmélienne.

It's a fairly new (opened only in 1978), sprawling, contemporary two-story structure directly on the beach at the edge of town. Everything about La Jacmélienne is light and airy and unpretentious—lobby and reception are open to the breezes; a covered dining room, on the second floor, is exposed on two sides; guest rooms are spacious and bright with private terraces facing the water. Even the spirit is open and expansive, due no doubt to the personality of owners/managers Erick and Marlene Danies. Crisply uniformed Jacméliennes take your order and graciously serve you lunch—simple, well-prepared Haitian specialties at reasonable prices.

La Jacmélienne can be a lively place, from the Haitian band that serenades you at dinner nightly and at lunch on weekends to the crowds who linger at the pool and beach. Although there are only 31 rooms, the hotel is a popular spot for day-trippers from Port-au-Prince, with the result that on busy weekends there might be upward of 150 people, including families, enjoying themselves. Beach and pool are both large, however, and there's plenty of room for privacy. In any case, the visitors clear out around sunset and you and the other guests have the place to yourselves.

The Jacmélienne's dark sand beach is unexceptional, but there are several white sand beaches nearby, considered to be among the best on the island. You can also explore the town with its colonial architecture (reminiscent of New Orleans) and art galleries. But best of all you can rent a horse, ride into the mountains, and spend an afternoon beside the waterfall of the *bassin bleu* (blue pool) looking for the nymphs who, according to legend, cavort in the mountain grottoes. *(S.F.)* 31 rooms. *Hotel La Jacmélienne, Rue St. Anne, Jacmel, Haiti, W.I. Telephone: 509-124-899.*

Villa Creole
Pétionville

This is a favorite of many longtime visitors to Haiti. A sprawling (80 rooms) white structure high in the hills of Pétionville (near the deluxe El Rancho, without a harbor view), it has a large swimming pool, attentive staff and restful atmosphere. The public and private rooms are tastefully if unexceptionally decorated. The outdoor dining areas on the other hand are charming. Guest rooms are a mixed bag. All are air-conditioned (necessary), but the hot exhaust ruins too many of the terraces. If you do stay here, I recommend the three "special deluxe" rooms (509, 609 and 710) in the new wing, built in 1977. Each has two terraces to capture the sun at all angles. They're private and quiet. Nelson Rockefeller once stayed in room H in the old wing; its large terrace is, unfortunately, enclosed, but the room is big, comfortable and quiet, and you can always imagine that the red carpet actually laid down for Rockefeller still leads to the door. *(S.F.)* 80 rooms. *Villa Creole, P.O. Box 126, Port-au-Prince, Haiti, W.I. Telephone 7-1570.*

Le Picardie
Pétionville

Yet another private home turned hotel, the Picardie has only 10 rooms, of average size and ordinary decor, each with private bath plus terrace or garden. Swimming pool and gourmet restaurant overlook Port-au-Prince and the harbor. One guest room has a huge terrace with the same view. Ask for it. This place rarely advertises (most people, even in Port-au-Prince, don't know it exists), but its rooms are always full by word of mouth. *(S.F.)* 10 rooms. *Le Picardie, P.O. Box 2150, Pétionville, Haiti, W.I. Telephone 7-1822.*

Prince Hotel
Port-au-Prince

Like many of the most charming hotels in Haiti, the Prince was originally a private home. Located in the hilly residential area of Pacot, just behind the Oloffson, it has 33 rooms, all with air-conditioning and small terraces (some with harbor views). There's a small swimming pool, a large public terrace with a magnificent view, and a pleasant if unextraordinary dining room. The public rooms are furnished with antiques, the walls adorned with

Haitian paintings. The private rooms, on the other hand, leave something to be desired—moderate size, small bathrooms, sturdy dark mahogany furnishings and rather somber atmosphere. Still the place has great charm and character, a European ambiance and reasonable prices. *(S.F.)* 33 rooms. *Prince Hotel, P.O. Box 2151, Port-au-Prince, Haiti, W.I. Telephone 2-2765.*

Manoir Alexandre

Jacmel

Perhaps the most adorable hotel in all of Haiti, the little Manoir Alexandre in Jacmel perches on a hill overlooking the bay, a private home before it was converted to a six-room hotel. Outside, a large flower-decked porch faces the sea, while inside, family heirlooms and bric-a-brac tastefully decorate the dining room and drawing rooms. The bedrooms, though, are strictly for travelers who want real island atmosphere—sparsely furnished, no private baths, only two rooms with double beds, and *they* don't seem too sturdy. But for charm and price this *manoir* would be hard to beat. *(S.F.)* Six rooms. *Manoir Alexandre, Jacmel, Haiti, W.I. Telephone 827-11.*

The Dominican Republic

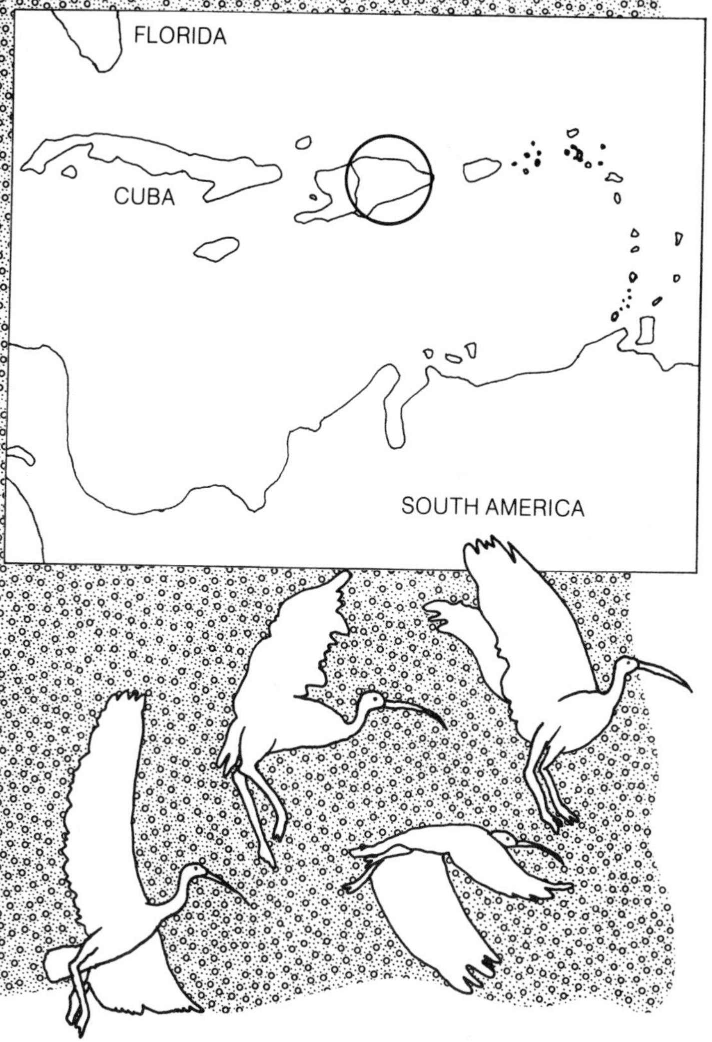

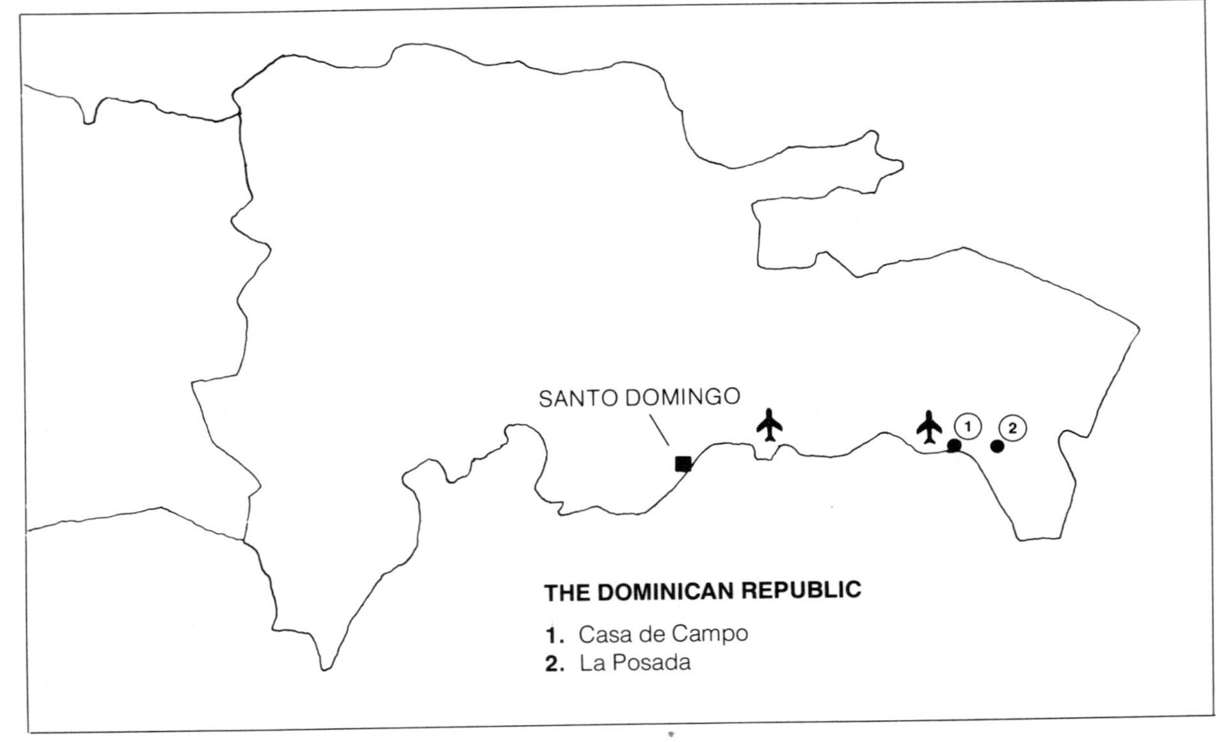
SANTO DOMINGO
1
2
THE DOMINICAN REPUBLIC
1. Casa de Campo
2. La Posada

The Dominican Republic

It's the other part of Hispaniola, Columbus's favorite *La Isla Española,* which it shares with Haiti. The first permanent European settlement in the Americas was here, in a place called Montecito, founded the year after Columbus stopped off in 1492. A few years later, Columbus's brother, Bartolome, founded a city on the banks of the Ozama River and named it New Isabella; we now know it as Santo Domingo. At one time Santo Domingo was the most important city in the Caribbean, and it was from here that renowned conquistadores set forth on their expeditions to colonize the surrounding islands—Diego Velázquez to Cuba, Hernán Cortés to Mexico, and Juan Ponce de León to Puerto Rico, which is less than 60 miles to the east. In recent years, the Dominican government has been forging ahead with an impressive program to preserve and restore the old colonial city. It's well worth a visit.

But Santo Domingo's surprises don't end with the old colonial section; it also has one of the largest botanical parks in the world, a zoological park with 5 miles of pathways and one of the largest bird cages in the world, and somewhere in the city there's a Museum of Miniatures with a fully clothed flea.

HOW TO GET THERE Daily nonstop flights from New York by American or Dominicana de Aviación, and nonstop from Miami by Pan Am, Eastern and Dominicana; there are also flights direct to Casa de Campo from Miami and San Juan. The Caso de Campo's airstrip is listed under La Romana in airline directories.

Casa de Campo

La Romana

The original "ambience" here was designed by Oscar de la Renta and the hotel brochure almost has you thinking that every last guest was designed by de la Renta.

True, many celebrities vacation here and several of them have built private homes on the property, but La Romana's "house in the country" is a pleasant, informal resort with few airs—designed not so much for beautiful people as active people. And how!

Two golf courses (one seaside, one inland) designed by Pete Dye are the pride of the project. With reason. Both are highly rated by pros, but for average duffers they promise more frustration than relaxation. Tennis facilities are so extensive they get a "village" all to themselves, across the main road, where you'll find both Har-Tru and clay courts (eight with lights), ball machines—even ball boys. There are, on a casual count, a dozen swimming pools, and 2,000 quarter horses and polo ponies in the equestrian center. Even the polo fields come in pairs.

William Cox was the architect who pulled the whole thing together and created a sprawling complex that nevertheless manages to be compatible, more or less, with its Dominican surroundings. Buildings (never higher than three stories, mostly two) are finished in stucco, with red corrugated roofs, native stone and rough-hewn local hardwoods. Interiors sport floors of hand-fired tile, screened-glazed-and-louvered doors, local paintings and boldly patterned fabrics. Every hotel room has a stocked refrigerator and patio or balcony; villa suites are larger and more luxuriously appointed.

All in all, Casa de Campo doesn't sound like the creation of a big, corporate conglomerate, but that's exactly what it is—or was. The Gulf & Western Corporation started the project in a corner of its 7,000-acre sugar plantation, but sold everything—sugar, land, hotel, horses, golf balls—a few years back to the Fanjul brothers of Palm Beach, Florida, a family also heavily into sugar plantations. As homeowners themselves on the Casa de Campo estate, they were probably eager to buy up a project 11 times larger than Monaco.

The problem is, Casa de Campo is getting to be more *casa* than *campo*, with new villas going up everywhere and a new 150-room hotel planned alongside an already crowded beach. Nowadays, you almost have to plan your travels around this *hotel* as diligently as you might plan a tour of Caribbean *islands:* tennis is here, golf is there, stables thataway and the closest beach is slated for a relocation. So the first thing guests do when they get here is rent an electric "villa cart" or Moped, to avoid standing around waiting for shuttle buses.

Here are some pointers to consider when you sit down to make your reservation. First, call 800-223-6620 and ask them to send you a map of the resort, then decide which sporting activity will take up most of your time, then pick out a room or villa close to golf or tennis or whatever. The hotel is organized around a handsomely designed core of restaurants, lounges, terraces, patios, courtyards and a spectacular split-level pool with swim-up bar and thatch-roofed lounge. Grouped around it are the hotel "casitas."

Golf villas are half a mile or so east, the equestrian center, polo fields and tennis courts are across the main two-lane highway, Altos de Chavon (see next entry) is a few miles farther east. There are private homes on the hill (some for rent, others like the Pucci place strictly private) and private homes (like de la Renta's) down by the spectacular shoreline—and adjoining the resort's private airport. In all, there are over 1,000 rooms at Casa de Campo, although only 700 or so are available for rent on a regular basis.

To fill all those beds, the resort has to haul in groups and conventions (a new convention hotel is in the cards), and since groups and conventions are unwieldy, many of them arrive directly at the airstrip—once the private preserve of corporate minijets, now growling with the roar of DC9s.

With all those rooms, all those acres and a staff of 1,500, management obviously can't keep an eye on every detail. Hence, some flaws in basic amenities: new villas with connecting doors between rooms are not soundproof, valet service is tentative (I had to bully a concierge—young and untutored but dressed by de la Renta—into having a pair of pants pressed, not even laundered); and how do you think Oscar de la Renta would feel if a waiter arrived at six o'clock the evening before he checked out to do an inventory of his refrigerator—then *locked* it? These gripes aside, it should be emphasized that the staff is pleasant even if not always polished, rates are reasonable, you can eat well at modest prices (there you are, out there in the boonies, miles from the nearest cantina, and they don't try to gouge you).

And even if you never catch so much as a glimpse of the polo-playing, party-giving, trendsetting socialites who fill the usual glossy articles about Casa de Campo, here's a place where you can never say you're bored. Ever.

NAME: Casa de Campo

MANAGER: Touran I. Rateb

ADDRESS: P.O. Box 140, La Romana, Dominican Republic

LOCATION: On the southeast coast, 1½–2 hours from Santo Domingo airport, 2–2½ hours from the capital itself; the resort has an air-conditioned lounge at the airport and hostesses to escort you to air-conditioned minibuses for the ride to La Romana ($50 per couple round trip), but have your travel agent look into the possibility of flying direct to the resort via Miami or San Juan on Air Puerto Rico (in case he or she has trouble finding them, the code for Air PR is FD, for Casa de Campo LRM)

TELEPHONE: 809-682-2111

TELEX: ITT 346-0398

RESERVATIONS: Own Miami office, 800-223-6620 or 305-856-5405

CREDIT CARDS: American Express, Visa, MasterCard

ROOMS: 740, including 268 hotel rooms (or casitas), the remainder, suites of various sizes in villas and homes of various sizes; all casitas have air-conditioning and louvers, wet bar and stocked refrigerator, balcony or patio, telephone

MEALS: Breakfast, lunch and dinner somewhere on the property from 7:00 A.M. to midnight in one or other of the 9 restaurants (some with taped or live music); dinner for 2 anywhere from $20 to $80; informal dress, but long trousers for men everywhere after 6:00 P.M. and jackets or long-sleeved shirts in the hotel's Tropicana Restaurant; room service, limited menu, $3.50 extra per tray

ENTERTAINMENT: Bars, lounges, taped and live music, dancing, disco, movies, folklore shows, occasional concerts and recitals at Altos de Chavon

SPORTS: 2 beaches, lots of pools (some semiprivate); you pay for just about everything else—boat trips to Catalina Island, snorkeling, windsurfing, Hobie Cats, Sunfish sailing, scuba, deep-sea fishing, waterskiing, tennis (13 Har-Tru courts, 8 with lights, full pro shop), fitness center (squash, racquetball, massage, sauna, whirlpool, exercise equipment), trap and skeet shooting (Olympic standards), horseback riding (Western and English, with *vaquero* guides only), polo instruction and rentals, golf (2 superb Pete Dye courses)

La Posada

Altos de Chavon

$

Cobblestoned lanes wind from *plazuela* to *plazuela*. A weathered campanile towers over a tiny chapel. Bougainvillea splashes on native stone walls. Terrace cafés shelter beneath cooling foliage. An amphitheater echoes the curve of the river far below in the gorge.

If this surreal spot puts you in mind of a scene from a Fellini movie, you're not far off the mark, because this "sixteenth-century" village, with peeling walls and exposed foundations, actually debuted 300 years late (in 1978) and the architect was, in fact, a set designer for Fellini.

Altos de Chavon was the brainchild of Charles Bludhorn, the man who put together the Gulf & Western conglomerate. To complement his main resort, he and his family dreamed of an artisans' village, where artists from the Dominican Republic could find an international showcase. Now its narrow streets are lined with art galleries and ateliers, the workshops of ceramists and woodcarvers, weavers and jewelers, not only from the *republica* but from all over the Americas.

The village is only 5 minutes from the main resort, but for those who prefer seclusion rather than bustle, there's La Posada. All sturdy stone and timber, it looks like a typical European inn, but the 10 rooms (choose the upper level for the view) go beyond typical auberge charm and amenities with modern plumbing, central air-conditioning and refrigerators. Apart from its modest rates (as little as $50 per day, per person in summer), La Posada has another attraction that makes it a beguiling alternative to its big sister—the swimming pool. Where the cobblestones end, a dozen stone steps lead down to a large terrace with a lovely free-form pool, surrounded by balustrades and lanterns, right on the edge of the cliff, looking almost straight down from the *altos* to the Chavon River and the coconut plantations lining its banks.

With a pool like that you may never get as far as Oscar de la Renta's village boutique, but don't let it keep you from all the cafés and bistros. Everything from pizzas and *pastelillos* to haute cuisine. The sidewalk El Sombrero is the sort of place where you may spy jet-setting homeowners chowing down their $8 Taco Ole while being serenaded by Mexican minstrels. The kitchens at La Piazzetta are headed up by a pair of chefs from Venice's Cipriani, and while the Café del Sol's menu wouldn't look out of place in Disneyland, the view from the upper terrace is breathtaking. But the grandest view of all is from the plush gorge-edge Zanzi Bar—all along the floodlit gorge awash in a mystic orange glow.

With luck your visit may coincide with a stellar concert at the 5,000-seat amphitheater (Sinatra and Iglesias have performed there), but more likely it will be a recital by a roving quartet or pianist. Even the local choir. Whoever performs, go—the magic of the setting will make it worth your while. To say nothing of the lamplit walk back to La Posada, serenaded by a million tree frogs. (Since La Posada is run by the Fanjul brothers' Premier Hotels Corporation, management and facilities are the same as those at Casa de Campo, with La Posada guests having full access to all the activities at Casa de Campo.)

Added Attraction

Hostal Nicolás de Ovando

Santo Domingo

The *palacio* of Diego Columbus, the Discoverer's son, is a few yards away at the end of Calle de las Damas; the Casas Reales, the former administration buildings, are directly across the street; a short stroll will bring you to the first city hall in the Americas, the first university, the first hospital and the oldest cathedral, where the remains of Christopher Columbus are said to be buried in a marble-and-bronze mausoleum.

The 55-room Hostal itself has been created from two fifteenth-century mansions transformed into one of the most charming small hotels in the Caribbean. Its weathered facade may look rather somber on arrival, but step into the lobby and you're in surroundings befitting the former home of the knight commander and governor for whom the hotel is named. Public rooms gleam with heraldic tapestries and bronze mirrors, guest rooms have hardwood furniture hand-carved in Spain to re-create the colonial era. Quiet patios echo with fountains, and one of them has been fitted with a full-size pool, sun terrace and poolside bar overlooking the port. 55 rooms. *Hostal Nicolás de Ovando, Calle de las Damas 53, Santo Domingo, Dominican Republic. Telephone: 809-687-7181.*

The U.S. Islands

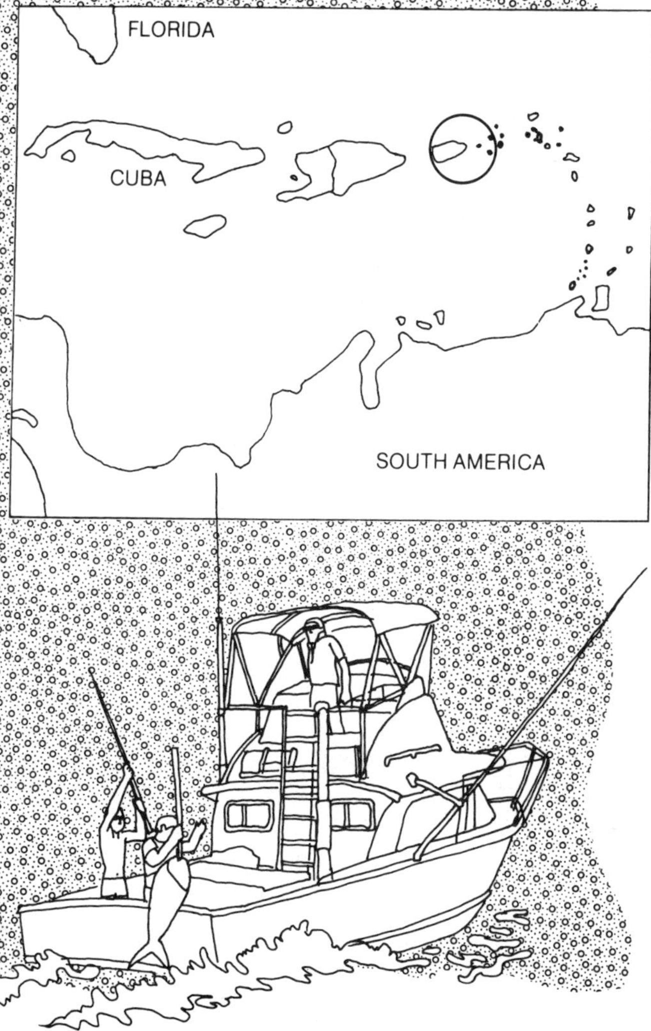

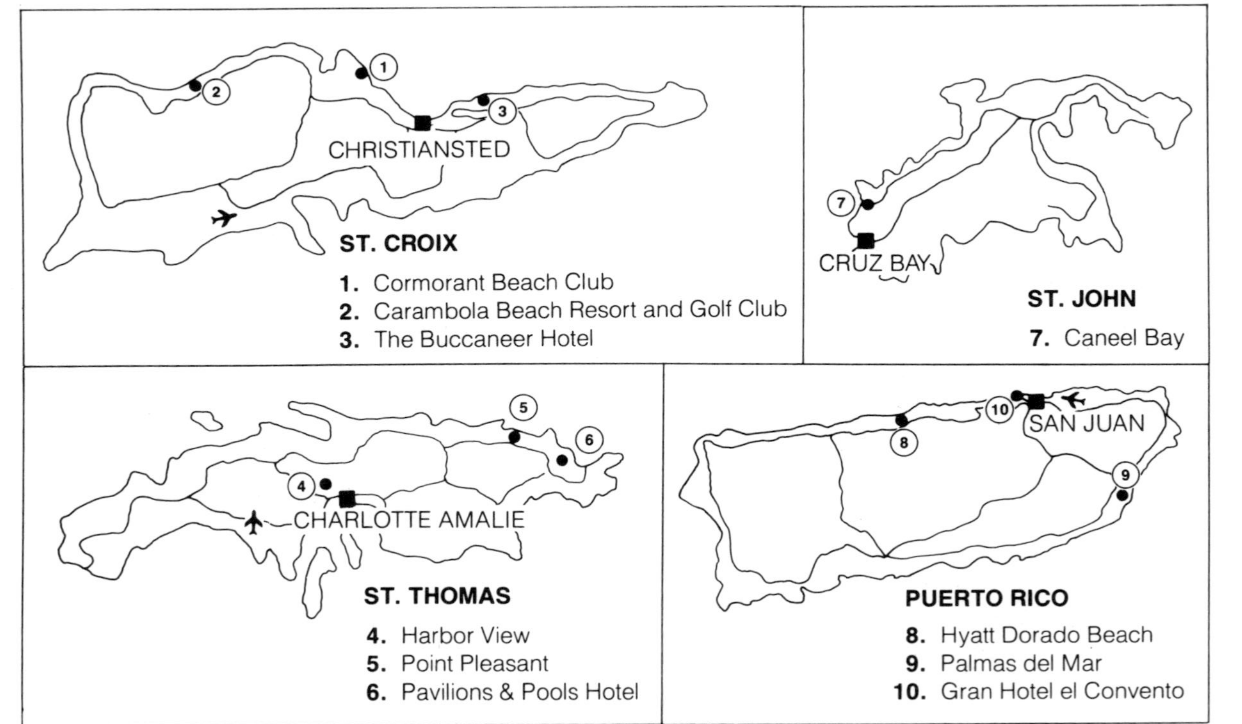

THE U.S. ISLANDS

The U.S. Islands

Suburbia south. With a few delightful exceptions, they're just about everything you're trying to escape—shopping centers, Kentucky Fried Chicken, real estate billboards, telephone poles, traffic jams, crowded restaurants. However, since they are politically part of the United States and get a lucky break on air fares, Puerto Rico, St. Thomas, St. Croix and St. John have their attractions, sometimes bountiful. Not least of these attractions is the fact that you don't have to worry about passports, don't have to fidget in long lines on arrival while some doltish official thumbs his way through immigration formalities, don't have to stand in line at customs behind returning locals laden with suitcases and cartons of contraband that have to be painstakingly inspected and evaluated. These islands need no introduction, but a few comments might be helpful.

When most people think of *Puerto Rico* they think of San Juan, which, impressive though it may be from a commercial and political point of view, is no longer a tropical hideaway. But how about *Old* San Juan? The Old City, with its narrow streets and fortresses, is still one of the unique places of the Caribbean. Even the United Nations thinks so: it designated *six* sites in Old San Juan as World Heritage Monuments. Moreover, when you get beyond the city, Puerto Rico can be a stunningly beautiful island. Head for the rain forest. Try a drive along the roadway that runs east to west along the Cordillera Central. And the modern *autopista* from San Juan to Ponce is a spectacular but effortless route across the mountains.

St. Thomas and St. Croix have had more than their share of problems. The islanders blame it on a hostile stateside press; but you should read the lurid headlines in their own local papers. Both islands are low on the list of priorities for this guidebook, not because of any latent unrest but because they are just too overdeveloped for comfort. Charlotte Amalie is an almost constant traffic jam. Poor Christiansted should be one of *the* gems of the Caribbean, but instead its lovely old Danish buildings are almost swamped by masses of power cables and carbuncled telephone poles. Your best bet on either island is to get to your hotel and stay put. Otherwise you'll have to deal with their taxi drivers, who are not the Caribbean's most obliging fellows.

St. John is the delightful, enchanting standout—just 28 square miles, almost half of them national park. Cruz Bay, the main town, looks nothing like a suburb of Florida, and there are enough beaches and coves and mountain trails for everyone.

HOW TO GET THERE San Juan's Luis Muñoz Marín International Airport is the largest in the Caribbean (they've spent millions in the past few years expanding and improving it), and it's served by nonstop flights from 10 cities in North America, one-stop direct service from as far away as Los Angeles. From New York alone there are almost two dozen scheduled flights every day. Both American and Eastern have expanded their activities at the airport, and for both airlines it's now the hub of new interisland services—on American Eagle and Eastern Metro, both flying small, efficient aircraft. When using these services, remember that what passes as carry-on, stowable luggage on a wide-body jet may have to be checked for the smaller flight, so pack accordingly.

Both St. Thomas and St. Croix are served by frequent flights from San Juan, but there are also direct services from Atlanta, Boston, Chicago, Miami and New York on American, Eastern and/or Pan Am; the same three airlines have daily flights to St. Croix from Miami and New York. For St. John, the quickest route is via St. Thomas, then the ferryboat from Red Hook at the easternmost tip of the island; there is also seaplane service from Christiansted in St. Croix (but not from the main jetport). Flights to St. Croix usually stop first at St. Thomas, so you can probably visit both islands for the fare to either.

Hyatt Dorado Beach

Dorado, Puerto Rico

🌴🌴🌴 ✗✗✗ ☻☻☻☻ $$$

Yes, despite the name it's the same classy, elegant Dorado Beach Hotel conjured up by the Rockresort people a quarter of a century ago.

But, it's been fiddled with during those 25 years.

Since it's now coming into its second full season under its latest owner (its fourth), perhaps it's more accurate to say it's *almost* the same classy, elegant resort.

The setting is still one of the most majestic of any resort in the Americas: an estate of 1,000 acres and thousands of coconut palms, of winding fairways and manicured lawns and a pair of crescent beaches. The grounds have been replanted with a botanical bonanza of African tulip and almond trees, sweet immortelle and spiceberry and fiddleleaf fig, et al.

When I first came here in 1963, a few years after it opened, those crescent beaches were ringed with just 150 guest rooms, in decorous two-story wings hidden among the leafy palms; today, the room count has doubled. The first-rate sports facilities, once the playground of a mere 300, are now shared among all those extra guests *and* a local country club numbering 500 members.

Moreover, the 1,000 acres are shared with a sister hotel of over 500 rooms, a mile down the coast. Nothing very new in that, of course: the eight-story Cerromar has been there for some time now and it, too, has come under the Hyatt banner (it's now the grandly named The Hyatt Regency Cerromar Beach Hotel). But since it's given over largely to groups and conventions, whose members have charge privileges at both hotels, the rickety school buses that shuttle between the two resorts seem to carry more bodies bound for Dorado than vice versa.

On a recent visit (admittedly out of season) the clientele at Dorado Beach was not at all what Laurance Rockefeller had in mind 25 years ago. They didn't add anything to the elegance of the original. They cluttered the dining facilities. To keep guests happy, slot machines have been installed in the mini-casino. And it's not unknown for the bar/lounge just off the lobby to have a large-screen television blaring boxing or football.

And there certainly are pluses: When you include the sports facilities at

Cerromar, you find you now have *4* championship golf courses (the original 2 Robert Trent Jones courses are still rated among the hemisphere's finest, and the Hyatt people have spent a small fortune rehabilitating them). There are now more than 20 tennis courts, a few of those at Cerromar lighted for night play. And it's still a rare pleasure to hop on a tandem and cycle along paths that weave between the fairways and the sea (although you're expected to return the bike to the rental people before 5:00 P.M.—just when the sun and the sea and the palms are at their most ravishing).

Water sports are limited, horseback riding is nonexistent, but the Hyatt people are building new stables on the grounds and a new water sports center on the beach, with everything from windsurfers to scuba, pedal boats to Hobie Cats.

What the Hyatt people have also done is lavished about $5 million on renovating the rooms, and almost everything they've touched is an improvement. Colors are sprightlier. New wicker and rattan furniture enhances the Caribbean mood. New additions to each room include minibars, safes and terrycloth robes. The centerpiece of guest rooms on the upper floors is a sturdy bamboo four-poster; beach level guests have to settle for a pair of double beds, but they have more floor space these days because the sliding glass doors have been repositioned halfway into the patios (which now have dividing walls to maintain a sense of privacy).

The original deluxe beachfront rooms are the favorite of longtime guests, but the top-of-the-line accommodations are actually the Casita Rooms, located between the pool and the beach with split-level layouts and skylights above bathsize shower stalls.

Which room should you choose? The dozen or so "Standard" rooms facing the fairways are the least expensive (and perfectly acceptable in terms of facilities); the "Superior" rooms are closest to the swimming pool and dining rooms; "Deluxe" designates rooms fronting the beach—with those in the East Wing (the originals) closer to the golf and tennis pro shops.

The Dorado kitchens are now in the care of a young Hyatt hotshot named Wilhelm Pirngruber. His Sunday buffet brunch of local specialties is not only stunningly presented in the classic Dorado manner, but at $22 it's an outstanding value. Especially good value, I might add, since your $22 includes seemingly endless flutes of Domaine Chandon *vin champenois* (the buffet officially lasts until 4:00 P.M. so you have plenty of time for seconds, on your plate and in your flute).

The Surf Room, where dinner is served, is hardly the most romantic room in the Caribbean, even with its 3,600 square feet of windows facing the sea. But Su Casa, the original estate house or *finca,* most certainly is romantic, with its candlelit tables, its cool courtyards and foliage-draped stairways—a welcome holdover from the original Dorado.

NAME: Hyatt Dorado Beach

MANAGER: Jorge Gonzalez

ADDRESS: Dorado, Puerto Rico 00646

LOCATION: On the island's north shore, 22 miles west of San Juan, about 45 mostly untropical minutes by limo from the airport ($9 per person each way, on request), 15 minutes and $29 per person each way by air to the private landing strip

TELEPHONE: 809-796-1600

TELEX: 3450196

RESERVATIONS: Hyatt Worldwide 800-228-9000

CREDIT CARDS: All major cards

ROOMS: 300 rooms and suites in two-story and three-story wings, most of them strung out along the beach; all with marble bathroom (bath and shower, bathrobes, amenities basket), lanai or balcony, air-conditioning and fan, refrigerator/honor bar, safe, radio/alarm, direct-dial telephone

MEALS: 4 restaurants—the 400-seat Surf Room, the redesigned Garden Terrace, the Golf Pro Shop (if you don't mind cutely named dishes such as "sandwitches," etc.) and the romantic Su Casa (dinner only)—jacket and tie in the Surf Room and Su Casa; room service, $2 per person extra

ENTERTAINMENT: Small casino, music for dancing, beach parties, movies, VCR in lounge for special programs, plus the assorted clubs and shows at the nearby Cerromar; live music in the Surf Room and Su Casa (mostly Spanish-style ballads by strolling musicians)

SPORTS: 2 reef-protected crescent beaches and lagoons (good swimming), 2 pools (plus a children's pool), pedalos, walking/jogging trails—free; at extra charge, tennis (7 courts, no lights, pro shop), golf (36 championship holes, carts obligatory, green fee $19.50 per day, pro shop), bicycles and tandems ($3.50 and $5 an hour); the golf and tennis facilities are augmented by additional courses and courts, with lights, at Cerromar

P.S.: In the slack months, the hotel hosts groups up to 300; in summer and during holidays there are lots of children, but youngsters from 5 to 13 have their own day camp

Palmas del Mar

Humacao, Puerto Rico

$ $ $

Cobbled *plazuelas* with splashing fountains. Walls of tiles hand-painted by craftsmen in the village across the hill. A big free-form pool with tiles in a vivacious psychedelic design. It may not sound like a big sprawling residential/condominium development but it is—it's just that architect/ developer Steve Padilla tried to keep the scale intimate by adding "visual delights," and decreeing that no building go higher than the palm trees. His 2,700 acres are located on a former sugar plantation, in an unhurried and scenic corner of the island, with the island of Vieques offshore and the rain forest an hour's drive up the coast.

This is a place for people seeking the outdoors—but with a dash of style and comfort. The 20 tennis courts are grouped in pairs, separated from each other by trees and flowering bushes, with a duck pond in front of the clubhouse snack bar. Hiking paths weave through bird sanctuaries and subtropical forests. Bridle trails and biking trails wind through navelike stands of coconut palms. The fairways are as challenging and sporty as a golfer could hope for. The mile of beach and the marina between them lay on just about every water sport the most ardent watersprites could cope with. It also happens to be pretty good value.

Accommodations come in a variety of villas and apartments (probably more suited to family than a couple) and a pair of attractive inns in Mediterranean style—the hilltop Palmas Inn and the Candelero Hotel (which is also, alas, the core of an executive conference center, but probably the best bet for one couple). Unlike so many resorts, Palmas del Mar has a room-only rate even in winter, allowing you to take advantage of the resort's varied dining facilities.

I lost track of all the dining spots—stylish Italian and French up the hill, Mexican and Brazilian in the inn, seafood at the marina, Polynesian by the beach (tasty chicken Bora-Bora for $10.50, with free delivery service to rooms and villas).

Don't expect unspoiled bliss, however; Palmas del Mar is still ablossoming, so you can expect earthmovers and concrete mixers around the property. But probably not on the beach. Not on the golf course. Not beside the psychedelic pool.

NAME: Palmas del Mar

MANAGER: Arnold Benitez (Candelero Hotel)

ADDRESS: P.O. Box 2020, Humacao, Puerto Rico 00661

LOCATION: On the southeast coast, near the town of Humacao; an hour from the airport by minibus ($20 per person when sharing); by car take the *autopista* to Humacao and Yabucoa, then follow the skimpy signposts to the resort

TELEPHONE: 809-852-6000

TELEX: ITT—3450830/Candlro

RESERVATIONS: Own New York office, 212-983-0393 or toll free 800-221-4874

CREDIT CARDS: All major cards

ROOMS: Several hundred rooms and suites, in villas, condominiums; 23 in the Palmas Inn, 48 in the Candelero Hotel; all with air-conditioning (necessary much of the time), telephones, radios and television; apartments also have full kitchens

MEALS: Breakfast 7:00–10:30, lunch noon–3:00, dinner 7:00–11:00 (approx. $50 for 2) in the hotel dining room; more extensive hours elsewhere; informal dress; no room service, except by individual restaurants

ENTERTAINMENT: Bars, lounges, taped music, live music, depending on the location

SPORTS: 3 miles of beach and coves, 4 freshwater pools—free; tennis (20 courts, 4 lighted, All American Sports pro shop), golf (18 holes, designed by Gary Player), horseback riding (30-horse equestrian center), snorkeling, Sunfish sailing, windsurfing, paddleboats, deep-sea fishing, sailboat trips, bicycles

P.S.: Lots of groups and seminars, lots of children (especially on weekends) but there are special playgrounds and pools for youngsters

Gran Hotel el Convento

Old San Juan, Puerto Rico

$$$

The love nooks here were once the cells of Carmelite nuns but don't let that inhibit your frolicking. The convent was established 300 years ago, when all those Spanish conquistadores were around and this sanctuary was probably the only place in town where a maiden could remain a maiden. The great mahogany doors of the convent still open onto the same tiny Plaza de las Monjas, which priests and penitents cross before disappearing into the tall blackness of the cathedral, and where old men occasionally play dominoes.

This historic convent in Old San Juan actually went through a period of martyrdom as a garage for sanitation trucks, before it was rescued over 20 years ago by a group of brave and farsighted people, including a Woolworth heir and a pair of local brothers, Ricardo and José Alegría, whose passion it is to restore and preserve all the beautiful buildings of Old San Juan. They imported authentic antiques from Spain, and when they couldn't lay their hands on authentic pieces of the period, they had reproductions made specifically for El Convento. They decked the halls and galleries with paintings and tapestries, conquistadorean swords and shields, the guest rooms with hand-carved chests and high-backed chairs upholstered in satins and velvets, wrought-iron lamps, elaborate headboards and canopied beds, louvered doors and beamed ceilings. The former cells are neatly spaced along graciously arched galleries around a central patio, which now sports a swimming pool where young women cavort in garments so skimpy the Carmelite ghosts blush.

Most visitors to Puerto Rico, of course, don't want to spend all their days in Old San Juan, and although El Convento has guest privileges with beachside hotels it has never become the great romantic hideaway it deserves to be. It seemed, too, that what I predicted in earlier issues of this guide may be true: some people find all the massive furniture, dark wood and filtered light a bit somber.

So what has transpired is that the government's tourism authorities bought the hotel, turned management over to a Mexican hotel chain, which set them "popularizing" the old convent. Their latest efforts were unveiled for Christmas 1986, and while they make the hotel more viable commercially, they certainly haven't done anything to enhance the romance. Many of the rooms have been modernized—that is, with light fabrics, rattan headboards and end tables, like any resort hotel; the windows are now fitted with glass panels that seal in the cool air (but can be opened in combination with shutters for anyone who still likes to see filtered sunlight); bathrooms have been upgraded (but who on earth decided to install those factory john–looking holders for oversize rolls of toilet paper?).

Downstairs is a mishmash. The lobby has lost some of its conquistadorean splendor; service is pleasant but hardly grand hotel standard; the patio has been covered over by tinted plastic, with a stage installed in one corner (but the buffet breakfast served here is a real buy at just $5.95). What was once the casino is now an acceptable dining room, but the magnificent Ponce de Leon Room, with its minstrel gallery and stained glass windows, was closed during my most recent visit, and no one seemed to be quite sure what would happen to it.

Nevertheless, this is a special place because of its location in miraculous Old San Juan, because of its historic overtones. Think of it not as a *gran hotel* but simply as a good first-class hotel, check into one of the remaining rooms with four-poster twin beds, dine at La Mallorquina a few blocks away, and El Convento is still worth a couple of nights of your vacation.

NAME: Gran Hotel El Convento

MANAGER: Guillermo Solorzano

ADDRESS: Calle Cristo 100, San Juan, Puerto Rico 00902

LOCATION: In the heart of Old San Juan, a 25-minute, $10 taxi ride from the airport

TELEPHONE: Direct dial 809-723-9020 or toll free 800-468-2779

TELEX: 3453199 CONVENT PD

RESERVATIONS: Utell International

CREDIT CARDS: All major cards

ROOMS: 100, all with air-conditioning, radio/television, wall safe, state-of-the-art telephones that let you dial your own wake-up calls

MEALS: Breakfast 7:00–11:00, lunch 11:30–4:30, dinner 6:30–11:00 (approx. $50 for 2), served in the air-conditioned restaurant, informal dress

ENTERTAINMENT: Some live music (amplified) and fashion shows; live music (guitarist) in the restaurant

SPORTS: Small pool in the patio; free transportation to Condado Beach (15 minutes away); tennis (nearby), golf (an hour away), water sports by arrangement

P.S.: Some seminars, some group tours, lots of day-trippers and cruise ship passengers; free parking across the street

Caneel Bay

St. John

$$$$$

Where else in the Caribbean, where else in the world, will $200 a day or thereabouts get you a resort with 7 beaches (each lovelier than the next), a private peninsula of 170 acres surrounded by 6,500 acres of national park on land and 5,600 acres of national park underwater; where you can hike along paths lined with flamboyant, tamarind and shower of gold; snorkel among peacock flounders and trumpetfish; spot a yellow-bellied sapsucker or pectoral sandpiper, maybe even a bobolink; build up your strength on a five-course breakfast, buffet lunch and five-course dinner in some of the best restaurants in the Caribbean, and then bunk down in a double-size love nest open to the breezes and birdsongs?

True, $200 plus a day is the summer rate, but you still get all the attractions that presidents, vice-presidents, bank biggies, gospel biggies, French counts and senators pay almost twice as much for in winter.

Caneel is Caneel 12 months of the year, in season or out of season—just about the ultimate in seclusion, tranquility, a sort of ecological euphoria. You almost have the feeling you're camping out here, but with a roof over your head rather than a tent, a bed under you rather than a sleeping bag, and real china rather than plastic plates.

There are 171 rooms at Caneel Bay (for every room an acre of landscaped parkland!) and most of them are right on beaches, a few are on headlands, 36 hillside rooms are in the Tennis Gardens, the rise behind the courts, with a few bungalows off by themselves on the edge of the national park. A pair of shuttle buses circle the grounds every 15 minutes, but it's still worthwhile to give some thought to *where* you'd like to be. Of the beaches, my preference is leeward Scott (single-story wing), but others prefer the windward Hawksnest (two-story) for its views of offshore islands. Rooms at Turtle Bay, perhaps the prettiest beach, are close to the old estate house restaurant (a few are actually in the estate house and may pick up the sounds of what passes as conviviality in these sedate parts, but room number 93 has a particularly bosky balcony).

The most secluded quarters are in the famous Cottage number 7, once the home (*a* home) of the Rockefeller family, now the haunt of assorted VIPs (Kissinger, Bush, Mondale, et al.) since they can conveniently park their bodyguards in the attached servants' quarters.

Adjoining Cottage 7, rooms 61 through 66 are on a headland, secluded from the rest of the hotel, with their own patch of sand; on Caneel Bay

itself, rooms 26 through 29 are especially popular because they're farthest from the public areas yet close to the main dining room. Up in the Tennis Gardens, rooms 132 and 133 are particularly spacious.

Not that you're likely to feel claustrophobic in any of the accommodations here. Larger than usual, the Caneel Bay rooms come with walls of louvers and another of glass opening onto a fairly private patio. No radios, no TV, no room phones here (so no calling up for a drink when you're thirsty, but the resort greets you with a complimentary bottle of rum and ice is delivered daily). Decor is low-key—"madonna gray" blends the exteriors with the environment. But during 1987, interiors have been getting a stylistic facelift and many of the rooms are now quite colorful—almost giddily so by traditional Caneel standards but still subdued and tasteful. Many of the bathrooms have been retiled, replumbed and enlarged, some of the old fuddy-duddy furnishings have been replaced with rattans and wicker.

This flurry of activity can be attributed, in part, to the fact that the Rockresort organization is now part of CSX—ominous intergalactic initials, perhaps, but in fact merely the old Chesapeake and Ohio Railroad. Where does that leave Caneel, being owned by a railroad? Fortunately, CSX also owns one of the grandest and finest resorts in the United States, the Greenbriar in West Virginia, and they seem to be genuinely committed to maintaining the standards of service and ecological husbandry set by Laurance Rockefeller 30 years ago. In any case, the on-the-spot management team is very much in the Caneel Bay tradition.

Last time I talked to them they were fidgety about a new pool (first ever at Caneel) being installed in the Tennis Gardens for the benefit of guests without direct access to the beach. Would it upset the resort's air of calm? How would regular guests such as Alan Alda and Mel Brooks react? The Caneel people were at great pains to point out that the new pool is only 4½ ft. deep and has no diving board to encourage boisterous leaps and shouts. That's Caneel for you.

NAME: Caneel Bay

MANAGER: Michael Neary

ADDRESS: Virgin Island National Park, P.O. Box 120, Cruz Bay, St. John, USVI 00830.

LOCATION: 4 miles across the channel from the tip of St. Thomas; the resort has an air-conditioned lounge at St. Thomas's airport and the hostess there will take charge of your transfer to the resort—by taxi to Charlotte Amalie, where you board a private 58-ft. launch, *Lady Caneel II,* for the 45-minute trip direct to the Caneel dock ($13 per person each way)

TELEPHONE: 809-776-6111

TELEX: ITT 3470019

RESERVATIONS: Own office in New York City, 212-586-4459; toll free 800-223-7637; New York State 800-442-8198

CREDIT CARDS: All major cards

ROOMS: 171 in a variety of one-story and two-story wings strategically located around the property, with a few suites in Cottage number 7; all with ceiling fans and louvers, balconies or patios, refrigerators (in most rooms)—but no telephones, no television, no radios

MEALS: Breakfast 7:15–10:00, lunch noon–2:00, afternoon tea 4:00, dinner 7:00–9:00 (approx. $80 for 2), in 3 breeze-cooled dining pavilions, including the lovely hillside Sugar Mill; jackets for gentlemen after 6:00 P.M., "dry bathing suits and beach wraps and sandals at all times, no shorts or blue jeans after 6:00 P.M."; occasional live music in the main dining room; room service for breakfast only, $3 extra per tray

ENTERTAINMENT: No taped music ever, live music every evening (guitar, combo, "slightly amplified"), dancing most evenings, movies twice a week, nature lectures, backgammon, Scrabble, chess (I still haven't succeeded in persuading them to install a putting green but we're working on it)

SPORTS: 7 beautiful beaches, good swimming and snorkeling, new freshwater pool up behind the tennis courts, Sunfish sailing, windsurfing, nature trails, tennis (7 courts, Peter Burwash pro shop, no lights)—all free; by arrangement—scuba (from the dock), sailboat cruises, boat trips to St. Thomas (popular for shopping) and Little Dix Bay; special package offering a few days ashore, a few days afloat in a Hinckley

P.S.: No children under 8 except at Christmas (but hardly a distraction), some small seminars ("but they have to fit in"), a few day-trippers (who are allowed to have lunch in the 90-seat Sugar Mill, which is why resident guests usually forego the daytime panorama from up there)

Point Pleasant

St. Thomas

$$$

Guest cottages here are so artfully tucked into the crags and cactus gardens, at first you think, *Oops*—must have blundered onto someone's private estate. On second glance, a few cedar-shake roofs peek discreetly out of the greenery. Here and there, you spot a redwood deck, weathered to a sea-salty silver, jutting from the face of a cliff that swoops 200 ft. beneath you to an aquamarine bay.

Although Point Pleasant is less than 10 years old, it has the ageless, settled look of belonging to its surroundings as rightfully as any gnarled old sea grape or mampoo tree. Colors, materials, designs are all just plain natural. From a 15-ft.-high redwood ceiling, a paddle fan whirs above your king-size bed. Walls are mostly windows and glass doors, and they can stay open to the trade winds, because there's nothing nasty to screen out. At this height, both humidity and mosquitoes are conveniently blown out to sea.

All Point Pleasant's accommodations are in these airy cliff dwellings, usually two or three to a cottage. They range from a single room with either balcony or sunken garden to a damn-the-expense five-room, three-bath villa.

A comfortable, affordable compromise might be what the management unfortunately calls an Efficiency—a sleeping-living room plus dining space, kitchen, and a deck with a gull's-eye view of St. John, Tortola and various other Virgins undulating into infinity.

You, too, can do some interesting undulating—down and around Point Pleasant's boulder preserve. The route you take is a fantastic journey through what must have been a very Big Bang. In fact, you're standing precisely on the spot where, several billion years ago, a monumental volcanic eruption took place, the results of which look as if some psycho fire god had scooped up an acre of nice, quiet boulders, squeezed premature wrinkles into their skins, and petulantly flung them down like a handful of hot potatoes. And they're still sitting right where they landed, one balanced topsy-turvy on the tip of another, with organ-pipe cactuses and century plants sprouting out of them like Sassoon hairdos.

Point Pleasant has thoughtfully spiked your route along their new nature trail with some civilized stopping-off places. A woodland glade. A shady gazebo cantilevered over the abyss, where you can catch your breath and sip a planter's punch. A big freshwater swimming pool. A tennis court. A brand-new sea deck with comfortable redwood benches and chaises. And finally, at the end of the trail, an immaculate little white sand beach.

In the bargain, the hotel supplies you with free use of a car—1 of a fleet of 25 compacts—to take you around the island to other sights, other restaurants, and back again to this very pleasant point.

NAME: Point Pleasant

OWNER/MANAGER: Ruth Pfanner; Timothy Reynolds (General Manager)

ADDRESS: Estate Smith Bay #4, St. Thomas, USVI 00802

LOCATION: In the southeast of the island, overlooking Pillsbury Bay and the islands of Tortola and St. John, half an hour and about $9 by taxi from the airport

TELEPHONE: 809-775-7200; 800-524-2300

TELEX: 3677305

RESERVATIONS: None

CREDIT CARDS: American Express, Visa, MasterCard

ROOMS: 132 total: 27 efficiencies, 82 studios, 12 villas, 4 bedrooms (no view); all with direct-dial telephones, breezes or air-conditioning

MEALS: Lunch noon–2:00, dinner 7:00–10:00 in the Agave Terrace restaurant (approx. $50 for 2), informal dress; room service

ENTERTAINMENT: Weekly managers' cocktail party, island shows, rum tastings, occasional barbecues; shopping, Megan's Bay and evening shuttle bus service (small charge)

SPORTS: Beach, 3 pools (1 with poolside bar), complimentary snorkeling, Sunfish sailing, windsurfing, scuba lessons, tennis (1 court, lights)—all free; boat trips, golf, horseback riding nearby; cars available to guests for 4-hour tours at no extra charge

Pavilions & Pools Hotel

St. Thomas

$$$

The genies who designed this place proceeded on the premise that if we all had three wishes, they would be for 1) a tropical house on a tropical island, 2) a private swimming pool, and 3) no down payment, no mortgage. And, sure enough, they've made all three come true. More or less.

The pavilion part of their wish fulfillment consists of a suite (there are two basic designs, one slightly roomier than the other) of big, open rooms with one long wall of sliding glass doors. On the other side of the door lies the pool part: a completely private patio with a completely private swimming pool that's yours to do whatever you've always wanted to do in a swimming pool. A stout wall and plenty of tall spiky tropical plantings guarantee Peeping Toms can't peep.

Unlike most hotels with individual pools, Pavilions & Pools gives you one big enough (16 x 18 ft. or 20 x 14 ft.) for something more athletic than dipping your toes. And with most Caribbean hotels still frowning on topless tanning, you may be grateful for the chance to color in your white spaces without causing a riot. The rigorous privacy of the place, however, extends beyond your doorstep. To some, that's a plus. To others, a minus.

Because there is no central pool, no beach, and a bar with only limited meal service, you're scarcely aware of anybody but the two of you and the friendly people who run the hotel and happily help you arrange side trips, rent cars, call airlines, reserve tables at restaurants, etc. All activities outside your own room are at the hotel next door on Sapphire Beach. That includes tennis, any water sport you can think of and meals (unless you prepare them in your own kitchen or drive around sampling the island's varied cooking).

P & P keeps right on being one of the Caribbean's most popular ways of getting away from it all. If you both agree that a king-size bed, a pool of salt water, and thou are enough, come and join the crowd. Even though you'll never know they're here. *(C.P.)*

NAME: Pavilions & Pools Hotel

MANAGER: Christopher B. Kanzler

ADDRESS: Star Route, St. Thomas, USVI, 00801

LOCATION: In the southeast, near Sapphire Bay, half an hour by taxi from the airport

TELEPHONE: 809-775-1110

TELEX: None

RESERVATIONS: Direct, 800-524-2001

CREDIT CARDS: American Express, personal checks with I.D.

ROOMS: 25 villas with private pools, kitchen, air-conditioning, telephones, cable TV

MEALS: Breakfast and lunch at the Fish Pond Terrace Bar; "cook-your-own" dinner set-ups available; one-entrée dinner served nightly, except on Tuesdays and Fridays

ENTERTAINMENT: You

SPORTS: Private pools; tennis, golf and water sports nearby

Harbor View

St. Thomas

$$

Harbor View is a discreet little secret, cautiously passed on from lover to lover like the password to some frangipani-scented nirvana. So is it fair to blab to the world about a place much of whose charm comes from its mysteriousness?

Of course, everybody already knows about Harbor-View-the-restaurant.

It's one of the best and best known on St. Thomas. But even people who have often eaten in this once scandalous old house rarely notice that those tall, dark doors off the dining room and the shadowy staircases going above and below lead to snugly shuttered guest rooms swathed in dusky chocolate tones and lit by antique lamps and with big gleaming brass beds.

For nearly two centuries now, people have been slipping quietly in and out of these rooms. At first, when the house was the French consulate and the island was ruled by the Danes, the meetings here were over plots and counterplots, until one day in one of the rooms the consul was stabbed to death. You can see his head—and the gash in this throat—over Harbor View's gate, where a sculpture of the martyred Frenchman was mounted to shame his assassin.

After the French diplomatically withdrew, the house became home to a rich and jaded native family, which apparently had more than its share of black sheep. Soon the halls of Harbor View were echoing with screams again—but of delight this time. So nobody was surprised when the house became "A House"; the classiest bordello in town. Nor were any eyebrows lifted when it was sold at a cocktail party and another long line of high-rollers moved in and out over the years.

By the time a bright young woman from Manhattan came to Harbor View in 1961, she found it going wearily to pieces. As she put it slowly, charmingly together again, she began to discover its passionate past. She also discovered that the ghost of the French consul still wobbles through the halls whenever a floorboard is ripped up or a wall torn down. Which wouldn't be worth noting if she weren't the last person you'd expect to tell you that she'd seen a ghost.

The place itself is a graceful manor house mitered into the hillside overlooking St. Thomas's famous postcard-perfect harbor. And what she and her partner have made of it is a dazzling tossed salad of styles and artifacts, none of them matching but all oddly made for each other.

Sydney Greenstreet paddle fans hang next to Marie Antoinette crystal chandeliers in the high-ceilinged dining rooms. On the terrace beyond, you can sip a drink beside jiggling beaded curtains and bronzed Venetian *putti.* There's a baby grand here, a piece of terrible kitsch there. Shiny vinyl sofas rest on handsome old hand-painted tiles. Yet put it all together, light the candles, and somehow it's irresistible.

Each of the 10 guest rooms has a slightly different view—and its own mix of antique and modern furnishings, the beds ranging from brass to mahogany four-posters to cots. One upstairs room has a window full of frangipani tree. Another opens onto a cluster of gardenias, so you can pick yourself a corsage before going down to dinner.

Rooms on the main floor have higher ceilings and one has a terrace running around two sides and looking out on the cruise ships in the harbor.

But if you mind late-night piano tinklings or the sound of laughter and champagne corks on the other side of your door, you're better off above. Or, better still, below.

There's one tiny suite of rooms below everything else at Harbor View. You can spend days—or weeks—here, unseen and unhassled. You have your own private stairway into it and your own private door out of it to the swimming pool. In fact, it's the only room where you don't have to go through any other room to get to the patio and pool. There are a lot of low little windows but no view except the street, an ancient mango tree—and the head of the French consul over the gate.

Keep in mind, though, that this is no gung-ho beach resort. Your only diversions here, besides each other, are the pool and the food. And because you're still on the fringes of town, horns honk and gears grind far into the night.

However, all of the above notwithstanding, you rarely hear anyone who has stayed at this singularly civilized old house complain about anything but having to leave. *(C.P.)*

NAME: Harbor View

OWNERS/MANAGERS: Arlene Lockwood and Lenore Wolfe

ADDRESS: P.O. Box 1975, St. Thomas, USVI 00801

LOCATION: In the hills above Charlotte Amalie, a $3 taxi ride from the airport, 15 minutes from the beach

TELEPHONE: Direct dial 809-774-2651

TELEX: None

RESERVATIONS: American International in U.S. and Canada

CREDIT CARDS: American Express, MasterCard, Visa

ROOMS: 10, with air-conditioning

MEALS: Breakfast 8:00–10:00, dinner 7:00–10:30 (except on Tuesday; approx. $60 for 2); informal dress; no room service

ENTERTAINMENT: Pianist/singer, taped music

SPORTS: Pool

P.S.: *Closed after U.S. Labor Day until mid-October*

Carambola Beach Resort and Golf Club

St. Croix

$ $ $ $ $

Tree-clad hillsides plunge into the sea. A narrow roadway winds among mahogany and saman trees. Reefs and headlands shelter a secluded bay with a curve of white sandy beach. A tiny lighthouse pokes above a distant headland. And not a fast-food stand for miles around.

If this is not everyone's image of St. Croix that's because not many people venture to the still undeveloped northwest corner of the island light-years from downtown Christiansted.

Until recently, Davis Bay was a "secret" bathing Eden with few people. There must be a few Cruzan sun worshippers feeling miffed because their pristine bay now sprouts red-roofed villas among the coconut palms and saman trees. But not guests at Carambola. They seem to have few complaints.

This new-in-1987 Rockresort venture tucks 157 rooms into a narrow 28 acres between hills and beach, its 26 villas ribboned among a grove of saman and coconut and mahogany trees. The porte cochere sets the architectural tone—red corrugated roof, steeply pitched roofline, hardwood ceiling with sturdy rafters from the entrance, and breezeways leading past the lobby, lounge, boutique, deli, bar and restaurants to end at a whimsical gazebo-cum-clocktower. By day it's part Caribbean, part Jutland, echoing the island's Antillean/Danish heritage; by night, it's pure Disneyland.

But in its quirky, understated way it all adds up to an attractive complex. The villas have the same red roofs and timber siding (except for one wall of pastel-colored concrete, presumably the "Caribbean" touch, but it looks almost as if the accountants gave the architect instructions to save money so he left one wall unfinished). Interiors feature masses of wooden louvers and brass fittings, screened doors and tile floors. Each spacious (520 sq. ft.) room is quartered into dressing room/shower, sleeping area, sitting area and (most attractive feature of all) screened porch with padded and cushioned banquettes around two walls—a reposeful, if not too practical, spot for breakfasting on McCann's Irish oatmeal and banana pancakes with mango-coconut syrup.

The furniture is custom-made—reproductions of somewhat staid Danish colonial sofas, chairs, rockers and dressers. A nice idea—one designer's stand against plush-and-trendy California/Caribbean pastels—but it would work even better if the pieces were set off against weathered brick or wood rather than white concrete. Or if the pieces were comfortable.

A few of the rooms are just a tad too close to their neighbors' air-conditioned hum, and some of the lovely screened porches are too exposed to neighborly gazes. They all cost the same, but upper floors have an edge because of their cathedral ceilings, and although all rooms are designated "sea view," the reality is that some have obstructed views. My suggestions would be rooms 141–147, 161–167 or 251–267, if you want to be on the beach; 221–227 if you like to be next to the tennis courts; 71–77 if you want to be close to the hub. Rooms 11–61 form a separate wing on the opposite side of what the hotel calls the Greathouse (i.e., the lobby, breezeways, etc.), a few paces from the beach but very quiet (definitely an upper room here, otherwise you'll be looking out on sea grape rather than sea).

The most impressive salons at Carambola are the dining rooms—the mahogany and the saman ceilings supported by massive tree trunks and festooned with scores (literally) of paddle fans. Air-conditioning supplements the fans and shutters in the carpeted, elegant Mahogany Room. Cuisine is more formal here, too—traditional continental with island accents. Thus an active day on the beach, courts or golf course might end sumptuously with coconut fried prawns and papaya lime coulis or herbed duck rillette with cassava bread; guava bisque with two tropical nuts or spice island coconut soup; steamed scallops with ginger nantua sauce or emince of chicken with pistachio and carambolas. All this is a sort of lead-up to bananas in armagnac caramel with chocolate granito and/or Caribbean lime mousse with papaya sauce. For the strict traditionalists the rack of lamb comes perfectly done.

The same cannot be said for the service, however. (At least in the opening months—things will probably have improved by the time you read this, but even so, don't come expecting polished Caneel-type service.) St. Croix isn't overflowing with talented waiters and chambermaids, so what you have here is a team of people hired not for experience but *attitude*. If service is sometimes slow, at least the staff (most of the time anyway) is friendly, willing and, it seems, eager to measure up.

But Carambola can probably never quite measure up as a worthy sister to its fellow Virgins—Little Dix Bay on Virgin Gorda and Caneel Bay on St. John. Or should it be "stepsister," since Carambola is *managed* rather than owned by Rockresorts? It's the beachside portion of an estate whose new owners plan to build scores of homes and villas here and there but with 4,000 bosky acres these new rooftops will be discreetly screened from guests at Carambola.

NAME: Carambola Beach Resort and Golf Club

MANAGER: Rockresorts

ADDRESS: P.O. Box AO Kingshill, St. Croix, USVI 00850

LOCATION: At Davis Bay, on the unspoiled northwest coast; 20 minutes and $12 by taxi from the airport, about 25 minutes from Christiansted (free shuttle bus daily)

TELEPHONE: 809-778-3800

TELEX: 1017

RESERVATIONS: Rockresorts in New York City, 212-586-4459; in New York State, 800-442-8198; 800-223-7637 nationwide

CREDIT CARDS: All major cards

ROOMS: 157 in 24 two-story villas, all with shower, dressing room, ceiling fan *and* air-conditioning, minibar, screened porch, clock radio; for suites, 2 rooms can be combined with a private entrance; the Davis Bay Suite, built on the remains of a sugar mill, has a large stone terrace, sitting room, 2 bedrooms, 2 bathrooms—but an obstructed view of the sea

MEALS: Buffet breakfast 7:30–9:30, lunch noon–2:00 in the Saman

Room, 11:30–5:00 in The Deli or at the golf course clubhouse, dinner 6:30–9:00 in the fan and air-conditioned Mahogany Room or fan-cooled Saman Room ($80 for 2); jackets for men in the Mahogany Room, casual but stylish (i.e., "no jeans") elsewhere; room service for breakfast only; no-smoking areas in both dining rooms

ENTERTAINMENT: Bar/terrace, music every evening (low-key, mildly amplified), parlor games and wide-screen TV in the Tamarind Room

SPORTS: Beach (good swimming, snorkeling), freshwater pool (no good for laps), two Jacuzzis, snorkeling gear, tennis (4 Laykold courts, pro shop, no lights)—all free; the resort's own Robert Trent Jones golf course 10 minutes away by shuttle bus (18 holes, $22 per round); sailing, scuba and horseback riding can be arranged

P.S.: Some seminar groups up to 200 ("but they have to blend in—no name tags allowed"); no restrictions on children, but the full rate is charged for kids over three, which effectively cuts down on numbers

Cormorant Beach Club

St. Croix

🌴🌴🌴 XXX ☺☺ $$$

Hammocks dangle between the tall palms (a thousand of them, I'm told) that rise straight from the sandy beach. Gentle trade winds skip ashore from reefs a hundred yards off the beach. Hi-tech mattresses float guests around the big freshwater pool.

And since there are never more than 76 guests at any time you never feel crowded, never have to "reserve" a hammock, never feel jostled at the breakfast or lunchtime buffet.

Better still, you never have to sign a check or pay a bill before 5:00 P.M. You just while away your days in an air of total relaxation and contentment. Which is just what Wally and Robbie Bregman had in mind when they opened their long-dreamed-of inn in January 1985 and introduced their "CBC Plan"—your room rate covers full American breakfast and lunch *and* all drinks until five. After five the resort's bar and dining room are open to outside guests so then you sign or pay for whatever you order.

First, some background. This Cormorant was once a Pelican—the Pelican Beach Club, which lay moribund for several years before Wally and Robbie

Bregman gave up their Connecticut/CEO life-style to plunge into the mad, mad world of Caribbean innkeeping. It's located on 12 quiet acres at the end of a rather domesticated drive from the airport, between a cluster of modest dwellings and a ribbon of beach that runs for probably half a mile in each direction. Not a *great* beach, but with its thousand palm trees and bedazzling background of reefs and multihued waters, it's all very tropical and soothing.

The Bregmans have made the most of the former Pelican's rather ungainly three-story lines, brightening and lightening the rooms with floral fabrics and rattan headboards, table and chairs. The lobby, bar and restaurant, trimmed with light wood, are open to the breezes and the beach; the barroom tables double as backgammon boards; a tidy little library, just off the lobby, has enough paperbacks and hardcover (obscurities) to fill a week of lounging in hammocks.

Because *lounging* is what this place is all about. It's a relaxing 12 acres where you can escape *or* mingle with like-minded idlers or find your very own corner or hammock. Apart from the earnest frolickers on the pair of tennis courts, guests move at a very, very lethargic pace; and with sprightly waiters to fetch your complimentary piña coladas or whatever, it makes more sense to loaf and lounge at the Cormorant than to go shopping or sightseeing in Christiansted.

The Bregmans claim they've applied to their club all the niceties they uncovered in years of visiting the world's other hideaways. Hence, bathrooms with oodles of fluffy towels twice a day and an amenities basket with sunblock and skin balm; fresh flowers in every room, king-size or two double beds; guests are invited to sit in the library to sign in and out; for tennis players who've just finished a rigorous set there's a canvas-covered shelter and a cooler full of complimentary beer and soft drinks right at the courts.

As newcomers to innkeeping the Bregmans suffered their share of tribulations, but one year later things were running smoothly. The dining room has a new chef but the kitchen's highlights are still local seafood cooked over beach kasha wood. The lobster is especially memorable.

The dining room staff has polished its collective skills, but the staff in general seems to have taken its cue from the hardworking, cordial Bregmans, so the welcome here is noticeably warm, smiles are genuine, tips are shunned. This is St. Croix? This is the Cormorant.

NAME: Cormorant Beach Club

OWNERS/MANAGERS: Wally and Robbie Bregman

ADDRESS: P.O. Box 708, Christiansted, St. Croix, USVI 00820

LOCATION: On the north shore, 20 minutes from the airport in one direction, 20 from Christiansted in the other, $8 per taxi in either direction (although the club operates a shuttle bus to town twice a day)

TELEPHONE: 809-778-8920

TELEX: None

RESERVATIONS: David B. Mitchell & Company, Inc.

CREDIT CARDS: American Express, MasterCard, Visa

ROOMS: 38, including 4 suites, in 2 two-story beachside wings, all with balcony or patio facing beach, ceiling fans, wall safes, direct-dial telephones that even dial your own wake-up calls; wet bars in suites

MEALS: Breakfast 8:00–10:00, lunch 12:30–2:00, dinner 6:30–10:00 (approx. $60 for 2), all beachside; island casual dress after 6:00; no room service, but tables with coffee and tea are set up in the breezeway of each wing from 7:00 A.M.

ENTERTAINMENT: Steel band on Fridays, dance combo on Saturday (lightly amplified), island troubadour for Sunday brunch, VCR for new and old movies in meeting room

SPORTS: Half-mile beach, big hexagonal swimming pool, parcours trail, snorkeling gear, tennis (2 courts, no lights)—all free; a highlight for most guests is a cruise to Buck Island ($70 per couple, including full lunch, or $50 for a half-day lunchless trip, maximum 6 passengers); scuba diving, golf and horseback riding (rain forest or beach) can be arranged

P.S.: No children under 16; a few small but discreet seminars in off-season

P.P.S.: As this edition was going to press, the Bregmans sold their dream resort to a group of Connecticut investors, who "promise to keep everything the way it is, including the Cormorant Plan." Except that the Bregmans won't be there keeping an eye on things.

The Buccaneer Hotel

St. Croix

$$$

Other guidebooks festoon the Buccaneer with their brightest stars and highest marks. Maybe because it's one of those doughty old enclaves of comforts and graces that have survived from the days when a trip to the Caribbean meant an expedition into the heart of darkness where if the piranhas didn't get you the tsetse surely would. On the other hand, maybe other writers of other guidebooks *like* this 1950s kind of "puttin on the Ritz." Except, alas, it ain't the Ritz.

Preserving the past can be a noble undertaking—depending on what the past *was.* But the Buccaneer, like so many of its big pink sisters in the islands, clings to a leatherette philosophy that makes you think the people who go to these places must never risk a visit to Little Dix Bay or Malliouhana. The main lobby, albeit refurbished—ceiling fans, tall wicker chairs with tropical print cushions, that sort of thing—still has that gaudy "island" wall mural and nonstop "mellow pop" taped music. Check in quickly, and step out on to the terrace lounge where you can still hear the music, but you'll also get a magnificent view of the sea, the coves and a corner of Christiansted.

While the main building, all formalities and false *luxe,* is indistinct and impersonal, there are two sets of accommodations—quite different in style and setting—that offer both privacy and unpretentiousness.

One set is called the Ridge. A parade of little row houses, each consisting of a small-scale bedroom and bath and sharing a communal terrace, sits on a hilltop overlooking just about everything there is to see, including golf course, tennis courts—and St. Thomas 43 miles out to sea. The Widow's Mite, with its two double beds and peaked wooden ceiling, is not only the nicest house in the row but the best buy as well.

Down below and right in the lap of the Buccaneer's perfect beaches there are two cabana colonies. One, the Doubloons, is just next door to the hotel's informal beach restaurant. The other, newer and more expensive, gives you a bigger room, a bigger bath and a private terrace facing the ocean. Each colony has a beach of its own, or you can wander on to a third, and more sequestered, stretch of silky sand called Whistle Beach, meaning: whistle just before you get there in case anybody else with the same romantic ideas is already there.

If you ignore the fake ceiling beams, the prefab arches and the kitschy decor of the air-conditioned main dining room, The Brass Parrott, you may enjoy the chef's *flambé* specialties—and a fiery sunset. For something lighter, there's the terrace dining room, breeze-cooled, but adjacent to the terrace lounge, where there may be some (loud) island combo playing. But the rates are EP, so why not hop aboard the shuttle bus and go sample the multinational cooking in town instead? Just a 10-minute ride from the hotel, Christiansted's historic old warehouses and government buildings, some proudly restored and some still prettily falling down, are honeycombed with lively little restaurants. The gourmet gamut runs from French and Danish to West Indian to every permutation of Oriental.

To sum up: if you must go to St. Croix, and you must stay at a big, fancy hotel with all the fixings, the Buccaneer it is. *(C.P.)*

NAME: The Buccaneer Hotel

MANAGERS: Robert D. Armstrong (owner), Carlos Duarte (manager)

ADDRESS: P.O. Box 218, Christiansted, St. Croix, USVI 00820

LOCATION: On the beach, about 10 minutes from Christiansted, $8 by taxi from the airport

TELEPHONE: 809-773-2100

TELEX: 347 1018

RESERVATIONS: Ralph Locke Islands

CREDIT CARDS: American Express, Visa, MasterCard, Diners Club

ROOMS: 144, all with air-conditioning, private bath, telephone, balcony or terrace

MEALS: Breakfast 7:30–10:00, lunch 11:30–3:30, dinner 6:30–9:30 (approx. $40 for 2 in the Brass Parrot); jackets; lunch outdoors at The Grotto or at the beachside restaurant; room service

ENTERTAINMENT: Taped music, steel band, guitarist, combo, piano, dancing, movie once a week

SPORTS: Beach, pool—free; tennis (8 courts, lights, $5 per hour, $10 per hour at night); windsurfing, snorkeling, scuba, sailing, boat trips, fishing, golf (18 holes), health club, horseback riding nearby

P.S.: Lots of families, some small groups

Added Attractions

Secret Harbour Beach Hotel

St. Thomas

No longer, apparently, a secret, judging by the private homes and low-rise condos that line the approaches. But secret enough to deter day-trippers, so once you're there, on a half-moon of sand studded with palm trees, you see only a few sun worshippers. This is basically a condominium resort with hotel services—maid service, restaurants, tennis, water sports. Accommodations, in four three-story balconied wings, are in air-conditioned studios and one-bedroom apartments, all facing the beach, all with kitchens and comfortable furnishings that vary to match the taste of the owners. (You want a studio or suite on an upper floor, since the lower level can't even see the sea.) The Bird of Paradise restaurant comes in two parts, both beachside. The classier of the two pavilions entertains its diners with an entirely superfluous local radio station (complete with commercials), and while the food is more than acceptable it hardly measures up to the expectations aroused by the maître d's fancy duds. 60 rooms, including 9 studios. *Secret Harbour Beach Hotel, P.O. Box 7576, St. Thomas, USVI 00801. Telephone: 800-524-2250. No credit cards.*

Sprat Hall Plantation

St. Croix

If you could invent your own relatives, surely you would want to come up with at least one set of rollicking extroverts complete with a stable of horses, uncounted dogs, cats, tame mongooses and resident frogs and doves, all spilling out of an ancestral manor house conveniently located on a sunny tropical island and a pebble's throw from white sand beach and sea.

If yes, then this jumbo serving of familial exuberance can indeed be yours. The mother of it all, and the chatelaine of Sprat Hall, is a blue-eyed, ruddy-cheeked fireplug of a woman whose great-great-great-great-great-great-great-grandfather sailed from England and settled in the Caribbean long before the first slave ever landed. She, her husband, their daughters and sons-in-law making up the Hurd family run things now.

Things being a 25-acre plantation, beach club, sailing, deep-sea fishing, scuba and—above all else—a riding school. Put one toe down here and you're swept into a rush of horse talk, family life and island gossip that swirls around you like a human Jacuzzi. You either love it or hate it. But one thing: it's genuine.

The 25 guest quarters are somewhat on the harum-scarum side, too. Sprat Hall is not for the seeker of *grande luxe*—or of perfect order. There's a scattering of guest cottages out among the horse pastures and show rings. A lane of wild orchid trees takes you to the doorstep of one, soursop trees shade the terrace of another. The furnishings are strictly Sears catalog: *too* bright prints, imitation French Provincial dressers, white leatherette couches, ceramic pineapple lamps, etc., but 17, a cozy little 1-bedroom cottage, has a nice wide terrace that looks off into the hills and through the frangipani trees to the ocean. You'd do better to take 1 of the 2 Astrodome-size rooms in the main house or a small but comfortable room-with-porch in the 6-room annex next door.

Built in 1670, the main house (a replica of a still-standing manor house in Brittany) is furnished in a good-humored motley of found objects and antiques culled from island homes and old Danish government buildings. One guest room has *two* huge four-posters, one Danish and one English. Which sums up the succession of invaders who ruled St. Croix before Americans took a turn, and gives you a nice little history lesson to sleep on.

Dinner is served at long, candlelit tables, family-style. Horse stories are told. And retold. There's a lot of laughter, a lot of life at Sprat Hall. Unless you're allergic to hay, you could do much worse for a weekend—and spend much more doing it. *(C.P.)* 25 units. *Sprat Hall Plantation, P.O. Box 695, Frederiksted, St. Croix, USVI 00840. Telephone: 809-772-0305. No credit cards.*

The British Virgins

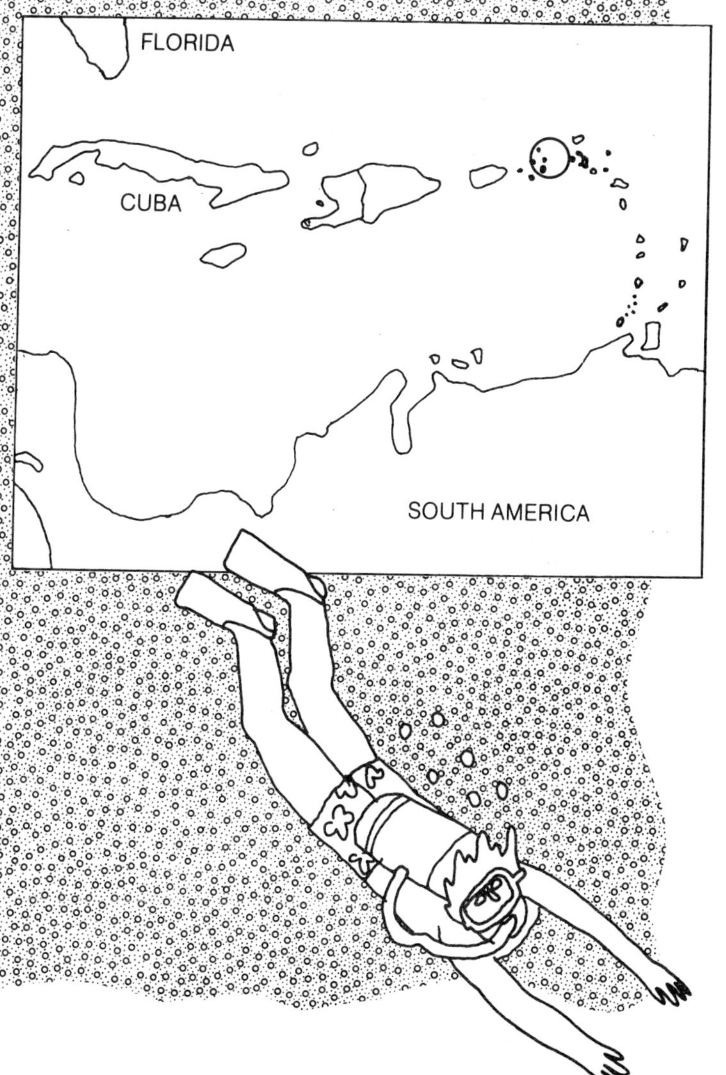

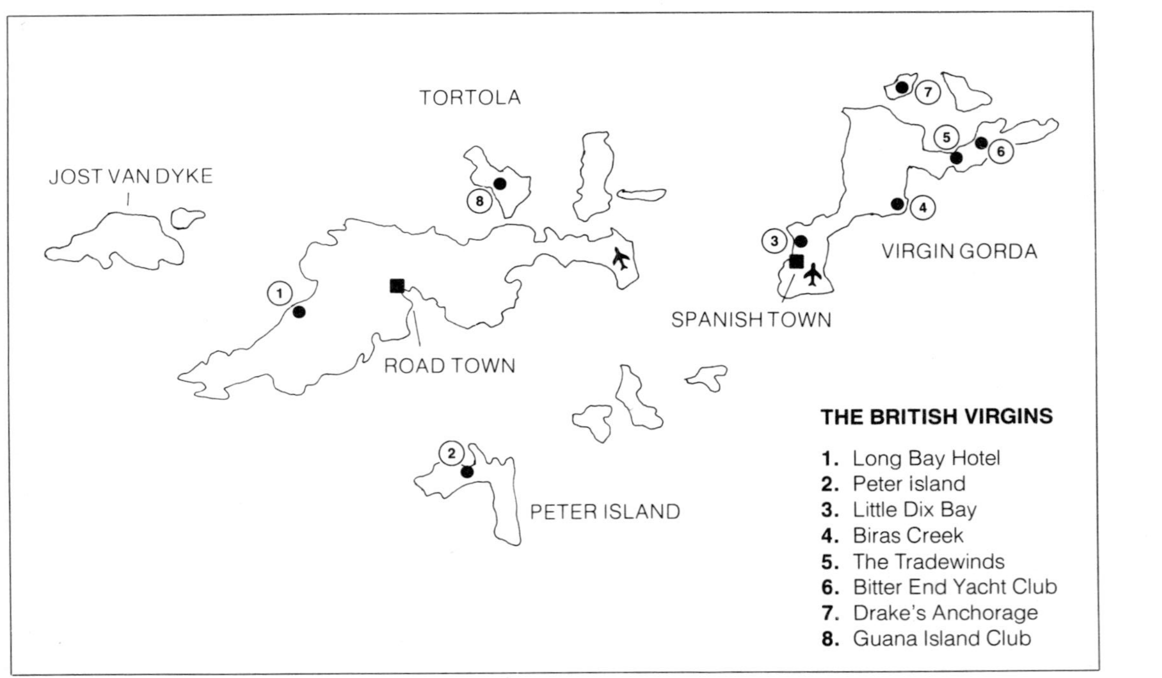
TORTOLA
JOST VAN DYKE
ROAD TOWN
PETER ISLAND
SPANISH TOWN
VIRGIN GORDA
1
2
3
4
5
6
7
8
THE BRITISH VIRGINS
1. Long Bay Hotel
2. Peter island
3. Little Dix Bay
4. Biras Creek
5. The Tradewinds
6. Bitter End Yacht Club
7. Drake's Anchorage
8. Guana Island Club

The British Virgins

Where are they? When Winston Churchill was asked this question in the House of Commons he is said to have replied: "Presumably as far as possible from the Isle of Man." In fact, the British Virgins are more than 3,000 miles from the Isle of Man, but only 60 miles from Puerto Rico and a 20-minute boat ride from St. Thomas. There are 60 of them strung out along Sir Francis Drake Channel, where the wily Elizabethan mustered his ships before attacking the Spanish garrison at El Morro in San Juan. The main islands are Tortola (Spanish for turtle dove), Beef, Peter and Virgin Gorda (the Fat Virgin—named by Columbus, who had obviously been too long at sea by this point); none of them is as big as Manhattan, and if you squeezed them all together, they would still be smaller than, say, Nantucket.

These virgins have no hangups. They're quite content to lie there drowsing in the sun, loyal outposts of Queen Elizabeth. Britain sends over a governor who nominally attends to matters such as defense and the law courts (which are operated on the British system). Otherwise, the islanders elect their own Executive Council and run their own affairs, such as they are. But they're no dummies, these islanders: legal tender is the U.S. dollar rather than the British pound sterling.

These are quiet islands for quiet people. There's no swinging nightlife here. No casino. What little sightseeing there is is usually done by boat rather than car. But what the Virgins dish out in return is glorious sea, glorious scenery, glorious serenity.

HOW TO GET THERE I had hoped to report in this edition that you could now get by jet direct from Miami to Beef Island (the main airport for the BVI, just across the bridge from Tortola); but that service, by British Caribbean, proved to be short-lived. Nevertheless, service has greatly improved in recent months with the introduction of dependable flights by Eastern Metro and American Eagle (and less dependable flights on Air BVI) from San Juan and St. Thomas. Two or three times a day each way, getting you to the remotest hideaway in time for a stroll on the beach before dinner. Air BVI also flies from St. Croix, and there is also a seaplane connection between that island's Christiansted and Tortola's West End.

Two points to remember: Always collect your luggage at San Juan or St. Thomas, rather than checking it through. The new Metro and Eagle services have cut down on the delays in transferring baggage, but it's still wise to handle the chore yourself, rather than have to wait for delayed luggage to arrive on the next flight (which may be the next morning). Also, although the schedules may list Virgin Gorda as the first stop for setting down passengers, your flight will first stop at Beef; there you'll have to get off to clear immigration and customs, then reboard for the 5-minute hop to Virgin Gorda. Tiresome, bureaucratic, penny-pinching.

There's an alternative transfer to the B.V.I, longer (1 hour) but less expensive ($13 per person each way): by twin-hulled, air-conditioned ferryboats, each carrying 60 to 80 passengers. The *Bomba Charger, Native Son* and *Speedy's Fantasy* leave from the ferryboat dock in Charlotte Amalie (about 10 minutes by taxi from St. Thomas airport) to West End or Road Town on Tortola, continuing, in some cases, to Virgin Gorda.

Long Bay Hotel

Tortola

$$$

Hens cackle. Burros bray. Pet ponies hustle you for a sugar cube on your way back from breakfast.

This bucolic hideaway is artfully designed to be just like home—or what most of us would like to call home. And on the theory that nobody posts rules and regulations at home, there's a liberating absence of them here. No dos and don'ts and checkout times, no bulletin boards with today's activities. In fact, you won't even find the name of the hotel posted anywhere. Not even on a matchbook cover.

For all its lack of pretensions, however, Long Bay is no mom-and-pop operation. The place is run by a very low-key Englishman, whom you may take for one of the guests until dinnertime when he comes to your table to ask if you want white wine or red.

The hotel's 50 acres, including a mile-long beach of powdery white sand, are immaculately kept. And what a revelation to find food like this in a faraway corner of a half-forgotten island. One of the best *coquilles St. Jacques* I've ever had (not too much cheese, for once, and not burned in a single spot) was followed by a superb loin of pork along with something rarely found on any British or American island—*fresh vegetables!* And neither overcooked nor oversauced at that.

(The wine, however, is of the Blue Nun persuasion, so you may want to convert to a good English beer or ale.)

This is one dining room where you will probably curse the service—for being too fast. You sit in amber candlelight, surrounded by wide airy arches opening onto a botanical gallery of tropical trees, each as dramatically spotlit as any Rousseau in a museum. Your table is set with the kind of linen, china and crystal ladies used to keep safely hidden in their hope chests when nobody had liberation but everybody had a trousseau.

Even before the coffee arrives, hands are held, sighs are sighed and guests begin to retire.

Eight cottages, twenty suites and twelve elevated beachfront cabanas with big decks are scattered up the side of a flowery hill. The view, naturally, is the bay and beyond that a lot of lesser Virgins parked out at sea. Architecture and furnishings are standard Caribbean Unobtrusive (everything painted white, inexpensive wall-to-wall carpeting, sliding glass doors, tiny balcony, big bed); beachfront rooms have ceiling fans and rugs and, like all the other rooms, kitchens.

Unless you're bananas for the beach, schedule Long Bay for five days or a week at most. The idle toe-dipper can play in the gentle rolling surf for yards and yards before it gets deep. Stronger swimmers have a quarter mile or so to get to a good snorkeling reef. And joggers have no excuse for breaking training with this beach's perfect measured mile.

But how much beach—and how much great food—can two bodies take? When you've reached your limit, take a taxi into town for a day's sail. The hotel will make arrangements for you. *(C.P.)*

NAME: Long Bay Hotel

MANAGER: (Name not available at press time)

ADDRESS: P.O. Box 433, Road Town, Tortola, B.V.I.

LOCATION: On the north shore, $10 for 2 by taxi from Road Town, $20 for 2 by taxi from the airport

TELEPHONE: 809-495-4252

TELEX: None

RESERVATIONS: American International

CREDIT CARDS: None

ROOMS: 40, in 8 cottages (breeze-cooled), 20 suites (with air-conditioning), 12 beach cabanas (with ceiling fans), all with kitchens

MEALS: Breakfast and lunch throughout the day at the Beach Bar, plus a la carte suppers 6:30–9:00, December–May; dinner from 8:00 (approx. $30 for 2); informal dress; no room service

ENTERTAINMENT: Taped music

SPORTS: Beach (1 beautiful mile of it), saltwater pool, tennis (1 court, no lights), 9-hole pitch and putt course—all free; snorkeling gear; scuba, boat trips nearby; day sails and car rentals by arrangement

P.S.: As this edition was going to press, Long Beach acquired new owners and management; so far, no plans have been announced that might alter the ambiance of the resort.

Peter Island

Tortola

🌴🌴🌴🌴🍴🍴😊😊😊$$$$

From the beginning, I never warmed to this place, a Norwegian shipowner's dull little Bergen-in-the-sun on a private 1,900-acre Virgin, and I wrote some unkind comments about it in the last edition of *Caribbean Hideaways*.

Now I have to rewrite that chapter: four years and a half-million-dollar upgrading later, there's been a complete turnaround. Now owned by the Amway Corporation, Peter Island still may not be the place most people think of as one of *the* fashionable and exclusive resorts in the Caribbean, yet if you had been here last year, for example, you might have found yourself shuffling through the buffet line next to a reigning monarch and his casually attired queen, or a Hollywood studio's grand panjandrum. Or you might have recognized the reclusive twosome in the hilltop villa as a movie star and a well-known violin virtuoso. Turnaround, indeed!

It's one thing to spend a bundle on building and decorating new accommodations (we'll get to them in a minute) and on planting hibiscus by the cartload, but the real surprise was the staff.

There was a period when service was a sometimes thing, the staff about as cheerful as a Bergen winter. Today the glowers and ineptness have been displaced by smiles, an urge to please and, by island standards at least, real competence. I assumed the old lot had been tossed into the channel and replaced. But no—same people. It's simply that they've been motivated, encouraged, trained (in some cases with stints at top-flight hotels and cooking schools in the States).

But the most striking difference between old and new Peter Island, at least for the lucky 40 who are able to book them, are the 20 new deluxe rooms, in 5 two-story bluestone-and-cedar villas tucked behind newly transplanted

palm and sea grape trees in a quiet corner of Deadman's Bay—without spoiling the looks of what is surely one of the most ravishing beaches in the B.V.I.

Let me tell you about my room there. To make sure that guests don't miss any of that picture-postcard view of Deadman, broad louvered doors fold all the way back and open onto a spacious patio (lower floor) or balcony (upper floor). This would be a great place to spend entire days admiring the view were it not for the fact that the interiors are so inviting it's difficult to decide how to divvy up your time—outdoors or indoors.

These spiffy interiors are done in a style that might be called Island Sophisticate. Mexican tiled floors, cedar walls, Brazilian walnut cabinets, wicker sofas and peacock chairs establish the island ambiance; custom-designed fabrics (silk-screened fishnet-and-shell motifs in subtle pastel hues) add a sophisticated touch to upholstery, bedspreads, drapes, even the frames around the native paintings on the walls.

Bathrooms come with fitted hair dryers, step-down bathtubs with floor-to-ceiling windows (and blinds), twin vanities, terry robes and heaps of towels—hand, bath and beach. The walk-in closets have coated wire baskets/drawers (to keep air circulating around your polos) and aerosols of Amway bug spray (about the only trace of the island's corporate ownership anywhere on the property).

If you ever want to have a pillow fight, by the way, this is a veritable Pentagon of pillows—overabundant, overstuffed, a dozen on the king-size beds, a dozen more on the sofas.

The really distinctive touch, though, is the tiny atrium garden between the floor-to-ceiling windows beside the bathtub; it creates a lovely sense of sleeping or bathing in a garden without going outdoors; it lets sunlight filter in yet screens you from the eyes of passersby.

One final note of extravagance: I counted *14* light switches in my room. Normally, on a Caribbean island, that would amount to overkill, if not overload; but so well did the Norwegian shipowner plan the infrastructure here that the problems plaguing many Caribbean islands are hardly a consideration: the electricity rarely (maybe never) gives out because the private generator is more than adequate for the demand, and when other islands are panting for water, Peter is drawing on enormous underground reserves—stored in earthquake-proof tanks! So what are the 14 switches for? *Two* ceiling fans, *two* bedside lights, overhead lights, one light each for patio, entrance, desk, reading, closet, mirror. There's even a night light in the bathroom, a spotlight over the toilet—and a dimmer switch for a lamp concealed among the greenery in the atrium.

The other new attraction at Peter is the smart 60-seat beachside bar/restaurant halfway along Deadman Bay, open to the breezes with some tables in the shade, others in the open. It's a welcome alternative both for guests who don't want to dress for dinner every evening and for visitors from the charter yachts who don't want to look like landlubbers when they come ashore (*Little* Deadman Bay, beyond the headland, is a favorite mooring for charter yachts). Menus here are less elaborate than the 5-course banquets in the main dining pavilion, where the original gymnasiumlike roughcast hall has been cleverly chopped into smaller, more congenial rooms.

If every dish here isn't a success, at least enough of them *are* to make dinner by candlelight something to look forward to. The best choices are, as you might expect, the fresh grouper and lobster or dishes with a local touch, such as the tasty breast of chicken stuffed with bananas, dipped in coconut and served on a bed of orange-flavored pumpkin. The wine list, appropriate for the cuisine and climate, offers choices from $10 to $100.

And what of the original resort? Still a little Bergen, but much less dull than before because the 32 A-frames on the broad breakwater now sport the same cheery fabrics and furnishings designed for the beachside rooms. These Harbour House rooms will appeal to vacationers who want to enjoy the privacy and facilities of a 1,956-acre private island without paying top dollar. Or vacationers who prefer to be near the swimming pool rather than the beach (this pool is a beauty). Or vacationers who welcome the option of being able to switch on air conditioners to supplement the cross ventilation and ceiling fans. If you stay in the Harbour Houses, though, I suggest you ask for a room on the second floor (better view) and as far from the main pavilion as possible (to avoid post-dinner festivities).

The one feature I still find disconcerting here is the music that accompanies dinner and post-dinner dancing. It's amplified and too loud (for just 120 diners!) and in any case, neither solo guitar nor native flute sounds its best when processed by electronics.

But now, of course, you can avoid the loudest of the musical evenings by dining at the beach bar where the accompaniment is the gentle sound of surf and swaying palms. But best of all, if you're lucky, is to retire to your private beachside patio, fetch the champagne from your private bar and settle down for a private session of stargazing.

NAME: Peter Island

MANAGER: Brian Webb

ADDRESS: P.O. Box 211, B.V.I.

LOCATION: Across the channel from Road Town on Tortola, a trip of 20 minutes aboard a 46-ft. or 65-ft. luxury power yacht (regular ferry service 9 times a day between the 2 islands)

TELEPHONE: 809-494-2561

TELEX: 318-7923

RESERVATIONS: Own U.S. office, 800-346-4451 or 616-776-6456; or Preferred Hotels 800-323-7500; or Reservations Systems, Inc. 800-223-1588

CREDIT CARDS: All major cards

ROOMS: 52: 20 in the new Beach Houses, 32 in the original Harbour Houses, plus 1 cottage and 2 villas; all rooms have private bath, refrigerator, balcony or patio, telephone ("confidentiality cannot be guaranteed" because transmission is by radio wave); Harbour House rooms have air-conditioning and fans, Beach House rooms 2 fans only

MEALS: Breakfast 8:00–10:00, lunch 12:30–2:00, dinner 7:30–9:00 (in 2 restaurants—main pavilion and beach bar, both cooled by the breezes); dress code casual at the beach bar, jackets in the dining room (in season); dinner for 2 $74 in the dining room (4 courses), $44 at the beach (3 courses); room service, no extra charge

ENTERTAINMENT: bar/lounge, parlor games, live entertainment (amplified) during and after dinner, for listening or dancing; beach barbecue on Tuesdays

SPORTS: Saltwater pool, several beaches (including isolated coves with transportation and picnic baskets supplied), windsurfers, floats, sailing (Hobie Cats, Squibbs, Sunfishes), snorkeling, tennis (4 Decoturf courts, lights on 2), bikes, horseback riding (hillside trails and beach)—all free; scuba diving, charter boats for fishing and sailing can be arranged

P.S.: "Due to the special design and structure of our resort, children under the age of eight years of age are not encouraged"; some small seminars and high-level meetings

P.P.S.: The resort also has 6 villas for rent, with 2, 3 or 4 bedrooms, 1 at shore level, the others hillside or hilltop

Guana Island Club

Guana Island

$$

The hotel boatman is waiting at Beef Island Airport to escort you the couple of hundred yards to the dock; there he stows your luggage and you step aboard the 28-ft. Bertram *Pelican* for the 20-minute ride to the island. Past Tortola, around Great Camanoe, around the rock formation that gave the island its name and so into White Bay. There you're greeted by a dazzling sight—glistening water, glistening sand. But instead of the inn being buried among the palm trees it perches on the hill, in the midday haze, looking for all the world like a hilltop village in the Aegean. As you approach the private dock the boatman sounds the horn and a Toyota pickup winds down the hill to meet you. Step ashore and you're in another world: even the run-of-the-mill Caribbean seems a long way from here. Guana Island Club was built in the thirties as a private club on the foundations of a Quaker sugar and cotton plantation. The native stone walls are 2 ft. thick, graying whitewash with green shutters. The rustic library and lounge suggest the country home of a well-bred but overdrawn gentleman farmer; the dining terrace is a pair of tables beneath a ramada and framed by pomegranate and ginger thomas trees, cape honeysuckle and white frangipani. From the Sunset Terrace, fragrant with jasmine and carpeted with blossoms from the pink trumpet tree, stone paths and steps wind through archways of trees and off into the hillsides. The loudest sound is a kingbird, perched on the highest bough of the highest tree. The views are stunning—hills and coves, slivers of white sand and polyblue bays, sailboats beating to windward, vistas of distant islands.

Guana Island is not a place you come to for stylish accommodations and luxurious conveniences (for that, head for Little Dix Bay or Biras Creek). Some people, indeed, may find it *too* rustic. Certainly (thank goodness) no one has made any effort to "style" the classic simplicity of the guest rooms. They are clean and comfortable, of course, with rush rugs, handwoven bedspreads, wicker chairs; bathrooms have showers only, and even then the shower is activated by a pull chain to discourage guests from lingering and wasting precious water. The original 10 guest rooms, perched on a ridge above the beach, were once part of the original plantation. Of these, the "Barbados" is perhaps most romantic—self-contained, spacious, with a very private balcony overlooking the Atlantic; guests in the "Fallen Jerusalem" share a common terrace, with stunning views all the way to St. Thomas. On the topmost hill, in the "New Villa," the views of islands, sea and sailboats are also stunning, but the furnishings are more contemporary, the decor mocha-and-ecru modern; rooms here can be reserved *ensuite* with private use of the patio pool.

This is a place that either embraces you instantly or leaves you cold. It has something of the charm and coziness of the best small inns of New England or Burgundy. Since new owners took over in 1976, it has not been operated as a formal club but there is still a clubby feeling. Guests mingle at sundown on the Sunset Terrace or in the tile-and-rattan lounge for cocktails at seven. Dinner is served by candlelight, family-style, everyone gathered around the two tables (unless any couple happens to request a table for two—rare). Dinner is a fixed four-course menu. "If the cook's husband goes out fishing we may have fish, otherwise roast leg of lamb with fried eggplant or guava potatoes . . ." Cooks Rita Penn and Rose Gerrald serve up traditional cuisine (roast stuffed veal, chicken Marengo, roast leg of lamb) with local home-cooking touches—Rita's Cold Curry Soup, Rose's Conch Fritters, home-baked breads and rolls, cassava bread prepared specially by an old lady on Tortola. After dinner, the party atmosphere continues on the Sunset Terrace, where guests reassemble for coffee and cognac and conversation. Officially the island generator is switched off at midnight, but if the guests seem to be so inclined, lights can be left on until the last guest retires.

By day, Guana Island is 850 acres of ineffable peace. Since the only way to get here is by boat, the island's seven beaches are virtually private, and two of them are so secluded they are accessible only to waterborne castaways. Indeed, so serene is the entire setting that when you finally hoist yourselves from your loungers on White Bay's 600 ft. of white sand and peer across the dappled water, all you see is another deserted beach—on the uninhabited side of Tortola. The meadow beside the beach is given over to a croquet court, new all-weather tennis court and a hint of a golf minicourse; the Salt Pond in the center of the island is heaven for bird spotters—a preserve for black-necked stilts and red-billed tropics, plovers and blue herons.

The main beach, a quarter-mile sweep of the whitest powder, is a stiff hike down the hill, a stiffer hike back up. Transportation is either by pickup truck with padded seats or on the not-too-padded backs of Jack and Jenny. Jack and Jenny are the island's mules. Sad to say, even in this demiparadise you have to be careful because things "disappear": apparently Jack and Jenny have developed an appetite for books. They're especially partial to the flavors of paperbacks with glossy covers (titles and authors irrelevant), so be warned.

As we were saying, this is not an everyday Caribbean island, but people who enjoy a relaxed, soft-spoken, almost genteel atmosphere will love it here.

NAME: Guana Island Club

MANAGER: Paula Selby

ADDRESS: Box 32, Road Town, Tortola, B.V.I.

LOCATION: A private island northeast of Tortola, 10 minutes by boat ($20 for 2 round trip) from Beef Island Airport

TELEPHONE: Direct dial 809-494-2354

CABLES/TELEX: Guanaclub Tortola

RESERVATIONS: Scott Calder International, Inc.

CREDIT CARDS: None

ROOMS: 15, in 7 buildings, breeze-cooled

MEALS: Breakfast 8:00–10:00, lunch at 1:00, afternoon tea at 4:00, cocktails at 7:00, dinner at 8:00 (6:45 for children); informal (jackets optional, but usually worn in January and February); no room service

ENTERTAINMENT: Library, Scrabble, backgammon, conversation

SPORTS: 7 beaches (2 accessible by boat only), snorkeling cove (gear available free), tennis, (1 clay court), croquet, 5-hole golf meadow, walking trails—all free; 14-ft. Phantom sailboat, windsurfer, waterskiing, powerboats for rent (fishing gear available), Bertram cruises for charter; scuba nearby

P.S.: *Closed August, September and October*

Little Dix Bay

Virgin Gorda

🌴🌴🌴🌴🌴🍴🍴🍴🏐🏐🏐$$$$$

The Fat Virgin turned out to be Cinderella after all. Her Prince Charming—Laurance Rockefeller, no less. Between the two of them they've created an idyllic, dreamy loveaway; a half-mile, palm-fringed crescent of soft, white beach, a protective reef on one side, low-lying hills on the other, with 500 acres of conserved landscape to screen out the everyday world.

You could say that Rockefeller spent $5 million creating this 82-room resort, but that would be doing him a disservice. Lots of people spend lots of millions on resorts. What Rockefeller has done here, as he did at Dorado Beach and Caneel Bay, is instill his Rockresorts troops with a delight in environment, an appreciation of good taste, a commitment to peace and privacy.

What's so impressive about Little Dix is the tender, loving dedication. Fifteen gardeners fuss over the trees and flowers as if they were paying guests; reception staff meet you at the airport, register you while you're collecting your bags and drive you straight to your room; lights are

deflected, signs are muted; no radios are allowed on the beach, no spear guns on the reefs, no hair curlers beyond the guest rooms. When you get to the beach you feel like you have the place all to yourself, and to make sure no roving charter boats encroach on the peaceful setting, Rockresorts built a 120-yacht marina to lure them to the other side of Cow Hill.

From the beach all you can see of Little Dix Bay Hotel are the four conical shingled roofs of the main dining pavilion rising above the trees. The guest cottages are cloaked by sea grape, tamarind and calabash trees, and almost disappear among the scarlet cordia, frangipani and fragrant Jerusalem thorn. The cone-topped, wallaba-shingled cottages blend natural stone and tropical hardwoods—red cedar, purpleheart, mahogany and locust; new interior decor brightens wicker and cane with Caribbean fabrics and wall hangings and new accents of bright cushions and bedspreads the color of the flowers. Walls of screens and louvers admit the trade winds, ceiling fans boost the breezes. For the benefit of longtime devotees of Little Dix: during 1987 many of the original rooms were overhauled, bathrooms and shower stalls enlarged, things generally livened up—nothing too drastic, of course, just enough to bring the rooms and facilities more into line with current trends while still retaining the resort's unique, and enviable, environmental harmony.

A few of the rooms have a view, others are coddled by greenery and flowers, but they all have a balcony, patio or terrace. It doesn't really make much difference which room you stay in, but my preference would be 1 of the beachside 30 hexagonal hives, 15 of them on stilts, with patios on the garden level and hammocks swinging from the stilts. Rooms 121 and 122, at the Cow Hill end, up a few feet from the beach, are quietest; any room from 29 to 44 is closer to the boat jetty, rooms 27, 28, 33 and 36 are closest to the tennis courts; while 60, at the far end of the beach, is the most secluded.

Little Dix is a place for doing lots of things in such a leisurely way you never have time to do them all. Swim out to the raft. Sunbathe. Swim back from the raft. Float around on a rubber float. Walk to the end of the beach. Skim across the lagoon in a Sunfish. Walk to the other end of the beach. Have a picnic on one of the untrampled beaches farther along the coast (the hotel will fix you up with a picnic lunch and sunshade, a boatman will take you there in a Boston whaler and come and fetch you again a few hours later). Play a set of tennis. Go for a sail on Laurance Rockefeller's 49-ft. Hinckley. Go scuba diving. Take a walk up Cow Hill. Ride horses. Drive over to the Baths and swim in the grottoes formed by giant prehistoric boulders. Take a safari in a Jeep. Wrap yourselves up in your hammock. Sip a Pimm's Cup on the terrace. In some ways, though, Little Dix is at its most Cinderellalike in the evening, when the tiny lamps guide you between the fragrant Jerusalem thorn and scarlet cordia to the hotel's most distinctive feature—the four-coned roof towering over the big breezy pavilion housing the lounge and bar and dining room. This soaring masterpiece, supported by huge beams of purpleheart (hoisted by hand because there was no equipment on the island strong enough to lift them) adds a touch of Polynesian magic. Here, or in the adjoining 60-seat Sugar Mill, any meal would be a banquet, but the food and cellar here are first-rate to begin with—like everything else at Little Dix.

NAME: Little Dix Bay

MANAGER: Peter Hamel

ADDRESS: P.O. Box 70, Virgin Gorda, B.V.I.

LOCATION: 5 minutes from the Virgin Gorda airport (in free shuttle bus), 5 minutes from the marina, light-years from real life

TELEPHONE: 809-495-5555

TELEX: 318-7916+

RESERVATIONS: Rockresorts

CREDIT CARDS: American Express, Diners Club, Visa, MasterCard

ROOMS: 82 double rooms, various combinations of one- and two-story villas, plus 2-bedroom cottages, all breeze-cooled, all showers (no baths), all with balcony or patio

MEALS: Breakfast 8:00–9:30, continental breakfast 7:30–8:00, lunch 12:30–2:00, afternoon tea 4:30, dinner 7:00–9:00 (approx. $65 for 2, in the Polynesian pavilion or the Sugar Mill restaurant, both breeze-cooled); jackets for men most evenings in the main dining room, informal in the Sugar Mill and for barbecues; room service for continental breakfast only, no extra charge

ENTERTAINMENT: Guitarist, steel band, combo, dancing 6 nights a week, library, games parlor with VCR, local bars and bands a short taxi ride away

SPORTS: Half-mile beach, snorkeling gear, small sailboats (and instruction), waterskiing, snorkeling trips, water taxis to adjacent beaches, tennis (7 courts, pro shop, no lights), bicycles—all free; day sails on Laurance Rockefeller's 49-ft. Hinckley yawl *Evening Star* ($90 per person, including lunch and open bar); horseback riding (with guide) $6.50 per hour per person; scuba, Jeep safaris can be arranged

P.S.: Small groups (10–15) for lunch once or twice a week, usually from another Rockresort; no children under 8; reservations from December to mid-March are virtually family heirlooms

Biras Creek

Virgin Gorda

$$$$

It looks for all the world like a Crusader's castle when you first see it as you cross North Sound: a circular stone fortress with a peaked roof. But when you climb the hill, there's no mistaking it for what it is: a one-of-a-kind luxury hideaway for people who want seclusion without giving up too many comforts. The turretlike structure turns out to be The Clubhouse, the bar and dining room—three shingled roofs over a framework of heavy hewn beams, opulently furnished with custom-designed rattan chairs and tables, boldly patterned Caribbean fabrics, island ceramics and a huge tile mural.

Biras Creek is part of a 150-acre estate owned by a Norwegian shipping company, which obviously doesn't have to count its *ore.*

All the guest rooms are spacious beachside suites, two to a cottage, recently redecorated with expensive-looking furniture indoors and out, tiled floors, ceiling fans, big patios, platform rockers, coffee makers, small refrigerators (stocked with rum and mixers) and—the nicest touch of all—neat little outdoor shower patios with potted plants and tall walls to hide your hides. Two new "super deluxe suites" (their words, not mine) have full walls of glass overlooking the sea and "three-room bathrooms" with sunken tubs.

The surrounding acreage is more than just scenery. It's a living, breathing nature preserve created with equal regard for the animals that live here and the people who come to look at them. Trails wind through a desert landscape so natural you can step right over a 3-ft. iguana and he'll never blink. A saltwater lake twitters and flaps with waterfowl and wading birds. Even the docks where Biras Creek's powerboats plow in and out every day are clean enough to support baby lobsters and thousands of delicate tropical fish. Take a flashlight down to the pier after dark and you can do some spectacular snorkeling—without a snorkel and without getting your feet wet.

Since the beginning, the Biras Creek kitchen has always ranked among the best in the Caribbean; even with a new chef (a talented young Ulsterman, on my most recent visit) this ranking still holds true—although more *local* seafood might be welcome. You'll be expected to make a reservation for a table in the evening, but it's a table *for* the evening. You can turn up whenever you feel like eating, not when they feel like serving. No one will hustle you to finish and make way for other guests, so you can relax and linger lovingly over your Château Montrose or Château Mouton Rothschild. Because what has really distinguished the dining experience here, what has always somehow justified that imposing Crusaders castle setting, is the wine cellar. Your choices are not merely good wines but—even rarer in the islands—good vintages.

Which is all the more remarkable when you see where Biras Creek *is*. Not even the dustiest road leads there. No airplane lands here. And boats are few and far between. So what do you do when you're up this particular creek? Well, you might start by wandering off together over miles of nature trails, by foot or by bike. Visit cactus forests and stands of turpentine trees (locally dubbed "tourist trees," because they're tall, bright red and peeling). Admire the newly luxurious gardens, coaxed and cosseted into blooming by a scientific green thumb from Georgia. There's shell gathering on the long breeze-swept beach outside your cottage, and floating, wallowing or swimming in another sheltered sandy bay. And now there are all the wind-powered activities at the sister resort around the bend, Tradewinds (see below), a whole new water sports facility at no extra charge for Biras Creek guests. The newcomer has opened up new options for sailing and windsurfing, drinking and dining while detracting in only the most marginal ways from Biras Creek's cherished solitude. Sophisticated solitude.

NAME: Biras Creek

MANAGERS: Maryan Elliott and Nigel Renouf

ADDRESS: P.O. Box 54, Virgin Gorda, B.V.I.

LOCATION: On North Sound, accessible only by boat; by air to Virgin Gorda airstrip, where you will be met by Mr. Potter's taxi, which will convey you over the hills to Gun Creek, where the launch will be waiting—a fairly efficient transfer organized by frequent two-way radio conversations (and if you're staying more than 4 nights, the cost of the transfer is included in the room rate)

TELEPHONE: 809-494-3151/2

TELEX: 7971 Trades VB

RESERVATIONS: Ralph Locke Islands

CREDIT CARDS: American Express, Visa

ROOMS: 32, all suites (including 2 new deluxe suites), all directly on the bay except for 8 rooms, all with ceiling fans, refrigerators (unstocked), coffee makers, "garden" shower

MEALS: Breakfast 8:00–9:30, lunch 1:00, dinner 7:30–8:30 (approx. $60–80 for outside guests), in the hilltop pavilion, except for beachside barbecue lunches; slacks required after 6:00, but no jackets; no room service; live music twice a week ("quiet during dinner, louder later")

ENTERTAINMENT: Mostly yourselves, except for the live music twice a week

SPORTS: Virtually private, sandy beach called Deep Bay on leeward side (3–4 minutes from rooms by bike, 5–8 minutes on foot, with bar service), freshwater pool on windward beach (beside the rooms), tennis (2 courts, with lights), water sports (everything available at Tradewinds [see below] is available to Biras Creek guests), hiking trails, garden walks, bicycles—all free; scuba diving and sailing trips can be arranged

P.S.: "While we welcome families, we regret we cannot accept children under school age"

The Tradewinds

Virgin Gorda

🌴🌴✗✗⚾⚾⚾$$$

Just down the beach from Biras Creek is its own $10-million sister resort. What a family! Biras Creek and The Tradewinds share the same Norwegian shipping company owner and the same 150-acre estate. But where Biras Creek is oriented toward relaxed but stylish vacations, the relatively new (spring 1984) Tradewinds is more casual and sports-oriented—with a flotilla of small sailboats and dinghies included in the rate.

On land, the Tradewinds' 19 timber cottages dot a hillside accented with prickly pear and mother-in-law cactus, landscaped with alamander, hibiscus and bougainvillea. But it's the interiors of these cottages that may set The Tradewinds apart from its neighbors—all warm wood tones, with doors of molded Oregon redwood, high wood-slatted ceilings with brass paddle fans, straw rugs on floors of terra-cotta tile. Each of the 38 rooms is spacious enough for sturdy designer rattan furniture *and* a pair of queen-size beds with 8 fluffy pillows. The 3-part bathrooms are practically suites in themselves—separate marble-tiled w.c., a larger dressing room with vanity and basin, and beyond that a sliding glass door leading to an indoor/outdoor shower with a mini-garden of tropical greenery.

There's nothing intrusive in the rooms (i.e., no television, radios, telephones), but there *are* lots of welcome touches such as minirefrigerators, clothes lines in the showers and skirt pins in the closets. In case you arrive with a thirst, the maids have stocked your refrigerator with rum and

Coke (on the house); and if you're early risers and want to keep the dawn all to yourselves, you can still enjoy your morning coffee or Darjeeling tea—all the fixings are there in your room.

When it's time for more substantial fare, you can hop a roving electric cart to take you down the hill to the main drinking/dining pavilion near the beach—for pepper-pot soup, shrimp and papaya, spicy gazpacho, grouper fresh from the waters you've been admiring from your veranda.

As you might expect from a sibling of Biras Creek, the wine list is above average for these parts, but the house wine itself is ideal for lazy tropical lunches. By the way, lunch is also served, for a change of pace, at the Beach Bar, alias the Traprian Law, a twenties Scottish cutter complete with its original masters' papers.

If you're not nautically minded, you probably won't want to pay Tradewinds rates, because apart from the tennis court at Biras Creek, there's little else to do. The manmade beach hardly justifies the roundabout trip to get to North Sound. Of course, if you want to spend your day lolling on fine sand, you can have one of the resort's boatmen take you to one of the deserted islands nearby. The hotel will fix you up with beach umbrellas, snorkeling gear, picnic lunch and chilled Bordeaux.

On the other hand, there's a lot to be said for lounging on your rocking chair and just surveying the channel and the offshore islands—Mosquito, Eustatia, Necker and Prickly Pear.

NAME: The Tradewinds

MANAGER: Dan Reid

ADDRESS: P.O. Box 64, Virgin Gorda, B.V.I.

LOCATION: On North Sound, via small plane from San Juan, St. Thomas or Beef Island to the Virgin Gorda airstrip, then by taxi to Gun Creek where the hotel boat will meet you (by taxi and boat it's a half-hour trip, more or less); if you're staying at the hotel for 4 days or more, taxi and boat ride are free, otherwise the taxi is $15

TELEPHONE: 809-494-3151

TELEX: Trades VB 7971

RESERVATIONS: See Bitter End Yacht Club, following

CREDIT CARDS: All major cards

ROOMS: 38 rooms in 19 cottages all with 2 queen-size beds, ceiling fans, minirefrigerators, furnished verandas

MEALS: Breakfast 8:00–9:30, lunch 1:00–3:00, dinner 7:30–9:00 (in the pavilion dining room, approx. $44–48 for 2); taped music (light classical mostly); no room service; dinner also available at Biras Creek

ENTERTAINMENT: Each other

SPORTS: Manmade beach, eight 14-ft. Holder sailboats, ten 12-ft. Holder sailboats, ten windsurfers, two 19-ft. Boston Whalers with 6 h.p. engine, snorkeling equipment—all free; tennis at Biras Creek at no extra charge; sailing and windsurfing *lessons* available, plus trips to nearby islands for picnics or snorkeling

P.S.: At press time, Tradewinds had just been acquired by its neighbor on the other side, Bitter End Yacht Club (see following). Its dining and water sports facilities will be incorporated into those of its new owner—but that means that anyone who wants to play tennis had better stay at Biras Creek.

Bitter End Yacht Club

Virgin Gorda

The first thing you discover about this wonderfully windblown little place is how apt its name is. To get here from the United States, your journey involves two, maybe three, flights, then a precipitous 20-minute ride over the Fat Virgin's hillocks, followed by a boat ride almost straight to your doorstep. Well, getting to heaven isn't easy, either.

As for Bitter End, it's worth the trip. How often, after all, do you have a chance to spend your days and nights on land *or* sea *or* both?

Choose *land* and you get a room in a big, airy guest cottage, fashioned from fir and topped with an Antillean-style red roof, meticulously outfitted in rattan and tile, decorated with serapes and batiks. Ceiling fans cool the interiors, acres of sliding glass doors open to semiprivate sundecks shaded by Mexican thatch. Some cottages stand on stilts a few paces from the shore, others are perched among hibiscus and hummingbirds on the boulders above. The latest hillside additions (identified as Beach Cottages, oddly enough) are particularly pleasant, a shade removed from all the action and bustle of the dock and public pavilions, but with undisturbed views of sea and the islet of Eustatia (not to be confused with the saint of the same name).

Choose *sea* and you get your own seagoing sailboat to stay in—a floating suite, fully equipped and provisioned even if you never leave your mooring. It's a Cal 27 sloop, easy to handle on voyages to The Baths, Peter, Norman, Treasure and other nearby cays. Yet whenever you come back, all the landlubber conveniences of the hotel are waiting for you—from hot showers to long and lavish menus in the shoreside thatch-roofed dining pavilion.

And if you can't decide between a sea or land vacation, you still get to spend your days afloat. You have at your disposal an entire fleet of sailing craft—all day every day and at no extra charge. To Bitter End's credit, when they list windsurfers as an attraction, they don't mean just a couple of boards—they mean by the dozen. Day sailers? By the dozen. Plenty for everyone. To say nothing of on-the-beach instruction and the resort's big launch, the *Prince of Wales,* to take you on day-long picnic cruises.

Although there's room for only 90 land-billeted guests, Bitter End is on nearly every seasoned sailor's Caribbean itinerary. The sea-breezy bar and dining pavilion flutter with hundreds of burgees left behind by the constant tide of salt visitors—from charter yachters lazing their way through the islands on a regimen of Mumm's and movie starlets to flinty Ahabs sailing around the world with nothing but Saltines and a sextant. Not to mention one of the hotel's more memorable stopovers: a couple kayaking from Venezuela to Miami Beach.

In spite of the barefoot informality that wafts through the place as naturally as all the sun-bleached sea dogs, Bitter End is run with great care—and a lot of largesse.

It happens to be the pampered pet of a tycoon from Chicago who himself came asailing in a big black ketch into the North Sound one bright day. He noted the deep, clear waters. He spied the white beach. He liked the looks of the clubhouse. "I'll buy it," he said to his captain, "and you'll run it." And that, of course, is how it has been ever since. But Myron Hokin isn't the kind of owner to sit in Chicago and pick up the phone occasionally to ask, "How many bodies this week?" He's his own most frequent guest, so the staff of 112 (112 for 45 rooms—that shows how many people they have looking after their boats!) is friendly, cheerful and on their toes, barefoot or otherwise.

If you don't consider yourself especially seaworthy, don't let that keep you from the Bitter End. Take a lesson. They're there for anyone who has never so much as hoisted a jib as well as for old salts who want to learn new twists on the spinnaker. Start with a small Sunfish and work up. Even the scuba diving here ranges from the simple to the serious. There's great coral hopping just about anywhere you stick your mask in the water. Deeper down, Horseshoe Reef is littered with the skeletons of doomed galleons. The resort will set up instruction, trips and dives.

And don't worry. When you get back, the sea dogs at Bitter End will still be sitting around nursing their grog and swapping salty tales.

NAME: Bitter End Yacht Club

MANAGERS: Don and Janis Neal

ADDRESS: P.O. Box 46, Virgin Gorda, B.V.I.

LOCATION: At John o'Point, at the east end of Gorda Sound; fly to Virgin Gorda, where Speedy Taxi Service will collect you and take you to Gun Creek, where the club launch will be waiting for you

TELEPHONE: 809-494-2745/6

TELEX: 02927995

RESERVATIONS: Own office, 312-944-5855

CREDIT CARDS: All major cards

ROOMS: 45, mostly 2 to a cottage, all with tiled showers, refrigerators, balconies, screens and ceiling fans

MEALS: Breakfast 8:00–10:00, lunch 12:30–2:00, dinner 6:30–9:30 (approx. $50–60 for 2), all in the beachside pavilion; casual dress; no room service; some taped music, loud at times

ENTERTAINMENT: Taped music (jazz, pop, modern), live music 3 nights a week, movies (classics and new releases) in the Sand Palace

SPORTS: Beach (but not terrific), snorkeling, windsurfing, sailboats (Sunfish, Lasers, Rhodes 19s), boat trips to Anegada or The Baths (lunch included), skiffs with outboard motors, sailing and windsurfing lessons—all free; scuba diving and Cal 27 sloops extra

P.S.: "Don't encourage preschool children"

P.P.S.: At press time, Bitter End had just taken over the neighboring Tradewinds, which gives the resort additional dining and sports facilities—and deluxe accommodations. Call the Bitter End number for details.

Drake's Anchorage

Virgin Gorda Sound

$$$

East-northeast from Tortola there's an island marked Mosquito on the charts—and bliss in the memories of escapists.

Now called Drake's Anchorage, it's all of 126 acres, each and every acre private, the playground of only 30 lucky sandaled sun worshippers. Ten wood frame, gingerbread-trimmed cottages perch on stilts along the shore, three rooms in each, furnished in a basic beachy sort of way. Bathrooms are strictly functional, paddle fans and ample louvers take care of ventilation, spacious sundecks overlook the beach (or, at least, *one* of the beaches).

A few shuffling steps away among the casuarina and sea grape trees you come to the main lodge, a low-slung, timber pavilion where the sea laps at your feet and the trade winds waft through the driftwood decor—turtle shells and fan coral and stuffed marlin and wahoo. Yachtsmen with the foresight to radio ashore for reservations will join you here for drinks and dinner, turning the driftwood pavilion into a merry salon. They've come ashore for the bounty of Brutus, a.k.a. Chef Martin Belmar, a longtime hero in these parts for a menu that's more sophisticated than you might expect in a backwater off a backwater. His personal recipe for chocolate mousse is guarded more zealously than pirate gold.

And that's about it. Drake's Anchorage is strictly a place for the Five S's—sunning, snorkeling, snoozing, smooching, sailing. And with only 30 overnight guests there's plenty of room for all five pastimes. Plenty of nature trails lined with frangipani and barrel cactus. Plenty of beach—the one on your doorstep, three more a few minutes' walk away. The most idyllic is Honeymoon (10 minutes, over the hill), especially if you don't have to share it with yacht people. Offshore, gardens of staghorn coral and reefs boggle the eyes of snorkelers. And enchant the student of nature: every summer, Jean-Michel Cousteau, son of the amphibious Jean-Jacques, arrives on Mosquito with a band of naturalists for weeks of sun-drenched study—above and below the water.

When you amble over to Lime Tree Beach you'll pass the island's big surprise: a pair of villas (belonging to the owners, MIT professors), as stylishly grand as the cottages are plain-Jane—with cathedral ceilings, fieldstone walls, bathrooms with sunken stone tubs, fully equipped kitchens and stereo. They're rentable, by the week only, but at rates that work out to be *much* less expensive than a mere room in some of the snazzier resorts on bigger islands.

Of course, if all that sand and solitude begin to pall, you can always charter a Boston Whaler and skim across the Sound to Bitter End—Manhattan to Mosquito's Staten Island.

NAME: Drake's Anchorage

MANAGERS: Peter and Janny Faust

ADDRESS: P.O. Box 2510, Virgin Gorda, B.V.I.

LOCATION: On Virgin Gorda Sound. To get there, first fly to Virgin Gorda airstrip via Beef Island (Tortola), then take a taxi (the resort can arrange to have it waiting for you) to Leverick Bay, where you'll be picked up by the resort's launch (the boat ride is included in the rate)

TELEPHONE: 809-494-2254

TELEX: None

RESERVATIONS: Own U.S. office, 800-624-6651

CREDIT CARDS: American Express

ROOMS: 10 (including 2 suites) in 3 cottages, all with shower, ceiling fan and breezes, terrace, big rechargeable flashlamps for the occasions when the lights fail; the suites also have refrigerators (in addition, the resort has 2 deluxe villas with sunken tubs and fully equipped kitchens)

MEALS: Breakfast 8:30–9:30, lunch noon–2:00, dinner 7:30 ($50–60 for 2), all served in a breezy surfside pavilion; informal dress; no room service (but you can probably persuade someone to bring breakfast to your terrace); taped background music (classical or jazz)

ENTERTAINMENT: Darts, chess, backgammon, library, VCR, guitarist on Wednesday (occasionally a steel band)

SPORTS: 4 beaches, snorkeling gear, Lasers, windsurfers—all free; scuba diving and sailing can be arranged

Added Attractions

The Sugar Mill

Tortola

Owners Jeff and Jinx Morgan are chefs/writers/food critics from San Diego so they bring an extra touch of sophistication to their restaurant, housed in the remains of a 300-year-old stone mill. It's sort of the tropical equivalent of one of those tiny *auberges* in Burgundy, with good food and a few rooms for staying over. But here you wake up to perfect days, a garden pool, beautiful sea. There's a beach bar and a patch of sand across the street (with a *mile*-long beach nearby), a quiet, congenial, relaxing ambiance and a steady flow of loyal guests. 18 rooms, kitchen facilities. *The Sugar Mill, Box 425, Tortola, B.V.I. Telephone: 809-495-4355. No children under 10 in winter.*

Sandcastle

Jost Van Dyke

Jost Van Dyke is the island off the northwest corner of Tortola—a Robinson Crusoe place with no airstrip, no electricity, not many inhabitants, and a few restaurants that cater mostly to people stepping ashore from charter yachts. Dinner is by candlelight, reading is by propane lamps, water is heated, if at all, by the noonday sun. Which is, for many escapists, what the Caribbean is all about. Sandcastle is right on the beach (a beauty, shared with maybe a couple of private homes that lie empty much of the time). There's no deck. You just roll up your trousers or skirt and paddle through the surf to get here, after a choppy ride by water taxi from West End (the hotel will make the arrangements). Activity revolves around the breezy beach bar, and the water sports—windsurfing, Sunfish sailing, snorkeling, rafts. But most of the time guests just seem to lounge around, wearing to dinner what they wore to breakfast. Rooms are functional, almost make-shift. Unfortunately, it's not as inexpensive as you hope it's going to be—over $200 a day for two in winter, with all meals. 8 rooms. *Sandcastle, White Bay, Jost Van Dyke, B.V.I. Telephone (Road Town office): 809-494-2462. No credit cards.*

The Dutch Windwards

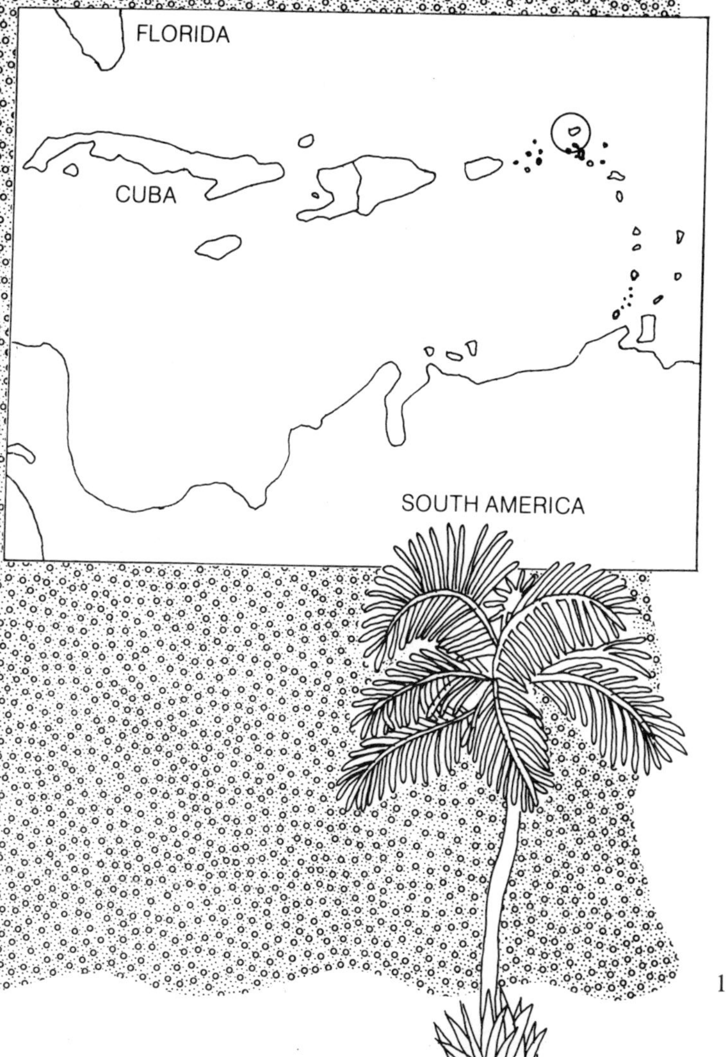

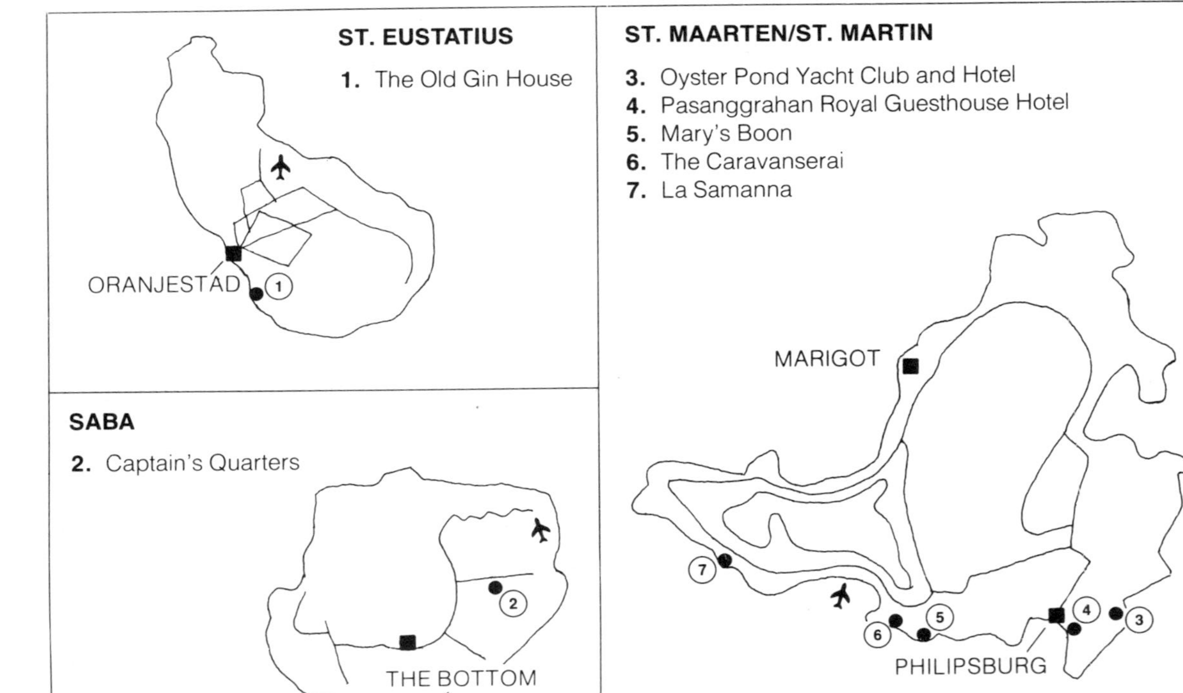

THE DUTCH WINDWARDS

The Dutch Windwards

The Dutch West India Company that sent Henry Hudson scouting around the northeast coast of America also sent its ships and captains to the Caribbean; and Peter "Pegleg" Stuyvesant, the hobbling Hollander who became governor of New York City, tried to dislodge the Spanish from St. Maarten only to have the Spanish dislodge his leg. What twentieth-century lovers will find in this corner of the Dutch Caribbean is a trio of islands—two totally unspoiled and serene (Saba and St. Eustatius), and one (St. Maarten/St. Martin) that offers pockets of serenity yet still manages to be a valid alternative to Puerto Rico and the U.S. Virgins for vacationers who want casinos and lively, varied nightlife.

Saba is the phantom silhouette you see on the horizon when you're sitting on the waterfront in St. Maarten. It's really the tip of a volcanic cone, a straight-up-and-down island with one roadway and a thousand inhabitants, completely unlike any other island in the Caribbean (it doesn't, for a start, have a beach). What it does have is a haunting, tranquil, otherworldly charm; but it's strictly for lovers who are content to be on their own (or, in recent years, for scuba divers who crave a change of aqueous scenery). St. Eustatius likewise, except that you'll find beaches (sort of) here. Statia should be popular with Americans for historic reasons: the Dutch garrison of Fort Oranje fired the first salute to the brand-new American flag during the War of Independence. For its pains the island was zapped by England's Admiral Rodney, and Oranjestad, once the busiest harbor in the Indies, is now a half-submerged ghost town—but a treasure trove for snorkelers and scuba divers.

Because the Dutch ended up splitting the island with the French, Sint Maarten is also St. Martin. When you go from one side to the other (there's no frontier, no customs), you're going from France to Holland—literally, because the French side is part of the Republic of France and the Dutch side is part of the Kingdom of the Netherlands. Between them, they offer you something like three dozen beaches—white, soft, powdery beaches, duty free shopping, nightlife and scores of interesting restaurants.

HOW TO GET THERE First nonstop to St. Maarten by American, Pan Am or ALM from New York; from Miami, by Eastern. There are also direct, one-stop flights from Boston (American and Eastern), Dallas (American) and Philadelphia (Eastern). From St. Maarten, take Windward Islands

Airways (Winair) to St. Eustatius or Saba, several flights daily, about $40 round trip to one or both islands. The 20-minute flight by Twin Otter DHT 6-300 to Saba is an experience in itself, because the only way the islanders could find a flat surface for a runway was by chopping the top off a hillock rising from the sea; touchdown here is like landing on an aircraft carrier, but no problem for an advanced STOL plane like the Twin Otter.

NOTE: If you're thinking of flying to any of St. Maarten's neighboring islands, buy your tickets before you leave home. The government of St. Maarten now imposes a stamp duty on airline tickets purchased on the island—not a token dollar or two, but $8 or thereabouts per ticket. Don't encourage them: buy at home—you can always cash in your tickets if you decide not to use them.

Oyster Pond Yacht Club and Hotel

St. Maarten

$ $ $ $ $

To get here, you have to drive all the way over to the other side of the island on a road engineered on the same basic principle as the roller coaster.

The final lurch brings you to the crest of a hill and your first heart-stopping glimpse of the eponymous pond—a circular lagoon with a circular hotel on the point of a promontory.

Until recently, that was about all you saw. That and St. Barthélemy off in the distance. But the island's concept of progress—where there's concrete there's cash—has been catching up on even this remote corner of the island, so there are now more homes, some condos, a resort (too crowded for your tastes) and restaurants strewn around the lagoon. Nevertheless, here are peace and seclusion in abundance. That hill you've just come over effectively shuts out the casual rubbernecker and bargain-hunting day-tripper. The background distractions of cars, planes and tour buses are effectively eliminated, and the only distraction is more likely to be the occasional whine of an outboard motor hauling waterskiers around the pond.

Tranquility reigns once you step through the entrance to the Yacht Club—a semicircle of natural stone with half a dozen arches, flanked by two square three-story stone towers. Within the arches, planters and white wicker with

a scattering of antiques turn the lobby into a conservatory; jaunty sun umbrellas turn the circular courtyard into an alfresco café at lunchtime. Beyond, a plushly cushioned bar-lounge and a breezy candlelit restaurant with arches opening to the sea—and glimpses of aquamarine and azure every way you turn.

Guest rooms ring the courtyard, all but six of them on the second floor, around a white-walled gallery with dark wooden arches and balustrades, their names on shining brass plates—L'Oiseau des Iles, Passage, Monitor, Nirvana, Tantrum, and so on, echoes of ocean-going ships of bygone times. Decor is more or less identical throughout: new owners who took over three years ago installed Jacques Pergay wicker from France, white on white set against russet tiled floors, the walls decorated with prints by Rothko or Liechtenstein. Variations in rooms are minor—patios on the ground floor, balconies (and higher ceilings) on the upper level, a few extra cubic feet for deluxe rooms. Oddly enough, the duplex suites in the towers have no balcony, and the duplex gallery, accessible by steep wooden steps, is really practical only for reading or siestas. The best views (that is, the peaks of St. Barthélemy) are framed by the windows of Monitor and Nirvana.

With the new owner (a hotelier from the French side of the island) came a new manager and chef. Kirsten Borjesson keeps the back-of-the-house running smoothly with Danish unflappability, and in the evening adds her own breezy class and elegance to the lounge and dining room. In the kitchen, Paul Souzette (a protégé of La Samanna) turns out the kind of cuisine—*soupe aux truffes, médaillons de langouste au gingembre, marquise aux fraises et bananes*—that has dedicated gourmets scrambling for reservations at one of the 14 Rosenthal-decked tables. Even though for outsiders dinner at Oyster Pond involves a helter-skelter ride on a roller coaster road.

NAME: Oyster Pond Yacht Club and Hotel

MANAGER: Kirsten Borjesson

ADDRESS: P.O. Box 239, St. Maarten, N.A.

LOCATION: On the southeastern shore, 35 minutes and $18 by taxi from the airport, 15 minutes and $14 from Philipsburg

TELEPHONE: 599-5-2206 or 3206

TELEX: 8030

RESERVATIONS: David B. Mitchell & Company, Inc.

CREDIT CARDS: American Express, MasterCard, Visa

ROOMS: 20, including 2 suites, all with ceiling fans, balconies or patios, showers only in the bathrooms

MEALS: Breakfast 8:00–10:00, lunch noon–2:30, dinner 7:30–9:30 (approx. $80 for 2); informal dress ("but no shorts in the evening, proper attire at all times"); room service for continental breakfast only, no extra charge

ENTERTAINMENT: Bar/lounge with taped music (usually bartender's choice), parlor games

SPORTS: Beach a 2-minute walk away through the gardens, sunning terraces with loungers, tennis (2 courts, no lights), pool to come in 1988—free; water sports—Sunfish sailing, Hobie Cats, waterskiing, windsurfing—in the lagoon at extra charge (private concession)

P.S.: "No children under the age of 10 years, please"

Pasanggrahan Royal Guesthouse Hotel

St. Maarten

$ $

There are not many authentic old West Indian guesthouses still in business but this is one of them—so authentic its very name is Indonesian for "guesthouse." This is the West Indies as they were back in the days when London and Paris and, in this case, The Hague, had to build government lodgings for roving royalty and officials because there was no other place to put them up. Holland's Queen Juliana stayed here at one point during World War II, after an unglamorous voyage aboard one of her destroyers. Royalty doesn't stay here anymore, but you may find yourselves downing rum punches in the company of publishers, art directors, executives, professors and students, people of all ages, sizes and incomes, but all with a common predilection for a relaxed, informal atmosphere, friendly when you want it to be, private if that's what you prefer.

Pasanggrahan is located on the main street in Philipsburg, between the street and the beach. It's a pretty little place—with a deep white porch, potted plants, rocking chairs, ceiling fans and an antique-filled lounge with an imperious portrait of Queen Wilhelmina of The Netherlands. Ahead of you, beyond the Dining Gallery, are the beach, the bay and the Garden Café—a cool jungle of knep trees and coconut palms, almond and avocado trees and a tree that's known within these precincts as the Buttercup-and-Stringbean Tree because no one can remember the proper botanical term. This is the most popular spot in the hotel by day, particularly at tea time; after sundown, imbibers withdraw to the Evening Bar with its four rattan stools, cowhide chairs, four-bladed fans, and a woven blue-and-white portrait of the founder—in fact, several portraits of The Founder. He (it) was the original rooster-in-residence immortalized in a poem published in *The New Yorker:* "And I could swear that I heard the rooster in the Pasanggrahan garden . . ."

The original 12 guest rooms are in a two-story veranda-trimmed wing (known as the West Wing) next to the Garden Café, screened from the beach by trees and hanging plants; they make no compromises with modernity—wicker chairs and tables, small tiled shower stalls, small carved wooden headboards. Probably the most romantic room is the Queen's Room (21) on the second floor of the main house, up a private spiral stairway wreathed with bougainvillea, a sort of tree house up among the birds. There are also 6 efficiency apartments in a new two-story wing on the other side of the Garden Café; these rooms are more comfortable (air-conditioned, too), but the price you pay for the extra touches is that you're closer to the garden. Most of the time, though, Pasanggrahan is quiet and relaxing. You go to the beach; you walk a hundred yards along Front Street to Sam's Place for lunch; you have a siesta; you sip afternoon tea in the Garden Café; you shower; you sip a rum punch in the Evening Bar before sitting down in the Dining Gallery, now magically lighted by Mexican lamps.

Pasanggrahan. It has just the right ring about it for this delightful little keepsake of an inn.

NAME: Pasanggrahan Royal Guesthouse Hotel

MANAGER: Peter de Zela

ADDRESS: P.O. Box 151, 13 Front Street, St. Maarten, N.A.

LOCATION: On the beach in Philipsburg, 20 minutes and $7 by taxi from the airport

TELEPHONE: 5995-2-3588

CABLES/TELEX: Pasanggrahan St. Maarten/8125 PASAN

RESERVATIONS: St. Maarten Reservations

CREDIT CARDS: Visa, MasterCard

ROOMS: 32, all but 4 of them on the beach, some with air-conditioning, all with ceiling fans, plus 6 efficiency apartments with pantries

MEALS: Breakfast 8:00–10:30, complimentary tea hour in the Garden Café, dinner at 7:30 (served on the veranda, $40–50 for 2 with complimentary French wine, and reservations are essential for outsiders); casual dress; no room service

ENTERTAINMENT: Weekly cocktail parties, weekend barbecues, movies, local "scratchy" bands

SPORTS: Beach and loungers—free; snorkeling, scuba, sailing, boat trips at the town pier, a 5-minute walk away; discotheques and casinos nearby

---

Mary's Boon

St. Maarten

$$

The Mary with the boon is Mary Pomeroy, one of the Caribbean's legendary innkeepers, but the inn is now owned by Rushton Little, known to many St. Maarten buffs as the long-term manager of Pasanggrahan.

It consists of six white-roofed bungalows with wraparound verandas and gingerbread trim garlanded with hibiscus, in a sandy garden of allamanda and shrubbery. It's right on the beach, practically in the water, on one of the longest stretches of sand on the island, and everything is designed to make the most of the setting. The sea beckons the minute you step through the main gate; lobby, dining room and bar are all open to the breezes and framed by sea grape, coconut palms and a wild cotton tree; the murmuring surf is right there all the time when you're drinking, eating, making love.

The rooms are really efficiencies, about half as large again as the average hotel room, fitted out with tile floors, ceiling fans, wicker furniture, a few antiques, original Dutch and Haitian paintings, and a few items that look as though they might have come from a millionaire's yacht. There's a kitchenette in case you feel like rustling up your own breakfasts, but the best feature of all is the bathroom: lots of toweling room, Italian white-and-sienna floor tiles, and tiled shower stalls. Since Rush Little took over six new rooms have been added (beside the bar) and the place has been spiffed up, top to bottom.

There's a great atmosphere at Mary's Boon. Pure beachcomber. The setting puts you in the mood for swimming and snorkeling, the exercise puts you in the mood for lunch, lunch puts you in the mood for a siesta. Before you know where you are you're involved in the favorite pastime at Mary's Boon, sitting around the bar chatting with all sorts of interesting people—a French painter and his mistress; a pretty young woman who looks very innocent but happens to work for a think tank in California and knows all about supersonic jets; a few airline people; a few island people, old friends of Mary Pomeroy or Rush Little from farther down the islands. The bar is operated on the honor system and drinks (for house guests) cost only a dollar, so most guests are quite happy to have a few before dinner; and since coffee is served in the bar after dinner (damned good food, too), the drinking and conversation continue until the last guest goes home.

Mary's Boon is the almost perfect resort for young lovers except for one drawback—the airport. The runway is a hundred yards away, which means that half a dozen times a day you'll be bombarded by a few seconds of appalling whine, mostly midafternoon, never after 9:30 in the evening. But the agony really lasts for only 60 seconds and only half a dozen times a day, which leaves you another 23 hours and 53 minutes to enjoy all the good things about Mary's Boon.

NAME: Mary's Boon

MANAGER: Rushton Little

ADDRESS: P.O. Box 278, St. Maarten, N.A.

LOCATION: On the long, long beach at Simpson Bay, 5 minutes and $3.50 or more from the airport

TELEPHONE: 5995-44235

CABLES: Marysboon St. Maarten

RESERVATIONS: None

CREDIT CARDS: None

ROOMS: 12 efficiencies, with breezes and ceiling fans, porches or verandas, showers

MEALS: Breakfast 7:30–9:30, lunch at 1:00, dinner at 8:00 ($50 for 2, on the beachside veranda; no dinner served Sundays); casual dress; room service 8:00 A.M.–9:00 P.M., 15 percent extra

ENTERTAINMENT: The clientele

SPORTS: Beach (more than 2 miles of it, one of the finest on the island), good swimming; water sports, golf and tennis nearby

P.S.: No groups, no children, no cruise ship passengers, no outsiders for meals except by reservation

The Caravanserai

St. Maarten

$$$$

Caravanserais along the camel routes of Asia had, we're told, a courtyard for "camel parking," complete with arcades, fountains and soothing greenery for shade, and that's basically what you find here. Arcades and soothing greenery—but with swimming pools rather than fountains, bikinied bodies rather than camels.

St. Maarten's legendary Caravanserai is a mirage on a prickly promontory of coral—a few pointy rooftops peeking above palms and casuarina trees, a big octagonal gazebo perching by the edge of the coral, low-roofed arcades inviting you in out of the glare, a pathway lined with lacy foliage and honey-colored stone winding around a tiny cove, past coral outcroppings to a crescent of soft white sand known as Maho Beach.

For almost 20 years The Caravanserai has been one of the places I really looked forward to seeing again. But in recent years its character drifted from its original exclusive dinner-at-eight clubbiness. When it was bought several years ago by the huge Mullet Bay resort nearby, new two-story wings of luxury apartments seemed to detract from the original low-profile hotel; a few years ago, additional wings were stuck down in the parking lot (which was miraculously transformed into a tropical garden). The original 20-room retreat had burgeoned into a miniresort of 85 rooms and apartments, the "club" had become a plaything for the fun-seeking guests of Mullet. Now the distinguished new owner of Mullet Bay (a former Iranian ambassador) has seen the light and pumped a couple million dollars into the inn to restore some of its old luster. Old-time guests may not recognize the new lobby, the new lounge (formerly the arcaded dining room) and the new rooms (brighter fabrics, new plumbing, more stylish furniture)—but they'll still be knocked out by the wondrous setting of sea and coral and beach and gardens.

Robert Dubourcq, one of the island's most respected innkeepers, has been brought in to turn the tide. The original intimacy can never be recaptured but he will, I'm sure, make The Caravanserai once more "the small gem" the brochures promise.

The one thing neither ambassadors nor Dubourcqs can do much about is the location. The setting, as I mentioned, is ravishing—but when my old advertising colleague Dave Crane pinpointed this promontory for his Caravanserai, the airport was a mere landing strip—half a mile away. Now the runway comes all the way to the beach, and although each year brings more jets (never early in the morning, never late at night), most guests don't seem to mind. Some, in fact, find the whole thing fun and after a couple of days can tell which flight is about to land without even checking their watches. It says a lot for The Caravanserai that so many people come back year after year (sometimes two or three times a year) despite the turgid roars of all those Pratt and Whitneys.

NAME: The Caravanserai

MANAGER: Robert Dubourcq

ADDRESS: St. Maarten, N.A.

LOCATION: 5 minutes and $4 by taxi from the airport, 25 minutes and $10 from Philipsburg or Marigot

TELEPHONE: 59954-2801

TELEX: 8019

RESERVATIONS: Own office (Gem Marketing, New York), 800-223-9815

CREDIT CARDS: All major cards

ROOMS: 85, including 24 apartments and 10 studios, in the main hotel and 3 garden wings, all with air-conditioning, patio or balcony, some with shower only, direct-dial telephone, radio, satellite TV

MEALS: Breakfast 7:30–10:00, lunch noon–2:30 poolside, dinner 7:00–9:00 (approx. $60 for 2), in the octagonal shoreside pavilion; informal but stylish dress; taped background music; room service for breakfast only

ENTERTAINMENT: Occasional live music, shuttle bus to casino, bars and nightlife at Mullet Bay

 SPORTS: Beach (beautiful sand, good swimming, but with those planes), 2 pools (1 fresh, 1 salt), snorkeling gear—free; complete water sports facilities at Mullet Bay

P.S.: No children under 15

La Samanna

St. Martin

🌴🌴🌴🌴🌴XXXX☺☺$$$$$

A couple of decades ago a New York businessman named James Frankel went cruising in the Aegean Sea and found in those whitewashed Greek fishing villages the inspiration for his dream hotel, but what he's finally hatched, with the aid of architect Amos Morril, is Aegean with overtones of Marrakech, New Mexico and Bel-Air.

Despite its seemingly jumbled pedigree, the 15-year-old La Samanna is a gorgeous spot, one of the most beautiful in the Caribees: gleaming white villas along a thousand yards of beach (a beauty in itself), rising in flower-decked terraces past a dazzlingly tiled swimming pool and the three-story main building to a pair of villas on a bluff above a cove. It's all arches and balconies and 55 acres of gardens, highlighted by blue doors and blue sun umbrellas (not the usual wishy-washy blue either, but a gutsy royal blue that makes even the Caribbean itself look sickly by comparison). The decor's artful blend of traditional wicker and rattan with contemporary lamps and chairs has stood the test of fashion (15 years ago, on reflection, it must have been well ahead of its time).

Rooms and apartments are divided among the three-story main lodge and villas strung out beside the beach, among luxuriant tropical plantings. Most guests prefer ground-floor suites, presumably to be closer to the beach or pool; but aficionados of escapism opt for the second-floor suites with big tiled sundecks on their roofs—some so spacious they also have shaded patios topped by thatched ramadas. Pick, for example, a suite on the second floor of Villas N and P (above the cove, to the left of the main lodge) and you get not only a dramatic view of the beach, but up on your rooftop deck you can do anything horizontally and only the pelicans will know.

Anyone wanting air-conditioning as a backup for their fans should check into 1 of the 14 rooms in the main lodge, but the best room here (and the best value) is room 110, a corner nook newly redesigned to incorporate 2 terraces—1 shaded by a ramada, the other an octagonal affair for taking in the sun, both furnished with armchairs and sofas of whimsical wicker.

Your room, your suite, your villa or whatever may be so appealing you never want to leave. Lounging on your sundeck. Lounging on your patio. But now and then shimmy into your smartest togs and head for the La Samanna dining terrace. If I had to name the Caribbean's 10 most romantic resort restaurants, this would surely be high on the list. It sits atop the coral cliff, open to the breezes, with frangipani and cup of gold framing glittering views of beach and sea. With its thatched ramada, red quarry tile floor and rush chairs, it's a setting that conjures up memories of long leisurely luncheons on Mykonos. Or St. Tropez. But the Rosenthal china and replica Orient Express table lamps whisper Monte Carlo, and the cuisine is unabashedly French: *mignons d'agneau grillés à la Provençale, saucisse de langouste et meron* and *filet de bar grillé avec compôte de tomates et basil.* Unlike so many Caribbean chefs, Jean-Pierre Jury has been tending La Samanna's stoves almost since the year the place opened—which gives the restaurant an air of consistency. Sure you hear snide remarks about La Samanna not being what it used to be. About things slipping. Some people have been saying the same things about Pavarotti and Sutherland and Rysanek almost since they started singing. Some critics mumble about La Samanna's guests being too flashy. Flashy? Peter Ustinov? Richard Nixon?

On various visits to La Samanna, I've spotted Billy Graham and Jackie Onassis, but I've never been especially impressed by most of the guests here. When, after dinner, you stroll through that lovely low-arched lobby and lounge for a nightcap, it's the taste and flair that impress—the low-lit seven-sided tented lounge with its hand-sewn Indian embroidery. And the gleaming white terrace. And the striking blue-tiled swimming pool. The stars, the moonlight on the sea. The white villas peeking above the glistening palms. Gorgeous.

NAME: La Samanna

OWNER/MANAGER: James Frankel

ADDRESS: B.P. 159, 97150 St. Martin, F.W.I.

LOCATION: On Long Beach, 15 minutes and $9 by taxi from the airport, about the same from Marigot

TELEPHONE: 596-875122

TELEX: 919892GL

RESERVATIONS: David B. Mitchell & Company, Inc.

CREDIT CARDS: American Express

ROOMS: 46 apartments, 10 bedrooms, in a variety of one- and two-story villas or the main lodge, all with balconies or patios, telephones, breezes and ceiling fans, some with air-conditioning (in main lodge only), some with kitchenettes, some with rooftop decks

MEALS: Breakfast 8:00–10:00, lunch 12:30–2:30, dinner 7:00–9:30 (approx. $100 for 2), in an indoor/outdoor terrace overlooking the beach; informal but stylish dress (cover-ups at lunchtime); room service for continental breakfast only

ENTERTAINMENT: Parlor games, soft taped music in the bar/lounge, which sometimes doubles as a low-key discotheque; casinos 5 minutes away

SPORTS: Mile-long beach, freshwater pool, snorkeling gear, Sunfish sailing, waterskiing, tennis (3 courts, no lights)—all free; boat trips extra, golf nearby

P.S.: No groups ever, some children during holidays

Captain's Quarters

Saba

You get a quick tour of this extraordinary island on the way up to the inn. Saba is higher than it is long: it goes up, up and up to 2,900 ft. within a sea-level distance of less than a mile. The largest village, Windwardside, is about halfway up, teetering on a ridge between two precipitous flanks of the volcano, one of which drops off in a blanket of greenery almost vertically to the sea. It's a hugger-mugger hamlet of whitewashed walls, red tin roofs, cisterns and family graves in the backyards, a few churches, lots of goats and an air of charming, total detachment. Back in the 1800s, a retired sea captain (by tradition the Sabans are, not surprisingly, great sailors) built a little square whitewashed cottage with a red tin roof and gingerbread veranda, just as his ancestors and neighbors had done, right on the edge of the ravine; he was joined a few years later by the village doctor, who built yet another small white house next door, practically swamped by hibiscus and orchids and snowflake. Several years ago the two homes were integrated and converted into the Captain's Quarters inn.

Coming upon Captain's Quarters is like discovering a New England inn on top of a magic volcano. All rooms are doubles (some have four-poster beds), with plenty of welcome cross-ventilation, modern tiled bathrooms with hot water and balconies with great views over the green cliffs to the sea.

Meals are served family style, simply but elegantly, in an arbor pavilion beneath breadfruit, papaya, and mango trees. There's a pool perched on the edge of the ravine adjoining a sundeck, and a casual, shaded bar close at hand—and that's it. There's nothing to do here but relax and take great chugalugging gulps of fresh pine air. Maybe you'll go for a hike up Mount Scenery, a drive down to The Bottom (Saba's capital) or a stroll through the winding streets of Windwardside. Most of the time you'll eat, have a rum punch in the sun, eat, snooze, take a dip in the pool, eat, make love.

NAME: Captain's Quarters

MANAGER: Steve Hassell

ADDRESS: Windwardside, Saba, N.A.

LOCATION: At the top of the hill, $25 plus tip from airport or pier with a tour of the island thrown in

TELEPHONE: 2201

TELEX: 8006

RESERVATIONS: International Travel & Resorts, Inc.

CREDIT CARDS: None

ROOMS: 10, no air-conditioning (up here you certainly don't need it), showers

MEALS: Breakfast 7:30–9:30, lunch 12:30, dinner at 8:00; informal dress (but bring along a jacket or sweater for the evening); room service for breakfast only

ENTERTAINMENT: The other guests, library, parlor games

SPORTS: Tiny freshwater pool, tennis, hiking—all free; dive shop

P.S.: In winter, expect lots of day-trippers around lunchtime; closed September

The Old Gin House

St. Eustatius

🌴🌴🌴🍴🍴🍴$

On an escapist island like Statia you probably don't expect to sit down to candlelit dinners served up on pewter and cobalt blue china. Or a meal of red snapper mousse, lobster soup Provençal, Chateaubriand Dijonaise, followed by *Marquise au chocolat* snow orange (vanilla ice cream blended with Cointreau and frozen in a scooped-out orange iced with sugar). There's not much to do on Statia when the sun goes down, so John May and Marty Scofield help you fill your evenings like trencherpersons, an apt pastime here among the ruins of eighteenth-century gin houses where the navies of the world caroused.

"We wanted to build a small inn that had island flavor, but we also wanted it to have good beds and good plumbing." So you'll find Sealy Posturpedic mattresses, modern bathrooms and hot water behind the warehouse doors and louver windows (all hand carved on the island). The bedspreads and curtains were hand-stitched by the ladies of the island, the armoires hand carved by the men. Everything else is antique, mostly French or Welsh, mostly eighteenth century "and violently anti-Victorian"—tea chests, captain's trunks and other pieces appropriate to a former trading post.

The first of the two inns, Old Gin House, consists of six guest rooms, sitting directly above the beach. Breakfast and lunch are served beachside, on a trellised terrace lined with ferns and crotons, shaded by palm trees, cooled by the breezes off the beach and decorated with ancient anchors and other doohickeys hauled up from the crumbled warehouses beneath the water. This is where *le tout* Statia gather—swimmers, snorkelers, scuba divers, other expatriate Americans, crews from the sailboats in the bay. So many visitors gathered here that John and Marty decided to produce a second small hotel with island flavor, across the street in the tumbledown ruins of an old cotton gin factory at the foot of the cliff. To everyone's surprise except their own, the Mooshay Bay Publick House went up in double-quick time—14 rooms furnished in island style, an antique here, Haitian decoration there, and bedside chests and lamps, even the door hinges, designed by Marty and crafted in the islands. All rooms have showers and individual water heaters. (Rooms 22 and 23, by the way, are the favorites of Holland's—and Statia's—Queen Beatrix.)

Evenings are passed in leisurely, congenial manner in the raftered Publick House, sampling strawberry daiquiries or playing Scrabble in the library on the wooden gallery. The big clock on the wall is 200 years old, and it's working again because one of the regular guests fixes old clocks as a hobby and spent a vacation getting this one into ticking order. When the hands get around to 7:30 Marty and John escort their guests, couple or foursome by foursome ("We're very adept now at mixing and matching") to the dining room. Soft candlelight glows on hardwood shutters and sturdy beams and walls of bare brick that once served as ballast on sailing ships. Which is more pleasurable—the setting or the hearty dinner? Both.

NAME: The Old Gin House

OWNERS/MANAGERS: John May and Marty Scofield

ADDRESS: St. Eustatius, N.A.

LOCATION: On the beach, beneath Fort Oranje, among the ruins of the eighteenth-century port, a 10-minute ride from the airport, $3.00 per person by taxi; Statia, in turn, is 20 minutes by Winair from St. Maarten (longer via Saba)

TELEPHONE: 599-3-2319

TELEX: None

RESERVATIONS: Scott Calder International, Inc.

CREDIT CARDS: American Express, Diners Club, MasterCard, Eurocard

ROOMS: 20: 6 in the Old Gin House (above the beach), 14 in the Publick House (facing the pool and courtyard)—all with ceiling fans, antiques, quarry tile floors, showers

MEALS: Breakfast 8:00–9:30, lunch noon–2:00, dinner at 7:30 (4 courses, wine, $50 for 2); informal dress, but not scruffy; no room service

ENTERTAINMENT: Conversation or parlor games in the pubby bar or elegant lounge, tasteful background music (Bach, jazz, "whatever's appropriate")

SPORTS: Beach (maybe—most of the black lava sand had washed away on a recent visit, but it's expected back any time now), freshwater pool, hiking up the volcano; Surfside Statia is a new dive shop (new for Statia, the company's been around many years) with complete, professional snorkeling and dive facilities, including underwater cameras—with several wrecks from several centuries only a few yards offshore (to say nothing of the tumbled foundations of the old warehouses)

P.S.: Children are "discouraged in winter"

Added Attractions

Grand Case Beach Club

St. Martin

Grand Case, the village, is the prettiest hamlet on the French side, its narrow main street lined with pastel-colored frame houses, boutiques, bistros, bistros and more bistros. At the far end of town, where the main road makes a sharp right toward the French side's airstrip, you keep going straight ahead along a dirt road barely wide enough for a Toyota, aiming for the red rooftops of the new-in-1984 Grand Case Beach Club.

What this lovely, quiet corner of the island calls for is a low-profile inn such as, say, Pasanggrahan or Mary's Boon, but what the Beach Club presents is an ungainly three-story facade, in a narrow 6½-acre plot between path and beach. That said, the rooms and studios are comfortably furnished in upholstered rattan and freshly decorated with batiks and framed mola cloths; each has a balcony or patio a few feet from the placid bay, and most of them have serene views of the village and bay (but 803, 804, 809 and 810, billed as "garden view" look into the parking lot). The location, compared to most of St. Maarten/St. Martin, is certainly secluded, and there are few distractions to intrude on your relaxation. This is another place worth considering if you want seclusion *and* condo-style wall-to-wall comforts and convenience, including fully equipped modern kitchenettes. Also, it's within walking distance of the fashionable bistros, so you, unlike everyone else, don't have to worry about parking. 76 units. *Grand Case Beach Club, Grand Case 97150, St. Martin, F.W.I. Telephone: 87-51-87.*

L'Habitation de Lonvilliers

St. Martin

Located at Anse Marcel, a relatively undiscovered bay between Grand Case and l'Orient, the new resort opened in December 1986 with only half of its projected 400-plus rooms open. Smart move—better to get it working smoothly first. Guest rooms are grouped in two three-story wings running parallel to each other along a decorative landscaped pathway that leads to an impressive pool, pool bar, then the even more impressive beach. The architecture is modeled on French Antillean plantation great houses, but the interiors are slick and modern. Best feature of L'Habitation is its hilltop sport complex (four tennis courts with lights, two squash courts, racquetball, open-walled exercise room, café/bar/lounge). Other features include two attractive fan-cooled restaurants, a marina and a shopping gallery. 250 rooms. *L'Habitation, P.O. Box 230, 97150 St. Martin, F.W.I. U.S. telephone: 800-847-4249.*

La Baie Heureuse

St. Martin

If you read the brochure you'd learn that this is "St. Martin's most famous hotel . . ." Most famous joke, maybe. The concept is very grand (probably too grand): superdeluxe suites (three telephones, two televisions, wet bars, champagne, etc.) in villas grouped around a central great house with snazzy dining terrace and pool; meet guests at the airport in a limo, give them a free Peugeot sedan for the duration of their stay. Since it's also on one of the most beautiful (and virtually private) cove beaches on the island it should be, as the brochure chirrups, ". . . catering to the world's elite. . . ." But something went wrong 'twixt concept and execution: physically the place doesn't hang together as an entity (you might find that the main use of your Peugeot is driving to the beach), the rooms are lavish but without personality. In three visits I've still to see the reception desk installed. Keep your eye on La Baie Heureuse, however—it might someday live up to its brochure. It may even stay open long enough for people to check in. 20 rooms, 40 suites. *La Baie Heureuse, P.O.B. 170, 97150 Marigot, St. Martin, F.W.I. Telephone: 590-875520.*

La Belle Creole

St. Martin

It was first supposed to open 16 years ago (and almost did), then was supposed to open last year. Now the deadline is February 1988, but don't hold your breath. Even with the Hilton organization behind it, this place seems to be jinxed. But it's another worth keeping in mind. It might someday be a unique resort, in an interesting location, in the manner of a French Riviera fishing village but with luxury accoutrements and facilities. For details, check with Conrad International Hotels—212-980-6680.

The Queen's Leewards

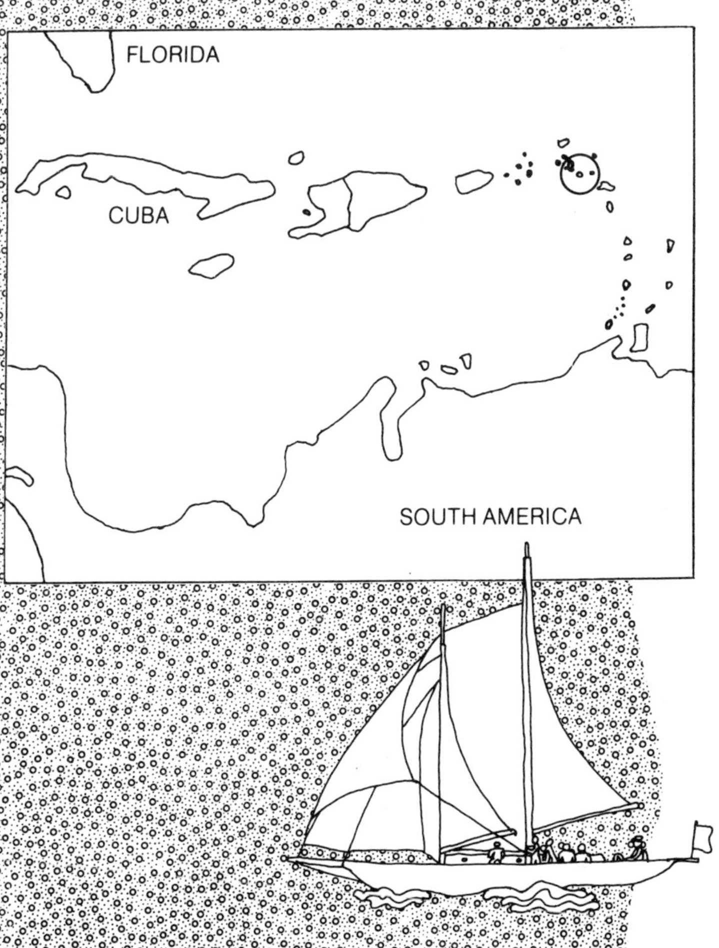

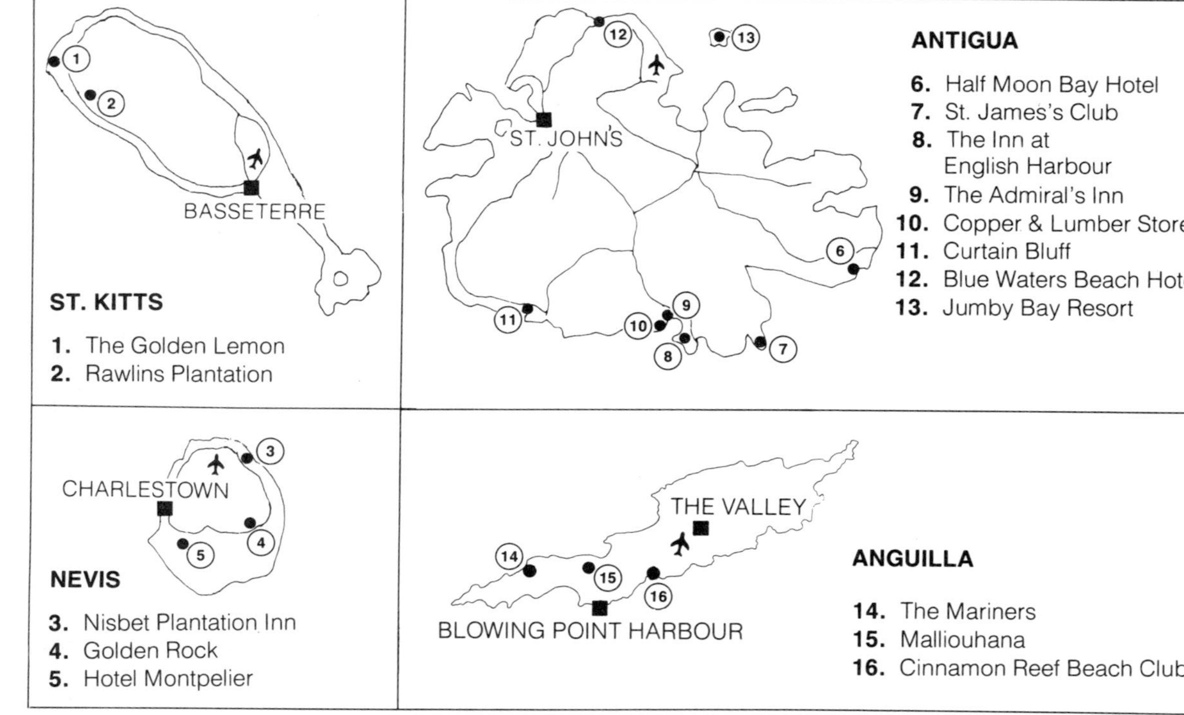

THE QUEEN'S LEEWARDS

The Queen's Leewards

The four islands that make up this group are, with one exception, former British islands that now owe allegiance to Queen Elizabeth as head of the Commonwealth. The exception is Anguilla, whose citizens decided to secede from the St. Kitts/Nevis partnership and remain a Crown Colony, governed directly by London.

Antigua claims that lovers can spend a year on the island and visit a different beach each day. Maybe so, but once you see the beaches at, say, Half Moon or Curtain Bluff you'll wave good-bye to the others. Most of the tourist resorts are in the northwest, vaguely between the airport and St. John's, the capital; with the exception of the newly deluxed Blue Waters and the offshore Jumby Bay, all the hideaways in this guide are toward the south of the island, where the country is lusher, the hills higher (all the way to 1,319 ft. at the curiously named Boggy Peak), and picturesque English Harbour fairly oozes with memories of those dashing young eighteenth-century officers about town, Commander Horatio Nelson and Prince William Henry, Duke of Clarence. Apart from Nelson's Dockyard, forget the sightseeing, enjoy the beaches, even if you don't make it to all 365 of them.

St. Kitts, alias St. Christopher, may not be the most gorgeous island in the Caribbean and you have probably seen more romantic beaches; the central part has been developed (hotel, condos, golf, casino) for a mass tourism that has yet to mass, but the mountainous western half is authentic Caribbean, foothills of sugarcane, narrow coast-hugging roads, huddled villages. Two attractions worth the bumpy drives: the spectacular fort perched on Brimstone Hill (take a picnic) and Romney Manor, a batik workshop in a lovely old plantation house.

Nevis—now there's a fabulous little island. Slightly mystical, slightly spooky, with centuries-old plantations, tumbledown hamlets, rain forest, a mountain with its head in the clouds (hence Columbus's designation—*nieves,* or snow). Alexander Hamilton was born here, the illegitimate son of a Scottish planter (his restored home is now a museum); Fanny Nisbet lived here with her husband until he died, and she was later wooed, won and wed by Nelson in the parish of Fig Tree. If they returned for a reunion, they'd find their island hadn't changed all that much—people still seek solace in the mineral baths where England's aristocracy came to frolic.

Anguilla is set apart from the others by geography as well as politics. It's just to the north of St. Martin, a 20-minute ferryboat ride from Marigot. It's long and flat and physically as undistinguished as the eel for which it's named, but if you want beautiful beaches here are Beautiful Beaches. And unaggressive, friendly people. In the past two or three years, a few new hotels have made people sit up and take notice, and another luxury resort is on the way. But Anguilla is a long, long way from being overdeveloped or crowded or spoiled. True, they do have a traffic light in the main village, mainly to handle the dozen or so cars going to and from church on Sunday.

Montserrat, 15 minutes by air southwest of Antigua, is one of the least visited of the Antilles—yet it's one of the lushest and prettiest, with its steep hills and dales, glens and glades. Some people compare it to Ireland (early settlers were Irish, the shamrock is the island's emblem). They wish. If Montserrat had beaches as beautiful as those in Ireland, we might have heard more of Montserrat. Another reason few people go to Montserrat is that getting there involves a flight on Montserrat Airways, a debt-ridden offshoot of LIAT, with only two small hand-me-down planes, only one of which seems to be capable of flying at any time. Usually late, usually overbooked.

HOW TO GET THERE For Antigua, American and BWIA from New York and Boston; American, Eastern and BWIA from Miami; Air Canada and BWIA from Toronto. For St. Kitts, fly to St. Maarten, St. Croix or Antigua, then connect with LIAT; or with Windward from St. Maarten, or American Eagle from San Juan. To Nevis, there are a few flights daily on LIAT from Antigua or St. Kitts, but the island's inns recommend (and arrange) shared-seat charters on Carib Aviation; it costs a few dollars more, but it saves a lot of time and anguish. There is also daily ferryboat service between St. Kitts and Nevis, a one-hour trip on the sturdy 85-ft. passenger/cargo m.v. *Carib* (to Nevis early morning, returning late afternoon).

For Anguilla, first fly to Sint Maarten and connect with Windward Flights (10 minutes); at press time, plans were afoot for American Eagle to operate two daily nonstop flights between Anguilla and San Juan. There are also small ferryboats several times a day between the island and Marigot on the French side, St. Martin.

Malliouhana

Anguilla

🌴🌴🌴🌴🌴 🍴🍴🍴🍴 ☺☺☺ $$$$$

When I first saw Anguilla's Mead Point in the early 1980s, it was a craggy coral headland flanked by two dream beaches—one a cove, one a ribbon of white sand—where "someone was planning to build a luxury hotel more beautiful than La Samanna." Ho-hum. How many times had we heard that over the years?

The next time I went there, someone was building a hotel. The stark headland was now a starker construction site, and during my tour of the cinder blocks and piled pipes, I met a young couple who had come over for the day from La Samanna just to see this new place they'd heard about. They were so impressed they left behind a $1,000 deposit for the following February, for a room that didn't exist in a hotel yet to be built. I knew then that I was present at the birth of a legend.

From the day it finally formally opened in November 1985, people have clamored to get a room at Malliouhana. And most of the people who go

there book on the spot for the following year. And who wouldn't want to return as often as possible to Malliouhana's delights? Thirty flowery acres with royal palms for shade, sea bean for greenery, purple and yellow allamanda for splashes of color, night-blooming jasmine for fragrance. Two beaches, one almost a mile long, the other a secluded cove, both with beach bars and loungers (the hotel assigns eight members of the staff just to look after two beaches!). A 30,000-bottle wine cellar, a kitchen headed by a Michelin two-star chef from the French Riviera. Villas whose bathrooms rival other hotels' bedrooms for size and appointments.

Step into the grand open-sided atrium lobby with its arched galleries and imposing paintings by Haiti's Jasamin Joseph and you feel like you're in a sort of Caribbean chateau. Settle into the plethora of pillows in the lounge's plump banquettes and admire the intricate raw silk tapestries and hand-carved wooden figurines (mostly lions in honor of owner Leon Roydon). The playground just beyond is a stunning landscape rather than a multilevel swimming pool.

The Roydons, on the spot day and night keeping an eye on things, have pulled out all the stops for their guests. Guest rooms are a carefree, non-bed-bumping 20 by 18 ft. (a couple of feet larger in the villas) with decks only a few feet smaller. Interiors were designed by the esteemed Larry Peabody, with the same sensuous ambiance he contrived for the much-lamented Habitation LeClerc in Haiti. Filtered sunbeams dapple hardwood louvers and quarry tile floors. Blossomy vines spill in profusion over balcony balustrades. Soft indirect lighting transforms lush planters and leafy ficus into mini-Edens. It's an atmosphere calculated to induce instant indolence. In addition, each villa comes with its own service pantry, a godsend for those of us who enjoy dawdly bathrobe breakfasts on the balcony, attended by not one but two maids—the first to set up the table and flowers, the other to serve piping hot croissants and pour freshly brewed tea. Granted, such a breakfast will set you back $15 a head, but think what it does to set you up for another day of dallying.

Interiors are basically the same throughout the hotel, but location may make a minor difference. Assuming you have a choice (which might mean going in, say, June or July), rooms 109, 209, 110 and 210 would be my choices, although Leon Roydon's favorite is 101, above the bar but with a particularly large balcony. The most popular villas are those on the cliff beyond the pool, for the view; the two directly on Mead's Bay for people who are water sprites. I spent time in a so-called Garden Villa (i.e., looking at the hotel rather than the sea but surrounded by flowers) and didn't feel deprived in the slightest. The newest (1987) accommodations are enormous two-bedroom suites on the bluff above the cove—quiet and secluded, but that much farther from the dining room and tennis courts (farther—all of 3 minutes' stroll).

Many people travel much more than 3 minutes, of course, to dine here, for the terrace restaurant is one of the undoubted lures to Malliouhana. Again, Leon Roydon wanted the best, and since one of his longtime friends was none other than Jo Rostang of the Michelin two-star La Bonne Auberge in Antibes, he invited him to direct the Malliouhana kitchen. Now even a Jo Rostang can't work miracles: Anguilla is no Riviera with an infinite supply of fresh produce. But given the shortcomings of a Caribbean island, Rostang and his corps do a commendable job of creating an Antillean Antibes. The setting helps immensely: an open fan-shaped pavilion above a sparkling sea, a hardwood canopy rising over giant ginger and stephanotis trees, with that final touch of civilized well-being—the pleasures of a well-endowed wine list, the product of Leon Roydon's long-standing oenophilia.

All of which may make dining at Malliouhana sound like a stuffy activity. Far from it. The cuisine may be French, the china Limoges and the cutlery Christophe, but the guests are as casually, but stylishly, dressed as they would be in St. Tropez. And the resort as a whole is as sports oriented as it is luxurious—and, from this year, almost all the sporting activities are available at no extra charge. Including the smart new gymnasium/exercise pavilion on a bluff above the cove, its walls open to the sea and sky. You'd expect to find a place like this on the French Riviera, but on an unspoiled Caribbean backwater such as Anguilla it's a marvel.

NAME: Malliouhana

OWNERS/MANAGERS: Leon and Annette Roydon

ADDRESS: P.O. Box 173, Anguilla, B.W.I.

LOCATION: On Mead's Bay, on the northeast shore of the island, about 10 minutes and $10 by taxi from the airstrip, 6 or 7 minutes and $10 from the ferryboat pier at Blowing Point

TELEPHONE: 809-497-2111

TELEX: 9316 MALHANA LA

RESERVATIONS: David B. Mitchell & Company, Inc.

CREDIT CARDS: None

ROOMS: 40 rooms, including 9 suites, in the main building or villas, overlooking beach or gardens, all with ceiling fans (plus air-conditioning in the villas), balconies or lanais, stocked refrigerators, wet bars, telephones

MEALS: Breakfast anytime in your room, lunch 12:30–3:00, dinner 7:00–10:00 (approx. $80–90 for 2, served in the breeze-cooled dining terrace above the sea); informal but stylish dress; room service 7:30 A.M.–11:00 P.M. (special menu)

ENTERTAINMENT: Elegant bar/lounge, TV room (satellite and video), library, backgammon, chess, cribbage

SPORTS: 2 beautiful beaches (1 long and public, 1 virtually private cove, both with beach bars, good swimming and snorkeling), 2 freshwater pools (chlorine-free), tennis (3 courts, pro shop, no lights), Sunfish and catamaran sailing, windsurfing, waterskiing, exercise room (Nautilus devices, Aerobicycles, weights)—all free; massage, scuba diving, 35-ft. powerboat for fishing and trips to adjoining islets available on the premises at extra charge

P.S.: One-week minimum stay

Cinnamon Reef Beach Club

Anguilla

🌴🌴🌴✕✕⚾⚾$$$

Take your pick: beach or bluff—either way you'll wallow in spacious surroundings at the Cinnamon Reef. All in individual bungalows, they're suites rather than rooms, all with big patios, dressing rooms and high ceilings. Half of them are set out beside the beach, the remainder on a bluff on the opposite side of the clubhouse. Otherwise, all the suites are identical, with those lovely big patios, loungers, ceiling fans, sitting areas with sofas and coffee tables, two double beds and tiled shower stalls (no baths).

Architecturally, the Cinnamon style is eclectic, white poured concrete that falls somewhere between Blockhouse Traditional and Mediterranean Fanciful, all arches and portholes and cathedral doors. Patios are shaded by arbors draped with wood rose, and when the bougainvillea blooms the bungalows are more Mediterranean than Blockhouse. The "clubhouse" (there's no significance to the word *club*) is a long, white arched temple abutting the bay, open to the breezes (but with electric-powered windows for those occasions when the breezes are too stiff), Italian tiled floors, pine-and-wicker/bamboo-and-canvas furnishings.

Pleasant setting, pleasant dining. The menu treads cautiously between Antillean and Manhattan; guests are expected to dress for dinner (that is, jacket and tie) during weekends in winter, and there's entertainment (delightful, not obtrusive) every evening by one of several local bands. Across the courtyard, the cavernous water tank provides an elevated

foundation for the hotel's playground—a 40 by 60-ft. pool, snackbar and three tennis courts.

It's a shame that on an island with so many beautiful beaches, Cinnamon Reef has to make do with a modest curve of sand at the end of a pondlike harbor; on the other hand, the reef creates a lagoon-smooth bay and the arms of Little Harbour frame a stunning view of the hilly, undeveloped corner of the French side of St. Maarten/St. Martin.

NAME: Cinnamon Reef Beach Club

OWNERS: The Hauser Family

MANAGER: Suzy Seitz

ADDRESS: Little Harbour, Anguilla, B.W.I.

LOCATION: On the south coast, at Little Harbour, 5 minutes and $5 by taxi from the airstrip and the ferryboat dock

TELEPHONE: 809-497-2727

TELEX: 9307 CINMON LA

RESERVATIONS: Ralph Locke Islands

CREDIT CARDS: All major cards

ROOMS: 18 suites, with spacious bathrooms, verandas, telephones on request

MEALS: Breakfast 8:00–10:30; lunch 11:30–2:30 in the main dining room or courtyard; afternoon tea at 4:00; dinner 7:30–10:00 (approx. $60–70 for 2), "long trousers for gentlemen in the dining room"; room service by prearrangement for breakfast

ENTERTAINMENT: Taped music, live music "that is, evenings the musicians show up"; Friday night barbecue, backgammon, chess, Scrabble, dominoes and Chinese checkers

SPORTS: Small beach, others nearby; 3 Deco-turf tennis courts, freshwater pool, windsurfers, Sunfish sailing, sailboats, paddleboats, floats, snorkeling, fishing gear—all free; island tours, sails and picnic lunches can be arranged

The Mariners

Anguilla

$$$

The Mariners, just a few years old, is already one of the true delights (and true *bargains*) of Anguilla. This hotel, bless its unprepossessing heart, strives to be true to its West Indies heritage: verandas trimmed with gingerbread, lattice screens and louvers, two-toned shutters, tray ceilings and wood moldings, showers rather than baths, ceiling fans and breezes rather than air conditioners. And the hotel dining room is just what you would hope to find in a backwater such as this—island-style, indoor-outdoor architecture, planter-and-driftwood decor, and a wooden beachside gallery with views of outlying islets—Salt, Dog and Prickly Pear.

Located on a crescent of beach adjoining the salt ponds and a somnolent, one-street hamlet called Sandy Ground, the Mariners' 27 rooms are divided among 9 cottages. Each cottage is ingeniously arranged so guests can have simply a double room or a studio with kitchen or a 1-bedroom suite or the entire cottage (a 2-bedroom suite), each unit with its own entrance (interior double doors enhance privacy). They're arranged in an arc around a young garden beside the beach and sea grape trees, except for 2 cottages right on the beach (of these, Cottage 6 is the prime location).

Though there are only 27 separate accommodations at The Mariners, you'll probably see more than your cottage mates in the dining room—it's a popular spot for guests in other hotels as well as day-trippers from St. Maarten because it's so deliciously inexpensive.

But even if the dining room is busy there's still the lovely peace of your veranda awaiting, where you can retire for the evening and think lazily about tomorrow.

NAME: The Mariners

OWNER/MANAGER: Clive Carty

ADDRESS: P.O. Box 139, Sandy Ground, Anguilla, B.W.I.

LOCATION: In the village of Sandy Ground, $5 by taxi and 5 minutes from the airstrip

TELEPHONE: 809-497-2671 and 2815

TELEX: 9319 MARINERS LA

RESERVATIONS: Direct, 800-223-0079; Robert Reid Assoc. in the United States; Ellan Vardy & Assoc. in Toronto

CREDIT CARDS: American Express, Visa, MasterCard

ROOMS: 27 in 9 cottages: 8 studios, 19 rooms converting to both 1- and 2-bedroom cottages; one 3-bedroom cottage

MEALS: Breakfast 7:30–9:30; continental only, 9:30 10:30; lunch noon–2:30; snacks/afternoon tea 2:30–6:00; dinner 7:30–9:30 (approx. $36 for 2) in beachside restaurant, informal dress; room service for continental breakfast 7:30–10:30 A.M., for bar service 10:30 A.M.–7:00 P.M.

ENTERTAINMENT: Live music (amplified) 1 or 2 nights a week; barbecue on Thursdays, West Indian Night on Saturdays; video/TV in the conference room

SPORTS: Beach; water sports rentals include scuba, snorkeling, water-skiing, windsurfing, Sunfish sailing; boat and picnic excursions to nearby Sandy Island, Little Bay or Prickly Pear can be arranged

---

The Golden Lemon

St. Kitts

🌴🌴🌴🌴🍴🍴🍴😊😊$$$

Take a seventeenth-century French manor house, in a walled garden beside a grove of coconut palms, and fill it with antiques and bric-a-brac. Paint the exterior a bright lemon yellow, tuck a tiny pool into a corner of the leafy garden and you'll have a handsome country inn in the tropics.

But you wouldn't have the legendary Golden Lemon.

The Golden Lemon is, indeed, all of these things—a seventeenth-century manor of coral-stone with a wood-framed upper floor, an eighteenth-century addition, surrounded by a gallery with a wide-plank floor. From the gallery you look out on unspoiled Caribbean—a reef, a lagoon, a beach of black sand and the palm trees, tall and spindly and well into their second century. In the walled garden, loungers and hammocks invite guests to relax among the trees, and white tables and chairs set up on the arcade beneath the

gallery beckon for a punch or lunch. All very romantic for escapists who want to savor authentic Antillean surroundings (the inn is located at the end of a narrow street in a simple fishing village). But there's more to The Golden Lemon than that.

It was the old manor's good fortune to be spotted by a connoisseur with a sharp eye who could recognize the house's thoroughbred qualities in its then dilapidated state. At the time, Arthur Leaman was an editor with *House & Garden* magazine, who also happened to be an avid collector with an eclectic array of antiques—four-poster beds, mahogany tables, Blue Delft tulipieres from Holland, clocks from Italy.

Leaman has an extraordinary and enviable ability of taking a castoff and, by deft juxtaposition or downright alchemy, turning it into an heirloom. Each room at the Lemon is different, each a masterpiece of composition and color (I have a hunch that if you stood on your head in one of the rooms here you'd still have a picture-perfect interior). I can never decide which is my favorite—the Hibiscus Room with its two white canopy beds, the Batik Room with steps up to the big antique double beds, the Victorian Room for its ornamentation, the Turtle Room for its carapaceous doodads. Every detail reflects Leaman's refined sense of style, so much so that you're so busy admiring the grace notes in the bathrooms you don't even notice you're stepping into a prefab plastic shower stall. Rooms on the upper floor, it should be noted, are wood framed and not infallibly soundproof, but your compensation for keeping your voices down or overhearing extraneous sounds is breakfast on the gallery. First the maid announces its arrival by the sounds of a table being set with a trayful of playful lemon-motif mugs and plates, then she returns with pewter dishes of homemade preserves, perfectly browned toast, perfectly timed scrambled eggs, a Thermos of coffee—all served course by course. It gets your day off to a very slow, very stylish start—just the way life should be at The Golden Lemon.

For guests who want more substantial accommodations, Arthur Leaman recently built a wing of townhouses across the garden, beside the coral shore, some with decks overhanging the sea, some with small private pools. The interiors, needless to say, are exquisite. The prices are extravagant at first glance, but, considering the setting and surroundings, not outlandish.

Evenings have always been special at The Golden Lemon. For one thing, the walled garden setting out front and the junglelike garden at the rear become quite magical with soft lighting and soft breezes. The antique-filled dining room sparkles in the soft light of candelabra and chandeliers. Traditionally Arthur Leaman has hosted a sort of captain's table, but tables are now set for twos and fours, with place cards (which Leaman discreetly rotates to give everyone a chance to mix, if that's what they want). But his patrician presence and wit still turn evenings into house parties. Especially since the guests next to you in the bar may be paying their twentieth visit in

20 years. Dinner is a fixed menu, with Mrs. Johnson's dishes a constant surprise, always something to look forward to. But repeat guests are looking ahead to Sunday brunch and the inn's West Indies Rum Beef Stew, liberally laced with Mount Gay.

The Golden Lemon, let me quickly add, is not for everyone. Its devotees are mostly designers and writers, young Kennedys, young Washingtonians, people in the theater (one of the condos is owned by playwright/librettist Hugh Wheeler; Graham Greene *was* a regular until he settled in Antibes), people who probably will not be startled to find suitless sunbathers around the pool. Gracious Arthur Leaman may be, but he doesn't want his inn (and the solitude of his guests) disturbed by cruise ship passengers, young people under 18, and because, he claims, "you can take only so much of paradise," no one is allowed to stay longer than 2 weeks.

NAME: The Golden Lemon

OWNER/MANAGER: Arthur Leaman

ADDRESS: Dieppe Bay Town, St. Kitts, St. Kitts and Nevis, W.I.

LOCATION: In the village of Dieppe Bay Town, on the northeast coast, about 30 minutes and $22 by taxi from the airport (let the hotel know when you're arriving and they'll arrange for a dependable driver to meet you)

TELEPHONE: 809-465-7260

TELEX: None

RESERVATIONS: Scott Calder International, Inc.

CREDIT CARDS: None (personal checks accepted)

ROOMS: 18, in 2 buildings, all with private bathrooms, ceiling fans, balconies or patios; kitchens in the 8 new condo units, some with shared pool

MEALS: Breakfast 7:30–10:00, lunch noon–3:00 in the patio, afternoon tea 4:00 ("real tea *not* bags"), dinner 8:30 ($40–60 for 2, in the fan-cooled main dining room); informal dress ("no wet bathing suits at lunch"); room service, no extra charge

ENTERTAINMENT: The bar, quiet taped music, backgammon, parlor games

SPORTS: Beach, 20 by 40-ft. freshwater pool (plus private or shared pools in the annex), snorkeling gear, "tremendous reef"—free

P.S.: "No young people under 18"; stay limited to 1-week minimum, 2-week maximum

Rawlins Plantation

St. Kitts

$ $ $

Don't be put off by the bumpy, hilly dirt road that meanders through the fields of sugarcane. Granted, 260 acres of the sweet stuff are hardly a romantic introduction to a hideaway, but press on up the hill and around one last bend and you arrive at a 25-acre oasis of clipped lawns and clumps of croton, breadfruit and Africa tulip trees. Up ahead, the cane fields rise to the foothills of forest-clad Mount Misery; behind you, the fields fall off to the sea and distant views of St. Eustatius. This is, as it has been since 1790 when the family came out from England, the home of the Walwyns, represented today by the young couple who will greet you—Philip and Frances.

At 350 ft. above the sea, Rawlins is exactly the sort of cool, calm place you relish returning to after a sticky day at the beach, or a hike through the rain forest foothills beneath canopies of trailing vines and wild orchids. Some guests actually make it all the way up to the peak, 4,000 ft. above the sea, where Misery must seem like Cloud Nine. The Walwyns will arrange picnic outings up the mountain, part of the way by Jeep, the rest on foot, fortified by their special rum punch. They've flattened a corner of their lawn as that rarity—a grass tennis court. If you can prove you're expert with horses, Frances can arrange for you to go riding through the plantation.

But essentially, this is an inn for relaxing. You'd never get me near the beach or up a hill. Sit on the picket-fenced porch of Mount Pleasant House and read a hefty book. Dunk in the spring-fed pool that was once the mill's cistern. Sit on the veranda of the great house at sundown, gin and tonic in hand, and listen to Philip Walwyn's accounts of his transatlantic trips on catamarans. Check out the library. Watch the sunset's glow on Statia. Listen to the birds and tree frogs. This is what people have in mind when they dream about a place to unwind, really unwind.

The inn still looks like a gentleman's plantation—white great house at the center, cottages for managers and overseers in the gardens, a white lattice gazebo beside the pool. The circular stone base of the seventeenth-century windmill is now a duplex suite, much favored by honeymooners—pretty red-and-white sitting room downstairs, white cast-iron double bed upstairs. The guest rooms reflect the ambiance of colonial times, mahogany floors and rush rugs rather than fitted carpet, ceiling fans rather than air-conditioning, wicker and rattan rather than leather. It's very tasteful and low-key. No television, no telephones. Plumbing and electricity are the sole concessions to the twentieth century.

The former boiling room, where the cane was converted to molasses, is now a flower-draped, stone-floored patio where guests gather for the buffet lunch. Dining has always been pleasurable here. Frances Walwyn has never promised "the finest continental cuisine" or any of the fatuous claims of some island inns. What she and her local cook serve are perfectly prepared local dishes or dishes with their own local embellishments. Thus guests gathered in the patio can while away sun-dappled noondays while nibbling on flying fish fritters, rice with ackee and dill, lobster quiche, soups (breadfruit, eggplant or cucumber with fresh mint), curries garnished with garden-fresh avocados and pawpaws. In the evening, candles sparkle on servings of, say, parrotfish stuffed with lobster and served with homegrown beans and cristofene or locally slaughtered roast shoulder of pork stuffed with homegrown herbs garnished with green pawpaw sauce. For dessert, passion fruit meringue pie or coconut pudding. Between them, Rawlins and Golden Lemon have created a haven for lovers of fine foods, who wend their way to this unspoiled corner of the Caribbean year after year—Rockefellers, Cabots, peers of the realm, doctors and lawyers and writers—and friends of the young and charming Philip and Frances Walwyn.

NAME: Rawlins Plantation

OWNERS/MANAGERS: Philip and Frances Walwyn

ADDRESS: P.O. Box 340, St. Kitts, W.I.

LOCATION: At Mt. Pleasant Estate, near Dieppe Bay Town; directly across the island from the airport, about 30 minutes and $25 by taxi (let the Walwyns know when you'll arrive and they'll send a driver to meet you, "probably Dash, who'll wait forever in case your flight is late")

TELEPHONE: 809-465-6221

TELEX: 6831 KANTOURS KC

RESERVATIONS: Own U.S. office, 617-367-8959

CREDIT CARDS: None

ROOMS: 10, in various cottages, including the Sugar Mill Suite and two 2-bedroom cottages with shared sitting room, all with breezes and ceiling fans, private bathrooms (some shower only), hair dryers, balconies or patios

MEALS: Breakfast from 8:00 on, lunch 12:30–1:30 in the patio, afternoon tea 4:00, dinner at 8:00 (approx. $60 for 2, fixed menu, in the dining room); informal dress, but conservative; Sunday barbecue in the gazebo; room service for breakfast only, no extra charge

ENTERTAINMENT: "Good conversation," parlor games, library with more reading material than you can handle on one vacation

SPORTS: Small spring-fed pool, croquet, tennis (1 grass court, no lights), snorkeling gear, transportation to the beach at Golden Lemon—free; full-day cruises on 45-ft. catamaran to Pinney's Beach on Nevis, including barbecue and drinks ($45 per person), crater trips by Jeep and foot, with refreshments and accompanied by a garden boy with two-way radio ($15 per person)

P.S.: Some children, but they have their own supper hour

Nisbet Plantation Inn

Nevis

✱✱✱ XXX ⊜⊜ $$$

Forty acres of coconut palms sound like a kind of romantic setting for a hideaway, and it is—provided you remember not to move your lounger directly under a tree and risk being bombed by the hirsute fruit. Forty acres, that is, minus a giant swatch cut through the trees to form a grassy grand allee stretching from the Great House all the way to the beach 200 yards away.

The Nisbet Great House follows the traditional Nevisian plantation pattern—square, two-story dwelling of native stone, with dining room and screened porches on the second floor, at the top of an imposing flight of steps. In bygone days when Nevis was wall-to-wall plantations, this was the estate of a Mr. William Nisbet, who lived here with his lovely young bride Fanny—who not so many years later, as a lovely young widow, went on to more universal fame as the wife of Horatio Nelson. The house you see today is not the one in which the Nisbets lived, since few of the old plantation houses survived intact. This is, rather, an authentic-looking reconstruction, with the atmosphere of a gracious, peaceful generations-old country house, complete with an inviting porch that serves as library/lounge/bar and antiques-filled salons that serve as dining rooms.

Socializing, dinner, and more socializing are the program for candlelit, congenial evenings, in a setting of polished mahogany and silver candelabra. There are tables for two, but more likely you'll find yourselves sharing tables with other guests.

The guest rooms themselves are in gingerbread-trimmed bungalows and

cottages dotted around the lawn, tucked in among the towering coconut palms, most of them with two rooms per bungalow, arranged so that bathrooms rather than bedrooms abut each other, and so that porches face away from their neighbors. Furnishings are island simple but comfortable and relaxing, and the newer bungalows have screened porches. The prize is a tiny pink-and-mint cottage called Gingerlands, wood-framed on stone foundations with antiques, a four-poster bed and a very private porch, screened by a flamboyant tree, with its back to the hotel and looking out on the plantation. Of all the rooms at Nisbet's, this is the one that most readily conjures up images of Fanny and her times. Gingerland is close to the Great House and the solitary tennis court, which is officially closed each morning until nine, for the benefit of late sleepers nearby. For the other rooms, if you plan to spend lots of time on the beach, specify a room at that end of the lawn and save yourselves a lot of walking. (That 200-yard hike between the honor guard of coconut palms is a cinch on the way out, but seems more like a mile after a day in the sun.)

The inn changed hands a few years ago, its new owner being a Mr. George Barnum, banker and descendant of the circus family. His new managers, who moved here in late 1986, are Ken and Sandra McLeod, a delightful, dedicated Scottish couple who have made many friends since they first came to the islands about 10 years ago.

NAME: Nisbet Plantation Inn

MANAGERS: Ken and Sandra McLeod

ADDRESS: Nevis, St. Kitts and Nevis, W.I.

LOCATION: On the northeast coast, just 1 mile from the airstrip, $4 by taxi, and 8 miles and $8 by taxi from Charlestown

TELEPHONE: 809-465-5325

TELEX: None

RESERVATIONS: U.S. office—613 Missabe Building, Duluth, MN 55802. Telephone: 218-722-5059 and 5046

CREDIT CARDS: None

ROOMS: 30, in 17 cottages and bungalows, all with private bathrooms (showers only, except 2 with tubs), porches

MEALS: Breakfast 8:00–9:30 (on the veranda), lunch 12:30–1:30 (at the beach bar), afternoon tea 4:00 (in the lounge), dinner 7:30–8:30 (in 2 small, fan-cooled dining rooms, $60 for 2); informal dress, but stylish; Sunday beach barbecue in winter; room service for breakfast only, no extra charge

ENTERTAINMENT: Bar, library, backgammon, Scrabble, TV/VCR in its own room, some taped background music

SPORTS: More or less private beach, snorkeling, tennis (1 court, no lights)—free; other water sports about 3 miles down the road

Hotel Montpelier

Nevis

$$

Horatio Nelson married Fanny Nisbet beneath a breadfruit tree on this hillside plantation, a few miles from Fig Tree Church where visitors can still see the couple's names in the wedding register. Or so goes tradition, and there's no need to ponder it too deeply as you lounge here, content in the shade of your own breadfruit tree. The estate now belongs to James Milnes Gaskell, whose family has lived in Nevis for generations, and it was he who transformed the 100-acre estate and great house into an inn in the early 1960s. "We made our home here and our life in the garden," he writes in his brochure. "We love it and you will, too."

The hub of the inn is the flower-draped gray stone great house, open to the breezes but with a cheery, floral-print clubhouse feel to it. This is the evening social spot; by day, guests tend to gather around the big swimming pool with its tropical murals and landscaping and the attendant bar/lounge/terrace. Dinner is served in a candlelit wing of the flower-filled great house or on the adjoining patio, beneath the stars, and Gwen Bartlett's home cooking is one of the features that sets Montpelier apart. Well, her cooking *and* James Milnes Gaskell's 3-acre fruit and vegetable garden that supplies the kitchen. Mention just the word "organic" and you may be led off for a tour of the host's organically grown cauliflower, papaya, avocado, eggplant and other staples.

The 16 guest rooms, renovated in 1980, are comfortable and efficient in a sort of traditional island way, located in 8 cottages angled and staggered in such a way that each patio or terrace has plenty of privacy and views across the estate or the surrounding hills. Regular guests (a cross-section of Americans and British) don't come to Montpelier for *House & Garden* styling—they come to enjoy the quiet, courtly tone set by the Gaskells and the calm, unhurried air of bygone days.

NAME: Hotel Montpelier

OWNER/MANAGER: James Milnes Gaskell

ADDRESS: P.O. Box 474, Nevis, W.I.

LOCATION: By taxi, 30 minutes and $14 from the airport

TELEPHONE: 809-465-5462

TELEX: 6898 HOMTRAD KC/6818 PUBTLX NVS KC

RESERVATIONS: Ray Morrow Associates in the United States, Morris Associates in London

CREDIT CARDS: None

ROOMS: 16 in 8 bungalows, all breeze-cooled, showers only, patios

MEALS: Breakfast 8:00–9:30, lunch 1:00, afternoon tea at 4:00 (not included in rate), dinner at 8:00, indoors or on the patio (approx. $50 for 2); informal; no room service

ENTERTAINMENT: Background taped classical music in the Great Room (the bar) and around the pool bar; dances, wine tastings—"Whatever seems right for the moment"; lunch barbecue on Saturday with The Honeybees

SPORTS: Large pool, games room, tennis (1 court, no lights, rackets and balls), free transportation to beach and water sports center

P.S.: Children under 12 not recommended, especially in winter. *Closed September 1 to October 15.*

Golden Rock

Nevis

The seeds of sandbox trees pop above your head, orchids grow in the stone patio, hummingbirds flit from blossom to blossom, from saman tree to saman tree. You're a thousand feet above the sea here, in a flowering 25-acre garden surrounded by 150 private acres of tropical greenery, with a misty rain forest an hour's hike from the pool.

Golden Rock is a 200-year-old sugar estate, its counting house converted into a guest cottage, its original windmill into an unusual duplex suite with stone walls, *three* antique four-posters and a private sun deck at the rear. The remaining rooms, in pastel-colored bungalows widely spaced among the allamanda and hibiscus, have one-of-a-kind bamboo canopy beds (designed and made by Leonard the bartender) and verandas with views of unspoiled countryside and unending sea. Three new rooms were added in 1987, between the rose garden and the herb garden, a few feet down the hill but still with that stunning view.

The dining room is a garden porch in the old vaulted "long house," where candlelit dinners might include pumpkin soup, lobster on the half shell or curried lamb with hot Nevis sauce, mango mousse or banana cream with meringue.

It's an unhurried life up here, at the end of a long bumpy driveway lined by poinsettia and flamboyant. Unhurried breakfast on your veranda, unhurried lunch on the patio, unhurried drinks in Leonard's bar, unhurried dinner in the garden porch. This is a place for reading (there's a reasonably eclectic library in the bar). For backgammon or Scrabble. Maybe a game of tennis, surely a dip in the big spring-fed pool. Twice a day Pam Barry offers her guests a trip to the beach or town, and twice a day many of them decide not to leave the garden or gazebo. A couple of evenings a week the gardener picks up his bamboo flute and leads his group, The Honeybees, through their repertoire of local airs.

But most of the time the loudest noise is one of those popping sandbox seeds.

NAME: Golden Rock

OWNER/MANAGER: Pam Barry

ADDRESS: Box 493, Nevis, W.I.

LOCATION: In the parish of Gingerland, a thousand feet up in the hills, give or take an inch or two, about 25 minutes and $20 by taxi from the airfield

TELEPHONE: 809-469-5346

TELEX: 6855 (Attn Golden Rock) JANSTRAV KC

RESERVATIONS: International Travel & Resorts

CREDIT CARDS: None

ROOMS: 16, including the Sugar Mill Suite (which sleeps 4), all with verandas, showers only (limited supplies of hot water), bamboo four-poster beds; the Sugar Mill Suite has an additional sleeping gallery, stone-walled shower and huge antique four-posters (king size upstairs, 2 queens downstairs)

MEALS: Breakfast 7:30–10:30, lunch noon–2:30 (both alfresco on the terrace), complimentary afternoon tea at 4:00, dinner at 8:00 (in the indoor garden dining room, fixed menu, $40 for 2); informal, but jackets not inappropriate (partly because of the elevation); room service for breakfast, lunch and afternoon tea, no extra charge

ENTERTAINMENT: Bar/lounge, parlor games, billiards, darts, some taped music in bar ("never in the dining room"), live music Tuesdays (calypso) and Saturdays (native band)

SPORTS: Spring-fed pool, tennis (1 court, recently resurfaced but with constricted alleys) in the garden, transportation to the inn's private 11-acre beach property twice daily, snorkeling masks, windsurfing—all free; hikes through the rain forest; other water sports can be arranged nearby

P.S.: "Not really suitable for children"

Jumby Bay Resort

Antigua

🌴🌴🌴🌴🍴🍴⚾⚾$$$$$

A private islet just off the northern coast of Antigua, Jumby Bay is one solution for escapists who want a resort that is at once secluded and accessible. Secluded because its 300 acres are shared by only 76 guests and a flock of wild sheep. Accessible because you take a taxi, 3 minutes, to the resort's dock, then, assuming schedules gel, a boat ride of 12 minutes to the island, with the crew dispensing rum punches and registration cards on the way over. When you arrive, a minivan or electric buggy takes you past trim lawns and the 200-year-old estate house direct to your room.

You have your pick of two styles of accommodation: the original octagonal guest cottages scattered around the cillamont-shaded lawns or the new two-story mission-style Pond Bay House at the far end of Jumby Beach. The rondavel cottages, two rooms to each, are draped in tropical foliage that screens the private porches from passersby and wafts the scent of tropical blossoms through the rooms; cathedral ceilings and anterooms with daybeds/sofas create a sense of space and comfort. Pond Bay House rooms are virtually minisuites, luxuriously designed with stylish teak furniture by McGuire, quarry tile floors and fabrics in soothing shades of peach and melon. The striking bathrooms have semisunken Roman tubs and breezy indoor/outdoor gardens.

Pond Bay House or rondavel cottage, all rooms have a few of those extra little touches that separate the good from the memorable: scads of big fluffy towels (18 per room!), cuddly terry cloth robes, golf umbrellas, walking sticks, wall safes. The welcome includes a refreshment tray with a bottle of Antiguan rum, cans of Coke, a bottle of Villa Banfi wine and bottles of Riunite cooler. Banfi? Riunite? Right, but let me back up a little. The resort, then known as Long Island, was started by the island's owner, Homer Williams, about four years ago. In 1986, he sold 80 percent to New York's Mariani brothers, who built a company called Villa Banfi into the largest wine importers in the United States. They have their own vineyards in Italy, and one of their best-sellers is the aforesaid Riunite. It's there, so they say, simply to cool you down after a hot set of tennis and not to test your palate as a wine lover.

What will happen under the new partnership is hard to say: one manager has departed, one chef has followed, the boss-on-the-spot is a developer rather than a hotelier, plans have been drawn up for the addition of private homes and a cluster of "club rooms" for new "members." I suspect that most of the development is a year or two off, in which case you can still enjoy the undoubted attractions of Jumby.

Not least of these is the beach known as Pasture, on the windward side of the island, accessible only on foot or by bicycle, a real Robinson Crusoe place with hammocks strung between the sea grapes and a conveniently placed cooler with soft drinks, beers, rum and ice. On the house.

Also on the house are cocktails from the bar, wine (Villa Banfi) with lunch and dinner, laundry, launch service, stamps for your postcards, most water sports and tennis. And, of course, nature: several beaches, 5 miles of walking trails and bike paths snaking through the box briar and pink cedar, through groves of turpentine and loblolly.

But you pay a price for Jumby Bay's accessibility; once or twice a day jets leaving the airport lumber upward close to the island, intruding on the tranquility, and once or twice a week a London-bound jumbo overflies Jumby late at night and has been known to awaken slumbering guests. But these distractions aside, Jumby Bay at its best is a ravishing hideaway.

NAME: Jumby Bay Resort

MANAGER: Marston Winkles

ADDRESS: P.O. Box 243, Long Island, Antigua, W.I.

LOCATION: On an offshore islet, 12 minutes by 48-ft. boat from the mainland (no charge), $3 by taxi from Antigua's Coolidge International Airport; if your flight misses the scheduled ferry, you can have drinks at the hotel beside the dock, but it's hardly a deluxe establishment

TELEPHONE: 809-463-2488 and 2176

TELEX: 2092 LONGISL AK

RESERVATIONS: Own U.S. office, 800-437-0049

CREDIT CARDS: None (personal checks accepted)

ROOMS: 38, in cottages, villas and two-story Pond Bay House, all with ceiling fans, porches or lanais, wall safes, bathrobes, some with showers only

MEALS: Breakfast 8:00–9:30, continental breakfast to 10:00, lunch 12:30–2:00 (at the beachside terrace, mostly hamburgers and variations!), afternoon tea at 4:00 in the Pond Bay House, dinner 7:30–9:30 (in the arcaded patio of the Estate House); weekly barbecue dinner at beach terrace; dress informal but elegant; limited room service

ENTERTAINMENT: Bar/lounge, library, backgammon, cribbage, etc.

SPORTS: 2 beaches (one leeward, one windward), windsurfing, Sunfish sailing, waterskiing, snorkeling, croquet, 40 bicycles, tennis (3 courts, 2

with lights, Peter Burwash pro), nature trails, boat trips to mainland—all free; scuba diving and sport fishing can be arranged (so can golf, but hardly worth the effort)

P.S.: There may be some construction going on, but management claims it positively won't interfere with guests

Blue Waters Beach Hotel

Antigua

🌴🌴🌴 XXX ☺☺ $$$

The waters are not just blue they're a palette of blues—and the hotel isn't going to let you forget it. Even the new bathrobes mirror the blues, every hue and shade of them.

Bathrobes? At Blue Waters? For years, this quiet, family-owned, family-run resort has been a dependable 46-roomer, with first-class facilities but accommodations that were outdazzled by all the flora and shrubbery. Last year, Blue Waters acquired a new owner ("a butcher's boy from London," is how he styles himself, but in fact a successful entrepreneur who went from butcher to processor to tycoon), with juicy plans to hoist the hotel up into the luxury category, then fill the rest of his 10 hillside/coveside acres with condos.

What remains is the lovely botanical-garden setting—down the steep hill, into the tree-encircled driveway, through the open lobby to the flowering terrace, pool and beach, with two-story wings of rooms fanning off on either side. Balconies are festooned with bougainvillea and plumbago, lawns are shaded by Antigua palms and flamboyants. There are so many plants and trees here that there are botanical walks through the grounds, and 10 gardeners are employed full time to keep everything spruce and dandy.

What remains, too, is the friendly, congenial atmosphere nurtured over a quarter of a century by the Kelsick family. Many of the senior staff are still holding fort, Chef Maddox is still in the kitchen, but now the team is headed by an esteemed local hotelier, the ever-smiling, unflappable Hamish Watson.

He, in turn, has installed his own concept of comforts and services. A new classy, a la carte restaurant has been tucked into an air-conditioned salon off the lobby. Meals are more inventive, well prepared, well presented

(but Maddox's famed Sunday curry brunch is still the culinary highlight of the week for many guests). New superior rooms have been made larger simply by extending the rooms to the edge of the original balconies and adding new ones. And all rooms now come with stocked refrigerators and individual safes—as well as the blue bathrobes.

The new rooms and sprightlier decor notwithstanding, what sets Blue Waters apart is the confluence of sea and beach and gardens (maybe the profusion of flowers is why it's so popular with the British), and the opportunities to appreciate the setting in romantic ways. Stroll past the plumbago and tamarinds to the breakwater known as North Point. There's a tiny gazebo there, just big enough for two, where you can get away from the chatter and laughter. Listen to the waves. Marvel at the water—maybe you'll discover yet another shade of blue.

NAME: Blue Waters Beach Hotel

MANAGER: Hamish Watson

ADDRESS: P.O. Box 256, St. John's, Antigua, W.I.

LOCATION: On the north shore, 15 minutes and $8 by taxi from the airport in one direction, from St. John's in the other

TELEPHONE: 809-462-0290

TELEX: 2066 BLUWTRAK

RESERVATIONS: David B. Mitchell & Company, Inc.

CREDIT CARDS: All major cards

ROOMS: 46 in two-story wings, all with balconies or loggias facing the beach, all with air-conditioning and louvers (some, upper floors, with ceiling fans), stocked refrigerators, closet safes, wall-mounted hair dryers, amenities trays, bathrobes, alarm/radios, telephones

MEALS: Breakfast 7:30–10:00, lunch 12:30–2:30, afternoon tea 4:00–5:00 (only $2.50), dinner 7:00–10:00 (approx. $60 for 2, on the veranda or in the air-conditioned Cacubi Restaurant); barbecue Tuesdays, buffet Fridays, curry brunch Sundays; informal dress; room service during dining room hours, no extra charge

ENTERTAINMENT: 2 bars, dancing, library, video and games room, dancing under the stars to live music 8:00–11:00 ("the bands have been chosen for how quietly they play"—which will be fine as long as the amplification plays as quietly as the band)

SPORTS: 2 beaches and a beachside manmade sandy terrace, freshwater pool, snorkeling, Sunfish sailing, Hobie Cats, pedalos, canoes, tennis (1 court, with lights)—all free; windsurfing you pay for; scuba, yachting, golf nearby

P.S.: Some children occasionally

Curtain Bluff

Antigua

XXX$$$$

Behold: one of the loveliest settings in the Caribbean. A 52-acre headland, lagoon-smooth beach on the leeward side, breezy surfy beach to windward, rocky bluff at the tip. The flowers are brilliant, the trees tall and stately, the lawns primped to the nearest millimeter. And with rooms for just over a hundred vacationers, there's more garden than there're guests.

Curtain Bluff also happens to be one of the most consistently dependable,

top-drawer resorts in the islands, thanks largely to the personality of its owner, the inimitable Howard Hulford. Thirty years ago, when he was piloting planes around the Caribbean for oil company executives, he used to fly over and lust after this south-coast headland, vowing that one day he would build a dream home there. Last year, he and his wife, Chelle, moved into a *spectacular* dream home on the very tip of the bluff; but in the intervening 25 years he had opened, modified, perfected his stylish resort and welcomed people to Howard's Headland year after year, decade after decade.

For some people, though, Curtain Bluff seems to be too cultivated, too country-clubby. You're expected to dress for dinner every evening, including Sunday, and judging by the sartorial splendor guests must send their togs ahead on container ships. Dinner is a serious affair, in an elegant garden pavilion surrounded by lawns, gazebo, Sugar Mill Bar and a dance floor beneath a tamarind tree. Add to that a well-rounded wine cellar that wouldn't look out of place in Beaune and you may decide that dining here is the sort of event that makes all the dressing up worthwhile. Of course, you may also decide to forego the dining room and the combo tootling Gershwin and have your dinner shipped over to your private balcony or patio, if you're lucky enough to snare one of the Hulfords' new suites (there are only six of them).

The suites are located in villas built step-fashion up the landward side of the bluff. Living rooms measure a generous 17 by 20 ft., bedrooms a few feet more; each room (not suite, room) comes with a comfy balcony overlooking the sea, and the suites with duplex configurations also have open dining terraces and secluded patios strung with hammocks. Everything in the suites seems to come in multiples. Two ceiling fans per room (again not suite, but room), plus another in the bathroom. His and Her lighted closets. Twin vanities, 2 double beds. Three, sometimes 4, telephones to a suite. The 1-bedroom suites are fitted with 18 light switches—for fans, vanities, dimmers, terraces and the track lighting that pinpoints gallery-caliber artwork, most of it commissioned for the Bluff. Fabrics and rugs are in delicate pastels, glass doors and screens positively *glide,* oversize rattan sofas and chairs billow with 18 cushions; Italian marble covers the walls and floors and separate shower stalls of the sumptuous bathrooms. Chelle Hulford designed and decorated these suites with great good taste—and has conjured up some of the grandest accommodations in the Caribbean.

The new suites are so exquisite, the Hulfords may have dumped a problem into the laps of their reservations staff: regular guests are going to want to trade up to the suites and there just aren't enough to go around. The remaining rooms, superior and deluxe and hitherto among the best on the island, now look a tad ordinary by comparison. They have more traditional proportions and accoutrements, but they too have had their own dose of prettifying, and now look all spic and span with rattan end tables and chairs, jollier fabrics and circular headboards. To conclude the resort's twenty-fifth anniversary splurge, the leeward beach has acquired a new drinking/dining pavilion, new loungers, new sun umbrellas, new sand chairs (not just a few here and there but one for each guest!). It's all very relaxed and genteel here (most guests don't even bother to lock their doors, since most of them know each other from previous visits), but despite its country-club flavor Curtain Bluff is far from being a pasture for geriatrics.

It's actually one of the sportiest small hotels in the Caribbean (see listing below). And, into the bargain, one of the best values despite what at first glance might seem like stiff rates. Most sports facilities are available at no extra charge. Even waterskiing. Even scuba diving. All you pay extra for is sport fishing or day sails on the resort's vintage yacht *Salamaat.* From its decks, Curtain Bluff looks even more stunningly lovely than it did from the air all those 30 years ago.

NAME: Curtain Bluff

OWNER/MANAGER: Howard Hulford (owner), Edward Sheerin (manager)

ADDRESS: Antigua, W.I.

LOCATION: On the south coast, next to the village of Old Road, 35 bumpy minutes from the airport ($17 by taxi)

TELEPHONE: 809-463-1115/6/7

TELEX: 2070 Curtain AK

RESERVATIONS: Own office, 212-289-8888; Relais Chateau/David B. Mitchell & Company, Inc.

CREDIT CARDS: None

ROOMS: 55, in two-story wings and the 6 new one- and two-bedroom suites, all beachfront with balcony or lanai, bathrooms (amenities trays, bathrobes, showers only in superior rooms), ceiling fans, louvers and screened glass doors, telephone, refrigerators in suites

MEALS: Breakfast 7:30–9:30 (continental 9:30–10:00), lunch 12:30–2:00 (in the open-sided garden pavilion or Beach Hut), dinner 7:30–9:30 (in garden pavilion, approx. $60 for 2); beach barbecue buffet on Wednesday; "we do request jacket and tie for the gentlemen after seven o'clock"; room service 7:30 A.M.–9:30 P.M., no extra charge

ENTERTAINMENT: Bar, lounge, library, parlor games, live music for dancing in the dining room every evening (combos, native bands, etc., amplified but not loud), steel band with beachside buffet

SPORTS: 2 beaches (1 windward, 1 leeward), hammocks, snorkeling, scuba, waterskiing, Sunfish sailing, seascopes (for fish watching), reef trips, tennis (4 courts, pro shop, no lights), putting green—all free; sport fishing and day sails on the resort's own 47-ft. sailboat cost extra

P.S.: "Please, no children in the bar after seven"; mid-May features a very popular pro-am tennis tournament

Copper & Lumber Store

Antigua

🌴🌴🌴XX$$

Four of the Caribbean's most stunning, most unusual suites can be found, not beside a beach, but in a dockyard—Nelson's Dockyards.

Don't let that faze you. No cranes and clatter, no grease and goo here—this is the National Park kind of dockyard, the former headquarters of

Britain's navy back in the days when Lord Nelson was still Captain Horatio.

The revered hero/admiral was billeted in a wood-frame mansion (now a museum), between the engineers' workshop (now the Admiral's Inn) and the warehouse that is now the dockyard's second inn, the Copper & Lumber Store. On a hillside across English Harbour stands Clarence House, the home of Nelson's buddy, the Duke of Clarence (Princess Margaret stayed here on her honeymoon); higher up the hill, on Shirley Heights, the former barracks have been restored as a museum, and on the battlements there's a pleasant pub/restaurant with panoramic views of mountains and yacht-filled harbor. For yachting buffs, Nelson's harbor is the Caribbean's most popular, best-equipped marina and revictualling base.

Throw open your shutters in the morning and you look out on a stunning setting of bollards and capstans, masts and rigging. The pride of the world's yacht builders spread out all around you—classic schooners from Maine, sleek 70-ft. ocean cruisers from Cowes, a brand-new ketch from Rio de Janeiro, mammoth power boats laden with antennae, radar scanners, flying bridges and unseamanlike names. Most of them are charter yachts, and many of the people staying or dining at either of the dockyard's inns are waiting to ship out—or have just returned from a cruise, unsteady of gait, getting back to normal before returning to the twentieth century.

The Copper & Lumber Store, in its current incarnation, is a sturdy, two-story structure in Georgian/Admiralty style, built of native stone and hefty rough-hewn timbers that wouldn't have looked out of place on a ship-of-the-line.

In keeping with its heritage, the four-year-old Copper & Lumber Store's owner/manager is, in Winston Churchill's memorable phrase, "a former naval person"—Commander Gordon Gutteridge R.N., Retired. In true mariner manner, young Gutteridge ran away to sea aboard a sailing ship, the *John and May Garnett* out of Chester; later he was an experimental (and not unheroic) diver in the Royal Navy; most recently he ran an industrial gas operation from the British Virgins. Apparently his wife, Gill, had a hankering for running a country house hotel in Wales but their navigation was flawed and they ended up in Antigua. With his bushy seadog eyebrows and commanding air, the Commander comes across to some people as gruff, but he is, in reality, a congenial, entertaining host and he and his wife run a tight ship.

Their "office" is a desk under the stairs. Not just any desk, but a sturdy seventeenth-century *escritorio* carted off as booty from a Spanish galleon. The lobby (weathered brick floor and walls, Oriental rugs, beamed ceilings, buttoned red leather wing chairs, breezes fore and aft) serves as an informal lounge/bar and opens onto the newest feature of the inn—the cloisterlike patio restaurant, its warehouse doors opening to the lawns and marina. The pub menu features traditional English items such as Scotch egg, Cumberland sausages, mango chutney, pickled onions and assorted cheeses. A welcome bargain, too, for these parts—$4.50–$7.50. (As of this writing, the pub menu is available in the evening also, augmented by more ambitious daily specials.)

All the guest rooms have views of the harbor and yachts in one direction or another, all are furnished with antiques and period pieces accenting the basic decor of raw brick and ceiling beams. Gill Gutteridge herself did all the hand stenciling and sewed most of the fabrics, but there's nothing "homemade" about the interiors. Even Nelson didn't live in such style.

The *pièces de résistance* are the 4 Georgian suites—Africa, Victory (1-bedroom suites) and Royal Sovereign and Brittania (studio suites), named for ships in Nelson's fleet. Africa, for example, is adorned with 200-year-old paintings, 400-year-old charts and a display of antique Wedgwood. The floor sports hand-stenciled pineapple motifs, the paneling is Philippine oak, the wallpapers and fabrics are replicas of 200-year-old patterns, the document chest is made of camphor wood on a steel frame. In the sleeping loft all the furnishings are authentic Chippendale, except for the double beds, which are replicas. What sets these 3 suites apart, though, are their bathrooms—paneling of Honduras mahogany, washbasins of Argentine brass, shower stalls of Welsh slate. It's all done with a sympathetic feeling for authenticity.

Although most people who stay here are overnighting, before or after cruises, these are suites to settle into for several days. Take time to explore the battlements on foot, for the 5-minute boat trip to the beaches in the outer harbor, to visit Shirley Heights for lunch, to row among the yachts at sunset. English Harbour was a "hurricane hole" for sailing ships, but the fact that it's so sheltered doesn't necessarily mean it's going to be hot and sticky; you can spend time there even in the summer without feeling uncomfortable.

There are several restaurants within walking distance of the Copper & Lumber (none of them, frankly, outstanding but at least they have some atmosphere); but there's less reason than hereto for eating out, now that the Copper & Lumber gives you the convenience of private pantries *and* the new restaurant.

NAME: Copper & Lumber Store

OWNER/MANAGER: Gordon and Gill Gutteridge

ADDRESS: P.O. Box 184, St. Johns, Antigua, W.I.

LOCATION: Anchored in the middle of Nelson's Dockyard in English Harbour, 25 minutes and $16 by taxi from the airport or St. Johns

TELEPHONE: 809-463-1058

TELEX: Antigua 2119 Yachts AK, attention Copper & Lumber Store

RESERVATIONS: None

CREDIT CARDS: American Express, MasterCard, Visa

ROOMS: 14, all suites (including 3 studio suites and 4 deluxe Georgian suites), all different, all with private bathrooms (showers only), kitchens (refrigerators stocked on request, commissary nearby), ceiling fans

MEALS: Breakfast 8:00–10:00, lunch noon–3:00, afternoon tea, dinner 7:00–10:00 in a courtyard restaurant overlooking the yachts and cooled by breezes and ceiling fans; pub lunch for 2 approximately $12, dinner for 2 $15–30; informal dress (but no shorts in the evening); taped classical eighteenth-century music; room service for breakfast only; C&L guests can also sign for meals at Admiral's Inn and the Inn at English Harbour

ENTERTAINMENT: The bar/lounge of the inn is popular with visiting yacht people, and it's not unknown to have an erudite conversation on Reaganomics continue into the wee hours; parlor games (Scrabble, wari, chess, darts, cribbage, shoveha'penny, backgammon); inn library with satellite TV and VCR

SPORTS: Beaches nearby (the inn will supply beach towels and arrange for a launch to the beach of the Inn at English Harbour, 5 minutes away across the bay); boats for rent, tennis across the bay, scuba and snorkeling by arrangement

---

The Admiral's Inn

Antigua

$$

In Nelson's pre-admiral days as commander-in-chief of the dockyard, this two-story weathered brick structure was an unglamorous corner of his domain—the storehouse for turpentine and pitch. You'd never suspect it today. It's now a lovely 25-year-old inn in a most unusual setting. A well-worn stone patio, set with tables and chairs, shaded by sun umbrellas and casuarina trees, leads to a lawn that ends at the water's edge. Just off to the right, a row of sturdy but stunted stone pillars are all that remain of the former boathouse, decapitated in a long-ago earthquake, and just beyond that another section of the dockyard has become an annex with 5 more guest rooms. Yachts lie at their moorings a few oar strokes offshore, and somewhere behind you the market ladies of English Harbour have hung the old stone walls with batiks and T-shirts, necklaces and baubles.

The inn's lobby is a tiny desk beneath the stairs in a beamy lounge, bar on one side facing French doors that lead to the dining terrace. A dart board adds the right Royal Navy touch, the burgees of a hundred yachts and yacht clubs remind you that the Admiral's Inn is a favorite gathering place for sailing buffs. If the Flying Dutchmen were to come ashore again one of these days, this would be a sensible place for them to come ashore and search for a latter-day Senta.

Being a gathering place for yachtsmen and yachtswomen, the inn may not be the serenest of hideaways, but it has a lot of charm and camaraderie. Guest rooms are small, simply but tastefully furnished, decked with Williamsburg fabrics by Schumacher, cooled by ceiling fans or air conditioners. The prime nest (indeed, one of the prettiest in all of Antigua) is number 1, a large corner chamber with lacy curtains, khuskhus rugs and canopied four-poster king-size bed (all the others are twins). Since it's right at the head of the stairs, number 1 gets a certain amount of inn traffic outside its doors, and since it's directly above the bar it picks up some of the chatter and jollity from rendezvousing voyagers. But the carousing generally ends around midnight, and then all you hear when you throw open the window shutters is the clank of the rigging on the sailboats.

The five rooms across the boatyard are a shade quieter—smallish in floor space but with high ceilings, whitewashed stone walls, built-in dressers, modern plumbing, fans and air conditioners. Room A is the biggest, and being at the harbor end of the row with louvered windows on three sides, is also the brightest and breeziest.

Even if you don't have time to stay here, stop in for a drink on the broad terrace. Or a meal—indoors beneath iron chandeliers, outdoors beneath the lacy casuarinas. The service is dilatory, the meals often disappointing, but the surroundings are delightful. It's another century. Even if the yachts have aluminum rather than wooden masts.

NAME: The Admiral's Inn

MANAGER: Miss Ethelyn Philip

ADDRESS: English Harbour, P.O. Box 713, St. John's, Antigua, W.I.

LOCATION: In Nelson's Dockyard national park, on Antigua's south coast; 16 miles directly across the island from the airport (40 minutes and $18 by taxi) and 14 miles from St. John's (30 minutes, $10 by taxi)

TELEPHONE: 809-463-1027

TELEX: None

RESERVATIONS: American International

CREDIT CARDS: None

ROOMS: 14, all with private bathrooms (showers only); 8 with air-conditioning, all others with ceiling fans, some with patios

MEALS: Breakfast 7:30–10:00, lunch noon–2:00, dinner 7:30–9:00 (approx. \$50 for 2, served indoors or on the terrace); casual dress (but not scruffy, despite the proximity of all those yachts); room service by special arrangement

ENTERTAINMENT: Combo Thursdays (in season), steel band Saturdays, dancing, some taped music, darts

SPORTS: Launch to beach at other end of harbor, snorkeling gear, Sunfish sailing—free; water sports, boat trips, tennis and golf nearby

P.S.: Some (sometimes lots of) cruise ship passengers, since you're right in the middle of what tourists come all the way across the island to see; especially busy during Sailing Week (late April, early May) and charter yacht review week (early December)

P.P.S.: The Inn's sister establishment, Falmouth Harbour Beach Apartments, is located 5 minutes away in the next bay; 25 twin-bedded apartments come with kitchenettes, private verandas and maid service—and bargain rates (\$80 double in winter 1986–1987)—but the beach is a 5-minute walk away

The Inn at English Harbour

Antigua

Rather than follow the low road to English Harbour take the road to Shirley Heights. Up there, among the fortress ruins and the dramatic views of the outer harbor, you'll also find a tiny sign with eighteenth-century script identifying the inn. Turn off, go down the hill and there, among the flowering shrubs and fruit trees, you come upon a lodge with a few cottages nestled among the trees. Actually, this is only the upstairs of this upstairs/downstairs inn, with the bulk of the rooms all the way down the hill beside the beach. No, you won't have to trek all the way up again for a drink or a lunch: there's a bar/restaurant on the beach. And when it's time for dinner upstairs, the lodge will send a minibus to collect you.

Hilltop or beach, the rooms don't vary much in terms of decor or facilities: island-style rush rugs, a blend of wicker and motel-modern furniture, bathrooms with separate showers and vanities, ceiling fans and balcony or patio. But where you unpack your bags can make a difference: if you want breezes and view—hilltop; if you want the sea a toe-skip away—the beach; if you want to isolate yourselves as much as possible from fellow guests—hilltop cottages or rooms 8, 9, 28 or 29 in the beach cottages (which have no second floor).

Not that there's anything unwelcome about your fellow guests. Judging by all the copies of *Punch* and *Country Life* lying around the lounge, the darts and skittles in the pub, most of the guests here seem to be English. And if you want to waft yourselves to Cornwall rather than Antigua, listen to the accents during the traditional afternoon tea.

One of the Inn's most famous guests was actually a Welshman, whose honeymoon visit is commemorated by the Richard Burton Memorial Table on the terrace, a cozy table for two, on its own little promontory, screened by a palm tree and with a majestic view over the entire harbor, the hills and the seas beyond.

Given the choice, I'd opt for staying with the view and making occasional forays to the beach, rather than vice versa.

NAME: The Inn at English Harbour

OWNER: Peter Deeth

ADDRESS: P.O. Box 187, St. John's, Antigua, W.I.

LOCATION: On the bay called English Harbour, on the south coast, 16 miles, 40 minutes and $16 by taxi from the airport, slightly less from St. John's

TELEPHONE: 4631014

CABLES/TELEX: Boreas Antigua/2063 AK

RESERVATIONS: American International; Robert Reid Assoc.

CREDIT CARDS: None

ROOMS: 28; 22 on the beach, 6 on the hill, ceiling fans and breezes; tiled bathrooms, balcony or patio

MEALS: Breakfast 7:30–10:30, lunch 12:30–2:30, afternoon tea 4:00, dinner 7:30–9:30 (approx. $30 for 2, on the hilltop terrace, or indoors on breezy nights); informal dress (but no shorts at dinner); room service 7:30 A.M.–11:00 P.M., no extra charge

ENTERTAINMENT: Taped music, steel band, combo, dancing, barbecues

SPORTS: Beach, snorkeling, windsurfing, scuba, Sunfish sailing, boat trips; tennis, golf, bikes and horses nearby

P.S.: *Closed September 15 to October 25*

Half Moon Bay Hotel

Antigua

$$

On an island famed for its extravagance of beautiful beaches, here is one of the most beautiful. Fortunately for us all, these pristine sands were spotted back in the forties by zillionaire Paul Mellon, who chose an adjoining headland for his members-only Mill Reef Club, which preserves one end of the half moon. At the other, this less snooty but tasteful, low-key resort.

Obviously, with a beach like this, Half Moon is heaven for sun worshippers—idle or active. If you want calm waters, flop down in front of the hotel. If you want breezes and surf, walk half a mile along the soft white sand and you've got what you want, without having to share it with more than a few other couples.

But Half Moon is also a mecca for tennis buffs. Singer Elton John often drops in during the January Tennis Weeks, which attract stars from two continents. Regular guests have a chance to attend clinics with the stars—or play in their pro-am tournaments.

That's not the end of Half Moon's sporty attractions, either; there's also golf. Not on the scale of Dorado Beach or Casa de Campo, of course, just a challenging but hardly exhausting nine holes up and down the slopes above the beach.

In such a setting—palm-fringed beach, a 150-acre estate—a hotel doesn't have to draw attention to itself with stunning architecture and this one certainly doesn't do that. Four two-story guest wings flank a breezy core built around a glistening free-form swimming pool. The poolside bar and lunch terrace lead to a lounge (popular with card players) and separate games room (the pool table looks a bit scrawny), then to a two-tiered dining room dressed in the hotel's trademark blues and whites.

Most of the guest rooms face the beach, with a few yards of lawn between your private patio and the sand; and of these, the best are in the new streamlined wing. Stylish furnishings don't seem to be high on the list of musts for Half Moonies, who keep coming back year after year (in winter, most of the guests are repeaters, mostly American). What they *are* interested in is dependable service and cuisine. They get both. Manager Keith Woodhouse is now in his thirteenth year here, the French-Swiss chef, Claude Barrière, even longer; and many of the 190 people on the payroll have become virtually personal retainers for the guests they've been attending to for generations.

Half Moon is not as classy as Curtain Bluff or as luxurious as Jumby Bay or as chic as St. James Club, but it has its own charms. Not least of them, of course, that expanse of soft white sand.

NAME: Half Moon Bay Hotel

MANAGER: (Not available at press time)

ADDRESS: P.O. Box 144, St. John's, Antigua, W.I.

LOCATION: On Half Moon Bay, on the island's southeast coast, 17 miles from the airport (45 minutes, $20 by taxi), about the same from St. John's

TELEPHONE: 809-463-2101/2

TELEX: 2138 JOHNANJO

RESERVATIONS: Robert Reid Assoc.

CREDIT CARDS: American Express

ROOMS: 100 in two-story wings plus 2 suites and 1 two-bedroom cottage, all with ceiling fans, showers only in most bathrooms, color TV/VCR (to be installed by winter 1987–1988)

MEALS: Breakfast 7:30–9:30, lunch 12:30–2:30, dinner 7:30–9:30 ($64 for 2), all served in an airy, glass-enclosed room overlooking the beach; informal dress (but no shorts or T-shirts), jacket and tie customary on weekends in season; room service for breakfast only, no extra charge

ENTERTAINMENT: Music every evening (mostly live, steel band, guitarist, combo, piano), dancing, some taped music, limbo dancing, barbecues and buffets (the St. James's Club is 20 minutes away if you want to go gambling)

SPORTS: Crescent-shaped beach (calm waters at one end, surf at the other), 78-ft. freshwater pool, snorkeling (gear provided), Sunfish sailing, windsurfing, tennis (5 Laykold courts, 2 with lights, pro shop), golf (9 holes, par 34)—all free; certified windsurfing instructor and simulator (extra charge), scuba and boat trips available nearby

P.S.: Open year round; no children under 4 during peak season

St. James's Club

Antigua

$$$$

"I don't collect antiques, I don't collect art, I enjoy having clubs and sharing them with people who like the things I like," explains Peter de Savary. The youthful English tycoon is probably wealthy enough to spend the rest of his days lounging on the deck of his America's Cup yacht; instead he has invested millions of dollars and lots of time and labor into making the Antigua club as chic and luxurious as its tony namesake in London.

The St. James's Club opened with great fanfare in 1985 and the staff had a chance to polish their act in front of inaugural celebrities such as Joan Collins, Michael York and Liza Minnelli. Elton John, David Frost and the Duke of Kent checked in shortly afterward and ever since the glitzy flow has continued unabated. What's the big attraction? At first glance, it's hardly the physical plant, which started out in the sixties as a formula two-story resort, first class rather than deluxe. Hardly an architectural gem, with little romantic character, the mildly Polynesian rooflines notwithstanding. But de Savary and his crew set about transforming this unpromising assortment of structures into a club worthy of the name St. James with 60,000 flowering shrubs, trees and plants carted in for camouflage. Indoors, however, all is spic and span and shipshape. Custom fabrics, bamboo étagères with bird figurines, bamboo four-posters and Dominican paintings add a dash of distinction to these basically standard-size rooms. In the suites, the double doors between bedrooms and sitting areas have been turned into graphic eye-catchers with hand-painted tropical flowers.

From the de Savary arsenal of nice touches come wicker baskets with toiletries, specially milled and wrapped soaps, fluffy white towels woven with the club insignia and white kimonos for each guest. Of the St. James's three residential blocks your best bet is probably Poinciana (rooms 180–190), if you want privacy, with balconies looking out to sea; Hibiscus (rooms 100–109), if you prefer to be close to the ocean beach and the tennis

courts (but avoid the ground floor rooms or you'll have a steady stream of sun worshippers trotting past your balcony); Bougainvillea (rooms 160–179), if you want a sea view but still like to be close to bars and restaurants. If you'd rather have breezes than air-conditioning, be warned that some of the lower rooms have a restricted flow of air. The quietest rooms of all are 14 and 15, in a string of villas with none-too-private patios, on a small peninsula facing Mamora Bay, a sheltered lagoon. The best quarters in the hotel, for anyone with moolah to spare, is the Roof Garden Suite, on the upper floor of the Poinciana block—the terrace is as large as the suite itself, ideal for very private sunbathing.

Two years ago, the resort decked the hillside behind the lagoon with 73 new cottages, all 2-bedroom, full-kitchen units, more plushly furnished than the hotel rooms. Since these cottages are priced for foursomes rather than twosomes (and since they're somewhat huddled together), you'll probably still prefer the hotel itself. But that still leaves the question: What do all these additional accommodations do to the overall ambiance of the club? They don't help, that's for sure. Unless you're interested in more action: With the additional rooms come a larger lagoon (twice the size of the original, or so it seemed to these eyes), more water sports equipment, 2 more tennis courts (for a total of 7) and a striking new multilevel bar/ restaurant, Savary's, for breakfast and dinner.

To oversee the upkeep of all these rooms and the comfort of his guests de Savary wisely installed a team of proven professionals. For his manager he went all the way to Bangkok and the esteemed Oriental Hotel to find Englishman Gregory Meadows. And to motivate his staff (not the easiest of projects in these parts) he instigated a system of bonuses: each day, management distributes a few tokens among the guests, who are invited to pass them along to waiters, maids, whoever, for exceptional performance. Since the tokens carry a cash bonus but the staff have no idea which guests will be making the decision, everyone is, at least in theory, treated like a VIP.

A few drawbacks aside (the food in the main dining room is disappointing, the Dockside Terrace is much more fun) few resorts offer guests so many diversions. Some may have horseback riding, but how many can boast stables with a dozen Texas quarter horses? Or seven tennis courts, and pro, *and* lights? Or a full-fledged marina with customs office? Or a casino? A small casino, for sure, but restricted to hotel guests and a few local members, this being in theory a private club. So for vacationers who want more than a patch of sand and the shade of a palm, the St. James's Club's hundred acres would seem to be as generous as they come—especially when you consider that most of the facilities come at no extra charge.

NAME: St. James's Club

MANAGER: Gregory Meadows

ADDRESS: P.O. Box 63, St. John's, Antigua, W.I.

LOCATION: At Mamora Bay, on the south coast, 30 minutes and $20 by taxi from the airport (the club has a rep at the airport to meet guests)

TELEPHONE: 809-463-1430

TELEX: 2088 STJCLUB

RESERVATIONS: First Resorts Management

CREDIT CARDS: All major cards

ROOMS: 105, including 15 suites, 5 villas (studios, 1 or 2 bedrooms) plus the 73 new 2-bedroom hillside condominium cottages, all with balconies or patios, air-conditioning and ceiling fans, telephones, bathrobes, amenities trays; suites with refrigerators, cottages with full kitchens

MEALS: Breakfast 7:30–10:00, lunch 11:30–3:30 (by the pool or beside the dock), dinner 7:30–10:30 (anywhere from $30 up, in 1 of 3 restaurants);

jackets for men for dinner in the formal dining rooms, casual on the terrace restaurants, but "guests are expected to be attractively attired at all times"; 24-hour room service (in hotel, not cottages)

ENTERTAINMENT: Something every evening—cocktail piano, combo, video disco, casino (blackjack, roulette, 1 crap table, 30 slot machines), pool table

SPORTS: 2 beaches (1 ocean, 1 lagoon), 2 freshwater pools (1 Olympic-size), Jacuzzi, gymnasium (Nautilus, weights, etc.), snorkeling, windsurfing, Sunfish sailing, catamarans, Lasers, pedalos, surfjets, waterskiing, glass-bottom boat trips, tennis (7 Laykold courts, lights, All-American pro shop)—all free; massage, horseback riding (with guides), scuba diving and sport fishing extra

Added Attractions

Cliffdwellers

Tamarind Bay, Nevis

If you don't mind a little legwork, you'll be well rewarded here—with a splendid view out to The Narrows and St. Kitts. This snug, cliffside enclave nestles around the sides of a 150-ft.-high volcano (extinct, don't worry), its spacious rooms, each with balcony, modern bathrooms (half tub/shower, hot water) and separate dressing rooms, spread out over half a dozen cottages. There's a small but erratic tramway that can shuttle you up and down from bedroom to beach, but you may be better off just hiking it on down to the sea, pool or tennis court. And when you hike back up, you'll find Cliffdwellers' comfortable (terrazzo, rattan and wraparound view) hillside terrace the perfect place to put your feet up, order a rum punch and watch the sun go down. 14 rooms. *Cliffdwellers, Tamarind Bay, Nevis, W.I. Telephone: 809-465-5262; U.S. telephone: 617-262-3654.*

Croney's Old Manor Estate

Nevis

At Croney's Old Manor Estate, you'll be whiling away your hours in a romantic, almost sultry hideaway burgeoning with monkey-no-climb and gooseberry trees. Owner Vicki Knorr and her son, Gregg, have revitalized the place, said to be the island's oldest continually inhabited plantation, with weathered gear wheels and pistons, the metal sculptures from another era, dotting the grounds.

Guest rooms are grouped around the Sugar Mill and the Great House; number 3 in the Admiral's House is a terrazzo-floored duplex with a king-size bed draped in mosquito netting; number 4 in the Executive House (the former blacksmith shop) is a cheery stone-walled suite, also with marble terrazzo and a bed tucked away in a cozy alcove.

When you tire of hiking around the slopes of Mt. Nevis or lolling around the Croney's tropically foliaged 40-ft. pool, you may start to think about dinner. And you're in the right place. Croney's is lauded for its dining room (the Knorrs even grow their own spinach and lettuce in what used to be the settling tanks).

In the breezy Cooperage Dining Room, surrounded by flamboyant trees, you can enjoy a tasty dish of shrimp dipped in coconut and sautéed with fruit juice and soy sauce, followed by a "Sinful Pie," coffee mousse with whipped cream and walnuts. Lobster's on the menu as much as possible (there's a special Friday night lobster and steak buffet). With such popular dining facilities, Croney's is probably the least "clubby" of the island's inns, especially in the evenings. 10 rooms. *Croney's Old Manor Estate, P.O. Box 70, Charlestown, Nevis, W.I. Telephone: 809-469-5445.*

Zetland Plantation

Nevis

A thousand feet above the sea, a park rather than a garden, this one-time plantation is dotted with cottages and two-story "chalets," some with three separate rooms, the two newest (1986) with four deluxe suites and shared plunge pools. Higher in Zetland's 750 acres of foothills, the estate's new owner/partner, Nigel Frazer (a retired British Army major and the staff had better believe it) and his new English manager, Nigel Adams, are building a few more one-of-a-kind private homes. The dining/lounging areas are attractive (refurbished in 1986), the gardens are spacious (with pool and tennis court), and children are now "discouraged" during the peak season. *Zetland Plantation, P.O. Box 448, Nevis, W.I. Telephone: 809-469-5454.*

Hermitage

Nevis

Horatio Nelson found it to his liking, we're told. So did Alexander Hamilton. And so do a bevy of contemporary knights and lawyers, actors and rock singers.

Certainly the place has been around long enough to have welcomed Nelson and Hamilton. The 245-year-old great house, all shingles and rafters and in remarkably fine fettle for its age, is more or less the original. Its laden lobby leads to a spacious lounge furnished with Victoriana and period pieces, the setting for house party–style gatherings before the lemon soup and beef Wellington (prepared with local beef), or after the cold rum soufflé. A brand-new dining veranda, just off the lounge, blends nicely with its surroundings. The Stable and Carriage House, in traditional Nevis style, houses a quartet of guest rooms; the remaining rooms are in a pair of newly built concrete villas in the garden, up the hill a few paces behind the swimming pool. Decor features four-poster beds (on a wood-and-foam base), Schumacher bedspreads with a pastoral pattern, frilly pillowcases and sturdy wardrobes, showers rather than tubs in the bathrooms. The newest rooms have kitchenettes.

Like so many Nevis plantations, Hermitage sits high in the hills, in a garden terraced by stone walls, flowering shrubs and fruit trees—tangerine and lime, tamarind and grapefruit and soursop.

Owners/managers Maureen and Richard Lupinacci built a reputation for fine cooking and genial hospitality when they ran the nearby Zetlands Plantation. They have quite a following, and their infectious charm brings "their" guests back year after year. Sometimes guests will gather around the veteran piano after dinner, sometimes they'll get involved in party games. But the Hermitage is the tropical cousin of a quiet little country inn in Vermont. So peaceful, movie producers settle in there for a week or two to work on scripts and shooting schedules. It's also moderately priced, a fact that wouldn't be lost on Alexander Hamilton if he were around today. 12 rooms. *The Hermitage, Nevis, St. Kitts and Nevis, W.I. Telephone: 809-465-5477. No credit cards.*

Ocean Terrace Inn

Basseterre, St. Kitts

Overlooks the entire town of Basseterre and South Friar's Bay, packing 30 guest rooms, 6 two-bedroom and 2 one-bedroom apartments into a garden setting beside the bay, on the edge of town. On the bayside there is also the new Fisherman's Village with 11 efficiency apartments. There are 2 freshwater pools, 1 with swim-up bar and an open-air Jacuzzi in the garden; guests are offered free transportation to nearby beaches, casino and 18-hole golf course. There are also free daily boat trips to a secluded beach for snorkeling and membership in the local tennis club (an attractive prospect for people who want to meet Kittitians rather than play serious tennis). 51 units. *Ocean Terrace Inn, Box 65, Fortlands, St. Kitts, W.I. Telephone: 809-465-2754. Telex: 6821 OTI KC.*

Banana Bay Beach Resort

St. Kitts

If your lover makes a living trading commodities futures or producing TV shows or something equally frenetic, take him/her here to unwind. Real escapist stuff, this. No telephones—the office can't call. No roads—no hopping into a taxi and heading for the nearest telex. Banana Bay is on the most easterly tip of St. Kitts, and only a few miles from Bassettere as the booby bird flies, but the only way to get there is a 45-minute trip by launch and Jeep (or a 20-minute boat trip from Oualie Beach on neighboring Nevis). Once there, there's nothing to do. Two lovely curves of beach, one of which you may have to share with wild monkeys. You can sail or windsurf. Or snorkel. Or read. The day is usually over by nine, unless someone suggests another round of passion fruit punch or another game of Scrabble.

The guest rooms are surprisingly stylish for this neck of the woods, located in two of the resort's three island-style bungalows. The inn was taken over at the beginning of 1987 by Colin Pereira of Ocean Terrace Inn, together with the adjoining seven-room Cockleshell. Refurbishing was still going on while this edition was being prepared, but latest reports are that only minor changes are being made, and most of them are improvements. 15 rooms. *OTI Banana Bay Beach Resort, Box 65, St. Kitts and Nevis, W.I. Telephone: 809-465-2754. No credit cards.*

Cul de Sac

Anguilla

Until recently, it was a moderately priced offshoot of Malliouhana, but it now has new owners, new chef, new menu, new decor—all arriving too late to be checked out for this issue. The inn perches beside the coral, between two swatches of sand on the south shore, close to the ferryboat landing. It's small (just six rooms)—the rooms themselves are relatively small but with kitchenettes—and the whole place revolves around a breezy terrace bar/restaurant that will feature Italian cuisine. Pool, limited water sports. 6 rooms, $165 EP. *Cul de Sac, Blowing Point, Anguilla, B.W.I. U.S. telephone: 212-696-1323 or 800-372-1323.*

Coccoloba Plantation

Anguilla

One of *two* deluxe resorts scheduled to open on Anguilla for the winter 1987-1988 season (see also Cap Juluca below), Coccoloba is actually a welcome reincarnation of a four-year-old resort, La Sante, that threw in the towel even before it had worked up a sweat. Location surely wasn't the problem—a charmed spot on a bluff above two lovely beaches. New owners have put the resort in the care of manager David Brewer (formerly of Rockresorts and Antigua's Jumby Bay), which, for many Caribbean buffs, is recommendation enough to go there; noted designer Carleton Varney is putting light and life into the hitherto dreary public spaces and beachside villas; a quarter of a million dollars is going into landscaping. Guest rooms have ceiling fans *and* air-conditioning, refrigerators and oversize bathrooms; sports facilities include a big pool with swim-up bar, Jacuzzi, tennis (the Peter Burwash people will be in charge) and an extensive range of water sports (including windsurfing and sailing). 50 rooms and suites, $290 to $460. *Coccoloba Plantation, P.O. Box 332, Barnes Bay, Anguilla, B.W.I.*

Cap Juluca

Anguilla

Another newcomer with not one but two beaches, this resort is on the southwest corner of the island, facing St. Maarten. Named appropriately for the Rainbow God of the Arawak Indians, it's the culmination of a longtime dream of Robin and Sue Ricketts, the English couple who first got Malliouhana off the ground; their resort began with a striking Moorish-style bar/restaurant, "Pimms," that has been serving acclaimed cuisine since December 1986. Cap Juluca's luxury beachside rooms and suites have ceiling fans *and* air-conditioning, patios/terraces, stocked refrigerators, bathrooms with private landscaped "gardens"; sports facilities include tennis (2 lighted courts), snorkeling, waterskiing, windsurfing and sailing. 18 rooms (60 more to come later), $225 to $375, including continental breakfast. *Cap Juluca, P.O. Box 240, Maundy's Bay, Anguilla, B.W.I. Telephone 809-497-6779.*

Note: I'll bring you updated reports on these and other new resorts in my newsletter, *Very Special Places* (see page 336 for details).

Vue Pointe

Montserrat

The view is coastline, black sand beach, a nine-hole golf course among the coconut palms, a few private villas on the hillside across the valley. The hotel consists of hexagonal rondavels on a grassy slope above the sea, each individual unit with fifties furniture, sitting area, shower and deck screened by flowering shrubs. It's comfortable, sensible—the Caribbean in its unspoiled simplicity. The main lodge houses a large bar/lounge/terrace and so-so dining room. Don't come here for haute cuisine but for peace and quiet and friendly folks. Since the owner is an eager tennis player, the hotel has two of the best-kept tennis courts in the Caribbean—with lights! There's a water sports facility on the beach, a pool up on the hill, and that uncrowded little golf course in the valley. 28 rooms. *Vue Pointe, Olde Town, Montserrat, W.I. Telephone: 809-491-5210.*

Galley Bay Surf Club

Antigua

Edee Holbert might almost have had this guidebook in mind when she envisioned her hideaway 20 years ago. Here's a place designed for lovers! Well, half a place.

On a secluded bay just west of town, Galley Bay sits between a marshy lagoon and a beautiful crescent of sand protected by a pair of headlands and rimmed with palms and sea grape. The centerpiece is a soaring timber pavilion in Polynesian style, with a grand piano and planters' armchairs (you know, the kind with an "armrest" for your legs and a holder for your rum), with a breezy beachside dining patio only a couple of steps away.

Half the club's guests check into so-called Beach Suites, directly on the beach but the kind of so-so rooms you've seen hundreds of times. The lovers' part of Galley Bay, the romantic fizz in Edee Holbert's dream, is across the lawn, beside the marsh-cum-lagoon, in the Gauguin Villas—a dozen dens in thatched Polynesian style, each consisting of two circular huts (one for sleeping, one for bathing) connected by a shoulder-high breezeway. Come off the beach, head for the shower to wash away the sand, then a quick towelless skip across the breezeway to bed. Native prints, bedspreads and wall hangings brighten up the cool, sunless interiors.

Galley Bay has lost some of its house-party verve in recent years, but it's still a nice quiet escape for people who want an unhurried, unfussy beachy lifestyle. 28 units. *Galley Bay Surf Club, P.O. Box 305, St. John's, Antigua, W.I. Telephone: 20302.*

Note: At press time, the Club had just been acquired by new owners.

The French West Indies

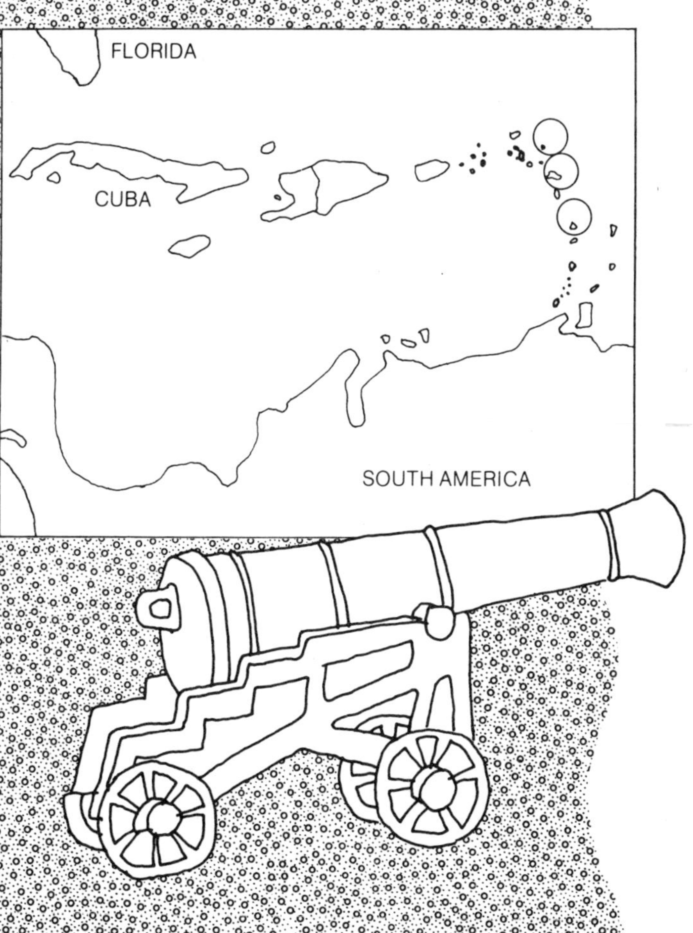

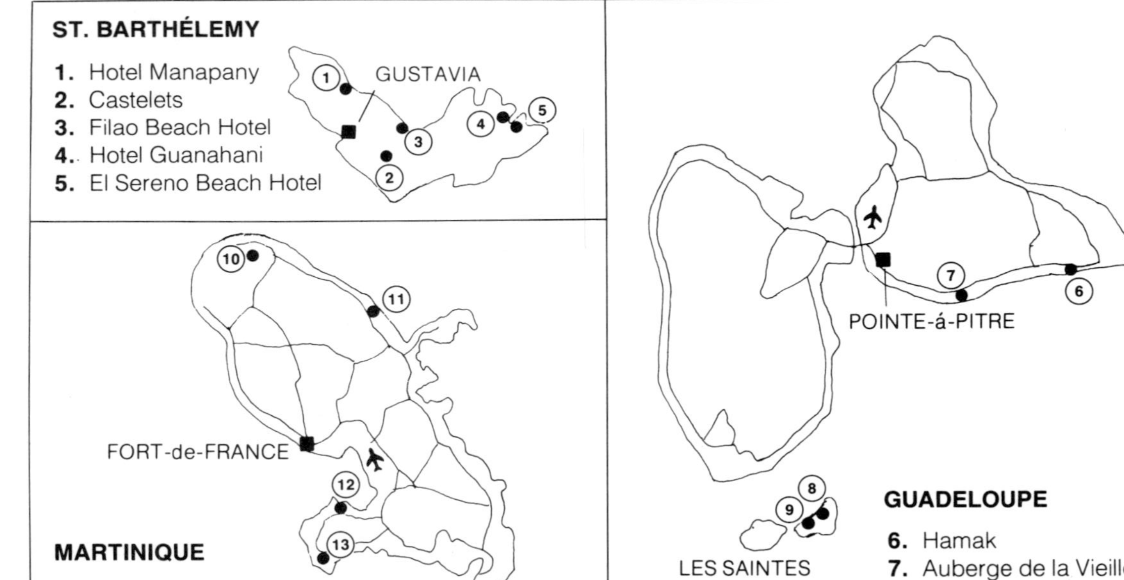

THE FRENCH WEST INDIES

The French West Indies

The *tricouleur* flutters over and micro-bikinis wiggle on Martinique, Guadeloupe, St. Martin (the French half of the island otherwise known as Sint Maarten), St. Barthélemy and a few out-islands; French *savoir-faire* and *joie de vivre* have been transplanted intact—in fact, they may even have gained from overlays of tropical sensuousness. You'll find some of the best eating in the Caribbean here, some of the sportiest highways, the most stylish dressers and, on the nudist beaches, the most enthusiastic undressers. These are great islands, or integral political units, of *la belle France.*

The largest of the islands is Martinique (48 miles long and 20 miles wide), a lush, mountainous land with rain forests, plantations, fishing villages and masses of wildflowers. It has enjoyed centuries of renown for its dusky maidens: Napoleon's Josephine is the most famous, but Martinique has also provided queens and consorts for a dozen other rulers—including Louis XIV and the Grand Turk of Stamboul. Fort-de-France, the capital, is an intriguing mishmash of West Indies seaport, the latest Peugeots, fishing boats, yachts, open-air markets, high fashion, and gourmet restaurants; but the most interesting part of the island for my money is the spectacular north around Mont Pelée, especially the tower of St. Pierre, once known as the Paris of the Caribbean, before it was destroyed when Pelée erupted one Sunday morning in 1902. The highway/road/path along the rugged northeast coast to remote Grand' Rivière is also worth an excursion and picnic.

Guadeloupe (from the Spanish "Guadalupe" and the Arabic "Oued-el-Houb," meaning River of Love) is really two islands, Grande-Terre and Basse-Terre, linked by a short bridge. The capital is also known as Basse-Terre, away in the south, shut off from the rest of the island by the magnificent Natural Park of Guadeloupe. But the action is up around Pointe-à-Pitre, which is rapidly beginning to look like a suburb of Paris. When *les citoyens* of Point-à-Pitre want to get away from it all, they head south to Trois Rivières (an hour's drive), where they board a ferryboat for the 1½-hour ride to Terre-de-Haut, one of the islets that make up the Les Saintes islands. It's about as quiet and unspoiled as they come, with an atmosphere that's French Antillean to the last Gauloise. This is one place where you may need an acquaintance with French beyond *bonjour* and *merci.*

Technically, St. Barthélemy, or St. Barths, is part of the *département* of Guadeloupe, although it's closer to St. Martin. "*Nudisme est interdit à* St. Barthélemy" is the first sign that greets you at the airstrip, but despite the ominous interdiction (which many people seem to ignore anyway), St. Barths is really a friendly little place. It's the tiniest (less than 10 square miles) of the French islands and something of a curiosity: It's the only island in the Caribbean with a predominantly white population (mostly descendants of the original Breton settlers), and its picture-postcard port of Gustavia was formerly an outpost of Sweden. Despite its modest size, St. Barths manages to accommodate three dozen restaurants and, at opposite ends of the island, the estates of the Rothschilds and the Rockefellers.

NOTE: Hotels on St. Martin, the French half of the dual St. Maarten/St. Martin, are listed under St. Maarten in the chapter on the Dutch Windward Islands.

HOW TO GET THERE From New York to Guadeloupe and Martinique: American to San Juan where you connect with AA's Eagle service to Point-à-Pitre and Fort-de-France; from Miami, direct service by Eastern and Air France; from Montreal and Toronto, direct service by Air Canada. You can also make connections at Antigua (Air Guadeloupe to Point-à-Pitre) and Barbados (Air Martinique to Fort-de-France).

For St. Barthélemy, the most convenient connection is via St. Maarten, on Windward or Air St. Barthélemy, 16 flights a day; the latter also has regular flights from San Juan with seven-seat Cessnas, or nine-seaters from St. Thomas. For the fainthearted, who may prefer not to endure the modified kamikaze approach to St. Barths' airstrip, there are also several sea crossings from St. Maarten's Philipsburg (power yacht or catamaran), but they all leave in the morning, which will involve an overnight stop in St. Maarten. *Reminder:* If you are flying to St. Barths from St. Maarten, be sure to buy your ticket before you leave home to avoid paying the outrageous stamp duty slapped on airline tickets by the St. Maarten authorities.

Castelets

St. Barthélemy

$$$

Perch by the edge of the tiny triangular pool, feet dangling in the water, champagne glass dangling from your fingers. Far below, one of the most breathtaking vistas in the Caribbean unfurls in a montage of silver beaches, rocky promontories, minimountains, craggy islets and scudding sails. It's like watching a movie while sitting in the balcony (remember big *movie* screens?), but without the soundtrack.

This panorama alone may well be worth foregoing a beachfront lair, but there's more to Castelets than the view. Is there ever! *La cuisine,* for example. The menu is a leatherbound volume the size of a citation, inviting leisurely browsing and the careful planning of dinner. *Chausseur de Camembert au cumin* (hot Camembert flavored with cumin in a popover) or *demoiselle des îles à la crème d'avocat* (lobster medaillons with avocado), *paupiette de meron au crabe* (grouper rolled and stuffed with crab) or *medaillons de veau plantation* (veal cutlets with banana garnish), *îles flottant aux amandes* (soft meringue with vanilla cream and crushed almonds) or *millefeuille* (thin flaky pastry layered with cream filling). There are, it should be noted, two dining rooms here: the fireplace room, where you'll be sharing the refectory table with other diners (perhaps not the romantic setup of your dreams), and the small enclosed terrace where—with the appropriate advance notice of four or five days—you can probably reserve a table for two.

On this Antillean hilltop, the inn seems more of a *gentilhommerie* that echoes the backroads of Burgundy, its dining salon resplendent with hefty refectory tables and chairs of wrought-iron and leather, the circular stone fireplace sports a canopy of copper, the walls glow with antiques and prints. Summon a vintage chateau-bottled wine from the extensive cellar ("we allow the wines to rest a good month and a half before serving," to let the Pommard and Château Margaux recuperate from their transoceanic voyage).

Each of Castelets' nine guest aeries is different, with a few common themes such as Breton-style trundle beds and rope balustrades, upholstered wicker and doors of Guayana greenheart, decorations of framed silk squares by Hermès and antique maps of the Lesser Antilles. The least expensive rooms are identified as Bistro West, meaning they're in the main lodge, above the kitchen; the remaining rooms and suites are in small villas, some with duplex sitting rooms and marble floors, bathrooms with fitted carpets, refrigerators and tape decks. Villa 2 is the favorite of Mikhail Baryshnikov (Castelets is popular with dancers and musicians—Beverley Sills is another regular—most of whom reserve their favorite rooms a year in advance).

Since last year, Castelets has sprouted a new room—tiny 2A, at the rear, with white walls and blue-gray trim and its own entrance from a small garden patio shaded by a flamboyant tree that puts on its fireworks display in August rather than July.

Each time I've come to Castelets over the past 12 years, it's been with a *frisson* of trepidation. Not because of the road that twists and curls its narrow way up the hill at an angle you wouldn't even want to experience in a biplane. No, but because of what *may* have happened in the interim to alter its *ambiance agréable*.

Fortunately, this little gem has turned out to be one of the most dependable inns in the entire Caribbean. The delightful Geneviève Jouany is still there to greet guests in her polished Parisian way; chef Michel Vilay is still tending the kitchen (although a couple of dishes disappointed on a recent visit); the family of banana quits is still nesting in the chandelier in Villa 3.

Only one thing seems to have changed: over the years I've watched *le jardin Jouany* blossom and bloom (with the help of a local gardener with a distaste for pruning) and it's now luxuriant by the standards of St. Barthélemy.

This is another Caribbean up here among the Jouany jasmine and hibiscus, lignum vitae and poirier, high on the coolest hill, with the bedazzling Baie-de St.-Jean spread out beneath you.

NAME: Castelets

OWNER/MANAGER: Geneviève Jouany

ADDRESS: St. Barthélemy, F.W.I.

LOCATION: In the hills above Gustavia, about 15 minutes and $8 by taxi from the airstrip

TELEPHONE: 596-287-6173

TELEX: None

RESERVATIONS: Jane Martin, New York, 212-571-0336

CREDIT CARDS: None

ROOMS: 9, in the main house and garden villas, all with breezes or fans, private bathrooms, some with tape decks

MEALS: Breakfast 8:00–10:00, lunch noon–2:00, dinner at 7:00 or 9:00 (2 sittings, approx. $80–100 for 2), in main dining rooms; restaurant closed on Tuesdays; informal dress, but no shorts; room service for continental breakfast only

ENTERTAINMENT: Parlor games, tape decks in villas

SPORTS: Tiny plunge pool; beaches and water sports just 7 minutes away

P.S.: "Not too suitable for children"

Hotel Manapany

St. Barthélemy

🌴🌴🌴🍴🍴🍴🍴🎾🎾$$$$

The Manapany is tucked away on one of the few coves left on St. Barths with no hotel—Anse de Caye—among unkempt, typically Antillean landscape. Nonetheless celebrities such as Mick Jagger, Peter Allen, Gianni Versace and tennis ace Yannick Noah have sussed it out and local cognoscenti praise its Ballahou Restaurant as one of the island's finest. Given the competition, gourmet and otherwise, on St. Barths, that's saying quite a bit.

Perhaps the staff have something to do with Manapany's popularity (the beach isn't the draw). Service here is definitely French rather than Antillean, with everyone more than willing to go that extra step to make your stay pleasant.

And pleasant it is. The Manapany's cottages are designed in traditional island style with red shingle roofs and gingerbread trim, and each consists of a suite-with-terrace and room-with-balcony. The rooms are small, but the suites are spacious and ideal for lounging and relaxing, with 20-ft. screened

terraces fitted out with wicker sofas, armchairs, coffee table, dining table and chairs and full kitchenette. Soothing pastel fabrics set off white-on-white walls, ceiling and floors. Beachfront rooms cost more, but since most of them tend to look out on other cottages (try to avoid the Lapis Lazuli and Chrysalite suites), you may want to opt for one of the upper cottages clinging to the steep, terraced hillside. They impose a bit of a hike down a somewhat precipitous path to get to beach, pool or restaurant, but they do afford more breezes and a stunning view.

Whether you walk down the hill, Minimoke it, or just step over from your beach cottage, it's worth the effort when you're bound for dinner at the Ballahou. Dinner is served on elegant Bauscher Weiden china. The menu is presided over by Chef Dominique Allegré who once ruled the private kitchen of Valéry Giscard d'Estaing. (Try his *terrine de requin au basilic,* shark fin pâté with fresh basil, or *filet de colas belle aurore,* yellowtail snapper with a delicate tomato cream sauce.) The Ballahou is attractive, with a bar at one end, its gingerbread trim fashioned from a single piece of timber about 40 ft. long and decorated with lobsters, seahorses and crabs. The dining and drinking venues curve around the big pool by the edge of the beach—a cool spot that seems to be one of the most congenial spots on St. Barths.

NAME: Hotel Manapany

MANAGER: Danielle Bollardière

ADDRESS: Box 114, 97137 St. Barthélemy, F.W.I.

LOCATION: On the bay known as Anse de Caye, about 5 minutes and $5 from the airstrip

TELEPHONE: 596-276655

TELEX: 919215 GL MAPY

RESERVATIONS: Mondotel

CREDIT CARDS: All major cards

ROOMS: 52, including 24 rooms, 24 suites, 4 new Club Suites, all with air-conditioning and ceiling fans, balconies or patios, private bathrooms (showers only in suites, bathrobes, wall-mounted hair dryers), clock radios, color TV (in-house movies, English and French), direct-dial telephones, pantries in suites

MEALS: Breakfast 7:30–9:30, lunch noon–3:00, dinner 7:00–10:00 (approx. $40–60 for 2, in the Ballahou Restaurant or Italian restaurant beside the beach); informal dress; 24-hour room service (including full menu during restaurant hours), no extra charge; piano player or taped background music

ENTERTAINMENT: Bar/lounge/terrace with piano, taped music and, horrors!, a big TV set on the bar ("for Americans who want to watch football"); big-screen video in the meeting room, chess, Scrabble, backgammon; to say nothing of oodles of bars 10 to 15 minutes away by Minimoke

SPORTS: Beach (windswept, with coral, not especially good for swimming or windsurfing), large egg-shaped freshwater pool with island deck for sunbathing, whirlpool (solar-heated, sometimes lukewarm), tennis (1 court, pro, lights), surfboards, snorkeling masks—all free; boat trips (with hotel-prepared picnics), scuba diving and sailing can be arranged

Filao Beach Hotel

St. Barthélemy

$$$

The ambiance around here is pure Côte d'Azur—but most resorts on the French Riviera would give an arm and leg to have a beach like the Filao's.

This plush little hideaway is on one of the prime locations on St. Barths, right on fashionable (and usually topless) St. Jean Bay, on that talcum-fine strand between the island's toy-town airstrip and the rocky promontory known as Eden Rock.

Hugging its plot of precious beach, the hotel meanders back along well-marked paths through gardens of sea grape trees livened with white hibiscus, allamanda and red cattail. Red-roofed bungalows house 30 guest rooms, each named for a château in France, with the name (Villandry, Montlouis, whatever) etched on a ceramic owl above the door. Rooms are generously furnished with double bed, daybed/sofa, plenty of chairs and tables, television, refrigerator, both air-conditioning *and* ceiling fan. Roomy baths incorporate tub, shower and bidet.

But it's in the niceties that Filao scores—fresh flowers in all the rooms, continually replenished supply of bottled water in the fridge, an electric hair dryer (unusual luxury in the Antilles) in the bathroom, and redwood chaises covered with comfy cushions in blue and white stripes on each private terrace. You'll probably do more snoozing than sunning on your terrace because of the copious shade from the sea grapes, but almost certainly you'll have breakfast there, seated at the glass-topped table with island chart, poring over the topography of St. Barth's, deciding which beach to visit once you've scooped up the last flakes of croissant.

After a morning's swim you can look forward to a pleasant (but uninspired) lunch at the Filao's bar/restaurant, a peak-ceilinged pavilion with lazily turning fans and baskets of colorful (but plastic) flowers. It opens directly onto a raised wooden deck and an angular swimming pool, with the flags of France, Sweden, the U.S.A. and Filao Beach fluttering fraternally in the trade winds. The Filao's light lunches draw a crowd from all over the island to nibble on cold lobster or cheese omelet, sip sancerre and look out across the sand to the far-off reefs. (But don't expect speedy, or even congenial, service.)

Afterward, if you're feeling too sated for much else, you have to walk only a few steps to one of the palm-thatched *paillots* on the beach and settle into a molded plastic lounger for a siesta. For something more active, the waters off St. Jean Bay, protected by those scenic reefs, are ideal for windsurfing—and there's a windsurfing concession right there to rent boards and offer instructions.

NAME: Filao Beach Hotel

MANAGER: Albert Veille

ADDRESS: BP 167, 97133, St. Barthélemy, F.W.I.

LOCATION: On St. Jean Bay, about 1 mile from the airport, $3 by taxi

TELEPHONE: 596-87-64-84 or 87-62-24

TELEX: FILAO 919 973 GL

RESERVATIONS: Direct

CREDIT CARDS: American Express, Diners Club, Visa

ROOMS: 30, all with ceiling fans and air-conditioning, refrigerators, hair dryers, TV

DINING: Breakfast and lunch only (the latter with raucous rock music), and the bar closes at 8:00; room service for breakfast only; there are lots of restaurants within walking distance

ENTERTAINMENT: Films (mostly French) in the Video Room

SPORTS: Freshwater pool, beach swimming, snorkeling—all free; windsurfing rentals

Hotel Guanahani

St. Barthélemy

🌴🌴🌴🌴🍴🍴🍴🍴🎾🎾🎾$$$$

A dozen swimming pools. A couple of tennis courts. *And* a two-star chef from Paris. St. Barths has never had it so lavish.

After a false start as Le Warwick, the island's largest resort finally opened its doors in December 1986 with a new name and new owner—the Banque Commerciale Prive de Paris. Whatever you may feel about banks as hotelkeepers, there can be few misgivings about Guanahani's setting: bay and beach, reef and islet, headlands and blue but breeze-whipped sea. The resort sprawls over several acres of landscaped hillside tucked into one corner of Grand Cul-de-Sac Bay, a reef-protected beach, with the low-profile but snazzy El Sereno Hotel on one side, a grove of coconut palms belonging to Edmond de Rothschild on the other.

Although it's the island's largest, Guanahani has well under a hundred rooms, deployed two or three to a villa. Furnishings and decor are more or less standard in all rooms—tasteful and luxurious but not overdone, Antillean with a dash of Rive Droite, white pencil-post beds with paisley sheets. Some suites come with kitchenette (indoors or on the patio), some with private pool, others with shared pool. Kitchen and pools aside, your options boil down to location—whether or not you want to be beside the beach and steps from the water or up on the hillside to catch the breezes and views. Tennis buffs might enjoy rooms 10, 11 and 12, overlooking one of the resort's two courts and sharing a pool for après-match dunking. (Conversely, those three rooms are less than ideal for late sleepers who prefer not to be awakened by thonk-thonks and assorted blasphemies.) Rooms 39 and 41 are particularly attractive because they're at the edge of the property, overlooking the Rothschild coconuts; at the Sereno side of the resort, room 61 has an exceptionally large and secluded terrace with uninterrupted views of the entire bay.

No one, private bank or private moneybags, can hope to run a successful hotel on St. Barths without paying almost as much attention to the kitchen as to the decor. Maybe even *more.* The most popular pastime on this island is not sunning but dining—here, there, everywhere, so that at times the entire island seems to be a stream of scooters and Minimokes puttering their way to the latest eatery. In case guests of Guanahani plan to follow the same trendy routine, the manager has installed a private fleet of rental mokes and scooters (rareties during the peak season), but you may quickly resolve that there's not much reason for Guanahanians to rush hither and yon to dine

out. Right from the start, the banker-owners lured a two-star chef from Paris to the Guanahani kitchens—Dominique Namias of the Jardin de l'Olympe. She is there off and on to inspire and consult, to create menus and maintain standards. Her right-hand chef from Rue Nicolas Charlet, Philippe Debize, is her resident *ambassadeur.* Between them, they have lobbed the Guanahani kitchen right into the topmost ranks, and this on an island not exactly lacking in outstanding restaurants.

You can sample their Olympian efforts in two restaurants. The Indigo, beside the beach, adjoining the pool, is a French-style casual café for luncheon grills to accompany bottles of Chablis or Muscadet; the Bartholoméo, a few terraces above the beach, sets a classier tone, with handsome mahogany-trimmed decor, tables set with Coldport, Cristofle and silver candleholders. It looks expensive—and it is (a fact of life on St. Barthélemy). But what appears on the table has a level of refinement you don't often find in the Caribbean. The service is professional and friendly, without, on the whole, the stumbling block of languages.

If you leave Guanahani to dine elsewhere, it is probably because Bartholoméo's 56 seats have been snapped up by people from other hotels, who have scootered and Minimoked here to sample the latest eatery.

NAME: Hotel Guanahani

MANAGER: Gerald Hardy

ADDRESS: Lieu dit Marigot, Anse de Grand Cul-de-Sac, 97133 St. Barthélemy, F.W.I.

LOCATION: On the Atlantic coast, about 20 minutes from the airstrip by courtesy air-conditioned minibus

TELEPHONE: 596-276660

TELEX: DOMTEL GUAN 771315F

RESERVATIONS: First Resorts Management

CREDIT CARDS: All major cards

ROOMS: 81 rooms and suites (junior, 1 or 2 bedrooms) in 30 villas, all with fans *and* air-conditioning, terrace/patio, refrigerator, satellite TV, radio, telephone, wall safe; some with kitchenette

MEALS: Breakfast 7:00–9:30, lunch 12:30–2:30, afternoon tea 4:00–5:00, all in the beachside Indigo Café, dinner 7:00–11:00 in the fan-cooled Bartholoméo Restaurant (approx. $100–120 for 2); informal but stylish dress ("shorts, T-shirts, swimsuits or other similarly casual clothing are inappropriate after dark in the dining room and bar"); room service for continental breakfast only; small commissary on premises

ENTERTAINMENT: Weekly barbecues, video films

SPORTS: Beach (with a second swatch of sand on the other side of the Rothschild coconut grove), 11 individual swimming pools (private or semiprivate), large pool and Jacuzzi beside the beach, snorkeling, tennis (2 courts, artificial grass, with lights)—all free; beach concession offering windsurfing, Hobie Cats, waterskiing, deep-sea fishing, sailing

P.S.: "Not appropriate for young children"

El Sereno Beach Hotel

St. Barthélemy

🌴🌴🌴🍴🍴🍴🍴🎾$$$

Despite the attraction of a secluded beach and protected bay, of a glamorous tiled swimming pool with sunbathing "islands," *dining* is the high point of a stay at this exquisite little hotel on St. Barths' Grand Cul-de-Sac.

The Sereno's managers, Marc and Christine Llepez, are also the owners of a popular Lyon brasserie, Le Café du Marche. When they took charge of the Sereno they brought along one of their friends, Jean-Pierre Fernandez, a chef who has sharpened his knives at the Hotel Majestic in Cannes and the Sahara Palace in Tunis. So special is the glittering dining room it was given its own name, Restaurant La Toque Lyonnaise. Chef Fernandez not only knows his way around a *beurre blanc,* but also embraces local seafood and produce with gusto. Lobster ravioli and truffles in cabbage butter share space on the menu with red snapper and mashed christophene. He even serves the traditional Lyonnaise green salad with poached egg, country bacon and garlic croutons. But figure also on Lyon prices—$100 for dinner for two, with wine.

The setting for all this gourmandizing is an open pavilion beside the beach and the pool, festooned with Haitian handwoven lampshades and wicker baskets, tables brightened by candles and sprays of anthuriums. In the evening the dining room takes on its fairyland quality. Tiny lights set into the deck twinkle in the twilight; fish swim in a four-sided aquarium that was once a grill, the mirror-encased chimney refracts the light from all directions; chicly clad guests lounge on comfortable sofas covered with Jean-Yves Fromant fabrics or around the bar where Marc and Christine welcome everyone to what appears to be a vivacious house party.

Visually, the hotel complements the restaurant—it's equally stunning. Set among low palm trees, it's a dazzle of free-form white walls, royal blue lampposts and the red-and-blue shiny tiled pool. Guest rooms surround a sandy center courtyard, each with a fragrant, private patio/garden of hibiscus and laurier and latanier. The rooms are all alike indoors—whitewashed, blue-beamed but small, with cot beds, closets in the bathrooms. Terraces have chaises, hammocks that look like trampolines and tables and chairs for your morning croissants—and since the foliage and wall offer some protection you don't have to be too fussy about dressing for breakfast.

Unfortunately, the cross-ventilation may prove something to fuss about—there isn't much, despite the sliding glass door that divides the rooms from the terraces. You'll probably have the air conditioner running more often than you'd like, although prime rooms 1, 2 and 6 get a few more riffles of breeze than the others since they face the bay (of these, 2 is the most private).

But don't let the lack of ventilation keep you away from El Sereno. You'll be skimpily attired indoors or out most of the time—paddling in a bay so shallow it's still no more than shoulder high some 200 yards out, sunning yourself on those "islands" in that stunning pool, lunching lazily on the trellised porch—or dozing on the beach, eyeing that beautiful dining room and dreaming of lobster ravioli.

NAME: El Sereno Beach Hotel

OWNERS/MANAGERS: Marc and Christine Llepez

ADDRESS: BP 19, 97133, St. Barthélemy, F.W.I.

LOCATION: On Grand Cul-de-Sac Bay, about 3 miles from the airport, about $10 by taxi

TELEPHONE: 596-87-64-80

RESERVATIONS: Jacques de Larsay

CREDIT CARDS: American Express, Visa

ROOMS: 20, all with patio/garden, showers only, TV, wall safe and air-conditioning

MEALS: Breakfast and lunch on the beachside glass-enclosed terrace, La Toque Lyonnaise is open for dinner only; dress code "elegantly casual" in the evening; dinner for 2 approx. $100; room service for breakfast only

ENTERTAINMENT: Video movies in your room

SPORTS: Swimming, freshwater pool; windsurfing, pedal boats, tennis nearby

Hamak

Guadeloupe

$$$$

Hammocks, hammocks everywhere. One waiting on your front patio. Eight more swinging over the bar. And embossed on every towel, plate and ashtray as well. The message here is clear: relax.

On an aquamarine lagoon where a perpetual ocean breeze cools the sunshine even at high noon, this is a place for doing everything or nothing in great style. A Technicolor botanical garden of 10,000 (the gardener keeps count) exotic trees and flowers undulates around 56 cabana suites. The glass wall of your bedroom opens into a private walled garden with a locked gate to which only you and the maid have a key. Along with hummingbirds, bougainvillea and beach chairs, each garden has a tiled open-air shower big enough for your own private splash party. But this is one of the few Caribbean resorts where you can do your topless tanning anywhere. For Hamak has both an openness and a privacy few other places have mastered.

A hundred other guests are here—somewhere. In their walled gardens. On a little scallop of private beach in front of their cabanas. Or out to sea waterskiing, pedal-boating, Sunfishing, windsurfing, etc. But the only spot where you're likely to encounter more than one body at a time is in the middle of Hamak's main beach, and most of them make very pleasant scenery. Even the adjoining sweeping Robert Trent Jones golf course is blessedly free of both crowds and the island's famous *yen-yens* (nasty gnats that make a buzzing sound just like their name as pronounced by a Frenchman).

As all good things usually do, Hamak's sophisticated simplicity emanates from an owner who runs the place for himself—and strictly to his own tastes. What Jean-François likes *you* had better like, too. And why not?

Every last matchbox and dinner napkin has been chosen with bull's-eye taste. And there's not a polymer in sight. Creamy stucco and poured concrete, dark woods and terrazzo tiles are the stuff everything's made of. The cabanas are simply but thoughtfully done: 10 ft. of soft sofa in the sitting room, floor-to-ceiling mirrors beside the king-size bed, roomy bath, nearly silent air-conditioning, and refrigerator.

But the instant you want to get away from it all, the hotel provides jitney, powerboat or private plane to take you where you want to go. With a landing strip right on the property, you can arrange to go on a day's island hop to St. Martin and St. Barths (both in one day), to the nearby islets known as Les Saintes or all the way to Mustique for lunch and a swim at the Cotton House.

NAME: Hamak

OWNER/MANAGER: Jean-François Rozan

ADDRESS: 97118 Saint-François, Guadeloupe, F.W.I.

LOCATION: On the beach, about 20 miles and $30 by taxi from Point-à-Pitre and the airport

TELEPHONE: 596-885999

TELEX: 919753 G.L.

RESERVATIONS: Jacques de Larsay and Robert Reid Assoc.

CREDIT CARDS: American Express, MasterCard, Diners Club, Visa

ROOMS: 56, in garden bungalows, all suites, all with garden patio, extra shower on patio, terrace with hammock, air-conditioning, refrigerator, pantry, wall safe

MEALS: Breakfast 7:00–10:00, lunch noon–3:00, dinner 7:30–11:00 (approx. $55–65 for 2); informal dress; room service

ENTERTAINMENT: Taped music, "mood music" combos; casinos and shopping nearby

SPORTS: 3 virtually private beaches, waterskiing, Sunfish sailing, windsurfing, tennis (2 courts, with lights, at nearby club)—all free; golf (Robert Trent Jones design, 18 holes) guaranteed starting times for Hamak guests *twice* a day, snorkeling gear for rent; excursions by boat and twin-engined plane can be arranged

Auberge de la Vieille Tour

Guadeloupe

$$$

Some travelers choose great hotels with a decent restaurant attached. *French* travelers choose great restaurants with a decent hotel attached. Hence, the never-ending popularity of this out-of-date fifties-style hotel. Yes, it has nice beaches, pool, tennis, boats and some newly refurbished guest rooms—but the real attraction here is what comes steaming out of the kitchen every night. Delicately prepared local fish in perfect sauces. Pink and tender lamb. A rolling silver cart of crisp, fresh Caribbean antipasto. Bries and Camemberts. Rum cordials with a headiness inherited from the exotic fruits you find lurking at the bottom. So, although that handsome eighteenth-century sugar-mill tower at the entrance is what gives the *auberge* its name, as soon as you step into the lobby you sense that eating is the main sport here.

Since the rate for every room here is precisely the same, reserve early and get a good one. Number 77, for example, is actually a bungalow; it sits all the way at the end of the garden completely refurnished and with a tiny terrace right over the beach. Its three matching neighbors aren't quite so private but otherwise have all the same advantages. Another stretch of 18 guest rooms has also been redone from stem to stern in simple white cottons and natural wood. Each has a vest-pocket refrigerator stocked with champagne, Schweppes, beer and fruit juice.

If the three beaches get too crowded for you, the hotel will send a boat around to take you to a nearby island where you can establish your own beachhead, break out a picnic lunch supplied by the hotel chef and still be back in time for one of Vieille Tour's outstanding dinners. (*C.P.*)

NAME: (PLM Azur) Auberge de la Vieille Tour

MANAGER: Jacques Serpollier

ADDRESS: 97190 Gosier, Guadeloupe, F.W.I.

LOCATION: About 10 minutes and $10 by taxi from the airport, or from Pointe-à-Pitre

TELEPHONE: 84 23 23

TELEX: 919751

RESERVATIONS: Frantel Hotels, Inc. in New York City 212-687-1210; toll-free 800-223-9862

CREDIT CARDS: American Express, MasterCard, Diners Club, Visa, Carte Blanche, Carte Bleu

ROOMS: 82, with air-conditioning

MEALS: Breakfast 7:00–10:00, lunch noon–2:30, dinner 7:00–10:00 (in the air-conditioned dining room, approx. $70 for 2); dress is moderately formal—jacket, but no tie; room service, 7:00 A.M.–9:00 P.M., no extra charge

ENTERTAINMENT: Steel band on Tuesdays, roving guitarists, dancing, orchestra from 9:00 to midnight every night except Sunday and Monday; casino nearby

SPORTS: Beach, freshwater pool, tennis (1 court, lights)—free; snorkeling, scuba, sailing, boat trips, golf (18 holes) nearby

P.S.: Occasional small groups, lots of outside guests for dinner; most of the staff speak English.

Auberge des Anacardiers

Terre-de-Haut, Guadeloupe

🌴🍴🏊$

Until recently, most visitors came over to Terre-de-Haut for the day because the few hotels on the island were barely the kind to tempt people to stay longer. That changed somewhat last year when two new lodgings opened, the most engaging of them run by Robert Joyeux, the dapper mayor of the island. He has simply converted his modest hilltop home into an amiable 10-room *auberge.*

Named for one of the many fruit trees that ring the house, this little plant-filled, tile-roofed charmer sits at the top of a hill with an unbeatable view of the bay. Monsieur le Maire speaks only French, but his small staff can interpret ably. Even without the translation, though, you get the feeling that guests are cordially invited to feel at home. So settle back. Admire the view from the arbor out front. Peek into the cages aflutter with prize French pigeons and the Technicolor parrot. Sample *le punch* the mayor loves to concoct with native rum and the fruits plucked from his garden—the bar sports apothecary jars filled with this heady stuff (which has nothing to do with the fact that the mayor's name is Robert Happy).

The inn's interior is simple, in keeping with the unspoiled ambiance of the island, featuring lots of wood paneling and sturdy hand-carved wooden rockers that are a specialty of local artisans. The front parlor is now a pretty little dining room in traditional French Provincial style. As you might expect, the kitchen's specialties come from the surrounding sea, but the menu also offers *filet de boeuf* or *entrecôte,* and the same grill that sears langouste or *merou* can also produce a tasty *brochette* of beef. Breakfasts (included with lunch or dinner in the rate) are generous—*café, thé, chocolat, pamplemousse, ananas, goyave, oeufs au plat, oeuf brouille, pain frais et grillé,* etc.

Guest rooms are small, as you might expect, but comfortable, with efficient plumbing (and air-conditioning, although that's something you can be without most of the time at this elevation). Four of the rooms have bathrooms just outside in the hall (but each reserved for a specific room, so still private)—and priced at bargain rates as a result. Rooms 1 and 2 (with fully private bathrooms) have the advantage of doors opening to the terrace beside the pool.

Everyone here, whether they speak your language or not, takes special care of you, running you into town or to the beach, doing your laundry, plying you with *le punch.* The *auberge* is a taste of a bygone, more personal Caribbean—all served up with inimitable French flair.

NAME: Auberge des Anacardiers

OWNER/MANAGER: Robert Joyeux

ADDRESS: La Savane, 97137 Terre-de-Haut, Les Saintes, Guadeloupe

LOCATION: In the hills, 5 minutes by hotel minibus from the dock (the island itself is 1 hour by ferryboat from Pointe-à-Pitre, 30 minutes from Trois Rivières, 15 minutes by Air Guadeloupe)

TELEPHONE: 590-995099

TELEX: None

RESERVATIONS: None

CREDIT CARDS: All major cards

ROOMS: 10, all with air-conditioning, 4 with private baths in the hall

MEALS: Breakfast 7:00–10:00, lunch 12:30–2:00, dinner 7:30–9:00 (approx. $50 for 2); informal; no room service

ENTERTAINMENT: Taped background music, TV set in parlor

SPORTS: Pool, free transportation to beach; bikes, snorkeling gear, water sports for rent nearby

P.S.: Not all the waiters and chambermaids speak English

PLM Azur Los Santos

Terre-de-Haut, Guadeloupe

$$

This colony of gingerbread-trimmed, red-roofed bungalows bears little resemblance to the hotels you expect to find in France's PLM chain. Los Santos has been aptly fashioned in the rakish style of its home port, the tiny fishermen's island of Terre-de-Haut.

The 27 bungalows are clustered on a hillside beside the deep blue of Marigot Bay. Each room has a loggia with a panoramic view of the bay and the small but virtually private beach; if it also had a skylight, you might catch a glimpse of massive Fort Napoleon on top of the hill. Some of the bungalows are sited too close for comfort and privacy, so insist on a front row location—you'll have nothing and nobody between you and the sea, and you won't have to pay a franc more. Otherwise, ask for rooms numbered 42–45, on the second floor, with higher ceilings and extra privacy. Interiors are on the small side, but they're pleasantly if simply dressed up, with contemporary white wicker furniture and matching yellow or cool green prints on the beds and wall-to-wall windows. The main building houses a bar, a small sitting room with television, and the dining room—a large pavilion with lots of windows and dark wood accents. The food may not rate a Michelin star but it's fresh and tasty, at its best with local fish and the smoked tuna that's an island specialty.

There's not much to do in Les Saintes, even less at their namesake Los Santos. Laze under a thatched sunshade. Swim out to the float moored offshore. The favorite island pastime seems to be watching the fishermen bring in their catch. Or, in an energetic frame of mind, you can make your way to the top of the hill and take in the breathtaking sea-and-islet view from Fort Napoleon.

If you're looking for the serenity of a fishing village and the conveniences of a small resort, Los Santos could be a prize catch.

NAME: PLM Azur Los Santos

MANAGER: Jean-Michel Martial

ADDRESS: Baie de Marigot, 97137 Terre-de-Haut, Les Saintes, Guadeloupe, F.W.I.

LOCATION: 5 minutes from town on a private bay; the island of Terre-de-Haut is reached by ferryboats from Pointe-à-Pitre (1 hour) and Trois Rivières (½ hour), or by Air Guadeloupe (15 minutes); hotel minibus meets guests, if requested

TELEPHONE: 590-995040

TELEX: 919346

RESERVATIONS: Mondotel

CREDIT CARDS: American Express, Diners Club, MasterCard, Visa

ROOMS: 54, all with showers only, air-conditioning, loggias facing the sea, minibars, direct-dial telephones; 16 with kitchenettes

MEALS: Breakfast 7:00–10:00, lunch noon–2:00, dinner 7:00–10:00 (approx. $45–55 for 2, in breezy La Caronade restaurant on the rocks above the beach); informal; no room service

ENTERTAINMENT: Taped music except for live music and dancing on Saturday, TV in lobby

SPORTS: Beach, sailboats, windsurfing, snorkeling gear—free; water-skiing, scuba, pedal boats, trimaran cruises at extra cost

P.S.: Lots of families on weekends and holidays

Hotel Plantation de Leyritz

Martinique

🌴🌴🌴🌴🍴🍴☺☺$$

You know there's got to be something special about a place when all the other hotels in the country (including Club Med, a 3-hour drive away) send their guests here by the tour-bus load. For Martinique has two glorious sights: the volcano Pelée and Leyritz.

Born before Mozart, before the steamboat, before even the United States, it is a living, working banana plantation three centuries old and as close to unspoiled as a national treasure can be that's not locked behind glass. The guardhouse, the slave quarters, the grand manor house are all intact—but now instead of *planteurs* bedded down in them, you find guests. The former chapel and sugar factory have been transformed into beamed, stone-walled dining rooms with stenciled ceilings. And at the bottom of a long emerald lawn, a swimming pool with fountains sparkles like a big, cool sapphire.

Accommodations here are comfortable but far from luxurious. What wins Leyritz its three-palm rating is that overworked catchall word, charm. Forget you ever saw it before. This is the place for which it was invented.

Everywhere you go, a miniature stone canal splashes fresh mountain water along your route. Through the garden, past the guest rooms of the carriage house, cascading over the walls. Engineered by the first French colonial owner to bring water down from the rain forests to the coffee and spices he grew here, the canal's role now is to provide water music for the guests.

Some people who come back to Leyritz year after year make a point always to choose different quarters—they say it's like staying at a different hotel each time. For instance, the 14 tiny cottages that once housed the plantation's slaves provide the most privacy—snug little bamboo-roofed warrens with foot-thick stone walls and windows discreetly screened by tropical flowers and mango trees. Or you can share the grand manor house

with the owners—and anyone else who happens to be sauntering its cool, airy rooms. Up the winding staircase, a guest room called Bergere gives you a view across the avocado orchard straight out to sea, and another, called the Blue Room, stares up at Pelée and the glowering rain cloud it wears nearly every day. Rooms in the carriage house all have sun decks and the easiest route to the swimming pool is 250 grassy feet down the hill; the smallest rooms are the newest—in a one-time dormitory. But probably the two most unusual places to hang your sun hat at Leyritz are what once served as the guardhouse and the master's kitchen. Now each gives you your own stone cottage surrounded by guava trees and manicured lawn.

Although it hasn't cooked up a meal in a hundred years, the kitchen cottage is still called Pan by the present lady of the house (but after the satyr, she says, not the utensil). Three-hundred-year-old beams crisscross above your bed, and if you hear a whistle it's only the ghost of a long-departed scullery maid. (The master demanded that the help always whistle in the kitchen—so he could be sure they weren't stealing a bite of his dinner.)

The guardhouse cottage gives you the best of both worlds: inside a cool and shadowy stone-walled bedroom with slit windows just wide enough to poke a musket through, and outside your own tiled patio with nothing in sight but a few million banana trees.

The old rum distillery on the plantation is now offering a different kind of relaxation as a spa where you can order up a massage or facial or soak in the hot tub on the sun deck, before retreating for a siesta in your private digs.

As to what to do between siestas, the main sport here is wandering. To the tiny village next door, where the local people always have a welcome mat—and a cold rum punch—for any guest of Leyritz. Or by car down to the beaches and fishing villages below, especially Grande Rivière at land's end, where the fishermen have devised their own ingenious navigation system for sailing out against the breaking waves. Saint-Pierre, "the Paris of the Caribbean" before being wiped out by Mont Pelée in 1902, is a short drive away. Or go off on a Tarzan and Jane adventure in one of the gorgeous gorges of the surrounding rain forests. Leyritz has one right on its own estate, but as of this writing it is impassable to anyone but a mountain goat, thanks to the last hurricane. However, there's an even more spectacular climb down the Gorge de Falaise nearby: under giant fern trees and wild orchids and up a racing river of mossy rocks and icy pools to a 200-ft. waterfall you can have all to yourself.

By the time you make it back to the real world, trade winds will be rocking the birds to sleep in Leyritz's ancient mango trees, and the candles will be lit for a dinner of baby lamb and *papaya gratinée.* Pour the wine and drink a toast to the impresarios of Plantation de Leyritz, M. et Mme. de Lucy de Fossarieu. And if that's too much of a mouthful for one toast, drink two. They deserve it. (*C.P.*)

NAME: Hotel Plantation de Leyritz

OWNERS/MANAGERS: Charles and Yveline de Lucy de Fossarieu

ADDRESS: 97218 Basse-Pointe, Martinique, F.W.I.

LOCATION: In the north, 35 miles from Fort-de-France, or $55 and an hour's drive by taxi from the airport; most people rent a car to get there, but if you will be arriving after dark, let the hotel know and they'll arrange to have a reliable taxi driver waiting for you at the airport (you pay the fare, of course)

TELEPHONE: Basse-Pointe 596-755308 or 755392

TELEX: 912 462 MR

RESERVATIONS: Jacques de Larsay

CREDIT CARDS: American Express, Visa, MasterCard

ROOMS: 52, 4 in the main building, the remainder in former plantation annexes, all with telephone, some with air-conditioning

MEALS: Breakfast 7:30–10:00, lunch noon–2:00, dinner 7:30–8:30 in dining pavilion, informal dress; room service for breakfast and drinks only

ENTERTAINMENT: Dancing to live music twice a week, some local folklore groups or bands

SPORTS: Pool, tennis, walks through the plantation; beaches 30 minutes away

P.S.: Tour groups for lunch almost daily (eat early or late or request seating in the smaller room adjoining the noisy main dining room); several staff members speak English, but expect a few verbal hitches

Hotel Bakoua Beach

Martinique

$$$

If you're rich and lucky you may get to do what Jean-Paul Belmondo, Darryl Zanuck, Prince Napoleon and Aretha Franklin did—spend a few coddled, stylish nights in the Imperial Suite, a dazzling boudoir in period decor with sunken tubs of green marble, a dainty yellow four-poster bed and a private circular porch perched right above the sea at the end of the garden.

Chances are, though, you'll spend more modest nights in less imperial surroundings in one of this 20-year-old hotel's regular rooms. Still, the Bakoua Beach is probably your best bet for a *resort* hotel in Martinique. It's surrounded by gardens of frangipani and coconut palms. The rooms are comfortable, amply equipped, recently refurbished with spanking new tiled bathrooms. The 20-odd compact *casitas* between the garden and the sea are probably the best buy, with modern fitted wall units, balcony, sliding screen doors, tiled floors, tiled showers and double beds.

The distinctive feature of the Bakoua is a cluster of orange conical rooftops representing the *bakoua,* or conical native hat, for which the hotel is named. They cap a colorful, open dining pavilion seating 500 (that is, two and a half times the guest count), where fresh anthuriums and crotons climb the columns, the table linen matches the anthuriums and waitresses in local costume serve the Bakoua's French and Creole delicacies (Sunday is "lobster night," with island crustaceans cooked half a dozen different ways). Expect distractions, though—the dining area abuts a dance floor covered by an orange-and-yellow awning, next to a circular open bar.

Originally sole guardian of a quiet peninsula, the Bakoua Beach has managed to keep its calm and its distance through all the development on its doorstep and now offers the best of both worlds. If you want beach, you have a beach, of sorts, and lots of water sports and tennis; if you want a disco or casino, they're just a stroll away in the big hotels, and if you want the markets, shops and nightlife of the city, they're just across the harbor, a 15-minute trip by *vedette*. And if you want a good dinner and a quiet drink on your own terrace, you can have that, too. That's why it remains the choice of fun-loving celebs.

NAME: Hotel Bakoua Beach

OWNER/MANAGER: Guy de la Houssaye

ADDRESS: P.O. Box 589, Fort-de-France, 97207 Martinique, F.W.I.

LOCATION: Across the harbor from Fort-de-France at Les Trois-Îlets, 15 minutes and $2.50 round trip by ferry, but 30 minutes and $23 by taxi from the airport ($30 after dark)

TELEPHONE: 596-660202

TELEX: 912666 MR

RESERVATIONS: David B. Mitchell & Company, Inc.

CREDIT CARDS: American Express, Visa, MasterCard, Diners Club

ROOMS: 98 rooms, 2 suites, some on the beach, the remainder in three-story wings with sea view, all with balcony or patio, air-conditioning, telephone, radio

MEALS: Breakfast 7:00–10:00, lunch noon–3:00, dinner 7:30–10:00 (in the big open dining terrace, approx. $50 for 2); informal dress, but no shorts in the evening; room service 6:00 A.M.–3:00 P.M. and 7:30 P.M.–10:00 P.M., $1 extra

ENTERTAINMENT: 2 bars, dinner dancing nightly to local live music; folklore dance show on Fridays; steel band and show Saturdays; discos and casino nearby

SPORTS: Beach (now enlarged, with thatched *bohios* and umbrellas), freshwater pool—free; tennis (2 courts, lighted, free by day, $6 an hour with lights); snorkeling gear, scuba, waterskiing from the beach (extra charge); helicopter trips from the hotel's pad to outlying islands; golf 5 minutes away (18 Robert Trent Jones holes), horseback riding nearby

P.S.: Some groups, some children, some cruise ship passengers (but *not* by the busload); most of the staff speak English

St. Aubin Hotel

Martinique

🌴🌴🍴🍴$$

Could it have been a playful time warp—or an addled travel agent? You get on a jet for Martinique and end up on a Louisiana bayou plantation complete with miles of filigreed veranda and sunny sugarcane fields.

But look again, and beyond the cane you see blue sky meeting even bluer sea. St. Aubin has recently been restored, if not to its original French colonial grandeur, at least to a night's colorful, comfortable stopover.

Nobody comes to Martinique to flop in just one spot. There's probably no more glorious ride between California's Big Sur and the Riviera's Grande Corniche than along this island's west coast. So rent a car, ooh your way up the Caribbean side, aah it down the Atlantic side, and you'll find St. Aubin a handy half hour from the airport. The second-floor rooms all open on the veranda (most have sea views-cum-breezes). And the pretty pool near the garden is the perfect refresher after a day in the car.

As for dinner, the owner himself, who previously ran the best restaurant in Fort-de-France, will prepare for you three courses of French Creole cooking to remember, served up with a fine chilly bottle of Muscadet. (*C.P.*)

NAME: St. Aubin Hotel

MANAGER: Guy Foret

ADDRESS: Petite Rivière Salée, B.P. 52 97220 Trinité, Martinique, F.W.I

LOCATION: 30 minutes from the airport, about 19 miles from the capital

TELEPHONE: 596-693477

TELEX: OFTOUR 912 678 MR

RESERVATIONS: None

CREDIT CARDS: Visa, Diners Club, Eurocard, MasterCard

ROOMS: 15

MEALS: Breakfast 7:00–9:30, no lunch, dinner 7:30–8:30 (approx. $30 for 2); no room service

ENTERTAINMENT: Eating

SPORTS: Pool; swimming and other water sports nearby

Manoir de Beauregard

Martinique

$ $

If you feel as though you're in a church when you enter the tiled-floor beamed-ceiling lounge here, it's not surprising, since the cathedral of Fort-de-France supplied much of the decor—the wrought-iron reredos that separate the lobby from the lounge, the chandeliers and candleholders, the stair rail (once the communion rail). The illusion soon disappears, though, with the constant toing-and-froing of some very skimpy bikinis under some very diaphanous caftans. There are more antiques (secular, this time) in the 11 guest rooms in the main building—big bulky plantation beds, double beds with *colonnes torsades,* a marquetry dressing table from French Guyenne; the rooms have solidity rather than charm, but those stout walls should give you plenty of privacy. They have been there since 1715 when the house was built by a planter named Beauregard; Saint-Cyrs have lived here for 25 years, but the *manoir* became a hotel less than 20 years ago. The stone building up on the hill now has 4 new suites furnished with antique four-poster beds, tile floors, tile bathrooms and tiny sitting rooms; at the end, the two-story tower has been transformed into a wood-paneled suite with circular staircase and conical ceiling. But the whole place needs refurbishing (some chaises need repairs, some walls are cracking).

What you have here, basically, is a fine old manor house in 50 acres of countryside just beyond the town of Ste-Anne: a useful and inexpensive place to have around when you want to get away from the crowds, stay close to a beach (one of Martinique's finest expanses of sand is only 5 minutes away by car) or sit down to a first-rate meal in the leisurely evenings. In fact, the best thing about the Manoir is its cuisine—*brochette de lambis, crabes farcies, côte d'agneau*—all done to something close to perfection. And the wine list has some worthy vintages to send you on your mellow way to a double bed with *colonnes torsades.*

NAME: Manoir de Beauregard

OWNER/MANAGER: Marcelle Saint-Cyr

ADDRESS: 97227 Ste-Anne, Martinique, F.W.I.

LOCATION: In the south, 1 hour from the airport, slightly more from town (and since the cost of taxis each way is the same as renting a car for a few days, you might as well rent—since you really need transportation to get you from the hotel to the lovely beaches of this corner of Martinique)

TELEPHONE: 596-767-346

TELEX: 912 349

RESERVATIONS: None

CREDIT CARDS: American Express, MasterCard, Diners Club

ROOMS: 23 rooms and 3 new suites, with a/c

MEALS: Breakfast 7:30–9:30, lunch 12:30–2:00, dinner 7:30–8:30 (approx. $30 for 2); informal dress; room service during dining room hours, no extra charge (bartender on duty around the clock)

ENTERTAINMENT: Taped music

SPORTS: Pool, bicycles; beach nearby, boat trips with local fishermen

P.S.: Some small groups, and avoid holiday weekends when there may be lots of children

Added Attractions

Hôtel l'Hibiscus

St. Barthélemy

From your private hillside terrace you look down on an authentic Old West Indian harbor. Red tin rooftops line a rectangle of *quais,* interisland freighters creakingly unload their cargoes, charter yachts bob at their moorings. The beach may be a 5-minute walk away, over the hill, but all of Gustavia's lively bars, boutiques and bistros are right there at your feet. If, on the other hand, you prefer to stay around your terrace and enjoy the view, just fasten the rope with the *occupé* sign across the path to your cottage and your enjoyment will be undisturbed.

L'Hibiscus is the best place to stay if you want to savor the charm of Gustavia. Its dozen white-walled cottages cover a terraced hillside draped with, of course, hibiscus. Rooms are modern and efficient, with contemporary island decor of native hardwoods and rattan and native paintings. Each has a view of the harbor from a private terrace, but what may appeal to many visitors is the outdoor Pullman kitchen (eye-level oven, two-ring cooker, refrigerator, china and cutlery for six), transforming your deck into an intimate outdoor dining room.

The core of the Hibiscus is a midlevel terrace decorated with wicker elephant planters and macrame hangings, with sun deck and pool at one end; at the other, a bar and dining room where you can sample the continental and Creole cuisine prepared by the Belgian *patron.* 12 units. *Hôtel l'Hibiscus, B.P. 86, Gustavia 97133, St. Barthélemy, F.W.I. Telephone: 596-87-6482.*

Village St. Jean

St. Barthélemy

A hillside garden full of rooms (6) and villas (20), with kitchenettes, air-conditioning, telephone, TV, comfy furniture, terrace or garden and maid service (including dishwashing). It's a steep hike up the hill from the beach (say, 5 minutes down, 10 up); open-air restaurant by the beach, boutique, minimarket with meats and liquor in the village. The attraction is the rates, from $84 to $226 with breakfast in winter, just $45 to $108 in summer. 26 rooms. *Village St. Jean, 97133 St. Barthélemy, F.W.I. Telephone: 596-27-61-39. Telex: 919057 GL.*

Emeraude Plage

St. Barthélemy

Another garden full of bungalows, this time by the edge of the beach. All 14 rooms have kitchenettes, sun decks and maid service, the atmosphere is totally beachcomber and there are water sports facilities on the doorstep. Season rates are approx. $135 to $300, room only, in winter. 14 rooms. *Emeraude Plage, B.P. 41, St. Barthélemy, F.W.I.*

Taiwana

St. Barthélemy

It's one of those hearsay hideaways that no one I know has ever actually stayed in—small site, tucked into one corner of a good but not great beach. There's one sexy suite almost in the surf; the remaining four units (all smaller) are on an elevated terrace behind the parking lot, minuscule pool and stylish dining pavilion. Outlandishly expensive ($400 and up for the kind of rooms that cost half that elsewhere) and terribly chic; but why celebrities would want to seek seclusion and anonymity in a tiny enclave where outsiders can come to lunch and swim in "their" pool is a mystery. Service, if not quite sullen, is not exactly outgoing (at least, not to noncelebrities). Owner Jean-Paul Nemegiey doesn't solicit guests and accepts only those referred by other guests. Let them have their privacy. 5 suites. *Taiwana, St. Barthélemy. Telephone: unlisted (ask Billy Joel or someone else who has stayed there).*

Jardin de St. Jean

St. Barthélemy

Perched on a hillside, with stunning views over the Bay of St. Jean, this cluster of un-formula condos includes a dozen one-bedroom apartments (some duplex), all with terraces, kitchenettes; some have private gardens, some have television. Each apartment is furnished differently (1B is particularly attractive), some of them are no match for the view, but they're comfortable and convenient. There's a shopping mall at the base of the hill, water sports and restaurants across the street. Rates, by St. Barths' standards, are reasonable, the management friendly (they speak English). 20 rooms and apartments. *Jardins de St. Jean, 97133 St. Jean, St. Barthélemy F.W.I. Telephone: 590-823154.*

The Queen's Windwards

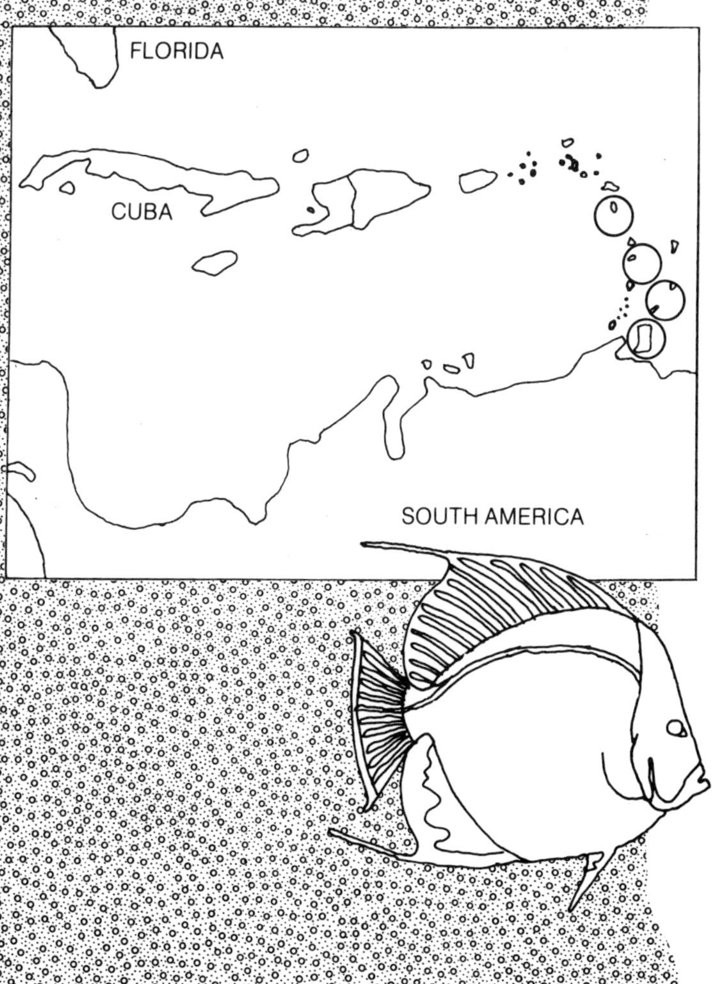

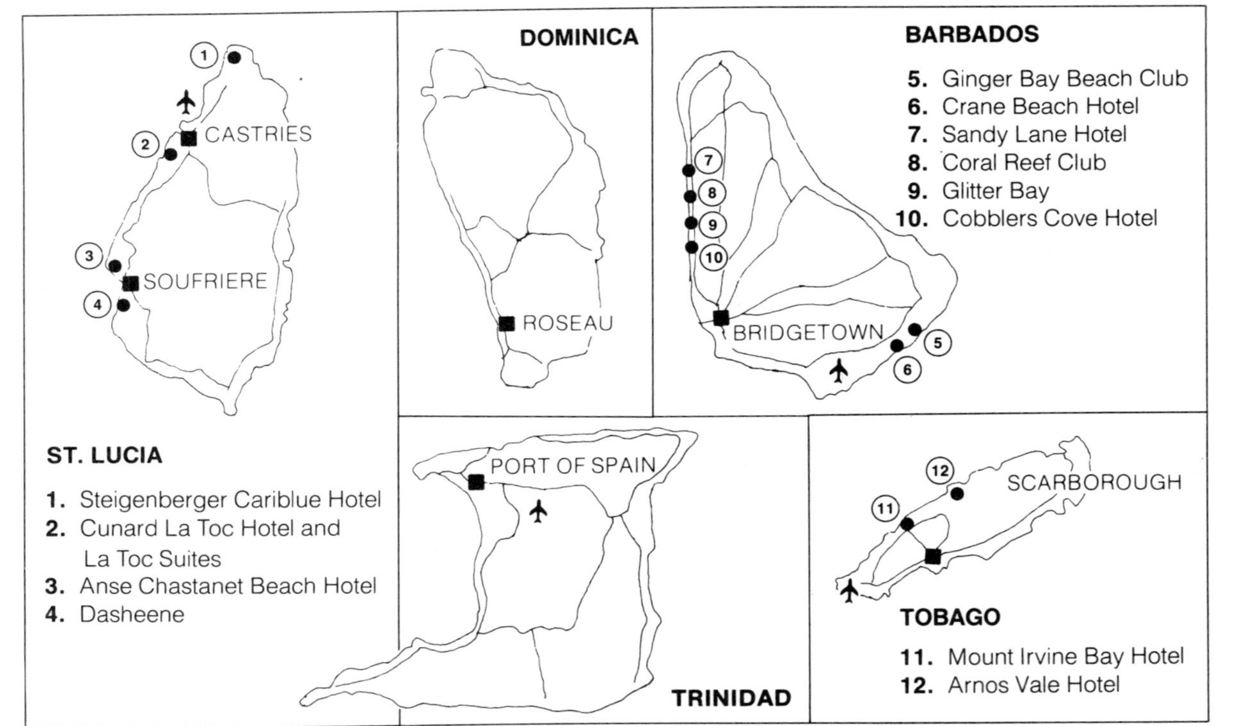

THE QUEEN'S WINDWARDS

The Queen's Windwards

Dominica, St. Lucia, Barbados, Trinidad and Tobago are not, strictly speaking, a geographical entity, and any sailor who thinks of them as "windwards" may find himself way off course; but for lovers and other romantics this is a convenient, if grab-bag, grouping. What these islands have in common is that they were all at one time British dependencies.

Of the group, Dominica is the most fascinating—the Caribbean as it must have been at the turn of the century, or, once you get up into the mountains and rain forests, as it must have been when Columbus arrived here one *dominica* in 1493. This is an island for travelers rather than vacationers, with real me-Tarzan-you-Jane countryside—untamed, forbidding landscapes, mountains a mile high, primeval forests, waterfalls, sulphur springs, lava beaches and communities of the original Carib Indians. But for lovers I haven't been able to find a suitable hideaway since my previous favorite was wiped out by a hurricane.

St. Lucia has much the same topography as Dominica, but somehow this one is a gentler island, its landscape softened by mile after mile of banana, spice and coconut plantations, by bays and coves of white sand beaches. The new road from the international jetport takes you along the windward Atlantic shore and across the mountains, but if you have time, return to the airport by the old road down the west coast. It winds and snakes and twists and writhes forever, but the scenery is impressive, and you pass Marigot Bay (good lunch stop), Soufrière, the famed Pitons, with possible side trips to volcanoes, sulphur springs or rain forests. The problem with this idea is that you'd have to rent a car, trot round to the police station to get a local driving permit (I also got zapped for a donation to Police Week) and when you leave the car at the jetport, you may be asked to pay an outrageous drop-off charge. But I'm almost persuaded it's worth the effort and expense.

Barbados is hardly a St. Lucia or Dominica in terms of scenery (it's relatively flat and pastoral except for a hilly region in the northeast) but it has a cosmopolitan air that few other Caribbean islands have, maybe because it has always been a favorite with the English gentry. Its main attraction, of course, is its scalloped western coastline, each cove with a lagoonlike beach. It may be rather crowded these days, but it still shelters most of the island's finest resorts. When it's time to take a break from sunning and swimming, however, Barbados rewards the leisurely tourist with an unusual variety of sights, from caves and flower forests to plantation houses and forts and venerable churches. There's even a house where George Washington slept when he visited his brother Lawrence.

Trinidad you can keep. At least as a lovers' hideaway. This island seems to get by on the strength of its carnival and, to some extent, the bustling, swinging, melting-pot qualities of its capital, Port of Spain. Its airport would be high on the list of places to avoid at all costs, if it weren't for the fact that you have to transit there to get to a gem—Tobago.

Tobago is another story: 114 square miles of lush mountains, backwater fishing villages, beautiful beaches and Buccoo Reef. This is the sort of island where the local bobbies hitch a ride in your taxi because they can't afford patrol cars and their chief is using the official bicycle. It's certainly worth the trouble it takes to get there, if you want someplace offbeat and secluded.

HOW TO GET THERE Barbados's Grantley Adams International Airport is one of the major gateways to the Caribbean, from North America and Europe, so there are daily nonstops from New York (American, Pan Am, BWIA) and Miami (Pan Am, Eastern and BWIA); and frequent nonstops from Toronto (Air Canada and BWIA).

St. Lucia needs a little more attention, because it has two airports: Hewanorra International in the south for jets, Vigie in the north for small planes. There are commuter flights between the two. Otherwise, there's a lengthy drive (at least an hour) from Hewanorra to the hotels near Castries and beyond. You can get to Hewanorra on Eastern and BWIA from Miami, from New York and Toronto on BWIA; otherwise, you can make connections to Vigie via Barbados (several times a day) by LIAT and Martinique by LIAT and Air Martinique.

For Tobago, you must first fly to Trinidad's Port of Spain, which is served from New York by Pam Am and BWIA, from Miami by Eastern and BWIA (some nonstops in each case). From Canada, there are direct flights on BWIA and Air Canada. BWIA also operates the 20-minute jet flights from Trinidad to Tobago. Leave yourselves plenty of time to negotiate the tediously officious formalities at Trinidad; even with a confirmed ticket try to check in for the Tobago flight a full hour before departure, especially on weekends when everyone in Trinidad, it seems, is heading for Tobago. Some of the North American flights arrive too late to make the Tobago connection; your best plan in that case is to head straight for the Trinidad Hilton.

Steigenberger Cariblue Hotel

St. Lucia

🌴🌴🌴🍴🍴⚽⚽⚽⚽$$

In this luxurious spot the welcome brochures are in German and English, the newspaper rack offers yesterday's news in *Zeitung* as well as the *Times*, and bronzed Isoldes whisper into their Tristans' ears. The Steigenberger Cariblue is the first (late 1973) venture in the Caribbean for a solidly established German chain. It stands guard over 300 yards of sandy beach, its arched coral-colored facade dominated by a campanilelike tower. The architecture owes as much to Garmisch-Partenkirchen as it does to Bermuda. Wooden alpine walkways with shingle roofs shield you from the sun, as you walk from the tower building or the beachfront wing to the open lounge and dining pavilion beside the beach. Apart from bamboo-and-rattan furniture, your room won't give you much clue to your location—wall-to-wall carpet, polished oak headboards, color schemes in green or yellow. You may have to use your air conditioner more often than you'd like to (not much cross-ventilation), but in terms of taste and comfort the Cariblue rooms are among the best in the islands. (The four categories of rates are related to location—least expensive in the main building, most expensive in the two-story beachfront wing.) The Teutonic starkness is now softened by masses of tropical blossoms spilling over terraces and balconies, splashing the coral-colored walls with pinks and blues and yellows. Alps and Antilles finally get together in the lovely dining pavilion—shingled chalet roof over Barbados stone, flowers, hardwood pillars, rattan chairs upholstered plumply in tropical pink, green or burnt orange. It's the sort of restful setting—soft lighting, gentle surf in the background, trade winds in the palm fronds—where you tend to arrive in time for two drinks before dinner, and it's hard to resist a nightcap afterward. Dinner itself can be variable here, since Steigenberger rotates its head chef every two years or so (though they always maintain a good German/Alsatian wine list). Likewise their managers. Currently the Herr Direktor is a genial, on-the-ball gentleman from Switzerland, George Brown.

NAME: Steigenberger Cariblue Hotel

MANAGER: Jean-Philippe de Muyser

ADDRESS: P.O. Box 437, Castries, St. Lucia, W.I.

LOCATION: On the northern tip of the island, 20 minutes and $12–15 by taxi from Vigie Airport, 1½ hours from the Hewanorra jetport ($40 per taxi, or less by Eastern bus if you reserve in advance)

TELEPHONE: 8551

TELEX: 6330

RESERVATIONS: Steigenberger Reservation Services in the United States; St. Lucia Centre in Toronto: 416-561-5606; SRS offices in Europe

CREDIT CARDS: All major cards

ROOMS: 100, plus 2 suites, all with air-conditioning, screened windows, radios, phones, safes

MEALS: Breakfast 7:30–10:00, lunch 12:30–2:30, dinner 7:00–10:00 (in the beachside pavilion, approx. $35 for 2); informal dress, "nothing too elegant, please"; full room service 7:30 A.M.–10:30 P.M., $1 extra charge

ENTERTAINMENT: Taped music, steel bands, folklore shows, dancing, barbecues and buffets 2 or 3 times a week, movies, bingo evenings and other exotica

SPORTS: Good beach, freshwater pool; tennis (2 courts, lighted), snorkeling, Sunfish sailing, catamarans, windsurfers, waterskiing, squash, golf (9 holes, $6 per day; and an unusual special golf package); horseback riding (15 horses); scuba and boat trips by arrangement

P.S.: Small conventions in summer, a few group tours year round; clientele about 40 percent German speaking, remainder mixture of other Europeans and North Americans

Cunard La Toc Hotel and La Toc Suites

St. Lucia

🌴🌴🌴 XXX ●●●● $$$$

Judging by the accents all around you, you could be in Brighton or Blackpool, but step out into the sun, look at the expanse of pinkish beach and the free-form pool with the tree in the middle and you know you're nowhere near England's favorite resorts. This is the Caribbean with a capital C. Palm trees, soft trade winds, clear water, blue skies. Nevertheless, La Toc breaks so many of my yardsticks (see Introduction) it almost shouldn't be included in these pages: it's big, it hosts cruise ship passengers, it indulges in "crab-racing" and other buffooneries to keep its guests amused. And yet . . . La Toc has so many attractive features that you'll probably be happy to overlook any shortcomings and enjoy its comforts and facilities—not least, the new deluxe suites.

The owners, Trafalgar House Investments, are London-based property development specialists (they also own the Cunard Line, hence the name). Their property here is a valley of 100 acres opening onto a half mile of curved beach, protected on either side by low headlands and the entrance to Castries harbor; their development consists of a 170-room cantaloupe-and-white hotel, a cottage colony, a 9-hole golf course, tennis courts and a few score private homes dotted around the valley and the golf course. It all sounds overwhelming, and in fact your first glimpse of the 4-story Tower Wing from the top of the hill hardly signals "hideaway," but when you get into the swing of things you don't really notice the hotel's size. You can thank nature a lot for that; in St. Lucia's fertile climate a matchstick can grow into a coconut palm, and here at La Toc the grounds are vivid with red ixorra, Christmas candle and purple eranthemum. Despite the size and the slabs of cantaloupe stucco, you're never far from the sounds of tree frogs, crickets and birds.

There was a time, a few years back, when La Toc lapsed into the doldrums. Maintenance was slack. Staff was surly. The beach was often overrun by passengers from Cunard's cruise ships. But beginning in 1986, the Cunard people spotted the trend to Caribbean Deluxe and decided to spend something like $3 million refurbishing the entire property. Especially the pastel-colored villas. Into the sea went the concept of self catering, and with it went the kitchens. They've been replaced by stocked refrigerators and wet bars. Stylish new furnishings include cabinets with television and VCR. The best of these villas have private plunge pools just outside the window (some also have private Jacuzzis). In theory, all the villas have ocean views, some more so than others; but the choice locations are those farthest from the hotel—beside the beach or up on the bluff. Over here you not only have a splendid sea view and cooler breezes, you're also screened from the comings and goings at the hotel; yet one of the pools, the Crow's Nest Bar and Les Pitons (the smartest of the resort's three restaurants) are within easy walking distance (on lazy days you can always call for the minibus to come to collect you). Cunard refers to its new villa suites as "a hotel within a hotel"—you don't check in at the main desk, you're simply whisked directly to your suite to sign in at your convenience.

If you decide to save a few dollars and opt for the hotel itself, the best bets are the rooms numbered 101 through 112 (at the far end of the beach wing, away from the bustle of the pool and terrace), and they're priced accordingly. Medium-price rooms are housed in the four-story Tower Wing; the least expensive accommodations face the garden and driveway but are probably quieter than those adjoining the main pool.

The remaining revampings are decided improvements, especially the smart new Crow's Nest Bar and Les Pitons Restaurant. The kitchen has improved, the staff is sharper and friendlier. And the Cunard people, realizing that you can't have a top-of-the-line resort swarming with day-trippers, have decided to bite the bullet and restrict the number of cruise ship passengers visiting La Toc. And then making those visitors pay for water sports.

Overnight guests, of course, enjoy the sports facilities at no extra charge. With a wide array of water sports, a dandy little golf course and 5 tennis courts—to say nothing of its 46 plunge pools—La Toc now has to rate as one of the classiest sporting resorts in the islands.

NAME: Cunard Hotel La Toc and La Toc Suites

MANAGER: Michael Marko

ADDRESS: P.O. Box 399, Castries, St. Lucia, W.I.

 LOCATION: Just south of Castries, the capital; 10 minutes and $10 from Vigie Airport, 1 hour and $35 by taxi or 20 minutes and $60 per person by helicopter from Hewanorra Airport

TELEPHONE: 809-452-3081 and 3089

TELEX: 6320 LC

RESERVATIONS: Cunard, New York, 800-229-0939, or Scott Calder International, Inc.

CREDIT CARDS: All major cards

ROOMS: 160 rooms and 12 suites in the hotel, 54 luxury suites in garden villas, all rooms with air-conditioning, patios or balconies, telephones; all suites with patios or balconies, stocked refrigerators, wet bars, VHS videotape player, some with ceiling fans, some with private plunge pools, some with Jacuzzis

MEALS: Breakfast 7:00–10:00, lunch noon–2:30, dinner 7:00–10:00 (approx. $30–60 for 2, in one of 3 breeze-cooled dining rooms); informal dress, but stylishly so in Les Pitons; live music with dinner at the main terrace; room service to 10:30 P.M., no extra charge

ENTERTAINMENT: 3 bars, tennis club pub, library (with VHS tapes), movies, live entertainment every evening (amplified, combos, folklore shows, etc.)

SPORTS: Sandy beach (good swimming), 2 freshwater pools, 46 plunge pools, snorkeling, Sunfish sailing, windsurfing, waterskiing, tennis (5 courts, 3 with lights, pro shop), golf (9 holes)—all free; pedalos, scuba diving, sport fishing and horseback riding can be arranged

P.S.: Some children, some cruise ship passengers (but they now have to pay to use the beach and facilities, which effectively cuts down on the numbers)

Anse Chastanet Beach Hotel

St. Lucia

$$$

Don't come here for three-speed showerheads and Porthault sheets. The luxuries at Anse Chastanet run deeper, and dearer. First, there's the Caribbean's most spectacular view, a Bali Ha'i of jagged mountains soaring

out of the sea that would have sent Gauguin diving for his umbers and indigos. Then there's the hotel's simple good taste, from handmade mahogany bed tables to the twist of immaculate madras on every waitress's head.

But you find something else here that is all too rare in the Caribbean these days: a caring and a closeness not just between owner and guests or staff and guests, but with the whole tiny community—taxi drivers, schoolgirls, fishermen, banana cutters. Consider what happened to the guests here on Christmas Eve. As they sat sipping their after-dinner cognacs high above the darkened beach, suddenly a flaming torch appeared in the sea. Then another and another and another. The villagers had come to sing carols from their canoes. No hats were passed, no bows were taken. It was just to say Merry Christmas.

Artfully tucked away in one of St. Lucia's remotest back pockets, Anse Chastanet proves hard to get to even once you get there. Its private roadway rocks 'n' rolls you up and up and up until at the end of it all you discover the beginning of the hotel, spiraling down the other side of the mountain to the sea.

Octagonal, whitewashed guest cottages cantilever out from the hibiscus like vacationers who can't get enough of that Gauguin view. The style is Beach Functional: wraparound windows and terraces, paddle fans, island-crafted furniture of local wood, crisp madras and muslin at the windows and on the beds, no-frills showers. All of it born of the theory that beach houses are for sleeping. (Best views, by the way, are from rooms numbered 5, 6 and 7.) Owner Nick Troobitscoff added 12 new rooms in 1986 without upsetting the scenery. They're tucked behind the beach (behind the kitchen, too, alas) but to compensate for what could be a breezeless location they're luxurious, 6 of them 1-bedroom suites with private plunge pools. For the rest, there is a series of multilevel open-air terraces, dining rooms and bars—and, at the bottom of a long hillside stairway, a graceful quarter-mile beach of fine volcanic sand the color of pussywillows.

But who says you have to be a stay-at-home? Take a picnic lunch to the hotel's private waterfall. Get a native guide to paddle you around the neighboring mountain islands. Give your camera a workout in Soufrière, a tumbledown fishing village as scrubbed and picture-perfect as a movie set. Tour an authentic French colonial banana plantation. Soak your weary bones in the hot mineral baths of a tropical rain forest. Visit a volcano you can drive into (and *out* of). And in the evening, try the Hummingbird. It's one of the West Indies' best restaurants, and it's right at the start of Anse Chastanet's roadway.

Then, if all this hasn't exhausted your pluck, leave in grand style. Skip the tortuous taxi ride to Vigie Airport and take the *Family Bible* instead. It's a pirogue, a dugout canoe owned by a local fisherman who cheerfully takes you and your luggage the 25 miles in 1 sea-breezy hour right to the terminal's front door. Just remember not to wear your Guccis—it takes a few steps in the ocean before you step into the terminal.

NAME: Anse Chastanet Beach Hotel

MANAGER: Peter Pietrouszka

ADDRESS: P.O. Box 216, Soufrière, St. Lucia, W.I.

LOCATION: On the southwest coast, 50 minutes and $35 by taxi from Hewanorra airport, 1½ hours and $40 from Vigie or Castries (but if you're staying 4 nights or longer, the fare may be included—and in any case, the hotel will have someone meet you at the airport if you let them know when you'll be arriving)

TELEPHONE: 809-455-7354/5

TELEX: 0398-6370

RESERVATIONS: Scott Calder International, Inc.

CREDIT CARDS: American Express, Diners Club, Visa, MasterCard

ROOMS: 37, 20 in the hillside cottages, 12 in three new plantation-style villas at beach level, all with ceiling fans, balconies or patios, 6 with private plunge pools

MEALS: Breakfast 7:30–10:00, lunch noon–3:00 (at the beachside bar), dinner 7:30–10:00 (approx. $40 for 2, in one of two hillside terraces); informal dress; coalpot barbecues Friday evenings, Creole buffet Tuesdays; room service for breakfast only, $1 extra

ENTERTAINMENT: Quiet taped music, folklore shows, dancing, local "shake-shake" band, steel band

SPORTS: Beach (volcanic sand), snorkeling, windsurfing, Sunfish sailing, pirogue trips to the Pitons, tennis (1 court, no lights)—all free; complete scuba facility with 3 dive boats and photo lab extra (no spearguns—the sea around here is about to be declared a national preserve)

Dasheene

St. Lucia

Waking up here in the morning is like being present at the Creation. Immediately below, an amphitheater of hillside thick with tropical greenery drops off precipitously to a coconut plantation, then the Caribbean glistens and glitters all the way to the horizon. And framing the view, the picturesque Pitons, those postcard-perfect twin volcanic cones soaring straight from the sea to about the same height as your bed, 1,200 ft. above the yachts bobbing at anchor in their secluded bay. And it's all right there before your bedazzled eyes without the effort of opening the windows or pushing back the shutters, because your hilltop aerie has no west wall. In some suites, you can ooh and aah at the panorama without even getting out of bed.

This most unusual inn, part Big Sur, part Bali Ha'i, sits atop the ridge of an extinct volcano (which you would never guess in a thousand nights was a volcano, given the surrounding foliage), a 4-acre plot in a 200-year-old working plantation that still produces cocoa, coffee and copra. Conceived some 15 years ago by an American designer/sculptor to be environmentally harmonious, the villas and public rooms are constructed of timber and native stone, camouflaged by flowering shrubs, all with the "invisible" west wall. Even the name comes from its surroundings, a dasheene being the St. Lucian version of the taro root. You enter via a gatehouse, a driveway that brings you to a series of terraces and decks, a tiny rock pool that seems to be trickling over the side of the hill and a cathedral-ceilinged, shingle-roofed dining pavilion that is at once simple and sophisticated.

Each of the wood-framed villas and suites is different, each a designer's fantasy, with splashes of color, tropical and otherwise, livening the stone and wicker and bamboo. In one, a gallery bedroom with open shower, in another the bathroom is in the style of a Polynesian grass hut. Some rooms come with coalpots for heating your toes or cooking hors d'oeuvres, some have indoor gardens. Suite L has semicircular banquettes and a circular plunge pool at the edge of the ridge, Villa C has a plunge pool *and* Jacuzzi. Suite K sports a mahogany four-poster with Indian fabrics; in others, double beds pose on platforms beneath clouds of mosquito netting. They're all quite special—Dasheene dashing, as it were.

Certainly Dasheene's villas and suites are not for everyone. The fitted-carpet-fastidious might balk at the missing wall and the resulting invitation to moths and lizards (too high for no-see-ums). And it should be noted that the inn has changed ownership recently and there's talk of installing a branch of a well-known Swiss clinic (I suspect that's a long way down the line); and the new manager, Rudy Blaha (formerly at Brias Creek in the British Virgins) will have to balance the wishes of guests and homeowners. But for the romantics among us, Dasheene is wonderful. Or "awesome," as singer/actor/entertainer Burl Ives called it when he came here a few months back to while away his seventy-seventh birthday.

From Dasheene, high on its hill, it's a twisty drive down to the village of Soufrière, a rickety backwater fishing village—so is there anything to do here? Apart from beaches and water sports, there are trips for would-be seafarers—by pirogue or sailboat to Marigot Harbour; Rudy Blaha can arrange to have you driven to the revitalized mineral baths (in the days of Louis XVI, the French aristocracy took the waters here); you can drive up to the extinct but bubbling volcano or the nearby rain forest.

However you fill the hours between spectacular sunrise and spectacular sunset, there's still another surprise about Dasheene: going to bed, with the moon shimmering on the sea behind the Pitons.

NAME: Dasheene

MANAGER: Rudy Blaha

ADDRESS: Soufrière, St. Lucia, W.I.

LOCATION: A few miles south of the town of Soufrière, 40 minutes and $32 by taxi from Hewanorra Airport

TELEPHONE: 809-454-7444

TELEX: 6239

RESERVATIONS: Own U.S. office, 800-DASHEEN

CREDIT CARDS: American Express, Visa, MasterCard

ROOMS: 18 suites and 3-bedroom villas, all different, all open to the breezes, some with shower only, villas with kitchenettes

MEALS: "Coffee is on the charcoal fire at 8:00 A.M.," breakfast 8:30–10:00 and lunch 11:30–2:30 on the poolside patio, dinner 7:30 in the breeze-cooled dining room (approx. $80 for 2); informal attire, "however, gentlemen are required to wear sport shirts and trousers to dinner"; soft classical background music; room service during meal hours, 10 percent extra

ENTERTAINMENT: The bar, the view, the moon and Venus

SPORTS: Pool (filtered, odorless water from the mineral baths), 6 plunge pools (1 with Jacuzzi), health club (exercise rooms, Nautilus equipment), trips to mineral baths—free; own dock and water sports facilities (including scuba diving) in Soufrière

P.S.: "Not suitable for children under 12"

P.P.S.: At press time, Dasheene was closed indefinitely, "but should be open for the winter season"—check with the number above

Ginger Bay Beach Club

Barbados

$$$$

To get to the beach here you walk through the garden gate, along a stone path to a cavelike gash in the coral cliff, then down, down 64 wooden steps *through* the coral cliff.

Sounds like work? Maybe. Especially on the return trip. But in either direction the hike is well worth the huffing and puffing since this is the northern end of Crane Beach, probably the island's loveliest (some reporters list it as the most beautiful beach in the world but that's fanciful). Sometimes there's a beach bar down under, sometimes not. But there's a Thermos bottle in your pantry, which you can fill with rum punch before you leave for the lower reaches.

Built in 1984, the Beach Club (a club in name only) sits romantically atop the coral cliff, three two-story villas all dressed up in coral pink. The suites (no rooms, just suites) come with air-conditioned bedroom, pantry and living room. But you may find yourselves spending most of your nonbeach hours on the spacious lanai, lounging in your hammock, listening to the surf pound the coral far below and watching the moonlight shimmer on the sea.

Furnishings and fabrics are more English country house than Barbados resort—fitted carpets, wingback armchairs, double beds topped with forest green spreads and baldachins with floral motifs.

There's a more tropical flair about the hub of the club—a compact courtyard given over to free-form pool and whirlpool, kiosk bar and open dining pavilion, with patio furnishings, umbrellas and even the bottom of the pool embellished with a stylish representation of the ginger lily, the hotel's insignia.

Ginger's, the club's pavilion-restaurant, puts you even more in an island mood: gray-stained hardwood beams and columns, waitresses in long native costumes with pretty pink chapeaux, candles in terra-cotta replicas of traditional Bajan homes. The young Bajan chef put in stints at the Culinary Institute of America and Washington's Vista (where he helped prepare banquets for Reagan and Bush) but hasn't forgotten his island roots—flying fish or dolphin smoked over pinewood, callalloo, breadfruit "vichysoisse," lobster and chubb from the reef beyond your windows, prepared with ginger and lime.

And when you've admired moon and reef for the last time and it's time to turn in, what do you find your maid has placed on your pillows? Ginger-snaps, of course.

NAME: Ginger Bay Beach Club

MANAGER: Jim Clark

ADDRESS: St. Philip, Barbados, W.I.

LOCATION: On the windward southeastern shore, 10–15 minutes from the airport, $11 by taxi

TELEPHONE: 809-423-5810

TELEX: 2564 (ADMIRAL) WB

RESERVATIONS: None

CREDIT CARDS: American Express, Visa, MasterCard

ROOMS: 16 one-bedroom suites, all with ceiling fans and air-conditioning, wet bars, balconies or lanais, direct-dial telephone, radio

MEALS: Breakfast 8:00–10:00, lunch noon–2:00, afternoon tea 4:00, dinner 7:00–9:30 (approx. $50 for 2); informal dress; room service at no extra charge

ENTERTAINMENT: Bar, parlor games

SPORTS: 1 mile of beach (good swimming and snorkeling, depending on the surf), freshwater pool, tennis (1 lighted court)—free; other sports by arrangement

Crane Beach Hotel

Barbados

$$$

Once the only thing that stood on this airy bluff was a gigantic wooden crane that handed down bales of sugarcane to British schooners bobbing in the sea below. By the turn of the eighteenth century, the gentleman who owned the crane had done so well that next to it he built himself a very small, very grand manor house. Close to 200 years later, that minimansion of gray-white coral stone is the east wing of the Crane Beach Hotel.

You can usually count on a couple of centuries to take their toll, especially in a windswept, spumeswept spot like this. But the miraculous thing about the old Crane is that its original seigneur would probably still feel right at home—even with the addition of a new wing in the nineteenth century and a swimming pool in the twentieth.

This pool, a spectacular Roman affair with Ionic columns, is scooped right out of the edge of the cliff with a backdrop of sea and beach and a full-blown coconut grove. It's the kind of vista that dreams are made of.

Unfortunately, it's also the kind of vista that attracts parties of sightseers in minibuses, and since the site and sight are also historic you have to pay an admission charge just to enter the grounds (you get a refund, of course, if you're checking into the hotel). Good-bye tranquility, farewell serenity, especially on weekends.

These trippers usually arrive at midday for a swim in the pool, drinks on the terrace, lunch in the terrace dining room—where, if the wind blows and the windows are closed, the noise level can be jarring. Escape *is* possible.

Your charming room or suite, your breezy balcony or patio. And since a few rooms have kitchenettes you may be able to rustle up your own light lunch without setting eyes on a single day-tripper.

The guest rooms may be outshone by the hotel's setting—but only just. They're closer to a country *auberge* than an Antillean resort. Floors of gleamingly polished wide-plank pine or cooling quarry tiles. Canopy beds and 16-ft. ceilings. Walls a foot thick. Antique chests and wardrobes. Tiled baths with both overhead and handheld showers.

Some favorites. Room 3 may be the most intimate of all the Crane's romantic nooks and crannies, with simple beachy furniture, refrigerator and honor bar, flowery brick patio. Above, Room 10A has a balcony that gives you a two-way view along the picture-book beach and east out to the reef and the sea. Rooms 1, 2, 7 and 8 have four-poster beds. For the more ascetic, there are nine secluded, much less elaborate guest rooms down at the hotel's beach house (known as Crane Bank House), with their own swimming pool and coconut grove.

But for going the whole hog, there's no place like Suite 8. Beyond the gleaming foyer waits a sitting room worthy of a governor-general: burnished wood ceiling, silken sofas, glass-doored bookcases imaginatively stocked. Beyond that is a *House Beautiful* kitchen, and beyond *that* a bedroom full of splendid antiques. In the middle of it all, on a carpeted platform of blue, looms a huge canopied bed, from which on a clear day, with the wooden louvered shutters pushed aside, you can view the same sunny sea lane those ancient sugar schooners followed home to Liverpool.

One caveat: the Crane Beach dining rooms are not the most attractive in Barbados and the cooking is nothing special, so you may want to dine around in the island's restaurants, most of which involve trips of 30 minutes or more (except for nearby Ginger Bay Beach Club or Sam Lord's Castle). A car will be useful, but during the winter months you'd better reserve your wheels when you reserve your room. The hotel will take care of both reservations.

NAME: Crane Beach Hotel

MANAGER: Peter McKeever

ADDRESS: The Crane, St. Philip, Barbados, W.I.

LOCATION: On the southeastern corner of the island, 15 minutes and $11 by taxi from the airport, 30 minutes and $15 from Bridgetown (free shuttle bus to town in winter)

TELEPHONE: 809-423-6220

TELEX: 2381 CRANE WB

RESERVATIONS: Robert Reid Assoc.

CREDIT CARDS: American Express, MasterCard, Visa

ROOMS: 25, including 10 suites and 9 cabana-style rooms at the Beach House, all with ceiling fans and telephones, most with balconies or patios, some with kitchenettes, some with four-poster beds and antiques

MEALS: Breakfast 7:30–10:00, lunch noon–2:30 in the glass-enclosed cafeteria overlooking the beach and reef, dinner 7:00–10:00 in the breeze-cooled, tented dining room (approx. $50 for 2); informal dress; full room service from 7:00 A.M.–10:00 P.M. (except in Beach House)

ENTERTAINMENT: Taped classical music in lounge, four-piece amplified dance band on Saturday

SPORTS: 1,000 ft. of white sand beach (down spiral steps), 2 freshwater pools (the largest with 160,000 gallons, every drop from a private well), snorkeling, tennis (4 courts, no lights)—free; horseback riding, sailing nearby

P.S.: "Not suitable for young children"

Sandy Lane Hotel

Barbados

$$$$$

When I reviewed Sandy Lane in the last edition of this guidebook, I noted that dining at the beachside terrace was like picnicking in an aviary. Birds everywhere.

The service, too, was for the birds.

Seems I wasn't the only one to grouse and the message got through to Britain's Trusthouse Forte Hotels, who recently completed a $5-million renovation and rehab. A large chunk of that sum ($250,000 or thereabouts) went to consultants brought in to motivate and train—maybe even just waken—the staff; a much smaller chunk went to wrapping the pink-and-white dining pavilions in fishnet to keep the birds out of your lunch.

Most of the $5 million, of course, went to sprucing up rooms and the accoutrements therein. New beds, new rattan furniture in the rooms. New refrigerators (full-size and rather ungainly) on the balconies. New tile floors, new bathrobes and marble bathrooms in the suites. And a new bar just off the lobby, where the lovely open-to-the-breezes, chandelier-draped lounge is about to become, in the words of an assistant manager, "a nice air-conditioned cocktail lounge." Next thing they'll be air-conditioning is the beach.

Another welcome innovation will be complimentary water sports. Hitherto, guests had to pay through the nose for a room and then pay through the nose to rent a snorkeling mask or sail a Sunfish. Now water sports are included in the rate. Ditto tennis—even with the lights. So rates that were once outlandish begin to look a shade more realistic (especially off season—about half off).

Physically, of course, Sandy Lane is still one of the class acts—imposing gateway and driveway, classy porte cochere and main lodge of pinkish gray coral stone, the lobby leading to a half-moon veranda overlooking a circular beachside patio where you dance beneath the stars in the classic Caribbean style. Since it opened to jet-set fanfare in 1961, this classy resort has always sounded like a nice place to be. And it is. Sort of.

But I still can't whip up much enthusiasm for a place that charges around $80 a couple for a mediocre Friday evening buffet—about 24 dishes, with only 3 hot entrées and a so-so selection of desserts. (The buffet at, say, Cobblers Cove—with *6* hot entrées—is a more appealing event and costs $20 less.) And even if the birds *have* left the lunch table, there are still too many rubberneckers, hawkers and radios on the beach for real seclusion (not the hotel's fault, the beach is there for everyone, but uniformed security men don't put me in a very jolly holiday mood).

So, even with a new chef and new manager (a Scot, despite his gallic-sounding name, and highly regarded by other hoteliers, I should add), even with its tony diehards who return winter after winter (just try getting a room in February), Sandy Lane is still largely coasting along on its sixties reputation.

But at least the message has been heard and Sandy Lane is finally sharpening up its act.

NAME: Sandy Lane Hotel

MANAGER: Peter Vacher

ADDRESS: St. James, Barbados, W.I.

LOCATION: On the west coast, 40 minutes from the airport (free pickup in limo, $30 by Rolls-Royce, $25 by Mercedes—on request), 20 minutes and $10 by taxi from Bridgetown

TELEPHONE: 809-432-1311

TELEX: WB 2225

RESERVATIONS: Trusthouse Forte (212-541-4400)

CREDIT CARDS: All major cards

ROOMS: 115, in 3 two-story or four-story wings, including 24 suites (avoid Garden View, even if you save a few dollars); all with private bathrooms (Nina Ricci toiletries, new bathrobes), balcony or lanai, central air-conditioning, refrigerator, wake-up radio; color TV (Barbados station only) in suites

MEALS: Breakfast 7:30–10:00, lunch 12:30–2:30, dinner 7:30–9:30 (approx. $60 for 2), in 2 beachside pavilions festooned with pink-and-white awnings; informal but dressy most of the time, jacket and tie Wednesday and Saturday from, for some inexplicable reason "October 21 through April 19"; room service during dining room hours, no extra charge

ENTERTAINMENT: Bar, lounge with big-screen VCR, live music most evenings, dancing under the stars, some folklore shows—including the inescapable limbo (even though you'd think that all those repeat clients might be bored with it by this time)

SPORTS: Long stretch of beach, freshwater pool up at the tennis club, tennis (6 courts, with lights, pro shop), snorkeling, windsurfing, Sunfish sailing—all free; own championship-caliber golf course ($20 for 18 holes or $100 a week for unlimited play for resident guests); yacht trips, scuba, waterskiing and horseback riding can be arranged at extra charge

P.S.: Member of Elegant Resorts (see under Cobblers Cove); some groups and seminars in the off-season

Coral Reef Club

Barbados

You stay in bungalows with names like Petrea and Allamanda and Cordia, and you walk to the beach past splashes of blue petrea and yellow allamanda and orange cordia.

You swim a few leisurely breast strokes to the coral reef offshore.

You dine off flying fish mousse and marlin pâté, tipsy trifle and coconut meringue pie.

Above all, you relax.

The Coral Reef Club is the sort of place where people go to wind down rather than dress up, where entertainers like Engelbert Humperdinck and Tom Jones or Olympic skating stars like Torvill and Deane go to find undisturbed seclusion. This clubby but unstuffy inn has been a standard-bearer among Barbados resorts for over 30 years, a prototype of the small Barbados retreat built around a coral-stone villa. And because it was there before the others, it managed to snare more beachfront acreage—more than a dozen acres of tropical greenery. Space enough for most of the rooms to be in semiprivate bungalows, spread out among cannonball and mango and mahogany trees.

The other attraction that sets Coral Reef apart is the O'Hara family. Budge and Cynthia O'Hara started the place all those 33 years ago (after a stint at England's famed Lygon Arms) and they haven't missed a year since, greeting every guest, overseeing gardens and kitchens, buying gifts for everyone staying at the club at Christmas. (Question: What do you get Engelbert *and* Tom when they're *both* guests over the same holiday? Answer: Each other's records.)

Now the torch has passed to a new generation of equally dedicated O'Haras. With the long-serving staff (some of whom have been with Budge since Day One) it all adds up to a special, warm feeling you can never find at a Sandy Lane, with its track record of what seems to be a different corporate manager every year. (How many resorts, for example, let you have continental breakfast any time between 8:00 and noon?)

The family feeling overflows to the large and airy guest rooms, which lean to almost defiantly *non*designer decor. Until last year, that is. Lounge areas and guest rooms have just been given a touch-up by the designer to the Duke and Duchess of York, no less. But before devoted Coral Reefers have palpitations, it should be pointed out that the place hasn't changed all *that* much, since the diffident designer has himself been a regular Reefer for years. A few new fabrics, a new sun terrace beside the dining room, the addition of ceiling fans and refrigerators in most rooms. Nothing major. Guests still have their own toasters, their own shelves of paperbacks, and, if they're lucky enough to be in a bungalow (specify Poinsettia, Frangipani, Cordia or Petrea to be closest to the beach), their own terraces draped with vines to match the name of the room—petrea or frangipani or cordia or whatever.

NAME: Coral Reef Club

OWNERS/MANAGERS: The O'Hara Family

ADDRESS: St. James, Barbados, W.I.

LOCATION: On the northwest coast, 35 minutes and $15 by taxi from the airport, 20 minutes and $10 from Bridgetown (free shuttle to town weekdays at 9:30 A.M.)

TELEPHONE: 809-422-2372

TELEX: 2407 CORAL WB

RESERVATIONS: Ralph Locke Islands

CREDIT CARDS: All major cards

ROOMS: 75, in garden bungalows, the Clubhouse, or in a two-story wing, all with private bathroom, patio or balcony, air-conditioning and ceiling fans, direct-dial telephones, toasters, wall safes, shelves of paperbacks

MEALS: Breakfast 7:00–10:00, continental breakfast 10:00–noon, lunch 1:00–2:30, afternoon tea 4:00, dinner 8:00–9:30 (approx. $45–55 for 2) in the breeze-cooled beachside pavilion; Sunday evening Bajan buffet; jacket and tie most evenings in winter, informal the remainder of the year; 24-hour room service at no extra charge

ENTERTAINMENT: Live music and dancing seven evenings a week year round (amplified "but not loud"), weekly folklore show and beach barbecue, parlor games, VCR

SPORTS: Good beach, good swimming and snorkeling, freshwater pool, tennis (2 all-weather courts, no lights, across the street and a 5-minute walk)—all free; water sports hut (a private concession, but one of the most experienced on the island) offers, for a fee, waterskiing, snorkeling, windsurfing, Hobie Cats, scuba diving, sailing cruises on a 30-ft. catamaran; golf at nearby Sandy Lane

P.S.: "Children welcome except from January 15 through March 15 when those under 12 years cannot be accommodated"; member of Elegant Hotels group, with dine-around privileges (see Cobblers' Cove)

P.P.S.: A sister resort, the Sandpiper Inn, is located just along the coast, on the beach; it has rooms or 1-bedroom suites with air-conditioning and balconies or patios overlooking tropical gardens, a swimming pool and pleasant timber-framed dining pavilion and a relaxed air. It's a dollar or two more expensive, so I'd put my money on the Coral Reef.

Glitter Bay

Barbados

🌴🌴🌴🍴🍴😊😊$$$$

The glitter comes from the play of sun on sea, but when the Cunard family of steamship fame took over the estate in the thirties, the *guests* were the glitter—Noël Coward and Anthony Eden, assorted lords and ladies and merchant princes. Ocean-going Cunarders putting into Bridgetown often found their ships' orchestras shanghaied to play for Sir Edward's garden parties. All very romantic.

Today, the sea still glitters, lords and ladies still winter here, and at least one Arab prince has settled in for 6 weeks on more than one occasion, accompanied by an entourage of 25. But Sir Edward Cunard's original coral-stone Great House is now the centerpiece of a small resort, created 6 years ago by a thirtyish Englishman, Michael Pemberton. He made his bundle in amusement arcades and real-estate developing, but with his prime Caribbean estate he has opted to develop it in the style of Andalusia rather than the Antilles—white stucco buildings rising three or four stories above the lawns, their ocher-tiled rooftops eye-to-eye with the coconut palms, their balconies and terraces angled for sea views. By confining the rooms to one side of the garden and by building up rather than out, Pemberton avoided that pitfall of so many of the newer beachside resorts in Barbados—rooms looking into rooms.

The rooms are attractively tropical with Mediterranean overtones, scatter rugs brightening quarry tile floors and (nice touch) cushioned banquettes on the stucco balconies. Since the new resort was conceived originally as a condo operation, most of the accommodations are suites with kitchenettes, in versatile configurations of duplex suites, penthouse suites and nests with one to three bedrooms.

But Glitter Bay is almost two distinct resorts, because the most appealing rooms, for my money, are located not in the new Andalusia-style villas but in a couple of beachside villas—Beach House and Bachelor Hall, the former a coral-stone replica of the Cunards' palazzo in Venice.

Glitter Bay also gives you a sense of space rare in Barbados—15 acres tended by a dozen gardeners, lawns shaded by royal palms and cannonball trees, pathways lined by frangipani and lady-of-the-night, sturdy saman trees embraced and entwined by traceries of wild orchids.

The old Great House sits well back from the beach, while the remaining structures are grouped around a split-level swimming pool with a wooden footbridge and waterfall. Down by the beach, the restaurant, Le Piperade,

enjoys fresh sea breezes and lavishes attentive service on its diners (the young staff are forever checking if everything is fine, heating plates for entrées, whisking plates away promptly). Prices are reasonable (for food *and* wine), and the menu runs the gamut from fried flying fish sandwich and fish cakes with spicy tomato sauce to *escalope de veau Cordon Bleu* and *noisette d'agneau.* My problem with Glitter Bay is reconciling the lovely natural setting and the thoughtfully designed guest rooms with what goes on at the Great House. The original hallway serves as reception area, opening onto lawns and a fountain—fine, very attractive. But a new wing, artfully grafted to the original and furnished like an English drawing room, should be a very congenial lounge/bar/games room; instead, it's been chilled to Arctic temperatures and the arcade-tycoon owner has lined one wall with (yuck!) slot machines. Glitter? They don't just glitter, they blaze, sparkle, flare and flash.

Skip this not-so-great house. Head straight for the gardens, the beach, Le Piperade and the plushly cushioned banquette lining your balcony.

NAME: Glitter Bay

OWNER/MANAGER: Michael Pemberton

ADDRESS: St. James, Barbados, W.I.

LOCATION: On the northwest coast, 40 minutes and $15 by taxi from the airport (you can also arrange to have the resort's Daimler sedan collect you, for $50), 20 minutes and $10 from Bridgetown

TELEPHONE: 809-422-4111

TELEX: 2397 WB GLITBAY

RESERVATIONS: Robert Reid Assoc.

CREDIT CARDS: All major cards

ROOMS: 93, in three- and four-story wings or beachside villas, all with air-conditioning and fans, terraces or patios, refrigerators, direct-dial telephones; suites also have kitchenettes

MEALS: Breakfast 8:00–10:00, lunch 12:30–3:00 and dinner 7:00–10:00, in the breeze-cooled, beachside restaurant (approx. $60 for 2); afternoon tea in the air-conditioned lobby/lounge; informal dress (but no shorts in the evening); room service during dining room hours

ENTERTAINMENT: Beachside bar, live amplified music for dancing, some folklore shows, slot machines and satellite TV and VCR in lounge (TV sets can also be rented)

SPORTS: Cove beach, raft, 2-tiered free-form freshwater pool, windsurfing, snorkeling masks, Hobie 16s, waterskiing, tennis (2 courts, with lights)—all free; sailboat and speedboat cruises and scuba can be arranged at the beach hut, golf and horseback riding 10 minutes away

P.S.: Expect lots of children during holidays (but they have their own planned activities) and a few seminar groups in the off-season

P.P.S.: As of Christmas 1987, Michael Pemberton was scheduled to open another luxury resort nearby, called Royal Pavilion. It's a renovation of an inspired first-class property and its site is less spacious than Glitter Bay's, so it may not have the same appeal, but most of the rooms will be beside the beach and will, no doubt, be eminently comfortable and well designed.

Cobblers Cove Hotel

Barbados

$$$$

Claudette Colbert lives two villas along the beach and when, a few years back, Ronald Reagan came a-calling and a-swimming, quiet little Cobblers Cove found itself awash with paparazzi and a perspiring Secret Service.

Next day, it was back to being its cozy, relaxed self. Just 38 suites, 76 guests. A stately drawing room. A charmer of a wood-framed dining pavilion beside the beach. A mini-swimming pool and a quarter-mile of unspoiled palm-fringed cove—with just the resort at one end, a fleet of fishing boats at the other, and Claudette Colbert in the middle, screened by a mass of sea grape.

The most northerly of Barbados's small hideaways, Cobblers is a world apart, the unsung rendezvous of actors from the United Kingdom, CEOs from the United States, professionals and romantics from hither and yon. For some it may be too small—3 acres of garden with 10 two-story shingle-roofed cottages, 4 suites to a cottage, arranged in a V around an 80-year-old castellated villa that looks like a setting for a Gilbert and Sullivan opera.

If the property is a tad cramped, the accommodations most certainly are not: suites only, each with a big hardwood balcony or patio, living room with a louvered wall that folds back, fully equipped kitchen, bathroom and air-conditioned bedroom, all stylishly designed and furnished. Suites located at the bottom of the V may have less privacy than you prefer (also, suites 19 and 20 may pick up some traffic noise from the road just beyond the garden wall); the best are the most expensive, closer to and, in most cases, facing the beach—1 through 8 and 33 through 36 (with even numbers—and higher ceilings—on the second floor).

But whatever your suite, you'll find a welcoming, instantly-at-home feeling to Cobblers Cove. Richard Williams is very much an on-the-spot, hands-on manager, his staff is pleasant and efficient (with maybe a couple of grumps out of a roster of 61). The kitchen has improved immensely, to the point where what was once a nice hotel with a fine kitchen is getting a reputation as an outstanding kitchen with a nice hotel attached.

So on balmy, candlelit evenings with the sea foaming just inches away, guests of the Cobblers now sit down to tempting dishes you might expect on St. Barths rather than Barbados—*mousseline d'homard à sauce croustade,* dolphin in champagne sauce, coco shrimp with guava sauce, *tournedos*

alexander à deux sauces, la coulis de fruits sous le sorbet citron, soursop lime or melon sorbet.

President Reagan couldn't have dined more splendidly at the villa along the beach.

NAME: Cobblers Cove Hotel

OWNER/MANAGER: Richard Williams

ADDRESS: St. Peter, Barbados, W.I.

LOCATION: On the sheltered northwest coast, adjoining the village of Speightstown (pronounced "spiteston"), 45 minutes and $21 by taxi from the airport, 15 minutes from Bridgetown (free shuttle/minibus daily or $11 by taxi)

TELEPHONE: 809-422-2291

TELEX: WB 2373 COBBLERS

RESERVATIONS: Robert Reid Assoc.

CREDIT CARDS: American Express, MasterCard, Visa

ROOMS: 38, all suites, with private bathrooms, air-conditioning and ceiling fans, louvered doors, kitchenette, balcony or patio, direct-dial telephones

MEALS: Breakfast 8:00–10:00, lunch 12:30–6:00, dinner 7:00–10:00 (approx. $50 for 2), in the beachside pavilion; barbecue buffet Tuesday, Bajan buffet Friday; informal dress; room service during dining room hours, no extra charge (see note below regarding dine-around plan)

ENTERTAINMENT: Lounge/bar, occasional live music (not too loud, not exactly pianissimo either), radio or TV for rooms available

SPORTS: Lovely beach and lagoon-smooth bay, small freshwater pool, snorkeling gear, waterskiing, windsurfing, Sunfish sailing, glass-bottom boat trips—all free; scuba diving, picnic sails, tennis and golf can be arranged, at extra charge

P.S.: Cobblers Cove has joined with 4 other hotels on the west coast to form Elegant Resorts of Barbados. Guests of one will have reciprocal privileges for dining, social and some sports facilities at the others—Coral Reef, Glitter Bay, Sandy Lane and Treasure Beach. There are also plans to run a shuttle bus between them each evening—a welcome bonus, since no matter how attractive each dining room is, it's always fun to sample others.

Arnos Vale Hotel

Tobago

$ $

When you sit down for afternoon tea, a giant flamboyant shades you from the sun, and a sprawling sea grape tree cools you when you sip a punch on the beachside terrace. You stroll to and from your room along pathways hugged by oleander and frangipani. Banana quits come to filch tidbits from your breakfast, and you lunch to the cries of parrots and jacamars, mockingbirds and motmots.

"We wanted the place to look as little like a hotel as possible," said the original owners. They certainly succeeded. What you see when you step through the lobby is an arena-shaped botanical garden, solid greenery accented with splashes of color, the sea glittering beyond the foliage. Look more carefully and you notice a building or two here and there at different levels, up there on the hillside, down there by the cove. The shingled, cut-coral cottage housing the lobby, lounge, dining veranda and 3 of the 28 rooms is perched at the 100-ft. level. Follow the footpath 20 ft. higher and you come to half a dozen rooms in 3 cottages, including an aerie called the

Crow's Nest Suite. The remaining rooms are down by the beach and pool, each different, but simply furnished with few frills, even though they come in two categories, standard and superior.

The newest rooms are in the Jacamar Wing, a few paces from the beach; but the most romantic (and probably the tiniest), room 21, is right on the beach, with local fishermen's dugout canoes hauled up at the foot of the tiny stone stairway that leads to a small private terrace. Back in the days when Arnos Vale was a sugar plantation this was part of the storehouse where the cane was stacked before being shipped to England. What makes a real difference between the rooms is location—whether you want to be close to the beach and pool, or up in the hills with the birds and breezes.

There are plenty of paths to follow through virtually unspoiled tropical forest. Your best plan would be to ask the bartender to make up a flask of rum punches, then follow the path up the hill to Sunset Point, where you'll find a bench for two, strategically placed to face the sun.

Since the original owners left, so has much of the tender loving care a place like this needs to keep it spic and span, but it's still a place for true solitude. Maybe too much so—I met an Englishman there once who claimed, in impeccably clipped accents, that he could actually talk to the motmots.

At any rate, this is a great place for nature lovers and birdwatchers who're happy with basic comforts and convenience in a stunningly beautiful setting.

NAME: Arnos Vale Hotel

MANAGER: Adolf Kessler

ADDRESS: P.O. Box 208, Tobago, Trinidad & Tobago, W.I.

LOCATION: In a tropical vale beside a quiet cove on the southwest coast, 20 minutes and $15 by taxi from Crown Point Airport

TELEPHONE: 809-639-2881/2

TELEX: None

RESERVATIONS: Utell International

CREDIT CARDS: American Express, Visa, MasterCard

ROOMS: 28, divided between the hilltop main lodge, hilltop cottages and beachside wings, all with balcony or terrace, telephone and radio, standard rooms with portable fans and showers, superior rooms with air-conditioning and tub/shower

MEALS: Breakfast 8:00–10:00 and lunch 12:30–2:00 on the beachside terrace, dinner 7:30–9:00 (on the veranda of the main lodge, approx. $30

for 2); barbecues Friday or Saturday; informal dress (but trousers rather than shorts for men after 6:00); room service 8:00 A.M.–9:00 P.M., $1 extra per tray

ENTERTAINMENT: Taped music in the dining room, steel band 2 evenings a week ("no amplification—and early in the evening since our guests like to be in bed by 10"), large-screen TV on terrace adjoining the dining room (spewing forth "Down by the River Side" in the middle of the afternoon, with not even a bananaquit watching it)

SPORTS: Sheltered beach, freshwater pool, tennis (1 court, newly resurfaced, no lights)—free; snorkeling gear for rent, fishing, golf, excursions to Buccoo Reef and bird sanctuaries can be arranged

Mount Irvine Bay Hotel

Tobago

$$$

It's constructed around an old sugar mill, fitted with a shingle-roofed ramada and stylishly transformed into an open bar and dining terrace.

A two-story wing of balconied guest rooms forms a protective L around a big blue-tiled swimming pool with a swim-up bar in one corner. Other rooms (46 out of 100) are housed in little square bungalows engulfed in heliconia and thumbergia. But what makes this 1970s resort so attractive is the setting—27 acres of tropical flora surrounded by 130 acres of fairways and coconut palms, laid out on a bluff above the curve of Mount Irvine Bay, with the famed Buccoo Reef breaking the sea just beyond the headland.

Most of the balconies and loggias are sited to make the most of the gardens and the views (except for 10 "standard" rooms facing the fairways) and without the views the room would be fairly conventional. New owners (a Trinidadian company) who took over the resort 3 years ago have recarpeted the rooms and cottages, replaced the plastic slat patio furniture with tubular loungers and chairs in tropical colors. Again, with the exception of the standards, the rooms are quite large, with double the usual closet space.

The bungalows, the priciest accommodations, have large loggias that are

virtually breezy outdoor living rooms with terrazzo floors and khuskhus rugs; the bedrooms, with new beige-plum wall-to-wall carpeting, are smaller and probably need the air-conditioning unit stuck in the wall.

The pièce de résistance of Mount Irvine is its Sugar Mill Restaurant, especially in the evening with the candlelight flickering, its raftered ceiling, its gray stone walls softly lighted, the scent of jasmine wafting in from the garden. (On my last visit the new owners were talking about installing a second air-conditioned restaurant for quote, gourmet dining, unquote, but my bet is you'll prefer the open terrace.)

For guests who enjoy a round of golf, earnest or casual, the Mount Irvine might rate high there. Not because its lovely, rolling fairways are a challenge for players of all handicaps. Not because the green fees are a mere $14 *a day.* But because anytime I've been there I had the fairways and greens (and, alas, traps) almost to myself. Even if you're not a golfer, take a walk or bike ride along the courses' winding pathways to enjoy the views of the bay and the reef and the tropical greenery.

NAME: Mount Irvine Bay Hotel

MANAGER: Brandon Mural

ADDRESS: P.O. Box 222, Scarborough, Tobago, Trinidad & Tobago, W.I.

LOCATION: 10 minutes and $10 by taxi from the airport

TELEPHONE: 809-639-8871/2/3

TELEX: 294 384 63 GULFTEL

RESERVATIONS: American International in the United States; Brodie/Cairs in Canada

CREDIT CARDS: American Express, Diners Club, Visa, MasterCard

ROOMS: 110, including 54 superiors and 10 standard rooms in the main building; the remainder in 2-room bungalows; all with private bathroom (showers only in standards), air-conditioning (cross-ventilation in bungalows only), balcony or loggia, telephones, wet bars and refrigerators in bungalows

DINING: Breakfast 7:00–10:00 (continental breakfast to 10:30), lunch noon–2:00 (the quietest spot is the golf course clubhouse), snacks at the beach pavilion all afternoon, dinner 7:00–9:00, at the open-air Sugar Mill Terrace of the air-conditioned Jacaranda Room; dinner for 2 $40; jacket and tie in the Jacanada, informal on the terrace, but "we do believe that informality has its acceptable limits within a hotel and house rules do not permit T-shirts or sleeveless vests in the public areas after 6:00 P.M."; room service 7:00 A.M.–10:00 P.M., $2 extra; taped music or radio on terrace, possibly live music in the Jacanada Room

ENTERTAINMENT: Occasional steel bands, movies in video room

SPORTS: So-so beach across the road, with beach bar and local fishermen and their boats (there are better beaches nearby), freshwater pool with swim-up bar, tennis (2 courts, no lights), sauna—all free; snorkeling gear, bikes and scooters for rent, golf (18 holes, $14 a day green fees); excursions (to Buccoo Reef to watch the fish, to Mrs. Blefounder's estate to watch the birds) can be arranged

P.S.: The hotel can handle groups of up to 200, but they are usually low-key

Added Attractions

Coconut Creek Club Hotel

Barbados

The setting here is modified Barbados—the usual quiet cove and sandy beach, but this time with a few coral cliffs added. And, of course, some coconut palms to justify the name. A few of the rooms and suites are perched on the coral, with balconies facing the sea, the remainder are grouped around the central pool area; they are comfortable but unremarkable. A dozen of the newer rooms are the Club's most luxurious and attractive—done in Moorish style with tiles and columns, walled flower gardens, posh rattan furniture and solid mahogany captains' chests. The striking feature here is the drinking-dining enclave, a cross between an adobe hacienda and an English pub, its walls decorated with Britannic nostalgia—pewter mugs, dart board, cricket bats and photographs of ships of the Royal Navy. You will be regaled with music most evenings of the week (steel bands, guitarists, combos), while you dine on *callaloo* soup or chilled cream of christophine, Creole carp imperial or roast shoulder of pork. We sat down to lunch recently at the awkward hour of three but the service was friendly, courteous and attentive—one of the specialties of the Coconut Creek. 40 units. *Coconut Creek Club Hotel, St. James, Barbados, W.I. Telephone: 809-42-20803.*

Treasure Beach

Barbados

Charles and Mary Ward's small 10-year-old resort is the fifth member of the Elegant Resorts of Barbados—and closest to Bridgetown. Its restaurant, highly acclaimed on the island, lives up to its ambitious menu (*Ecrevisses Provençale* and *filet de boeuf au Roquefort* are 2 of the specialties), served in a cool, comfortable rattan-decorated pavilion. Accommodations are 1-bedroom suites, recently renovated and restyled, housed in two-story wings along each side of the garden (with rooms facing rooms rather than the sea, except for a few beside the beach), with full kitchens and balcony or patio. Service is friendly, housekeeping immaculate, the beach uncrowded, with facilities for most water sports right on the premises. No children under 12, music 2 evenings a week. 24 units. *Treasure Beach, St. James, Barbados, W.I. Telephone: 809-432-1346 (in the United States, 800-223-6510).*

St. Vincent-Grenadines and Grenada

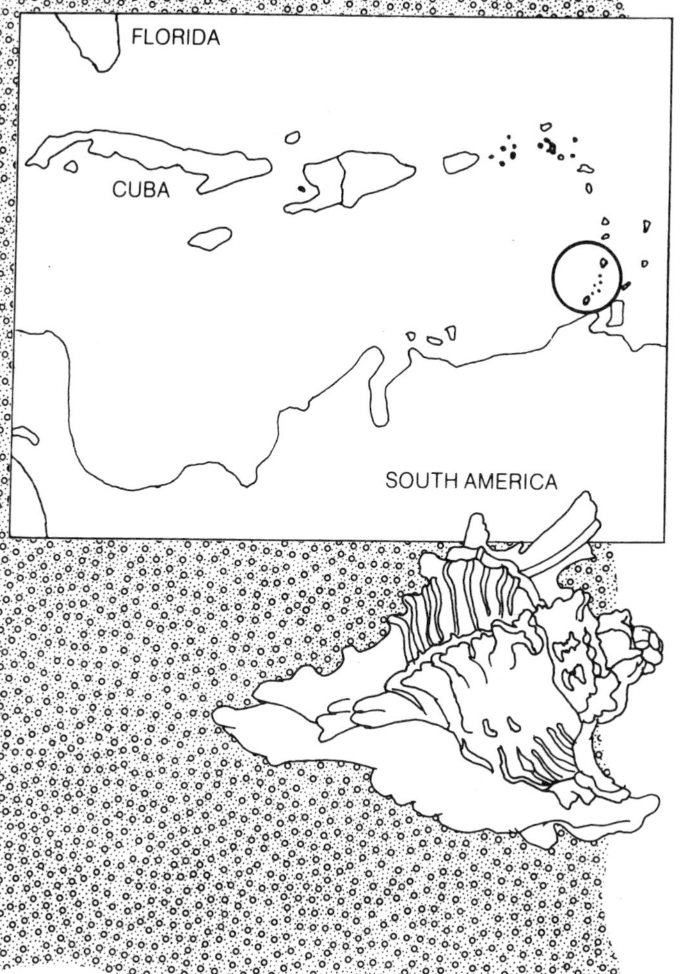

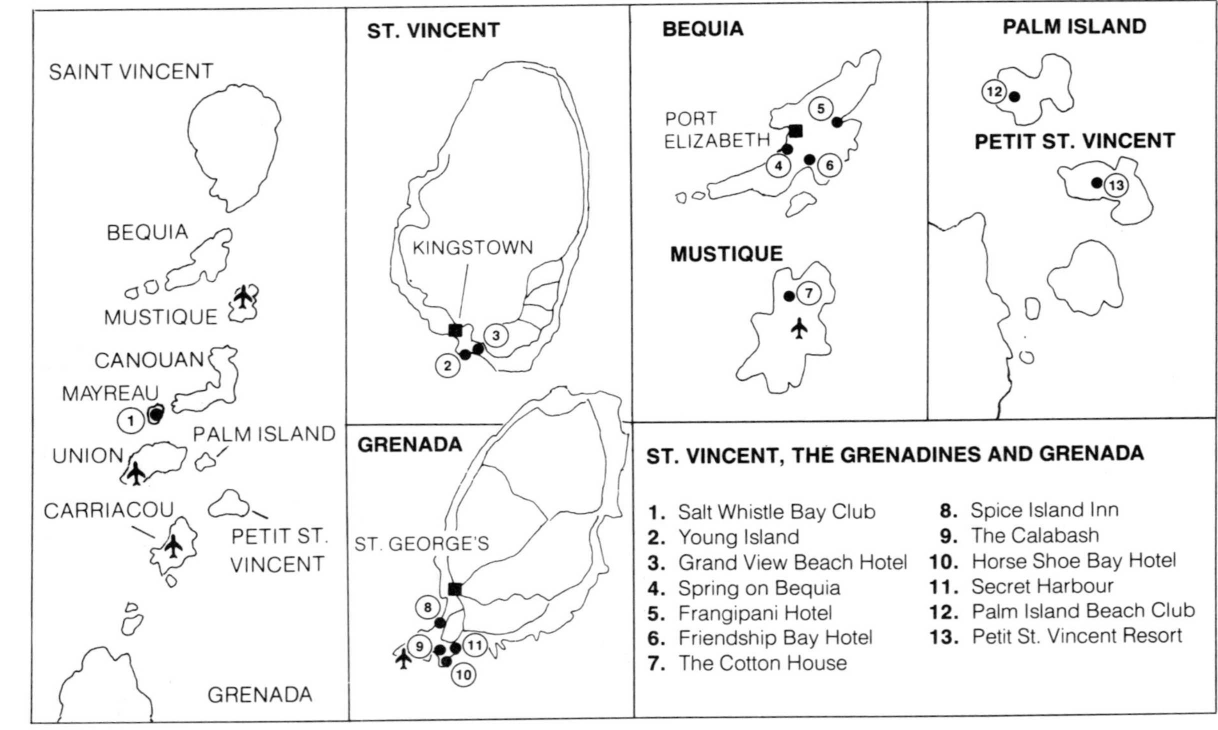

ST. VINCENT, THE GRENADINES AND GRENADA

1. Salt Whistle Bay Club
2. Young Island
3. Grand View Beach Hotel
4. Spring on Bequia
5. Frangipani Hotel
6. Friendship Bay Hotel
7. The Cotton House
8. Spice Island Inn
9. The Calabash
10. Horse Shoe Bay Hotel
11. Secret Harbour
12. Palm Island Beach Club
13. Petit St. Vincent Resort

St. Vincent-Grenadines and Grenada

The most desirable islands, like the most desirable lovers, make extra demands. That's how it is with the Grenadines; they'll reward you with seclusion, serenity and privacy, but you first have to get there, switching planes at least once, maybe twice. These islands are really part of the British Leewards, but they're so special, so totally Caribbean, that they deserve a category all to themselves.

They are, in fact, two quite separate and independent nations—St. Vincent-Grenadines (consisting of, for the purposes of this guide, Bequia, St. Vincent, Mustique, Palm Island, Petit St. Vincent and Union, which is the transit airstrip for Palm and PSV) and Grenada.

Bequia is a dream. The only way to get there is by boat. Not a big, powerful cabin cruiser or twin-hulled ferry, but by cargo/passenger ferry-boat or island sloop stacked with chickens, toilet paper, kerosene, Guinness Stout and Heineken Beer, bags of cement, a carburetor, more Guinness, more Heineken. If you see a man get aboard carrying bags of money accompanied by a guard with a discreet gun, you know you're on the "bank boat." The trip takes about 40 minutes or an hour, and you arrive in one of the most beautiful and most sheltered harbors in the Caribees, in the town of Port Elizabeth. There's not much more to Bequia than the hills you pass on the way into the harbor, but it's one of the most charming, most idyllic islands of all. Nothing much happens here, except once or twice a year when whales are spotted, and the men go out in their small boats armed only with hand harpoons—the only remaining fleet of hand-harpooners in the world.

St. Vincent is a mountainous island, lushly forested, incredibly fertile, brimming with papaws, mangoes and breadfruit. The bustling capital, Kingstown, is in the south, surrounded by towering hills, but the main scenic attractions are day-long excursions along the Leeward Highway to the foothills of 3,000-plus-feet Mont Soufrière or via the Windward Highway to Mesopotamia and Montreal—all very picturesque.

Mustique, Palm Island and Petit St. Vincent are privately owned and when you read about their hotels you're reading about the islands themselves.

Grenada, like St. Vincent a lush volcanic island, is the largest of the group (21 miles long, 112 miles wide) and scenically one of the most beautiful of all the Antilles. Still. Despite the efforts of modern firepower to wipe the island off the charts. You remember the events of October 1983. Some people called it an invasion, others a rescue mission. The official island description is a diplomatic "United States/Eastern Caribbean Intervention." Whatever, not much has changed, give or take a pock-marked wall or two. The Grenadians are pro-American (they always have been); one of my favorite inns has now become the American Embassy; the Holiday Inn is now a $15-million Ramada Renaissance; some of the roads have been resurfaced, mostly those between the Government House and the new airport. The major improvement these days is, of course, the airport, Point Salines International, which started it all. It's located in the southwest, near the hotels, thus eliminating the hour-long drive from the old Pearls Airport. Does this mean cheaper taxi fares? No. Taxis serving the airport belong to a special association, most of whose members still live in villages near the *old* airport, and since they now have to drive all the way across the island to the *new* airport, visitors—a.k.a. you—have to pay through the nose. Why, you might ask, don't they use taxi drivers who live near the *new* airport? Because those taxis belong to another, ineligible association—either the "hotel" association or the "cruise ship" association. It's all very simple. If you're a taxi driver. But these are inconsequential matters if you're simply planning to find a great little hideaway and flake out—and Grenada has plenty of pleasant, friendly places for doing just that. Into the bargain, to try to lure back their old North American clientele (the British kept on coming), the local hotels have been raising their rates by minuscule smidgens, so you may find your vacation dollars will go further here.

HOW TO GET THERE There are some nonstop flights from New York and Miami to Grenada (by BWIA or Grenada Airways), but otherwise to get to any of these islands you have to switch planes at Barbados or Martinique (you can also catch connections at Trinidad but I don't recommend that because it's such a hideous airport, or at St. Lucia, where you may waste time because of the difference between the international and regional airports). Barbados is the simplest route—nonstop or direct on American, Pan Am, Eastern, Air Canada and BWIA. From there you can catch a scheduled LIAT flight to St. Vincent, Mustique (occasionally), Union and Grenada. But, as mentioned in the introduction to the guide, your best bet is to allow your hotel to arrange seats on a shared charter, probably on Air Mustique or Tropicair, probably a seven-seater Islander or a Cessna. This arrangement costs a few dollars more but can save a lot of aggravation. (Just trying to determine the LIAT schedule is aggravation enough.)

Bequia involves a trip across the waters—either by charter launch from Mustique (which your hotel can probably arrange, but it's expensive) or by *The Admiral,* the ungainly but efficient Danish coaster that shuttles back and forth between St. Vincent and Bequia two or three times a day. The last departure from St. Vincent is 4:30 P.M., which allows at least some passengers from North America to get to Bequia the same day. You can also go the romantic way—on one of the 35-ft. interisland sailing sloops. If you find you have to spend the night in St. Vincent, Grand View Hotel is a convenient address. In town, the restored Cobblestone has local color and tends to be rather noisy but within walking distance of the jetty, if you're not carrying too much luggage.

Young Island

St. Vincent

$$$$

A Carib Indian chieftain, they say, once kept his harem on this islet, and generations of Vincentians used it as their vacation escape from the "mainland," a couple of hundred yards away across the lagoon. Now Young Island is 25 acres of petaled Polynesia. Half a million plants clamber up the hillsides. It took almost as long to landscape the grounds as it did to build the cottages and pavilions, but that was 20 years ago and now the island garden luxuriates. White ginger and giant almond trees soften the sun's rays as you stroll along stone pathways to quiet benches where twosomes can enjoy the breezes and sunsets. Swimming in the free-form pool, canopied by bamboo and fern and mango, you half expect Lamour and Hope to go floating by. And you're still shrouded by shrubbery and flowers when you rinse the sand off, because each room has an open patio shower screened by neck-high bamboo fences.

Two hundred yards may not sound like much of a journey but once you board the dinky water taxis for the 3-minute voyage, you could be on your way to Bali Ha'i. Once guests step ashore and sip the zingy Hibiscus Special that's waiting for them on the dock, they usually find there's no compelling reason—not even the 200-year-old botanical garden, not the oddball 150-year-old cathedral—to board that dinky taxi again until it's time to head for home. (Actually, if they sip more than half of their Special they probably *will* see Lamour and Hope.)

Why escape tranquility? There are so many ways to enjoy the barefoot euphoria of Young when you put what's left of your mind to it. At the Coconut Bar, a thatched *bohio* on stilts about six strokes from the shore. Curled in a *bohio*-shaded hammock, within semaphore distance of the shorebound bar. Flat out on the sand. Climbing the hundred-odd steps to the

peak of the island for an isolated stroll in one direction or the tennis court in another. For any guest who finds a 25-acre islet and some 50 guests claustrophobic after a while, owner/manager and 18-year-veteran Vidal Browne has his boatmen whisk the guests over to the most romantic manager's cocktail party in the Caribbean—on the nearby chimney rock known as Fort Duvernette, complete with native bamboo band, barbecue and flickering torcheurs.

But maybe the most sensuous way to enjoy the serenity of Young is to stay put in your own wicker wonderland: guest rooms feature lots of rush matting, native fabrics, terrazzo-and-shell floors, screened windows with jalousies and hardwood louvers. For anyone who has been to Young in the past, the rooms were refurbished in 1986/7, and although the overall Polynesian ambiance remains, they're brighter, more inviting. The cottages are located at various elevations up the jungly hillside, accessible by stone steps; the higher the cottage, the cooler the air but the wider the panorama. Of the beachside cottages, number 10 still has the fairest breezes and the most private of patios.

While the original rooms were being prettified, Vidal Browne was installing three new hilltop cottages, each a spacious deluxe suite (a first for Young Island) with huge semicircular deck/terrace with loungers and hammock, living room with rattan sofa and swivel chairs, wet bar and stocked refrigerator, toaster, kettle and the makings for a pot of coffee or tea. The louvered bedrooms have two double beds, separate dressing room paneled with greenheart, with bathrobes and amenities, twin vanities and open-to-the-breezes shower stall with its own water heater. The views are eye-filling, the breezes rejuvenating, the solitude complete. Just *how* far you've gotten away from it all is brought home to you when, thumbing through the welcome booklet, you come upon this sentence: "Keys for the cottages are available at the front desk, if this is considered necessary."

NAME: Young Island

OWNER/MANAGER: Vidal Browne

ADDRESS: P.O. Box 211, St. Vincent, W.I.

LOCATION: Just east of Kingstown, 200 yards offshore, about 10 minutes and $6 by taxi from the airport, shuttle launch to the resort free at all times; the hotel can arrange a "shared seat" charter flight from Barbados to St. Vincent for about $10 more than the scheduled one-way fare

TELEPHONE: 809-458-4826

TELEX: 7547 YOUNGISLE VQ

RESERVATIONS: Ralph Locke Islands

CREDIT CARDS: American Express, Visa

ROOMS: 29 in 29 cottages, some beside the beach, others on the hillside, 1 with air-conditioning, all with ceiling fans, patios or verandas, indoor/outdoor showers, some with wet bars and/or refrigerators

MEALS: Breakfast 7:30–9:30, lunch 1:00–2:30, dinner at 7:30–9:30 (approx. $50 for 2, in one of the breeze-cooled beachside pavilions); informal dress; room service for breakfast only, no extra charge

ENTERTAINMENT: Live music 4 nights a week—Bamboo Melodion Band on Tuesday, guitarist/singer on Thursday, steel band on Saturday, the Melodions again on Friday at the spectacular lantern-lit cocktail party on Fort Duvernette ("no amplification ever . . . request guests not to use radios/tape recorders"—which, alas, does not deter the disco owners on the "mainland" from occasionally bombarding the world with heavy metal, regardless of the protestations and petitions of Vidal Browne and his guests)

SPORTS: Beach with offshore Coconut Bar, saltwater lagoon pool in the garden, snorkeling, Sunfish sailing, windsurfing, glass-bottom boat trips—

all free; tennis (1 court, free by day, $5 per hour with lights); scuba, waterskiing and cruises (to Bequia, Mustique) on the resort's 44-ft. yacht by arrangement

P.S.: No children under 12, no groups ever, a few (very few) cruise ship passengers and day-trippers on weekends

Grand View Beach Hotel

St. Vincent

$

Your Grand View grand view is made up of islands, lagoons, bays, sailboats, Young Island, a fort, mountains, headlands and dazzling sea that turns into dazzling sky somewhere beyond Bequia. The hotel itself is a big, white, rather ungainly two-story mansion on top of a bluff (not on the beach, despite its name) between 2 bays, and surrounded by 8 acres of bougainvillea, frangipani, palms and terraced gardens. It's a beautiful location (breezes, flowers, birds, trees) if you don't mind climbing up and down to the beach. About 150 years ago it was a cotton-drying house, the private home of the Sardines, whose ancestors came over from Portugal; Frank Sardine, Sr., converted it into a hotel about 15 years ago, and despite its longevity, it's in spanking fresh condition. It's homey, pleasant and very relaxed, like the sort of small hotel Europeans would flock to on the Riviera (and, in fact, the hotel gets lots of visitors from Europe); the guest rooms are plain and unadorned—but who needs decor when you have a view like this?

NAME: Grand View Beach Hotel

OWNER/MANAGER: Tony Sardine

ADDRESS: P.O. Box 173, St. Vincent-Grenadines, W.I.

LOCATION: At Villa Point, 5 minutes and $6 by taxi from the airport, 10 minutes from town

TELEPHONE: 84811

TELEX: 7557 GRANDVIEW

RESERVATIONS: Robert Reid Assoc. in North America and United Kingdom

CREDIT CARDS: American Express, Visa, MasterCard

ROOMS: 12 rooms, 2 with air-conditioning, private bathrooms, showers only

MEALS: Breakfast 7:30–9:00, lunch noon–2:00, dinner 7:30–9:00 (approx. $40 for 2); casual dress; room service (no extra charge)

ENTERTAINMENT: Pleasant lounge with wicker armchairs, a vintage radio, a few books; maybe a cocktail party once a week in season, depending on the guests

SPORTS: Beach at the base of the cliff, swimming pool; snorkeling gear for rent; new tennis court ($7 with lights), 31-ft. fishing boat, squash court; scuba by arrangement

P.S.: No groups, some children

Spring on Bequia

Bequia

🌴🌴🌴🍴🍴🎾🎾$$

You're sitting on the terrace of your room, maybe lounging in a hammock, looking across a valley of coconut palms toward a bay, a pair of headlands and a sheltering reef. What you see is a working plantation that produces mangoes and avocados and plums and melons—to say nothing of all those coconuts; and what you are staying in is a 12-room jewel on a very quiet hillside in a very quiet corner of a very quiet island.

The 250-year-old Spring Plantation was bought up about 15 years ago by an Iowa lawyer, who planned to build a few unobtrusive homes among the trees of the hillsides (they're there, but you may not see them!) and a small inn to house prospective buyers and visitors. Part Japanese, part Finnish, part Caribbean, the hotel's clean, contemporary lines enclose open-plan rooms with native stone walls, stone floors, furniture fashioned from wood right there on the plantation, khuskhus rugs, whole walls of purpleheart louvers that push back to bring the outdoors right inside. Spring now has electricity, so the stone-floored, stone-walled shower stalls gush hot water.

All the guest rooms are charmingly rustic. The half dozen rooms in the old plantation Great House, draped in frangipani and cordia, are close to the swimming pool and tennis court, but since they're also next to the kitchen some guests prefer to be higher up the hill in one of two cantilevered wings: Gull, with four rooms, halfway up the hill, the Fort with two and higher

still. They're a stiff climb from the dining room, even more so from the beach; but if you've come here for seclusion, this is *seclusion*—with a beautiful view thrown in for good measure.

Spring's lobby/bar/dining room attached to the old Great House is open on two sides and overlooks the old syrup mill and slave quarters, a pleasant, breezy gathering place, with a rustic roof of beams and planks, walls of canvas and matted bamboo screens. The bar stools are the stumps of coconut palms with purpleheart seats, the native stone walls are covered with vines and planters, decorated with turtle shells, anchor chains and Arawak ax heads. But mostly the decor is the trees and the flowers and you're more aware of plantation than inn. Having dinner here is a bit like dining out in a cage of tree frogs and crickets—real Caribbean flavor. Elfie Grant's home-cooked meals are no letdown, either.

The good news, of course, is that Spring is still there and receiving guests. Closed for a few years, it is now the pride of the Rudolph family from Minnesota (who attribute their fascination with inns to an earlier edition of this guidebook); daughter Candice may be the only innkeeper in the Caribbean who speaks fluent Chinese. Wish them well, since Spring is still one of the most romantic tiny inns in the islands—even with its newfangled electricity and hot water.

NAME: Spring on Bequia

MANAGER: Candice Leslie

ADDRESS: Bequia, St. Vincent–Grenadines, W.I.

LOCATION: On the southeast coast, but just 1 mile over the hill from Port Elizabeth; the inn will pick you up at the dock; for some guests, the inn is a pleasant 30-minute *walk* from town

TELEPHONE: 809-458-3414

TELEX: 7557 HOTEL SPRING

RESERVATIONS: Direct to the inn's U.S. office at 612-823-9225 or Scott Calder International, Inc.

CREDIT CARDS: American Express, Visa

ROOMS: 12, half in the main lodge, half in hillside cottages, with private bathrooms (showers only); breeze-cooled (now with electricity and hot water), most with balconies

MEALS: Breakfast 7:30–9:00, lunch noon–2:00, dinner 7:00 (approx. $30 for 2); informal; no room service

ENTERTAINMENT: Parlor games, conversation

SPORTS: 500 ft. of virtually solitary sandy beach (with beach bar), about 5 minutes away along a pathway through the coco palms and pride of Barbados, freshwater pool, tennis (1 worn court, rackets available), walking and hiking trails, snorkeling—all free; sailing trips to Mustique and the Tobago Cays

P.S.: "Not really suitable for children." *Closed July through October*

Friendship Bay Hotel

Bequia

$$

The location is superb—the flank of a low hill, overlooking a half-circle of bay and the islets of Sample Key, Petit Nevis, Île Outre and Ramière, with a mile of passable beach a 3-minute walk from your room. You may even sight the whale hunters returning to Petit Nevis with a hapless cetacean.

The island's largest hotel, Friendship Bay has new owners, an engaging California/Italian/Argentinian couple named Eduardo and Joanne Guadagnino. They've spruced up rooms, tennis courts, beach bar, water sports facilities, and generally turned this once-floundering, once-cranky place into a welcoming rendezvous spot.

You have a choice of a dozen standard rooms in the main building (not so good), 10 cottages along the shore, or 5 in duplex chalets. All have recently been refurbished. Inside you'll find louvered windows of purpleheart wood, overhead ceiling fans and batik wall hangings illustrating Bequia life in primitive style.

Dinner (prepared by the Friendship's new Bajan chef) is served in a glass-enclosed dining pavilion above the bay. But after a hard day of lying on the beach looking at the sky, you may want to end the evening with a 3-minute stroll to the beachside bar for a rum punch.

NAME: Friendship Bay Hotel

OWNERS/MANAGERS: Eduardo and Joanne Guadagnino

ADDRESS: P.O. Box 9, Bequia, St. Vincent–Grenadines, W.I.

LOCATION: On the south coast of Bequia; to get there, fly to Barbados, where you'll be met at the airport by Mustique Airways, transferred to a small plane for the 45-minute flight to Mustique ($65 per person one way); from there you'll be taken by boat (power or sail) direct to the hotel jetty ($35 per person each way)

TELEPHONE: 809-458-3222

TELEX: 7438 FRIENDBAY VQ

RESERVATIONS: Ralph Locke Islands

CREDIT CARDS: Visa, MasterCard, American Express

ROOMS: 27, 10 in beach cottages, 5 in hillside beach chalets, 12 standard in main house; all with ceiling fans, balcony/terrace or patio, showers only, maid service twice a day

MEALS: Breakfast 7:30–10:00, lunch noon–3:00, dinner 7:00–9:00 ($25–30 for 2 in the hillside restaurant); lunch and dinner also served at beach bar; Saturday night barbecue "jump-up," including combo (amplified); dress casual; room service for breakfast only

ENTERTAINMENT: 2 bars, library, VCR, parlor games

SPORTS: Half-mile beach, tennis (1 court, lighted), windsurfers, Sunfish sailing, snorkeling gear—all free; rafts, parasailing, waterskiing, scuba, island sailing trips aboard the Guadagninos' classic 45-ft. yawl *Sally Ann* and speedboat picnic trips to Pt. Nevis, all at extra charge

---

Frangipani Hotel

Bequia

✝ ✗ ⊜ $

They used to build island schooners in the front yard here, the lounge was a ships' chandlery back in the thirties, and the sea captain who built it disappeared with his crew in the Bermuda Triangle—while his schooner sailed on. His son, currently prime minister of St. Vincent, turned this white-walled red-roofed family home into an inn back in the sixties, and it's now one of the most popular watering places in the Grenadines. It hasn't lost touch with its nautical heritage, either: antique charts and seascapes decorate the lounges; the jetty at the bottom of the garden welcomes fleets of dinghies from the yachts moored just offshore; and sooner or later everyone who sails the Grenadines stops off at the Frangipani beach bar to greet old friends they last saw beating toward the Tobago Cays.

The Frangipani is a real wicker-decked West Indies inn. The half dozen rooms upstairs are scantily furnished, with mosquito nets, partition walls and a couple of shared bathrooms down the hall—like the deck of a schooner, functional rather than frilly. The exception is also upstairs, where two rooms have been blended into one charming, plank-floored nest with four-poster canopy bed and private, if tiny, toilet/shower. If you prefer bunking down in something more substantial, ask for one of the rooms in the stone-and-timber garden cottages—big comfortable cabins with big bathrooms, dressing rooms, grass mats and louvers. Each of these five rooms has beams and furniture crafted from a different local hardwood, each has its own sun deck draped with jade vine, bougainvillea or the inevitable frangipani.

There's absolutely nothing to do here, nothing but unwind. Evenings, you can nibble fresh seafood on the veranda or sit on the seawall and listen to rigging; you can swap a few fancy tales with yachtsmen or listen to a folksinger or have another beer and watch the last sailor row off zigzaggedly to his yacht. In the morning, grab a cup of coffee and settle into a large, purpleheart armchair beside the beach. Watch the schooners and ketches weigh anchor for the Tobago Cays or Martinique. Don't even bother waving good-bye—they'll soon be back at Frangipani.

NAME: Frangipani Hotel

OWNER/MANAGER: Pat Mitchell and Marie Kingston

ADDRESS: Bequia, St. Vincent, W.I.

LOCATION: On the waterfront, a 3-minute walk from the schooner jetty

TELEPHONE: 809-45-83255

CABLES: Frangipani St. Vincent

RESERVATIONS: None

CREDIT CARDS: American Express, Visa, MasterCard

ROOMS: 11, 8 with private showers and balconies; in the garden cottages, 3 in main house with washbasins but sharing bath and toilets; direct-dial telephones, mosquito nets, no air-conditioning

MEALS: Breakfast 7:30–9:00, lunch anytime, dinner 7:30–9:00 (approx. $20–30 for 2, served in the beachside patio); no room service; very casual dress

ENTERTAINMENT: Barbecue and "jump-up" every Thursday, string band every Monday, guitar player or impromptu entertainment most evenings

SPORTS: None on the premises; snorkeling, scuba, sailing trips, charters, tennis and windsurfing by arrangement

P.S.: *Closed September.* Lots of yachtsmen, castaways and beachcombers

The Cotton House

Mustique

🌴🌴🌴🍴🍴🏊🏊$$$$

It's that rare combination of informality and elegance, of pristine (well, relatively pristine) surroundings and civilization. Here you are, on a private tropical island with a permanent population of 300, a few coconut groves, a few citrus groves, a dozen deserted beaches.

You can spend an entire day here without meeting anyone other than your maid or waiter or gardener; you can disappear to a beach for a picnic lunch—not another soul in sight; you can spend hours snorkeling among fish that rarely if ever encounter *homo sapiens.* Then in the evening you mingle with escapists who turn out to be cosmopolitan, urbane and

sophisticated—maybe even celebrated. And, at the end of the day, you hop into bed in a dreamy boudoir designed by no less a talent than the late Oliver Messel.

Mustique, unique Mustique, is small (3 miles long, ½ mile wide) and flat (about 400 ft. at its highest point); you arrive by air in a seven-seater that sweeps in between a pair of breastlike hills, to touch down in a pasture with a runway and thatch-and-bamboo terminal. When Reynolds, alias Smokey, the hotel's effervescent porter/majordomo/greeter/chauffeur/guide, sees the plane coming in he jumps into his minibus, and by the time you've taxied to the toy terminal and cleared customs, he's there waiting to convey you to the hotel.

And what a hotel! The Cotton House itself is an eighteenth-century storage house of handsome proportions—two floors of mellowed stone and coral rimmed by deep verandas accented by cedar shutters and louver doors. A few yards away, on the peak of a knoll, Oliver Messel created a swimming pool surrounded by "Roman ruins," the sort of setting he might have designed for a Gluck opera at Covent Garden. Beyond the stone stump of the mill (now a boutique) a pair of handsome two-story Georgian-style villas house half the guest rooms, each room with a different decor and furnishings, but all with custom-designed bedspreads and matching drapes, plank floors with rush mats, ceiling fans, breezy balconies or patios. Color schemes are restrained and cool, with antiques and doodads adding delightful little touches of Messel charm. Other guest rooms are in three cottages fashioned in vaguely "native hut" style, in a new two-story wing in vaguely Motel Georgian style; the newest of all, three guest rooms in a villa, Cuoutinot House, formerly owned by the Guinness family (smaller bedrooms, but with a big open-to-the-breezes common room lounge/terrace). The latter are closest to the beach at Endeavour Bay, but the prime quarters have to be the original Oliver Messel rooms in the Georgian villas (a shade less exquisite than they were when first renovated, but recently refurbished with newly sanded floors, new wooden balustrades and colors that recapture the originals).

But none of the guest rooms quite match the exquisiteness of the main lounge in the Cotton House itself—with its Messel-designed blue-gray acorn fabrics, its raftered ceiling, its hand-carved bar and masses of antiques—Lady Bateman's steamer trunks, a scallop shell fountain on a quartz base, Spanish silver mirrors. Messel took all these motley bits and pieces, blended them with his armchairs and sofas and created one of the most beautiful rooms in the Caribbean. In the hemisphere. The veranda facing the sunset is given over to comfy armchairs and loungers, another corner, shaded by shutters and foliage, is an enchanted dining room where candles flicker on rustic tables and straw-seated chairs and the air is filled with the sounds of tree frogs. In a setting as romantic as this, who cares if the cuisine is not three star? The owner shipped his cook off to Italy last year for exposure to Italian cooking, so a few pasta dishes appear on the evenings' fixed menus, but the most successful dishes are more local—fish soup, lobster, eggplant Mustique.

In the last edition of this guidebook, I quibbled about the massive speakers perched on Lady Bateman's trunks. They've gone. So has the inappropriate pop music (to be replaced by quiet classical tapes at teatime, a young Vincentian playing the precariously tuned piano during cocktails). Service is friendlier, sharper. Alas, the manager who turned the place around has since left, and the newcomers, though experienced, are unknown quantities in a setting such as this.

But regardless of personnel, the Cotton House is still a special place. Too quiet for some, no doubt. Yet, for all its isolation, the Cotton House can on occasion plunge its guests into nightlife larger islands envy. For a start, there's Basil's Bar, a raucous wood-and-wicker deck on Britannia Beach, blaring rock-and-roll even at noontime, positively hopping at the Wednesday barbecue, popular with homeowners and yachters, so you might find yourselves at three o'clock some morning, beneath a full moon and a myriad stars, listening to bamboo flute and "shake-shake," mingling with princesses, viscounts, rock stars, fishermen and CEOs masquerading as swingers.

NAME: The Cotton House

MANAGERS: Yvonne Cato and Thomas Shaw

ADDRESS: Mustique, St. Vincent–Grenadines, W.I.

LOCATION: On a private island, 35 minutes by twin-engined plane from Barbados (the hotel will arrange space on a charter flight); there is also frequent scheduled service from Martinique, St. Vincent and Grenada; the hotel, 4 minutes from the airstrip, will collect you by minibus, free of charge

TELEPHONE: 809-456-4777

TELEX: 7562 COTTONH VQ

RESERVATIONS: Relais Chateaux/David B. Mitchell & Company, Inc.

CREDIT CARDS: All major cards

ROOMS: 22, in villas, cottages and a two-story wing, all with balconies or patios, ceiling fans, telephones, some with showers only

MEALS: Breakfast 7:30–10:00 and buffet lunch 12:30–2:30 served poolside, afternoon tea (with classical music) 4:00, dinner at 8:00 (approx. $80 for 2, on the candlelit veranda of the Great House); informal but "island elegant" dress; room service for all meals, no extra charge

ENTERTAINMENT: Bar/lounge, parlor games, taped music, "Flambeaux" beach barbecue Saturdays (with steel band), weekly managers' cocktail party for hotel and villa guests, piano bar twice a week, "jump-up" at Basil's Bar every Wednesday

SPORTS FACILITIES: 12 beaches (free transportation, with picnic lunch), freshwater pool, tennis (2 courts, no lights), snorkeling, windsurfing, Sunfish sailing—all free; waterskiing $75 per hour; horseback riding, scuba and cruises to Tobago Cays or Bequia can be arranged

P.S.: No cruise ships, other than yachts or small deluxe ships such as the *Sea Goddess* or the sail-powered *Dindstar*

P.P.S.: In addition to the Cotton House, Mustique has 30-odd one-of-a-kind luxury villas for rent, some perched on hillsides, some beside the beach. None of them are designed for twosomes, but if you decide to junket with friends, this could be a memorable way to spend a vacation à la jet set. Mick Jagger's new wood-and-bamboo home may or may not be on the list of rentals, but Princess Margaret's is (although it's quite modest compared to some of the others). Among the most attractive *two*-bedroom villas: Blue Waters and Pelican Beach House (both on the water), Camylarde and Marienlyst (in the hills). Current rates are no longer outlandish compared with some of the Caribbean's new hotels: in 1987 two-bedroom villas cost $1,700–2,100 a week in winter, $1,200–1,600 in summer, in each case with full staff, Jeep and laundry. Or, in other words, less than $100 per day per couple in summer. For details and a lavish color brochure, write to Mustique Villas; i/c Resorts Management, Inc.; 201½ East Twenty-ninth Street; New York, NY 10016. Telephone: 800-225-4255 or 212-696-4566.

Palm Island Beach Club

Palm Island

$$$

The beach curves on and on for a mile and a half, and you get so spoiled for space here that if half a dozen other sun worshippers get to the strand before you tumble out of bed in the morning, you'll probably walk around the next bend to yet another uncrowded spot.

Not too many tides ago there weren't even half a dozen people here—and the island was no more than a ring of beach around a swamp, on the charts identified prosaically as Prune. Then along came John Caldwell. Alias "Coconut Johnny." "Tree planting is my hobby . . . there's hardly an island in these parts where I can't go ashore and look at some trees I've planted." At Palm he can look at somewhere between two and three *thousand.*

Caldwell, now in his sixties, is a Texan who grew up in California, short, wiry, a mizzenmast of a man who bought a pair of shoes fifteen years ago and has been seen wearing them once ("I've lived for twenty-four years on twelve hundred dollars a year"). Over 20 years ago he set out to sail single-handed across the Pacific and ended up on a reef off Fiji; somehow he continued to Australia, where he built a 45-ft. ketch, loaded his wife and two young sons aboard and set off again—this time smack into a hurricane in the Indian Ocean and then through the Suez Canal and across the Atlantic to the Grenadines. He spent 5 years there chartering; on each trip he came ashore on Palm/Prune Island with his charterers, and while they were having a picnic or swim he was planting his coconut palms. Before long, the swamp was a grove, the Prune was a Palm, and John Caldwell had started to plant a hotel. He and his sons designed and built the entire place from scratch, putting in power, water, roads, an airstrip, a dock—and 18 months later, in December 1967, they were ready to open Palm Island Beach Club.

The club (it's a club in name only—you don't have to join anything) at first sight appears to be a white beach sprinkled with coconut palms, casuarina, sea grape and almond trees, dotted with brightly colored plastic loungers; a second look and you'll find that there are bungalows strung out along free-form stone paths rambling through lanes of sun-dappled greenery, a few steps from the edge of Casuarina Beach. "It's small because we want to enjoy it ourselves." The dozen two-room bungalows are half stone, half hardwood, with two walls of wooden-slat vertical louvers, a third of sliding glass doors facing a patio. Some have open-air shower stalls, where you wash out the sand with water heated by solar power. John Caldwell designed and built his own furniture—in the no-nonsense, shipshape manner of a man who's fitted out a 45-ft. ketch.

You spend your days at Palm Island Beach Club shuffling from your louvered room to the beach to the circular beach bar to the big open-air timber Polynesian longhouse for an informal Creole-dish dinner (note the ceiling, a superb piece of carpentry). Maybe at some point you'll grab your snorkeling mask and sneakers and go for a walk on the coral garden on the front beach, a hundred yards north of the beach bar. Maybe tomorrow you'll sail over to the Tobago Cays. Maybe you'll go diving. Maybe you'll join the visiting yachtsmen and women at the beach bar for a tall, cool drink and a tall, salty tale. More likely you'll just lounge around in a couple of chaises and look at Union Island—one of those enticing mirages whose contours change with the passage of the sun, revealing unsuspected hamlets or coconut groves sparkling in the afternoon light.

By sundown, the loudest sound on Palm Island is the rigging of visiting yachts.

By nine o'clock, you're in bed beneath your mosquito net—flicking flecks of sand from each other's cheeks.

NAME: Palm Island Beach Club

OWNERS/MANAGERS: John and Mary Caldwell

ADDRESS: Palm Island, St. Vincent–Grenadines, W.I.

LOCATION: The Club *is* the island, and the island is 15–20 minutes by a new, home-built 36-ft. launch (free) from Union Island; Union, in turn, can be reached by scheduled flight from St. Vincent by LIAT, from Martinique by Air Martinique, or by charter flight from Barbados (about $103 per person, and the hotel can help arrange the flight if you give them plenty of warning)

TELEPHONE: 809-458-4804

TELEX: 7500 C&W agency UQ

RESERVATIONS: Caribbean Information Office, Chicago; Scott Calder International, Inc.

CREDIT CARDS: American Express, Visa

ROOMS: 24, in bungalows, breeze cooled, refrigerator

MEALS: Breakfast 7:00–9:30, lunch 1:00–2:00 (buffet), afternoon tea 4:00–4:30 on your patio, dinner at 8:00 (family-style, barbecues Wednesday and Saturday); casual dress, barefoot if you wish; room service for breakfast, lunch, dinner

ENTERTAINMENT: Barbecues twice a week, calypso night on Wednesday, Saturday evening "jump-up"

SPORTS: 5 beaches, paddle tennis (1 untended court), games room, snorkeling gear, windsurfers—all free; sailboats for rent; scuba equipment, diving off Palm or at nearby Tobago Cays; day sails to Tobago Cays and Mayreau

P.S.: At press time, John Caldwell had just taken on a new partner, who plans to spend money on improvements—and, I'm told, eliminate the weekly visits by cruise ship passengers, which had become an unpleasant intrusion for the resort's guests

Saltwhistle Bay Club

Mayreau

🌴🌴🌴✗✗☺$$$

Real barefoot, flake-out, crash territory this—an unspoiled bay on an unspoiled cay in the unspoiled Grenadines. To get there you first fly to Union Island, where you'll be met by the resort's 42-ft. catamaran, *Skywave,* which will skim you across the channel past Saline Bay, then finally around a headland and into Saltwhistle Bay.

Tom and Undine Potter, a young Canadian/German couple, settled here almost a decade ago and built a beachside restaurant catering to passing yachts, then just over a year ago opened their hotel. When you sail into the bay, with its glistening semicircle of sand, and beyond the beach, dwarf palms and sea grape trees that part to reveal glimpses of another shining sea beyond, you may well wonder where *did* they build their hotel?

Go in a bit farther, it's all there nestled into 22 acres of coconut palms, more sea grapes, that great curve of soft white sand and a windward beach that's pure Robinson Crusoe.

Though the landscape may be lush, there's nothing plush or luxurious about the Saltwhistle's accommodations—but there's nothing uncomfortable about them either. The guest quarters are in sturdy native stone and timber cottages at one end of the beach, each with hardwood louvers, handcrafted furniture, ceiling fans and showers supplied with water heated by the noonday sun. At the other end of the beach, there's a sprinkling of circular gazebos in matching stone with stone banquettes and palm-thatched shades. The two-room cottages share a spacious rooftop gallery with loungers, tables and chairs. The Potters' dining room is an ingenious collection of circular stone booths topped by thatched canopies where you can stuff yourselves with local delicacies like curried conch, turtle steaks and lobster, all fresh from the surrounding reefs.

There's not much to do at Saltwhistle—delightfully so. It is, as their brochure puts it, "an island where you start the day with nothing to do and finish it only half done." Of course, for the truly ambitious there's snorkeling gear, picnics to the wild and windswept beach with views of Palm Island and Tobago, fishing with the locals in their gaff-rigged sloops, a walk up the hill to the village for a warm beer and a sweeping view of all those cays and reefs, or a hike down to Saline Bay to watch the mail boat come in. And if any or all of these possibilities (or just the thought of them) exhaust you, there's always the lure of a good book, a rum punch, and a nice big hammock.

NAME: Saltwhistle Bay Club

OWNERS/MANAGERS: Tom and Undine Potter

ADDRESS: Mayreau, St. Vincent-Grenadines, W.I.

LOCATION: South of St. Vincent, a few miles from the islands of Union, Petit St. Vincent and Palm; to get there, you fly from Barbados or St. Lucia to Union, where the hotel collects you by boat, but since the Club (with advance notice) will make all the arrangements, all you have to do is get to Barbados or St. Lucia

TELEPHONE: Radio only

TELEX: 06-218309

RESERVATIONS: North American office, 800-387-1752; in Toronto, 416-366-8599

CREDIT CARDS: None

ROOMS: 21, including 7 standard, 10 superior, 4 junior suites (under construction); all with sun-warmed showers, ceiling fans (and steady cross-ventilation); superior rooms also have shared rooftop decks

MEALS: Breakfast 8:00–10:00, lunch 12:00–2:00, dinner 8:00–10:00 (approx. $40 for 2), all served in beachside booths; occasional beach barbecues; casual dress; taped music; room service for breakfast only

ENTERTAINMENT: Hammocks strung between the palm trees, conversation in the bar, darts, backgammon, a moonlight stroll on the beach

SPORTS: 300–400 yards of beautiful beach, snorkeling, windsurfers—all free; scuba diving, boat trips to Tobago Cays, "Sundowner" rum punch cruises, excursions with local fishermen at extra charge

P.S.: *Closed September and October*

Petit St. Vincent Resort

Petit St. Vincent

🌴🌴🌴🌴🌴 XXX ●●● $$$$

"Some of our guests never put on any clothes until dinnertime." Not in public, perhaps, but on their private terraces, because all but half a dozen of the rooms here are self-contained cottages, widely dispersed around this 113-acre private out-island. It may well be the most secluded, most private of the Caribbean's luxury hideaways.

It's certainly one of the most consistently dependable. Not for PSV any of the problems of revolving-door management. Any good resort manager knows where the pipes and power cables are, but in the case of Haze Richardson, he not only knows where they are, he put them there in the first place. He helped lay the cables and the pipes, helped quarry the stones for the cottages, installed the refrigeration in the kitchen, built a desalination plant, planted the fruit trees. Now the resort even makes its own fiberglass Jeeplike Minimokes. Richardson came to the island by way of a 77-ft. staysail *Jacinta,* which he skippered. One of his charterers was the late

H. W. Nichols, Jr., then the top man at a big corporation in Cincinnati, who bought this dinky Grenadine from a little old lady in Petit Martinique, the island just across the channel. They started building in 1966 and slaved for three years, working with whatever was available (mostly bluebitch stone and hardwood), planning the location of the individual cottages to make the most of the breezes and vistas.

It may sound simple and rustic, but it's really quite lavish in terms of solitude and seclusion—all that space for only 44 guests. And a staff of 60 to boot. The cottages follow a basic U-shaped pattern: big open sun deck, big shaded breakfast patio, big glass-enclosed lounge separated by a wall of bluebitch from a big sleeping area with twin queen-size beds, separated in turn from a stone-walled dressing room and bathroom with curtain-enclosed shower. There are no newfangled gadgets such as television, radio or telephone. For room service there's the unique PSV semaphore system: a bamboo pole with a notch for written messages (e.g., "2 piña coladas fast," "afternoon tea for 2") and two flags—red for Do Not Disturb, yellow for Come In. But the tactful maids and room service waiters first ring the little brass bell at the entrance—just in case you want to slip into your fluffy new PSV-crested bathrobes.

Guest room interiors follow a basic style of bluebitch walls, purpleheart louvers, khuskhus rugs on red tile floors. Jennifer Richardson's hand can be detected in the new fabrics—soft islandy shades of yellow, turquoise and terra-cotta. Where the rooms differ is in location: up on the bluff for the best breezes and views, down on the beach by the lagoon, on the beach beyond the dock. Cottage 1, on the bluff, is one of the most secluded, with a big deck overlooking a dazzling sea and the craggy silhouette of Union Island. For a beach right on your doorstep, Cottages 6 through 11 look out on unspoiled castaway beach. For total detachment, turn your back on the entire resort and check into Cottage 18, with a few stone steps to a private patch of beach, and beyond that nothing but ocean—all the way to Guinea-Bissau or thereabouts. Some of the cottages are what passes in these lazy climes as a stiff hike (all of 5 minutes) to the dining pavilion, but you can always arrange to be picked up by one of the ubiquitous "mokes."

This hilltop bar/dining pavilion is the focal point of the resort, with soaring hardwood roof and indoor/outdoor patios overlooking the anchorage and Petit Martinique. Beautiful place to sit and savor the twilight while sipping a Banana Touch or mango daiquiri. PSV meals are above average for these parts (meats, for example, are personally selected by Julia Child's butcher, a regular PSV guest, and flown in specially for the resort), the dining room staff is particularly attentive. Indeed, one of the main attractions of PSV, a feature that sets it apart from many of its peers, is its long-serving staff. They seem to care genuinely about making your vacation perfect. More often than not, Jennifer Richardson is at the dock to greet you with a rum punch when you arrive. The *Wakiva* skipper, Chester, is solicitous about getting you back to Union on time for your plane. There are totable beach chairs in your room in case you want to sample a nearby beach, but if you want to cart your *lounger* along, one of the roving stewards will pick you up in his Minimoke and transport you to whichever beach you choose (the one at the west end is particularly tranquil, with hammocks strung beneath thatch *bohios*). If you're bored with *that,* you can even have one of the boatmen transport you to PSR—Petit St. Richardson, a minuscule offshore cay with lots of sand and a solitary palm.

But why quit your own private deck in the first place—with or without swimsuits?

PSV may not be for everyone. You have to be your own entertainment. You have to forego the plushest amenities. You have to dine in the same dining room every evening, except one. But for anyone who genuinely wants a castaway setting with civilized comforts, who wants to get as far as possible from the everyday world without spending forever getting there, Petit St. Vincent is one beautiful, enchanting hideaway.

NAME: Petit St. Vincent Resort

MANAGERS (AND PART OWNERS): Haze and Jennifer Richardson

ADDRESS: Petit St. Vincent, St. Vincent–Grenadines, W.I.

LOCATION: An inkblot on the charts, just 40 miles south of St. Vincent and 20 minutes from Union Island, the nearest airstrip, by PSV's 48-ft. Grand Banks yacht, *Wakiva* (the ride is free); the easiest way to get to Union is by shared-seat charter from Barbados (about $103 per passenger), which can be arranged by PSV; there are also scheduled flights to Union by LIAT and Air Mustique, from Grenada, Barbados, St. Vincent and Martinique

TELEPHONE: 809-458-4801

TELEX: 7591 PSVRSRT VQ

RESERVATIONS: Own U.S. office (513-242-1333), Leading Hotels of the World, Robert Reid Assoc. and Relais Chateau, David B. Mitchell & Company, Inc.

CREDIT CARDS: None

ROOMS: 22 cottages, all with bedroom and sitting room, open *and* shaded patios or terraces, showers only (solar heated), amenities trays, bathrobes, hammocks, some with ceiling fans (otherwise acres of louvers take care of the cooling)

MEALS: Breakfast 7:30–10:00, buffet lunch 12:30–2:00, afternoon tea 4:00–5:00, dinner 7:30–9:30 (all in the hilltop dining pavilion); Friday beach barbecue, when the staff carts the entire dining room—chairs, tables *and* piano—to the lawn beside the beach; dress—informal but stylish (cover-ups required at lunchtime); room service all meals (including early morning coffee service), no extra charge

ENTERTAINMENT: Quiet taped music in bar, occasional live music (guitar, folk), backgammon and other parlor pastimes; the Wednesday "jump-up" with the staff's own steel band is one of the highlights of the Grenadines—yachts converge from far and near

SPORTS: Virtually continuous beach (plus the offshore cay), snorkeling, Sunfish sailing, Hobie Cats, windsurfing (with instruction by shore simulator), tennis (1 court with lights), croquet, table tennis, fitness trail—all free; waterskiing, scuba diving and day charters on the trimaran *Piragua* to Tobago Cays and Mayreau at extra charge

P.S.: Few children, no groups except visiting yachtsmen

The Calabash

Grenada

🌴🌴🌴🍴🍴😊😊$$

You never have to worry about making it to the dining room in time for breakfast because you have a kitchenette and maid (who has her own entrance to let herself in without disturbing you). So leave your order in writing the night before, or wake up and whenever you feel like breakfast, just tell your personal maid. She'll serve it to you in bed, in the sitting room or on your private patio. Eating, in fact, is one of the prime pleasures at The Calabash. Lunch and dinner are served in a pretty pavilion of native stone and local hardwoods, furnished with chairs and tables of polished saman. Flowering *Thunbergia grandiflora* dangles from overhead vines, threatening, it seems, to reach down and gobble up your lambis or swordfish pie Creole.

The Calabash is an old Grenada favorite. The British in particular have been wintering here loyally for a quarter of a century, with or without American marines on the beach. The intimate little resort circles 8 beachside acres, a "village green" dotted with lofty trees and fragrant shrubbery.

The 22 suites perfectly capture island atmosphere, comfortable but not plush, rustic but snug. For my money, the best buys are the suites in the two-story cottages on the west side of the lawn, and preferably the higher ceilinged units on the second floor: each suite subdivided with kitchenette, indoor sitting room, lazy breeze-cooled porch, small fan-cooled bedroom (showers only in the bathrooms). Room 1 is listed as a Honeymoon Suite, close to the beach, with a big hand-carved mahogany four-poster bed.

The prime quarters are now the two suites with private plunge pools, especially *the* Pool Suite, with a very large, very private indoor/outdoor living room, full kitchen and a giant calabash tree in the garden. But what brings the British and others back year after year to The Calabash is the long-serving staff—friendly, willing, attentive but unobtrusive. They make The Calabash an inviting, relaxed hideaway.

NAME: The Calabash

OWNER/MANAGER: Charles de Gale

ADDRESS: P.O. Box 382, St. George's, Grenada, W.I.

LOCATION: At L'Anse aux Epines (Prickly Bay) on the south coast, about 10 minutes and $12 by taxi from the airport, $14 from St. George's

TELEPHONE: 4234/4334

TELEX: 3425 GA (attn. Calabash)

RESERVATIONS: International Travel & Resorts

CREDIT CARDS: American Express, MasterCard, Visa

ROOMS: 22 suites, all with kitchenettes and porches, some with air-conditioning, 2 with private plunge pools

MEALS: Breakfast anytime, lunch 1:00–2:30, dinner 8:00–10:00 (in the arbor-covered dining terrace, approx. $50 for 2); informal (but preferably long-sleeved shirts for men in the evening); room service at no extra charge

ENTERTAINMENT: Some taped (or radio) music, steel band or country trio several times a week in winter, less frequently in the off-season

SPORTS: Beach, tennis (1 court, with lights), billiard room—all free; snorkeling, scuba, waterskiing, sailing can be arranged

P.S.: Occasional din of planes, rarely after 10:00 P.M.; some cruise ship passengers come to enjoy the dining and the beach

Secret Harbour

Grenada

For lovers, the secret harbors at Secret Harbour may be the bathtubs—sunken, free form, masses of colorful Italian tiles surrounded by masses of colorful Italian tiles, matching towels, potted plants and an unglazed "wagonwheel" window that lets you listen to the lapping of the water below as you lazily lap the water on each other's back.

Secret Harbour is the dream-come-true of an expatriate English lady, Barbara Stevens, a chartered accountant, who closed her books one day about 20 years ago and set sail with her first husband to cross the Atlantic in a 45-ft. ketch; after spending 4 years chartering in the Grenadines, she decided Grenada was her island and Musquetta Bay her mooring. This is where she built her hotel back in 1973.

It's more like a Spanish-Mediterranean village on a terraced hillside of gardens and greenery: a splash of red-tiled roofs, white stucco arches and hand-hewn beams among lime and papaw trees, frangipani and triple bougainvillea. At the top of the hill, the lobby-lounge and restaurant; the guest bungalows are a few feet above the water, and between top and bottom there's a big, tiled free-form pool as colorful as your bathtub.

Secret Harbour welcomes you with luxury—but luxury in keeping with the Spanish-Mediterranean theme: a big, semicircular balcony overlooking the bay, with padded loungers and enough room for a dinner party; arched glass-paneled doors leading into a small sunny lounge foyer with bright two-toned banquettes; a pair of authentic four-poster double beds from island plantations, with matching fabric on canopies and walls; stained glass windows to cast spangled light, and candles with dimmer switches beside each bed to set just the right romantic mood. To say nothing of your tasteful bathroom.

NAME: Secret Harbour

MANAGER: Grace Steele

ADDRESS: P.O. Box 11, St. George's, Grenada, W.I.

LOCATION: On a quiet bay (Musquetta) on the south shore of the island, a few miles from the resort hotels along Grand Anse beach, 10–15 minutes from St. George's ($10 by taxi), 1 hour and 10 minutes from the airport ($10 by taxi)

TELEPHONE: 809-440-4439 or 4548

CABLES/TELEX: 3425 GA SECRET HARBOUR

RESERVATIONS: None

CREDIT CARDS: American Express, Visa, MasterCard

ROOMS: 20 suites in 10 cottages, some with air-conditioning and ceiling fans and verandas

MEALS: Breakfast 8:00–noon, lunch 12:30–3:00, afternoon tea at 4:00, dinner 8:00–10:00 (approx. $50 for 2, but the wines are very expensive); room service at no extra charge; informal dress (but preferably slacks rather than shorts at dinner)

ENTERTAINMENT: Piped music, amplified combos, steel bands frequently

SPORTS: Small (but private) beach, sand-topped sunbathing terrace, pool; Sunfish sailing, motorboat for rent, snorkeling, pedal boat, tennis (1 court with curious markings, lights, $10 per hour); scuba, waterskiing, yacht trips and snorkeling trips (bring your own masks) by arrangement

P.S.: At press time, Secret Harbour had acquired new owners/partners who plan to turn the resort into an "all-inclusive"—that is, charge a weekly rate that pays for everything, including drinks and water sports. This is a whole new ball game, so the resort has not been rated for this issue.

Horse Shoe Bay Hotel

Grenada

🌴🍴🎾🎾$$

You almost can't see this small hotel for the foliage, beginning with the giant banyan tree at the entrance. Step through the door and you're already in the dining pavilion, with fern- and flower-framed views of seascapes and sunsets. On either side, breezy nooks decorated with island paintings and antiques invite you to sit down with a good book or play backgammon, another to play billiards, another for darts, another for imbibing.

All these facilities and the Horse Shoe's hillside of gardens are lavished on just 18 rooms, 6 of them brand-new in 1987. A new owner (a Grenadian lady living in New York) has pumped the necessary dollars into sprucing up the rooms, reequipping the kitchenettes and pantries, installing a new fitness club. Let's hope it all comes together—it's physically a very attractive spot, the staff is eager to please.

And the dozen rooms with lacy canopied beds are among the prettiest on the island.

NAME: Horse Shoe Bay Hotel

MANAGER: Eric Wardally

ADDRESS: L'Anse aux Epines, Grenada, W.I.

LOCATION: On the south coast, 5 minutes and $10 by taxi from the airport, $12 from St. George's

TELEPHONE: 809-440-4410 or 4424

TELEX: 3425 GA Horseshoe Beach

RESERVATIONS: International Travel & Resorts

CREDIT CARDS: American Express, Visa, MasterCard

ROOMS: 18, in two-story villas, all with air-conditioning, telephones, some with canopied four-poster beds, 12 with full kitchens (radios and satellite TV to be installed)

MEALS: Breakfast 7:30–11:00, lunch noon–3:00, afternoon tea 4:00, dinner 7:30–10:00 (approx. $40 for 2), all in the breeze-cooled dining pavilion; informal dress; pianist/organist twice a week; room service 7:30 A.M.–10:00 P.M., no extra charge

ENTERTAINMENT: Taped music, billiard room, darts, parlor games

SPORTS: Beach, freshwater pool, Sunfish and Sailfish sailing, snorkeling, fitness club (exercise machines, weights, whirlpool)—all free; scuba diving and sailing can be arranged

Spice Island Inn

Grenada

$$

Begin the day by slipping out of bed, sliding back the screens, and plopping straight into your private plunge pool. When the bell by the garden gate rings, it means the waiter has arrived with your breakfast, which he'll set up on your private, shaded breakfast patio. Dawdle over the fresh island fruits and cassava bread—the hot plate will keep your coffee piping hot. After breakfast, step down onto your private sunning patio and spread out on a lounger—the garden wall screens you from passersby, the doorbell guards you against maids and waiters, so you can shuck your bikini or robe or whatever you have half on, half off. Spend the entire day here—sunning, dipping, eating, loving, dipping, sunning, all in your own private little sun-bright world.

Your suite, if you take time to notice, is craftily designed: the terrazzo sun deck is in the sun all day, the breakfast patio is in the shade all day. In addition to your tiny garden and 16 by 20 ft. freshwater pool, your suite has tiled floors with soft scatter rugs, wicker chairs and fitted dressers crafted from local hardwoods; the bathrooms are like locker rooms—big tiled shower stalls, double washbasins, separate johns, magnifying mirrors. The 20 beach suites, the original 15-year-old accommodations, are less opulent, but still way above average—with a small inner garden patio that separates the sleeping quarters from the bathroom. All Spice Island's suites, beach or pool, have louvers and air-conditioning for cooling and individual gas water heaters to give you reliable supplies of hot water to steam up your tiled, sunken shower stalls.

When you get curious about the rest of the world, stroll a few yards across the lawn, among the coconut palms and flowering shrubs, to Grand Anse Beach—2½ miles of fine white sand. Jog. Walk. Work up an appetite or thirst, both of which you can satisfy in pleasant surroundings in the inn's big bamboo-and-wood beachside pavilions. But no matter how tasty the bread-fruit vichyssoise or nutmeg ice cream, no matter how jolly the music of the folk trio that serenades you, it's always a delight to slip off to your private patio and your private pool for a midnight swim beneath your private stars.

NAME: Spice Island Inn

MANAGER: Coleman Redhead

ADDRESS: P.O. Box 6, Grand Anse, St. George's, Grenada, W.I.

LOCATION: On Grand Anse Beach, 10 minutes and $8 by taxi from St. George's, 15 minutes and $10 by taxi from the new airport

TELEPHONE: 809-440-4258 or 4423

CABLES/TELEX: Spiceland Grenada/3425 GA SPICELAND

RESERVATIONS: International Travel & Resorts, Inc. in the United States, Robert Reid Assoc. in Canada

CREDIT CARDS: American Express, MasterCard, Visa

ROOMS: 28, including 10 pool suites and 18 beach suites, all with air-conditioning and louvers, all with patio or lanai

MEALS: Breakfast from 7:00, lunch 1:00–2:30, afternoon tea 3:00–6:00, dinner 7:00–9:00 (approx. $35–40 for 2); full room service (extra charge during off-season); informal but stylish dress

ENTERTAINMENT: Video movies (Sunday, Tuesday, Thursday), barbecues and steel bands, local bands

SPORTS: 2½-mile beach (hotel's frontage about half-a-mile), 10 private freshwater pools; tennis, snorkeling gear, scuba, sailing and waterskiing at the Ramada Renaissance, a short walk along the beach

P.S.: Few groups, no cruise ship passengers in the hotel (the beach is a different story, since it's public, but it's big enough to accommodate everyone)

Added Attractions

Twelve Degrees North

Prickly Bay

Another spot worth looking into, although it's not a hotel: Twelve Degrees North, a group of 8 self-contained apartments (6 of them with 1 bedroom), each with its own maid, who prepares breakfast, lunch, fixes the beds, tidies up and does your personal laundry. The apartments are immaculate (the kitchens are so clean they look like they're newly installed every day), attractively decorated with simple island-style furnishings, and each has a large balcony or patio overlooking Prickly Bay. On the beach, at the foot of the hill, you'll find a Sunfish, 17-ft. sailboat, 23-ft. launch, 2 windsurfers, freshwater pool and beach bar operated on the self-service honor system; up top there's a Plexi-Pave tennis court in tiptop condition (but bring your own rackets and balls). Twelve Degrees North, owned and operated by a former New York executive, is in the residential area of L'Anse aux Epines, a short taxi ride from several good restaurants. Children not encouraged. By the week only. 8 apartments. *Twelve Degrees North, P.O. Box 241, St. George's, Grenada, W.I. Telephone: 809-440-4580.*

Blue Horizons Cottage Hotel

St. George's

For many visitors to Grenada, this is the garden they pass through on the way to one of the island's finest restaurants, La Belle Creole. Diners have a hillside view over the bay as they sit down to Conch Scram and Deviled Langouste, recipes familiar to guests of Ross Point Inn (where the owners, the Hopkin brothers, learned the art of Creole cooking from their mother); beneath La Belle Creole, hidden among the saman and cassia trees and coral plants, are the cottages housing the guest rooms. Each room has air-conditioning and a small kitchenette, and the newest (1986) are especially comfortable. Communal areas include a pavilion lounge beside a freshwater pool, shaded by a tall Barringtonia that blossoms for 2 hours every evening at twilight. Two blocks from Grand Anse Beach, and ideal for lovers on a tight budget, although the restaurant, of course, is not inexpensive. 24 rooms. *Blue Horizons, P.O. Box 41, St. George's, Grenada, W.I. Telephone: 809-440-4316.*

The Dutch Leewards

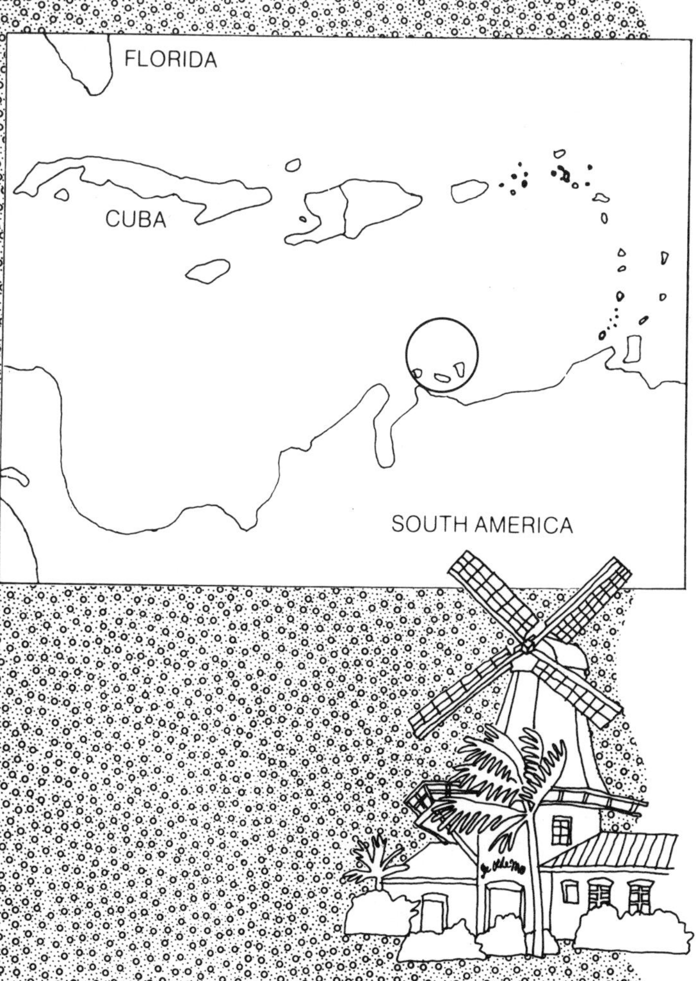

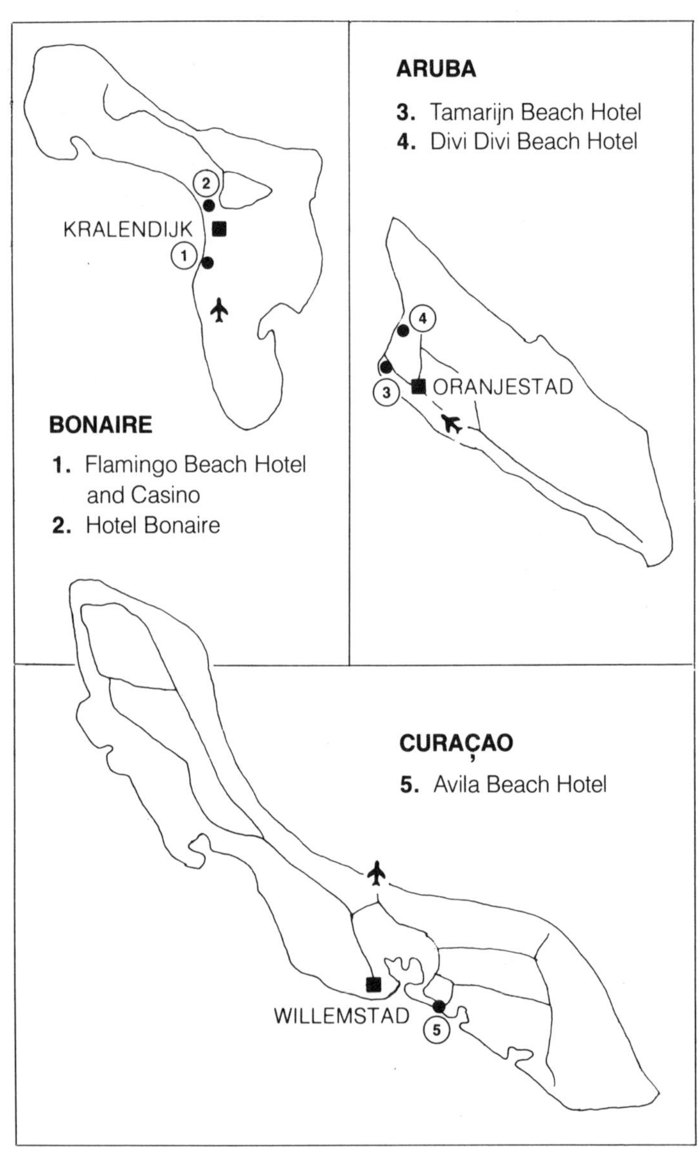

THE DUTCH LEEWARDS

The Dutch Leewards

They're ledges of coral rather than volcanic peaks, they're covered with cactus rather than jungle, and they have a personality all their own—part Dutch, part Indian, part Spanish, part just about everything else. They even have their own language, *Papiamento,* which grabs a few words from any language that happens to come along, shakes them around like a rum punch and comes up with something as infectiously charming as the people themselves. Thus, *Carne ta camna cabes abou, ma e sa cuant' or tin* means, "He is as innocent as the babe unborn," although the literal translation is "The sheep walks with its head down, but it knows what time it is"; or *stropi cacalaca,* which means "sweatheart" or "darling" although its literal translation means something quite unsuspected.

Bonaire is the loveliest of the trio, a coral boomerang 24 miles long and 5 miles wide, a world all its own, a world so bright, so luminous from coral and sand you practically get a suntan crossing the street. It has more goats than cars, and almost as many flamingos as people; one-third of the island is national park, and another large chunk is salt flats cultivated by Dutch seafarers a couple of centuries ago. The capital, Kralendijk, has 1,000 inhabitants, 1 discotheque and 2 Chinese restaurants.

Curaçao is the largest of the three, and its main city, Willemstad, is the capital of all the Netherlands Antilles. Willemstad is utterly unique, almost a miniature Caribbean Amsterdam with gingerbread houses the colors of a coral reef. Of late, it has become a bit grungy and slightly overcommercial, so maybe you'd better skip town and head out to the *cunucu,* or countryside, to find yourselves a quiet cove for the afternoon.

Aruba is all beach, but a beach unsurpassed by any other island, with mile after mile of some of the whitest sand in the Caribbean. It's the smallest but the liveliest of the Dutch Leewards, with high-rise hotels, nightclubs, casinos and lots of restaurants to keep you from enjoying the moon and the stars.

HOW TO GET THERE From New York, American flies wide-body jets to Aruba and Curaçao, nonstop to one, one-stop to the other, or vice versa, depending on the day of the week; from Miami, ALM and Eastern to both islands; from Baltimore and Washington via Eastern; and, good news, ALM now flies DC-9 jets from Miami direct to Bonaire, nonstop on Saturday and Sunday, via Aruba or Curaçao (no change of plane) the remainder of the week. Otherwise, to get to Bonaire you switch at Aruba or Curaçao to an ALM jet. You may also be able to fly *direct* to Bonaire from New York on once-a-week charter flights operated as inclusive packages that give you air fare and a room at either the Hotel Bonaire or the Flamingo Beach Hotel. It's a charter only in the sense that everyone flies down on the same plane and returns a week later on the same plane, but you don't have to mix with the other passengers if you don't feel like it—and you do get to fly to Bonaire nonstop from New York.

Divi Divi Beach Hotel

Aruba

$$$$

There's probably more sand on this beach than there is on a half dozen other islands put together. Shimmering, glistening, beckoning sand. Sand about as white as a beach will ever be. It's called Eagle Beach at this point, and it sweeps off into the distance on either side, 1 mile to the south, about 6 miles to the northern tip of Aruba.

The slightly Miami-ish Divi Divi appears in these pages by courtesy of this beach—and courtesy of its *casitas* and lanais. The *casitas,* 40 of them, are in staggered rows among tailored lawns and hibiscus in many hues; the 20 new lanai suites are next door to them, right on the beach.

Each *casita* has a patio on the lawn with a shaded breakfast alcove and a Spanish-Mexican interior, with tile floors, overhead ceiling fans, Mexican carpets and hand-crafted hangings from Colombia, wood-and-leather chairs, wrought-iron lamps, big tiled bathrooms and fresh flowers on the *two* double Sealy Posturepedics with hand-carved headboards. The new lanai suites have similar decor, with, of course, lanais facing the beach and a cool, quiet palm court.

Both the *casitas* and the lanais are to the left of the Divi Divi's open, breezy lobby; to the right there are a couple of two-story wings on the beach but in general appearances much like a motel; the focus of activity is the big, palm-encircled swimming pool off the main lobby and adjoining the bar and snack terrace. The public shenanigans here almost put the Divi Divi beyond the pale for lovers—there's music in some loud, amplified form or another almost every night of the week, often until 1:00 or 2:00 A.M. Fortunately, most of the *casitas* (except for those ending in 26, which are the noisiest, unfortunately, since they do have the best views) and lanais are upwind of the noise—you could be in a different hotel over there.

You could also feel like you're in a different hotel if you opt for the Divi Divi's deluxe hacienda-style rooms. These three-story Spanish villas all have suites with windowed patios and ocean views; cool breezes, overhead fans *and* air-conditioning; full bathroom and dressing room, pretty floral printed fabrics, lattice grillwork separating refrigerator/sink area from the bedroom. All rooms come with the luxury of a continental breakfast quietly dropped off in the dumbwaiter built into the dressing rooms and there's a separate whirlpool–swimming pool–lily pond–deck area for deluxe guests exclusively.

You have, actually, plenty of opportunities to escape the bustle and brouhaha—the beach is so vast a short walk will isolate you from just about everything except yourselves and the sand (turn left when you get to the beach, walk a few hundred yards, and you'll come to one or two great spots for coral and conch shells; turn right and you will pass a bit of construction inland). If worse comes to worst, call Avis for a car, order a couple of the Divi Divi's "Lovers' Lunch Boxes" and head for some totally secluded cove on the wild unswimmable north coast. In the evenings, stay upwind of the action in your *casita* or lanai. Call room service and have them send over your dinner. Afterward, take a stroll on the beach. Come, if you can, when the moon is full—then the great beach is pure scintillating magic.

NAME: Divi Divi Beach Hotel

MANAGER: Bernie Gassenbauer

ADDRESS: Aruba, N.A.; or 520 West State St., Ithaca, NY 14850

LOCATION: On the west coast beach, 10 minutes and $10 by taxi from the airport, 5 minutes from town, about the same from the casinos and nightclubs along hotel row (buses every 45 minutes, $.50 a ride)

TELEPHONE: 23300

TELEX: 444-2016

RESERVATIONS: Divi offices in United States and Canada 800-367-3484 or 607-367-3484

CREDIT CARDS: American Express, Diners Club, Visa, MasterCard

ROOMS: 202, including 40 *casitas* and 20 lanais, all with air-conditioning, most with cross-ventilation, all with balconies or patios, plus the new studio apartments

MEALS: Breakfast 7:30–10:00, continental breakfast 7:30–11:30, lunch noon–6:00, dinner 6:30–10:00 on the terrace or in the air-conditioned Red Parrott (a few dollars and up on the terrace, $22 and up a head in the Red Parrott); casual dress on the terrace and dining room

ENTERTAINMENT: Piped music on terrace, live music most evenings, steel bands, folklore shows, barbecues, buffets, Sunday brunch, beach parties; sunset sails on the 76-ft. ketch, *Mi Dushi;* casinos and nightclubs nearby

SPORTS: Beach (and how!), freshwater pool, loungers (no extra charge), tennis (2 courts lighted), "only half an hour per day per couple," Jacuzzi—all free; snorkeling gear for rent; scuba, sailboats and waterskiing nearby

P.S.: Many groups in main hotel

Tamarijn Beach Hotel

Aruba

$$$

The Tamarijn is the kid brother of the Divi Divi Hotel but costs a few dollars less, a point in its favor right there. Inspiration for its design is the typical country cottage you see out in the *cunucu,* Aruba's scrubby countryside, but instead of individual cottages, the Tamarijn strings them together in three or four clusters, red-tiled and white-walled, strung out along the beach. Interiors recently have been warmly refurbished—earth-colored tiles, orange wicker headboards, seashell colors on printed bedspreads and drapes; every room has two full-size double beds, small wall safes in the bathrooms and sliding screened doors opening onto patios with *bohios* or balconies, all with ocean views. You may find the rooms in wings 17 through 22 quietest, and (lucky break) they're also the least expensive rooms because they're farther (2 minutes, say, instead of 1) from the lobby, bar and dining terrace.

The hotel revolves around the Cunucu Terrace with its beachside/poolside bar (the enclosed Palm Court restaurant was closed for renovations) botanically boxed in by rows of cayena or hibiscus. Above you the palm trees, above the palms the stars, and with candles flickering on the table it would be one of the most romantic as well as one of the prettiest dining spots on the island if it weren't for the nondescript music blaring from the overhead speakers. (Make a point of avoiding the number 14 wing series—who needs to listen to an amplified combo version of "Feelings" when you'd rather sit quietly and feel the trade winds cool off your tan?)

The other hub of Tamarijn and Divi Divi nightlife is the "freestanding entertainment complex'' (that should tell you something), the brightly lit Alhambra Casino. Inside is an all night "New York" deli, theater nightclub, boutique mall and incredibly noisy casino where everything that can whirr, whistle, buzz, beep, clang, ring and light up does.

Since the Tamarijn and the Divi Divi have the same owner, the Wiggins family of Ithaca, New York, guests at either have access to the facilities of the other, and a golf cart known as the Panther shuttles between the two at regular intervals. There's also a paved path (a 7-minute walk); but if you decide to drink here and dine there, the thing to do is kick off your espadrilles, roll up your pants and stroll along the edge of the sea.

NAME: Tamarijn Beach Hotel

MANAGER: Bernie Gassenbauer

ADDRESS: Aruba, N.A.; or P.O. Box 686, Ithaca, NY 14850

LOCATION: On the west coast beach, about 10 minutes and $10 by taxi from the airport

TELEPHONE: 4150

RESERVATIONS: Own U.S. office (see above)

CREDIT CARDS: American Express, Visa, Carte Blanche, Diners Club, MasterCard, Amoco

ROOMS: 204, in beachside bungalows, with breezes, air-conditioning, wall safes, patios or balconies

MEALS: Breakfast 7:30–11:00, continental breakfast to 11:30, lunch noon–5:00, dinner 6:30–10:00 (approx. $30–35 for 2, served in the open garden terrace); casual dress but "coats and ties are permitted, reluctantly"; room service from 7:30 A.M.–11:00 P.M., $1 per order

ENTERTAINMENT: Piped music at dinner, steel bands, amplified combos in conical band shell, casinos, ketch sails (see above)

SPORTS: Freshwater pool, Ping-Pong; 1,000 ft. of virtually private beach (which is not as spectacular as the strand at the Divi Divi, a short walk away); tennis (2 courts, free by day, $5 per half hour at night); snorkeling gear for rent; waterskiing, scuba diving, sailing, boat trips nearby

P.S.: Some charter groups, noticeable only at check-in and check-out times (mostly weekends)

P.P.S.: A new time-sharing property, Dutch Village, has opened up on the Tamarijn property, without causing too much disruption in hotel services or to the hotel environment. The studio, one- and two-bedroom apartments all have air-conditioning, full kitchens, cable TV, Jacuzzi and patio or balcony, with a lushly planted grotto in full view. They're furnished with carved and painted wood furniture, canopied king-size beds, big bathrooms, all done up in brownish tones. Hopefully, this Tamarijn development will not impinge on the workings of the rest of the hotel.

Hotel Bonaire

Bonaire

$$

Roll over on your back. Float out to the raft through the cleanest water you've ever seen and haul yourselves aboard. Look around: lagoonlike bay sheltered by an uninhabited island; a stretch of sand, 600 ft. of it; a few palm trees, a half dozen *bohios,* a hammock or two, a pair of Sailfish flapping the breeze on the beach beside a thatch-roofed bar; a scuba shack and a jetty with a couple of dive boats moored alongside. No traffic. No planes. No ungainly resort developments (there are condo plans in the works, but we're on Bonaire time here, so not to worry *yet*). Just the steady lapping of calm water and the occasional splash of a hungry pelican. It may not be the most ravishing setting in the Caribbean, but the infectious charm of Bonaire and the Bonaireans make this odd-looking hotel one of your best bets for a few days of total detachment.

Swim ashore for a bit of lunch at that thatch-roofed beach hut and a chance to meet a few of these Bonaire charmers. Sooner or later the ebullient Cai-Cai will come bounding in, a one-man carnival, dazzlingly turned out in tropical whites with a peaked cap and name tag identifying him as the island's official tour guide (he knows all the official and *unofficial* news of the island—just ask).

The entire coastline of Bonaire is a coral reef. Scuba divers don't have to take a boat ride for an hour—they just step off the beach or take a short boat ride to Klein Bonaire; so while other divers on other islands are hanging over the side of a boat in choppy seas, the divers on Bonaire are already ogling the parrotfish. And while some guests in the Hotel Bonaire are settling down for an hour or two in the casino, it's not unknown for the dive master to muster his mer-people and take them for a moonlight dive.

Don't get the idea, though, that the Hotel Bonaire is not for you if you're not an avid scuba diver. Just think: If half the guests are underwater, you have all that extra room on the beach. And if you're jealous of their moonlight dives, rent one of those funny VW beachcars, put the top down and go for a leisurely drive to the white, scintillating, eerie moonscape of the salt flats.

A few years ago the island government bought this hotel, pumped in a half million dollars and turned the management over to Copthorne Hotels; since then the Bonaire has been restyled (albeit functionally): polished wooden floors and headboards, muted greens for rugs and spreads, underwater photos on the wall, fresh flowers on the nightstand. Second floor rooms have balconies, first floor rooms patios, some facing the sea, some with courtyard garden views (others look over the roadway into Bonaire's scruffy middle ground, so do specify your choice); and two new lighted tennis courts have been added. The enclosed, air-conditioned dining room, pleasantly but unimaginatively turned out yacht-style with fittings of canvas, wood and brass, features nightly "theme cuisine," Indonesian, Surf & Turf, etc. A better bet would be to stroll down to the Flamingo Beach Hut for a more romantic, breezy supper by the sea beneath the stars.

NAME: Hotel Bonaire

MANAGER: Kees Fekkes

ADDRESS: P.O. Box 34, Kralendijk, Bonaire, N.A.

LOCATION: 15 minutes and $6 by taxi from the airport

TELEPHONE: 599-7-8448

TELEX: Hobon/384-1291

RESERVATIONS: Robert Reid Assoc.

CREDIT CARDS: American Express, Visa, Diners Club, MasterCard

ROOMS: 147 rooms, all with air-conditioning or cross-ventilation, telephone

MEALS: Breakfast 7:00–11:00, lunch 11:30–4:30, dinner 7:00–10:30 (in the air-conditioned Neptune Room, $32–35 for 2); "theme cuisines"; folklore show Saturday; no room service; casual ("but not *too* casual") dress

ENTERTAINMENT: Live music in the Neptune Room (sometimes amplified); weekly barbecue with folklore show; Tuesday night cocktail parties; casino (with free drinks for players)

SPORTS: Pool, beach, golf (9 holes), tennis (2 courts, lights), Sunfish sailing lessons, windsurfers—all free; waterskiing extra; Bonaire Dive Shop offers instruction, diving trips by land and sea, guided snorkeling tours at any of 40 locations around the island; horseback riding, bicycle rental nearby

P.S.: Some small groups in summer, local families on the beach weekends

Flamingo Beach Hotel and Casino

Bonaire

$$

What you slip into in the morning here is probably what you'll slip out of at bedtime—bikini, swim shorts, diving tanks (or snorkel for the uninitiated), maybe even a pair of sandals. This is a down-to-coral resort ("where toes are in and ties are out"), which reflects the unspoiled, uncomplicated life-style of the island of Bonaire and the zealous, underwater life-style of the divers who come here.

If you're one of the discerning band of Bonaire buffs who would grow gills if you could, you already know what I'm talking about. If you've never heard of Bonaire or have never checked an air tank, no matter. When you finish breakfast in the open-air Calabas Terrace, just take three steps down to the beach, don snorkel and fins and float through schools of smallmouth grunts, listen to the spotlight parrotfish munch on some coral, keep an eye out for the shy Royal Blue, a real beauty. When you finally surface, you may want to pop over to the Flamingo Nest for an aqueous refreshment, a cool Mai-Tai perhaps, while you take in that stunning view: the multihued, multi*blued* Caribbean, the tiny coral mass, Klein Bonaire, the northern tip of boomerang Bonaire and one spectacular sunset.

Just about the most formal place at the Flamingo Beach is the Chibi-Chibi, a wood-beamed, red-shingled two-story terrace restaurant overhanging the water. Shoes and shirts are considered formal. Here you can watch the tropical fish, even moray eels, frolic and fight over the crumbs that drop through the wood-planked floors, while you savor a tasty Antillean *bouillabaise* or *keshi yena,* a local dish of chicken, spices and vegetables baked under a Gouda cheese dome. If you fancy wine, there's a surprisingly extensive French list.

Guests at the Flamingo tend to retire early, unless, of course, they're going to pay a visit to the "first barefoot casino in the world," just past the Calabas in a restored Bonairean mansion.

However directly or indirectly you do come to your rooms, you'll find comfortable accommodations when it's time for bed. Stay in the original cottages on the horseshoe path behind the terrace and you can relax on a patio shaded by gnarled old bean trees, behind a white "picket fence" of upended conch shells. All these cottages have recently been renovated to include new tile showers and sliding glass doors. The two-story ocean front deluxe rooms beside the coral beach feature big, wooden-railed balconies built right out over the gently lapping sea, and are tastefully appointed in wicker and batik, with double beds and half canopies. Over by the muraled, free-form pool and courtyard, superior rooms are done up Mexican style, with carved wooden bedposts and bureaus, tiled floors; some rooms have sea views, some are shaded by palms and overlook the gardens.

Recently the hotel completed a new wing of time-sharing units called the Divi Club Flamingo, which may sometimes be available to the hotel's guests. The 40 units are in a self-contained, two-story ell, just past the casino, and designed to blend in with the rest of the grounds—light lattice-work partitions separate the screened-in porches, the slanted roof is edged with Caribbean-style green gingerbread, there's all-new landscaping and a blue-tiled pool and Jacuzzi. The studio apartments are air-conditioned and are decorated with custom-designed, light-colored Haitian furniture.

Despite the expansion, Flamingo Beach remains strictly a place for relaxing. Nothing but sea, sand, sun, sun, sand, sea; rum punches in the beach bar; lazy dinners in the pavilion with moonlight shimmering on the bay; an evening stroll along the jetty—and if you're lucky, a split-second glimpse of Bonaire's mysterious, watery "green flash."

NAME: Flamingo Beach Hotel and Casino

MANAGER: Monte Hollander

ADDRESS: Kralendijk, Bonaire, N.A.; or 520 West State St., Ithaca, NY 14850

LOCATION: 3 minutes and $4 by taxi from the airport (but although it's so close you won't be disturbed by aircraft noise)

TELEPHONE: 8285

TELEX: 384 1293

RESERVATIONS: Divi offices in United States and Canada 800-367-3484 or 607-367-3484

CREDIT CARDS: American Express, Diners Club, Visa, MasterCard

ROOMS: 150 rooms, all with air-conditioning, many with cross-ventilation, half with balconies or patios, deluxe rooms have bath tubs, others showers only

MEALS: Self-service breakfast buffet 7:30–10:00, continental breakfast 10:00–12:00, lunch noon–2:30, dinner 7:00–10:00 (approx. $40–45 for 2, served in open pavilion beside the beach); no room service; "ties and jackets absolutely prohibited"

ENTERTAINMENT: Trio 4 nights a week in winter, Antillean Night with steel band (slightly amplified), Calypso Night with combo on Saturday; casino with open-air Players Bar

SPORTS: Pool with Jacuzzi, small beach; snorkel gear, bicycles, boat trips to offshore islands for a small fee (sometimes without charge in special packages); complete dive shop, underwater photo center and car rental on premises

P.S.: Occasional small charter groups, some seminars, lots of scuba divers, "We welcome children as long as they're done well"

Avila Beach Hotel

Curaçao

🌴🌴🍴🍴☺$$

The driveway with its jungle greenery and the glimpse of sun-dappled patio at the rear says "tropics," and so does the Avila's owner Nic Møller. "I like to give my guests a feeling of the tropics; I like to find things to make it interesting." *It* being a four-story colonial governor's mansion built in a time (1811) when ships had to fire gun salutes for the mansion as they bobbed down the coast to the harbor. The yellow, impeccably kept mansion with white trim and red-tiled roof, sandwiched between a former desalination plant and the octagonal home where Simón Bolívar used to visit his sisters, could still receive a governor at a moment's notice. And it's certainly *interesting.*

The lobby has been recently lightened and brightened with a cultivated Caribbean/European air: smooth pale paint replaces the heavy wood paneling, Oriental rugs blend with smart cane furniture, a grand piano stands ready for the occasional concert, large mirrors are guarded by life-size ceramic dogs.

Follow the sun through this pleasant lobby and you come to a breezy patio/terrace with flagstones and ceramic lamps, a sunshade of twining palms and flamboyants, cacti and rubber plants, with white wooden chairs grouped around white wooden tables with cheery red cloths. Further down there's a second arbor shading rustic lounging chairs and the Schooner Bar, which is shaped like a ship's prow with a roof of thatch projecting from the mast. Then comes the beach. Well, something like a beach. The Avila is indeed on the seafront but on this stretch of the coastline there's precious little natural beach; so with typical Dutch ingenuity, someone has fashioned a small breakwater to create a small lagoon with a sandy beach in one corner, ringed by a sunbathing terrace with a layer of sand and shaded by half a dozen *bohios.* Two years ago, Møller added a string of iron-poled, orange-capped gas-lamp-like lights to guide you to a romantic little stone bench at the end of the breakwater, perfect for private stargazing.

The Danish-born owner has been in possession of Avila for the last 10 years. His first major undertaking was a new bungalow near the seawall (very private at night, when everyone has left the beach), decorated with ships' lamps and portholes, furnished with refrigerator, cooker and bright Danish Contemporary chairs and tables. All the rooms in the main house and its wings have recently been redone in crisp Scandinavian style—cool, striped cloth blinds, sleek-lined wooden beds and couches, framed antique maps or pretty little watercolors on the walls. The standard rooms are fairly small; if you have a choice and can afford a sea view, ask for rooms 125, 235 or 345, on the upper floors, facing the tankers and cruise ships maneuvering for the run into the harbor channel. Rooms 344 and 345 have terrace/balconies for afternoon sunning.

The Avila is by no means a plush hotel, but in its unpretentious, friendly way it has a lot of old colonial charm. Especially in the evening, when you're sitting around the Schooner Bar sipping a Heineken, the pelicans are diving for their suppers, a cruise ship passes like a wall of lights and you'll soon be sitting down to a dinner of fresh fish smoked in the kitchen's spice room, topped off by handmade sorbet, all beneath the twining palms and flamboyants. And there're still the moon and that little bench at the end of the breakwater.

NAME: Avila Beach Hotel

OWNER/MANAGER: Nic Møller

ADDRESS: Penstraat 130-134, Willemstad, Curaçao, N.A.

LOCATION: On a residential street beside the sea, a 10-minute walk from the shopping center, $10 by taxi from the airport

TELEPHONE: 614377

TELEX: 1178 AVILA MA

RESERVATIONS: Utell International

CREDIT CARDS: American Express, Diners Club, Visa

ROOMS: 45, all with air-conditioning, plus 2 suites

MEALS: Breakfast 7:00–10:00, lunch noon–2:00, dinner 7:00–9:30 (approx. $42 for 2, fixed price, served on the open terrace beside the beach); special *Fondue Bourguignonne* on Monday, *smørrebrød* on Sunday; casual dress; no room service

ENTERTAINMENT: TV lounge; barbecue night on Saturday

SPORTS: Beach of sorts, loungers, free snorkeling gear

P.S.: Some cruise ship passengers, beach club families on weekends

The Rates

and how to figure them out

BEFORE YOU GO ANY FURTHER: ALL THE ROOM RATES QUOTED IN THIS GUIDEBOOK ARE FOR TWO PEOPLE.

Islands have different ways of establishing their rates, and individual hotels have their own little methods. The variables include twin beds versus double beds, rooms with bath or without bath, rooms on the beach or near the beach, facing the front, facing the back, upper floors versus lower floors, cubic feet of space. Some rooms may cost more because they have air-conditioning, others because they have small refrigerators, and so on. It would be a lifetime's work to figure out all the odds. If you have any special preferences, let the hotel know when you make your reservations.

Hotels in the Caribbean Quote Four Different Types of Rates:

EP	European Plan	You pay for the room only. No meals
CP	Continental Plan	You get the room and breakfast (usually a continental breakfast of juice, rolls and coffee)
MAP	Modified American Plan	You get room with breakfast plus *one* meal—usually dinner
FAP*	Full American Plan	You get everything—room, breakfast, lunch, afternoon tea (where served), and dinner

*Sometimes known as American Plan and abbreviated to AP.

FAP and MAP rates may mean that you order your meals from a fixed menu, rather than from the à la carte menu; in some Caribbean hotels this is a racket because the choice you're offered is so limited or unpromising you're almost obligated to order the items that cost a few dollars more. That happens in only a few of the hotels in *this* guide; although in many of the smaller inns you will be offered a fixed menu for dinner (identified in these pages as "family style").

Which rate should you choose? They all have their advantages. Usually you're better off having the EP or CP rate, because this gives you the flexibility to eat wherever you want to eat—for instance, to sample a *rijsttafel* in Aruba or Curaçao, to dine in some of the bistros on Martinique. On the other hand, in many cases the hotel dining room may be the best eating spot on the island (in some cases the *only* spot), and you'd want to eat there anyway; or the nearest restaurant may be a $10 or $15 cab ride away on the other side of the island and not worth the fare.

On some islands, as in Barbados, some hotels have wisely banded together to arrange an exchange program—in other words, you tell your hotel that you want to dine in hotel B, in which case they arrange to have hotel B send the bill to them. On other islands, you encounter a tiresome attitude among hotel managers in which each one claims to have the best restaurant on the island and therefore everyone wants to dine in his place anyway.

Rebates on Meals

Many hotels allow you a rebate on the dinner portion of your MAP or FAP rate—probably not a full rebate, but most of it, and only if you let them know before lunchtime that you're not going to dine there that evening.

The reason why hotels put you through this hassle is that their supplies are limited, and they have to know in advance how many dinners they must prepare (in the case of steaks, for example, how many they have to unfreeze), without entailing a lot of waste.

In the hotel listings elsewhere in this guide, I've included the price of dinner where a hotel offers a choice of EP or MAP/FAP rates. Usually, the cost of dinners on a one-shot deal is more expensive (a couple of dollars or so) than the MAP/FAP rates.

Taxes

Most islands entice you to their island and then clobber you with a tax, sometimes two. These taxes may go under any of several euphemisms—room tax, government tax, airport tax, departure tax, energy tax—but what it boils down to is that you're going to pay more than the advertised hotel rates. Some are as high as 8 percent on your total bill, some are 3 percent on your room only. If you're on a tight budget, or if you simply don't feel like being taken for a ride, choose an island with no tax. In any case, check out such things if you're watching your pennies.

Service Charge

Most hotels in the Caribbean now add a service charge to your bill, usually 10, 12½ or 15 percent, ostensibly in lieu of tipping; in some hotels you may tip in addition to the service charge, in others it's positively forbidden to tip and any member of the staff caught taking a *pourboire* is fired on the spot. The system has its pros and cons: from your point of view, it means you can relax and not have to bother about figuring out percentages, sometimes in funny currencies; on the other hand, a flat fee doesn't reward individual feats of activity, initiative and personal attention, and without that incentive service can be lethargic. But the chances are service will be lethargic either way. If tipping is included, don't encourage layabouts who hover around looking for an additional tip—send them on their way; and if service overall is so bad it almost ruined your sex life, just refuse to pay the service charge.

Additional Notes on Rates

In the list of rates that follows, please remember that "summer" is really spring, summer *and* fall: in other words, these seemingly horrendous peak season rates are in effect only 4 months of the year, the lower rates the remaining *8 months.* For most hotels, the peak season runs from December 15 through Easter, but this may vary by a few days; if you check into the matter carefully, you may find that in some hotels the higher rates do not begin until Christmas, or even until late January, and you can grab a few unexpected "peak" season bargains. Still others will give you a reduced rate during the *first 2 weeks in January.* A few of the hotels listed here have 3 or 4 seasons; keeping track of them for this guide would be a round-the-year vocation, so the range of rates for those hotels represents the lowest and highest for the 2 winter and 2 summer seasons *combined.*

REMEMBER The figures quoted are not the full story—to get a more accurate comparison of rates between hotels you should also check out the paragraph marked "sports" in the individual hotel listings, to determine what activities are *included* in the rates at no extra charge. For instance, Guadeloupe's Hamak and Jamaica's Half Moon Club give you free golf on Robert Trent Jones courses, Bitter End in the British Virgins includes unlimited sailing.

Special Packages

As we mentioned in the introduction, and remind you here, your wallet may benefit by looking into special packages offered by individual hotels and airlines. For example, Young Island in the Grenadines treats "Lovers" to their own special off-season rate that includes everything but drinks and postage stamps.

You might also want to check out Eastern Airlines' packages on what they call their Vacation Islands. American has an even more extensive selection of "Pleasure Islands" that includes 3-night or 7-night stays (usually including round-trip airport transfers, which can be costly otherwise). Check with your travel agent for details.

Beware

We've double-checked all the room rates in the guide, and at the time of writing, they were all as accurate as can be, given conditions in the Caribbean. In the best of times, it's difficult for a hotelkeeper to estimate rates for two seasons hence; in these inflationary times it's virtually impossible. So, alas and alack, some of these rates will be wrong by the time you get around to escaping. It's not my fault. It's not my publisher's fault. Blame it on oil sheiks, bankers, gold speculators, trade unions, fishermen and the sailors who man the island schooners. In any case, the prices will still be valid as a *comparison* between hotels and resorts, even between islands. The differences shouldn't be more than a few percentage points, but always double-check the rates before you go.

Please note: N/A (not available) indicates that rates were not available at press time, summer 1987.

The rates are arranged alphabetically by island and are quoted in U.S. dollars.

TYPE OF RATE	RATE (U.S. $)	PEAK SEASON	SERVICE CHARGE	OFF-SEASON REDUCTION

Anguilla
(8% tax)

Cinnamon Reef Beach Club				
EP	$250	12/16–4/15	10%	40%
Malliouhana				
EP	$350	12/16–4/5	10%	30%
The Mariners				
EP	$180–285	12/15–4/30	10%	30%

Antigua
(6% tax)

The Admiral's Inn				
EP	$74–86	12/15–4/14	10%	25%
Blue Waters Beach Hotel				
MAP	$250	12/15–4/15	10%	25%
Copper & Lumber Store				
EP	$135–155	12/15–5/4	10%	40%
Curtain Bluff				
MAP	$360–440	12/19–4/14	10%	30%
Half Moon Bay				
MAP	$260–410	12/16–4/9	10%	50%
The Inn at English Harbour				
MAP	$280–450	12/15–4/15	10%	25%
Jumby Bay Resort				
FAP	$600	12/16–4/9	10%	25%
St. James's Club				
MAP	$375–450	12/20–1/3	10%	15–30%

Aruba
(5% tax)

Divi Divi Beach Hotel				
EP	$200–400	12/19–4/9	15%	30%

TYPE OF RATE	RATE (U.S. $)	PEAK SEASON	SERVICE CHARGE	OFF-SEASON REDUCTION
Tamarijn Beach Hotel				
EP	$180–200	12/19–4/9	15%	30%

Barbados

(5% tax)

TYPE OF RATE	RATE (U.S. $)	PEAK SEASON	SERVICE CHARGE	OFF-SEASON REDUCTION
Cobblers Cove Hotel				
MAP	$370–450	12/16–4/15	10%	25%
Coral Reef Club				
FAP	$275–410	12/16–4/15	7½%	25%
Crane Beach Hotel				
EP	$70–250	12/15–4/14	10%	30–40%
Ginger Bay Beach Club				
MAP	$632–732	12/15–4/14	10%	N/A
Glitter Bay				
EP	$260–340	12/22–4/15	10%	25%
Sandy Lane Hotel				
MAP	$430–510	12/23–3/31	10%	30%

Belize

(5% tax)

TYPE OF RATE	RATE (U.S. $)	PEAK SEASON	SERVICE CHARGE	OFF-SEASON REDUCTION
The Belizean				
FAP	$380	12/22–4/2	15%	30%

Bequia

(5% tax)

TYPE OF RATE	RATE (U.S. $)	PEAK SEASON	SERVICE CHARGE	OFF-SEASON REDUCTION
Frangipani Hotel				
EP	$45–75	12/15–4/19	10%	25%
Friendship Bay Hotel				
MAP	$200	12/15–4/15	10%	30%
Spring on Bequia				
MAP	$165	12/15–4/15	10%	30%

TYPE OF RATE	RATE (U.S. $)	PEAK SEASON	SERVICE CHARGE	OFF-SEASON REDUCTION

Bonaire
(5% tax)

Flamingo Beach Hotel and Casino				
EP	$90–200	12/19–4/9	15%	30%
Hotel Bonaire				
EP	$100–180	12/19–4/9	15%	25%

Cayman Islands
(6% tax)

Hyatt Regency Grand Cayman				
EP	$200–350	12/19–4/14	10%	45%
Tortuga Club				
N/A	N/A	N/A	N/A	N/A

Curaçao
(5% tax)

Avila Beach Hotel				
EP	$88–98	12/19–4/9	10%	25%

The Dominican Republic
(11% tax)

Casa de Campo				
EP	$180–340	12/21–4/3	10%	30%
La Posada				
EP	$125	12/21–4/3	10%	30%

Grenada
(7½% tax)

The Calabash				
MAP	$200	12/21–4/9	10%	45%
Horse Shoe Bay Hotel				
EP	$110	12/21–4/9	10%	10%

TYPE OF RATE	RATE (U.S. $)	PEAK SEASON	SERVICE CHARGE	OFF-SEASON REDUCTION
Secret Harbour				
	($2150 for two per week, all inclusive)			
Spice Island Inn				
MAP	$190–230	12/21–4/9	10%	30%

Guadeloupe

(tax included in rates)

TYPE OF RATE	RATE (U.S. $)	PEAK SEASON	SERVICE CHARGE	OFF-SEASON REDUCTION
Auberge de la Vielle Tour				
CP	$150–200	12/15–4/15	(included)	N/A
Auberge des Anacardiers				
MAP	$90–125	12/15–4/15	(included)	N/A
Hamak				
CP	$280–430	12/19–4/22	(included)	35%
PLM Azur Los Santos				
CP	$127	12/15–4/15	(included)	40%

Guana Island

(7% tax)

TYPE OF RATE	RATE (U.S. $)	PEAK SEASON	SERVICE CHARGE	OFF-SEASON REDUCTION
Guana Island Club				
FAP	$345	12/16–4/1	12%	40%

Jamaica

($12 per person per day)

TYPE OF RATE	RATE (U.S. $)	PEAK SEASON	SERVICE CHARGE	OFF-SEASON REDUCTION
The Admiralty Club				
EP/CP	$75–140	12/15–4/14	10%	N/A
Half Moon Club				
EP	$200–340	12/19–4/15	10%	30%
Jamaica Inn				
FAP	$275–350	12/15–4/16	10%	30%
Plantation Inn				
MAP	$280–355	12/15–4/19	10%	30%

TYPE OF RATE	RATE (U.S. $)	PEAK SEASON	SERVICE CHARGE	OFF-SEASON REDUCTION
Round Hill				
MAP	$310–485	12/15–4/15	10%	30%
Sans Souci Hotel				
EP	$240–280	12/21–4/15	10%	30%
Sundowner Hotel				
N/A	N/A	N/A	N/A	N/A
Trident Villas & Hotel				
MAP	$300–500	12/16–4/15	(optional)	40%
Tryall Golf and Beach Club				
MAP	$260–310	12/15–4/14	10%	40%

Martinique

(tax included in rates)

TYPE OF RATE	RATE (U.S. $)	PEAK SEASON	SERVICE CHARGE	OFF-SEASON REDUCTION
Hotel Bakoua Beach				
CP	$205–275	12/15–4/15	(included)	40%
Hotel Plantation de Leyritz				
CP	$71	12/15–4/14	(included)	30%
Manoir de Beauregard				
EP	$95	12/15–4/15	(included)	30%
St. Aubin Hotel				
CP	$71	12/14–4/14	(included)	N/A

Mayreau

(5% tax)

TYPE OF RATE	RATE (U.S. $)	PEAK SEASON	SERVICE CHARGE	OFF-SEASON REDUCTION
Saltwhistle Bay Club				
MAP	$320	12/16–4/15	10%	30%

Mustique

(5% tax)

TYPE OF RATE	RATE (U.S. $)	PEAK SEASON	SERVICE CHARGE	OFF-SEASON REDUCTION
The Cotton House				
FAP	$384–400	12/17–4/17	10%	35%

TYPE OF RATE	RATE (U.S. $)	PEAK SEASON	SERVICE CHARGE	OFF-SEASON REDUCTION

Nevis
(7% tax)

TYPE OF RATE	RATE (U.S. $)	PEAK SEASON	SERVICE CHARGE	OFF-SEASON REDUCTION
Golden Rock				
EP	$150	12/20–3/31	10%	50%
Hotel Montpelier				
MAP	$230	12/15–4/15	—	45%
Nisbet Plantation Inn				
MAP	$270–330	12/15–4/14	10%	N/A

Palm Island
(5% tax)

TYPE OF RATE	RATE (U.S. $)	PEAK SEASON	SERVICE CHARGE	OFF-SEASON REDUCTION
Palm Island Beach Club				
MAP	$300	12/15–4/14	10%	25%

Petit St. Vincent
(5% tax)

TYPE OF RATE	RATE (U.S. $)	PEAK SEASON	SERVICE CHARGE	OFF-SEASON REDUCTION
Petit St. Vincent Resort				
FAP	$520	12/19–3/20	10%	15%

Puerto Rico
(6% tax)

TYPE OF RATE	RATE (U.S. $)	PEAK SEASON	SERVICE CHARGE	OFF-SEASON REDUCTION
Gran Hotel el Convento				
N/A	N/A	N/A	N/A	N/A
Hyatt Dorado Beach				
EP	$275–440	12/20–4/14	—	40–50%
Palmas del Mar				
EP	$170–210	12/19–4/30	—	N/A

Saba
(5% tax)

TYPE OF RATE	RATE (U.S. $)	PEAK SEASON	SERVICE CHARGE	OFF-SEASON REDUCTION
Captain's Quarters				
EP	$95	12/16–4/15	10%	25%

TYPE OF RATE	RATE (U.S. $)	PEAK SEASON	SERVICE CHARGE	OFF-SEASON REDUCTION

St. Barthélemy

(tax included in rates)

TYPE OF RATE	RATE (U.S. $)	PEAK SEASON	SERVICE CHARGE	OFF-SEASON REDUCTION
Castelets				
CP	$140–285	12/20–4/10	10%	30–35%
El Sereno Beach Hotel				
EP	$216–233	12/19–4/16	15%	N/A
Filao Beach Hotel				
CP	$240–290	12/20–4/30	(included)	25%
Hotel Guanahani				
CP	$290–330	12/20–4/2	(included)	25%
Hotel Manapany				
EP	$270–370	12/22–5/1	(included)	25%

St. Croix

(7½% tax)

TYPE OF RATE	RATE (U.S. $)	PEAK SEASON	SERVICE CHARGE	OFF-SEASON REDUCTION
The Buccaneer Hotel				
EP	$165–285	12/15–4/15	(included)	30%
Carambola Beach Resort and Golf Club				
FAP	$450	12/20–4/16	10%	25%
Cormorant Beach Club				
*	$350	12/15–4/20	10%	35%

*Price includes breakfast, lunch and all drinks before 5 p.m.

St. Eustatius

(10% tax)

TYPE OF RATE	RATE (U.S. $)	PEAK SEASON	SERVICE CHARGE	OFF-SEASON REDUCTION
The Old Gin House				
EP	$130	12/15–4/14	15%	25%

St. John

(7½% tax)

TYPE OF RATE	RATE (U.S. $)	PEAK SEASON	SERVICE CHARGE	OFF-SEASON REDUCTION
Caneel Bay				
FAP	$365–575	12/20–4/16	(optional)	30%

TYPE OF RATE	RATE (U.S. $)	PEAK SEASON	SERVICE CHARGE	OFF-SEASON REDUCTION

St. Kitts
(7% tax)

The Golden Lemon				
MAP	$265–300	12/16–4/15	10%	20%
Rawlins Plantation				
MAP	$250	12/16–4/15	10%	N/A

St. Lucia
(8% tax)

Anse Chastanet Beach Hotel				
EP	$132–156	12/14–4/15	—	30%
Cunard La Toc Hotel and La Toc Suites				
EP	$155–350	12/16–4/14	10%	50%
Dasheene				
N/A	N/A	N/A	N/A	N/A
Steigenberger Cariblue Hotel				
NAP	$205–225	12/21–4/16	10%	25%

St. Maarten/St. Martin
(5% tax on Dutch side, $1 per person per day on French side)

The Caravanserai				
N/A	N/A	N/A	N/A	N/A
Mary's Boon				
EP	$120	12/15–3/31	15%	40%
Oyster Pond Yacht Club and Hotel				
EP	$320–340	12/15–4/14	15%	30%
Pasanggrahan Royal Guesthouse Hotel				
EP	$95–125	12/15–4/14	10%	35–40%
La Samanna				
MAP	$600–690	12/15–4/15	10%	20%

TYPE OF RATE	RATE (U.S. $)	PEAK SEASON	SERVICE CHARGE	OFF-SEASON REDUCTION

St. Thomas
(7½% tax)

Harbor View				
CP	$102	10/23–5/1	—	35%
Pavilions & Pools Hotel				
CP	$195–220	12/21–3/31	—	10–20%
Point Pleasant				
EP	$205–285	12/20–4/14	—	25%

St. Vincent-Grenadines
(5% tax)

Grand View Beach Hotel				
EP	$103	12/15–4/14	10%	30%
Young Island				
MAP	$275–425	12/15–4/15	10%	30%

Tobago
(3% tax)

Arnos Vale Hotel				
N/A	N/A	N/A	N/A	N/A
Mount Irvine Bay Hotel				
MAP	$230–400	12/18–3/31	—	30%

Tortola
(7% tax)

Long Bay Hotel				
EP	$105–172	12/16–4/1	10%	25%
Peter Island				
FAP	$380–450	12/18–4/15	10%	30%

TYPE OF RATE	RATE (U.S. $)	PEAK SEASON	SERVICE CHARGE	OFF-SEASON REDUCTION

Virgin Gorda

(7% tax)

TYPE OF RATE	RATE (U.S. $)	PEAK SEASON	SERVICE CHARGE	OFF-SEASON REDUCTION
Biras Creek				
FAP	$370–570	12/15–4/15	10%	25%
Bitter End Yacht Club				
FAP	$270–395	12/19–4/10	9% per person per day	25%
Drake's Anchorage				
FAP	$305–335	12/16–4/1	12%	30%
Little Dix Bay				
FAP	$485	12/20–4/16	(optional)	30%
The Tradewinds				
FAP	$270–395	12/19–4/10	9% per person per day	25%

Reservations and Tourist Information

The Reps

Hotel representatives keep tabs on the availability of rooms in the hotels they represent, and they'll handle your reservations and confirmations at no extra charge to you (unless you wait until the last minute and they have to send telexes or phone calls back and forth, in which case you'll be charged). The reps who have appeared most frequently in these pages are listed below; in the interests of simplicity, only the main offices are listed for each one. (The list is in alphabetical order in the sense that David B. Mitchell, for example, is listed under D rather than M.)

American International
6 East 39th Street Rm. 803
New York, New York 10016
212-725-5880 800-223-5695
Telex 422407

David B. Mitchell & Company, Inc.
200 Madison Avenue
New York, New York 10016
212-696-1323 800-372-1323
Telex 422123

Divi Hotels
520 West State Street
Ithaca, New York 14850
607-227-DIVI 800-367-3484
Telex 4442016

Elegant Resorts of Barbados
Golf Club Road
Sandy Lane
Barbados, West Indies

Elegant Resorts of Jamaica
1320 South Dixie Highway Suite 1100
Coral Gables, Florida 33146
305-666-3566 800-237-3237
Telex 1560

First Resorts Corporation
307 East 56th Street
New York, New York 10022
212-308-3330 800-235-3505
Telex 4947107

International Travel & Resorts
25 West 39th Street
New York, New York 10018
212-840-6636 800-223-9815 Canada 800-468-0023
Telex 225559

Jacques de Larsay
622 Broadway
New York, New York 10012
212-477-1600 800-223-1510
Telex 238095

Leading Hotels of the World
747 Third Avenue
New York, New York 10017-2847
212-838-3110 800-223-6800
Telex 420444

Mondotel
200 West 57th Street
New York, New York 10019
212-757-0225 800-847-4249
Telex 825315

Ralph Locke Islands
P.O. Box 800
Waccubuc, New York 10597
800-223-1108

Ray Morrow Associates
360 Main Street
Ridgefield, Connecticut 06877
203-697-2340 800-223-9838
Telex 962400

Robert Reid Associates
845 Third Avenue
New York, New York 10022
212-832-2277 call 800-555-1212 (information) for other listings

Rockresorts
30 Rockefeller Plaza, Suite 5400
New York, New York 10112
212-586-4459 New York State 800-442-8198 United States 800-223-7637
Telex 422020

Scott Calder International, Inc.
152 Madison Avenue
New York, New York 10016
212-535-9530 800-223-5581

Selective Hotel Reservations
19 West 34th Street, Suite 700
New York, New York 10001
212-714-2323 New York State 800-522-5568 United States 800-223-6764
Telex 237468

Steigenberger Reservation Services
40 East 49th Street
New York, New York 10017
212-593-2988 800-223-5652

Utell International
119 West 57th Street
New York, New York 10019
1-800-44U-TELL
(Sales & Marketing only)

Tourist Information

The function of this guide is to give you facts and tips on where to stay, rather than what to see; there just isn't time or space to do both. In any case, with the exceptions of islands like Puerto Rico, Jamaica and a few others, there really isn't much to see—a fort, a volcano, a native market or two. Many of the major sightseeing attractions (and a few offbeat sights) are mentioned in these pages; if you want more information on topics like shopping and sightseeing, I suggest you get in touch with the tourist office of the islands that interest you. The other possibility is to write to the

Caribbean Tourism Association (20 East 46 Street, New York, NY 10017, 212-682-0435) for information on most of the islands.

If you wait until you get to the island, you'll find no shortage of publications and notice boards with up-to-the-minute details on shops, restaurants, sights and tours.

Update

As this edition of *Caribbean Hideaways* goes to press, several new hideaways are on the drawing boards or under construction—places like Cap Juluca and Coccoloba Plantation on Anguilla and the Royal Pavilion on Barbados. Obviously, you'd like to know more about them. You can keep abreast of these and other developments by subscribing to my independent newsletter, *Very Special Places.* It reports on hideaways in the Caribbean and around the world, as well as keeping you posted on changes taking place in hideaways described in this guidebook (new additions, facilities, rates and ratings, managers, that sort of thing). For a special subscription offer, *exclusively for readers of this guide,* turn to page 336.

Special Half-Price Offer
Very Special Places Newsletter

Hotel brochures rarely tell you the whole story, do they?

And while *Caribbean Hideaways* gives you a more balanced picture of each hotel and resort than most guidebooks, it cannot keep you fully up-to-date. That's why you need to supplement your research with a newsletter like my *Very Special Places. VSP* brings you up-to-the-minute, up-front, objective reports on resorts and hotels *before* you commit a bundle of money and a hard-earned vacation.

Very Special Places is an independent, confidential report on inns, resorts, hotels and hideaways of exceptional character. Like this guidebook, no one can pay to be included in the newsletter, and all properties are personally inspected before being rated.

But don't take *my* word for it.

Read what Jerry Hulse, the widely respected travel editor of the *Los Angeles Times,* has to say about *VSP:* "Because so many travel newsletters are feeble payoffs to innkeepers . . . Keown's is refreshing. It has class." See for yourself. You have nothing to lose because you can have your money back in full if you don't agree with Jerry Hulse and the thousands of travelers who already subscribe to *VSP.*

Very Special Places is published eight times a year, with eight fact-filled pages per issue. Normally a one-year subscription costs $55, but as a reader of *Caribbean Hideaways* you can have your eight issues *for just $27.* Half price! Now, if *VSP* saves you just one night in the wrong resort or directs you to one that's more in tune with your needs, it has repaid that $27 ten times over, hasn't it?

To qualify for this special rate, you must send your application on this page. Please complete the information requested below and send the entire page, with your check for $27, to: *VSP/CH,* 280 Midland Avenue, Saddle Brook, New Jersey 07662.

Name____

Address______________________________________

City________________State______________Zip____________

*Overseas subscribers: Please add $20 to cover bank charges and airmail.

MONEY BACK GUARANTEE If, when you receive your first issue, you decide that *VSP* is not for you, keep that issue and drop me a line asking to have your subscription cancelled and your money refunded. I'll send it back pronto.